Textile Mills of South West England

Textile Mills of South West England

Mike Williams

ENGLISH HERITAGE

Published by English Heritage, The Engine House, Fire Fly Avenue, Swindon
SN2 2EH
www.english-heritage.org.uk
English Heritage is the Government's statutory adviser on all aspects of the historic environment.

First published 2013

ISBN 978-1-84802-083-2

Product code 51598

British Library Cataloguing in Publication data
A CIP catalogue record for this book is available from the British Library.

For more information about English Heritage images, contact Archives Research Services, The Engine House, Fire Fly Avenue, Swindon SN2 2EH; telephone (01793) 414600.

Brought to publication by Sarah Enticknap, Publishing, English Heritage

Typeset in Charter 9.5/11.75 and 9.5/12.75

Edited by Sue Kelleher
Indexed by Sue Vaughan
Designed by Hybert Design

Printed in the UK by Butler Tanner & Dennis Ltd.

CONTENTS

PREFACE

The manufacture of cloth, yarn, twine, rope, nets and a wide range of other goods is one of the longest established forms of industry in the South West. Evidence of the traditional textile industries can be seen throughout the region's towns, cities, villages, countryside and coastal areas. The vast range of historic buildings and landscapes associated with textiles include such diverse sites as medieval fulling mills, vernacular clothiers' houses, water-power systems, drying grounds, domestic workshops, workers' housing and some of the largest integrated factory complexes in the country. Textile processes in the region developed considerably over several centuries *before* the construction of powered factories in the Industrial Revolution. These industries became central to the way of life of local communities, having a profound influence on the development of historic townscapes and landscapes. In the later 19th century, the main national centres of textile production shifted to other regions, but the mixed economies of the South West ensured that many mills were converted for new uses, thus avoiding rebuilding or demolition. As a result, the South West retains an exceptionally wide chronological range of textile sites, with better survival of early industry than in areas dominated by later factory building.

The complex history of the South West textile industries has been recognised for decades, and was the focus of some of the formative works in the study of industrial archaeology. Previous publications have been of great value to this study, but by choice most have concentrated on a particular industry or a local area, with few, if any, aiming to compare the historic buildings of the South West industries with those of other regions. The heritage of textiles is closely connected to other subjects, including economic, social and political history, and to other building types, such as warehouses, farms, workshops and market halls, so it is only by examining this broader context that the significance of mill buildings can be assessed. Textile industry buildings contain a wealth of historical information which adds greatly to the documentary evidence in libraries and archives, but only if the buildings remain intact. With the decline of all forms of traditional industry, demolition has inevitably been considerable, and alterations to their defining historic features continue as the surviving mills are protected and conserved.

This book builds on the expanding range of published research, and on the previous recording of textile mills by the Royal Commission on the Historical Monuments of England and English Heritage in other regions, to compare all of the main textile industries and assess the historical significance of their buildings. The emphasis in the text is firmly on context rather than detail, with an account of the early origins of the industries leading into descriptions of some of the best-preserved surviving sites. The most effective approach to textile mills research involves the combination of documentary information with on-site observation and the recording of historic features; in many cases, physical information from fieldwork adds considerably to the functional history of a textile mill. The development of each of the main industries is described in chapters 2 to 7, with those containing the most sites dealt with first. The varied content of these chapters reflects the widely differing histories of the industries themselves. More detailed information on individual sites can be found in the English Heritage Archive, county and local archives and other publications. A list of sites which are open to the public is included after-chapter 8. A full list of sites mentioned in the text is also included. This lists sites by name and parish and this convention has been followed throughout the text.

The earliest industries are still closely associated with the areas where they were established, the extant buildings following the distribution of earlier generations of mills which do not survive, and textile history is strongly reflected in the region's vernacular architecture. Later industries were more widely scattered, and their buildings show greater similarity to those in other regions. The form and construction of the buildings was largely determined by the processes they were built to contain; the influence of processes on buildings is discussed in chapter 1, with more specific descriptions of the different processes in each industry in the later chapters. Further background on machinery and processes can be found in the glossary.

A general aim throughout has been to encourage readers to look beneath the surface of textile industry buildings. Understanding textile mills as historical documents requires an appreciation of how the appearance of the buildings reflects their original function. To do this we need to look beyond the façades and consider the layout, construction and functional features of the interiors (when these are accessible), including the evidence of machinery and power systems. A wide range of annotated drawings and photographs are included to illustrate the internal features of the buildings and expand on the descriptions in the main text. *In situ* mechanical features, such as waterwheels or machinery, are now extremely rare, so selected examples have been illustrated with larger-scale 2D and 3D survey drawings.

As in other areas with traditional textile industries, the demolition of historic mills has been considerable, and many of those that survive have been extensively altered. A particular problem with industrial buildings is the removal of the historically significant details or functional features, which are often essential to the character of the buildings. The conservation of textile mills has seen notable successes, however, some of which are highlighted in chapter 8, and their statutory designation or protection through other means has generally preceded that in other regions. In recent decades, the conversion of mills, warehouses and related industrial townscapes for a surprising variety of new uses has significantly increased, but many more historic sites remain in a perilous condition, despite their obvious contribution to the heritage and landscapes of the region. Experience in both the South West and in other areas has shown that these historic industrial sites certainly can have a viable future, often providing the central focus of regeneration schemes, but successful conservation always begins with the full appreciation of their architectural character and undoubted historical importance.

ACKNOWLEDGEMENTS

This book is largely based on studies of textile industry buildings by the English Heritage Assessment Team and, in the 1980s and 1990s, by the staff of the Royal Commission on the Historical Monuments of England. The author wishes to extend his sincere thanks to the many professional colleagues, in English Heritage and other organisations, who have contributed to the work. The South West Textile Mills project was overseen and advised by a Project Board headed by Keith Falconer, Martin Cherry and John Cattell, comprising Barry Jones, Jill Guthrie, Nicholas Molyneux, Jenny Chesher and Caroline Power. The publication draft was read by Barry Jones and Professor Marilyn Palmer. Jenny Chesher contributed text on conservation and planning issues for chapter 8. The book was brought to publication by Sarah Enticknap of English Heritage Publishing. In the project team itself, Rebecca Lane carried out the research for chapters 6 and 7 and wrote the Glossary. Additional research and investigation was contributed by Lucy Jessop, Ursula Dugard-Craig, Olivia Horsfall Turner, Agnieszka Sandraei, Sheila Ely, Allan Brodie and Gary Winter. Alan Stoyel made an invaluable contribution to the initial stages of the project, and later provided detailed advice on water-power systems. Publication drawings are by Nigel Fradgley and maps by Jon Bedford. Professional photography is by Mike Hesketh-Roberts, Peter Williams and James O Davies.

The staff of libraries, archives and museums across the West Midlands and the South West have given valuable assistance throughout the project. These include the county records offices of Gloucestershire, Wiltshire, Somerset, Dorset, Devon, Worcestershire and Warwickshire, and the collections of Birmingham City Archives, Coldharbour Mill Museum, Stroud Museum, Tiverton Museum, Trowbridge Museum and the Allhallows Museum of Honiton. The records and expertise of specialist local societies have also been of great help, including the Stroudwater Textile Trust, the Gloucestershire Society for Industrial Archaeology, the Bristol Industrial Archaeological Society, the Somerset Industrial Archaeological Society and the Campden and District Historical and Archaeological Society. Many individuals have also contributed detailed knowledge of the subjects covered, notably Ken Rogers and Ian Macintosh. Thanks are also due for access to privately held archives, particularly those of Fox Brothers and John Boyd Textiles. Finally, we would like to express our thanks to the owners and occupiers of the buildings described or illustrated in the book. They should be given a great deal of the credit for the successful conservation of the textile heritage of the South West, and without their support a project of this nature would not be possible.

1

Introduction

The textile industries have been a central theme in the history of the South West from at least the 14th century. Evidence of the industries is widely distributed around the region, making a significant contribution to the historic character of its towns, rural landscapes and coastal areas. A wide variety of historic buildings and landscapes are associated with the textile industries, reflecting both the prolonged importance of textile manufacture to local communities and the diverse range of products that were made from different raw materials. The heritage of the region's textile industries also covers an exceptionally wide chronological range. The mills that survive in Gloucestershire, Wiltshire, Somerset, Dorset, Devon and Cornwall were preceded by a larger number of traditional buildings and landscapes, and these were often associated with the textile trades for considerably longer than the later factories (Figs 1.1 and 1.2).

The influence of the textile industries on historic buildings in the South West extends far beyond the mills that are synonymous with 19th-century industry in other regions. In many parts of the South West, textile trades were not separate or exclusive activities, and in some cases they did not completely dominate the local economy. They were traditionally combined with other types of work, becoming closely associated with the way of life in town and countryside. The result was that the buildings of the early industries were intimately connected with the region's traditional vernacular architecture. The distribution of the main industries was achieved centuries before the factory building of the Industrial Revolution, but the physical evidence of early textile production is largely hidden by changes of land use and the later alterations to vernacular buildings.

The geography of the South West textile industries

Local specialisation in particular textile industries had begun to develop by the late medieval period, and the distribution of the historic industries reflects the prolonged influence of such factors as the availability of water-power sites, the type of agriculture, traditional communication routes and the location of ports along the coastline (Fig 1.3). The counties of Gloucestershire, Wiltshire, Somerset and Devon, for example, each had historic woollen industries that were established long before the construction of the first factory buildings in the late 18th century. The early industries benefited from the availability of a variety of locally produced raw materials, notably high-quality wools. By the 16th century, the nationally important west of England woollen industry was one of the largest industries in the South West region. It extended across Gloucestershire, Wiltshire and Somerset, together with adjoining parts of Oxfordshire and Hampshire. This extensive industry included many local variations, however, in particular the development of distinctive products and building types in Gloucestershire and Wiltshire, and had itself emerged from an earlier cloth industry in the medieval towns. Its main products were a wide range of fine-woollen cloths, many of which were exported to be dyed and finished in Europe. Local variations in this late medieval woollen trade continued to influence the distribution of mill building throughout the later history of the industry.

The early industry in Gloucestershire was concentrated in a distinctive area of narrow valleys converging on Stroud, which provided an unusually large concentration of water-power sites (Fig 1.4). The industry was dominated by its many water-powered fulling mills, leading

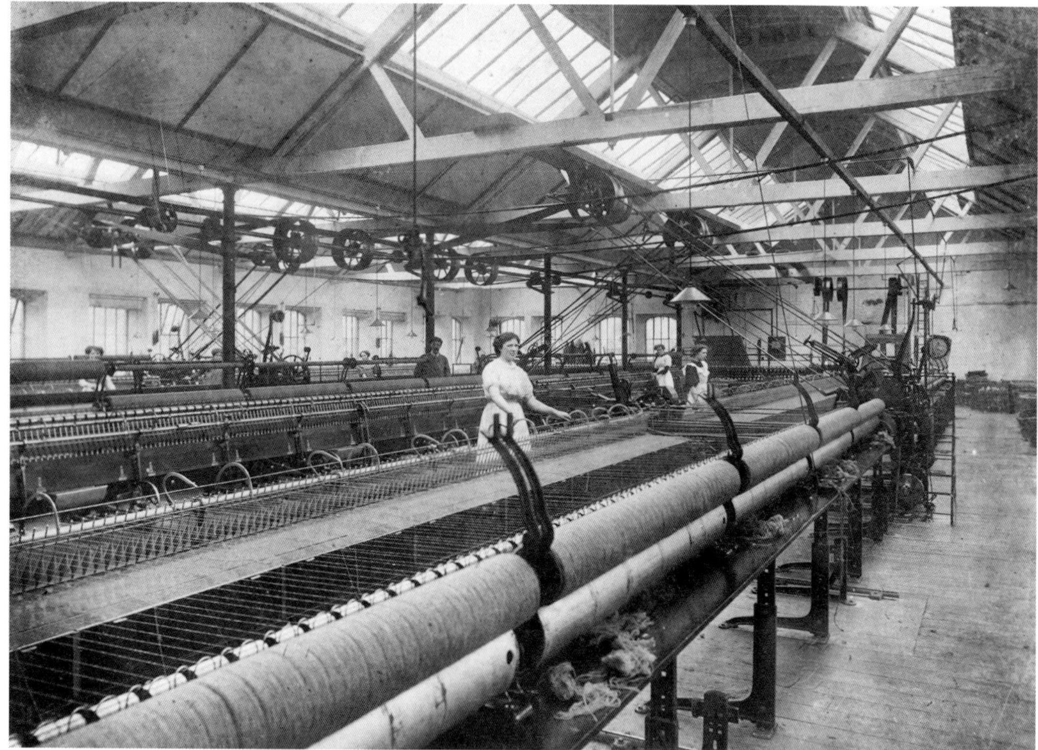

Fig 1.1
Woollen yarn spinning with steam-powered mules at Longfords Mills, Gloucestershire, c 1912. The processes and architecture of the later mills were the result of a prolonged development that began centuries before the introduction of the factory system.
[Reproduced courtesy of the Stroudwater Textile Trust. BB040975]

Fig 1.2
Cloth finishing at Longfords Mills, c 1912, representing the final stage in the wide range of processes at an integrated mill. The history of the region's textile industries often involved the gradual reorganisation of existing processes, rather than the introduction of completely new types of machinery.
[Reproduced courtesy of the Stroudwater Textile Trust. BB040980]

to a local emphasis on the production of the finest grades of woollen cloth, while the many streams also enabled the development of a cloth-dyeing industry. The early sites continued to be occupied by a succession of mills in the later development of the industry, resulting in a highly distinctive combination of vernacular buildings and factory architecture. To the

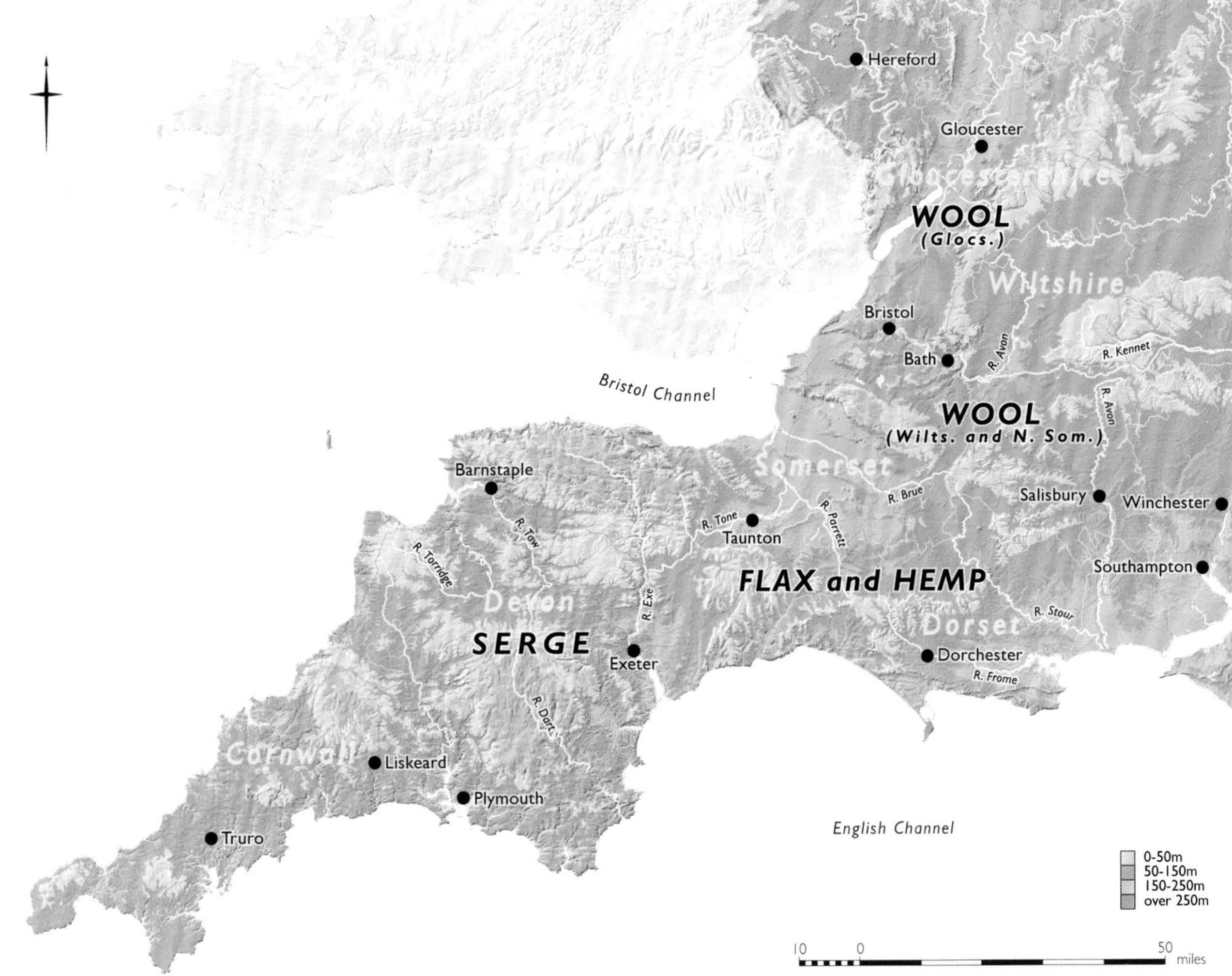

south, the woollen industry developed over a much more extensive area in Wiltshire and Somerset. Water power was also vital to the early industry in this area, but by the 16th century, market towns were already developing as the main centres for both the clothiers and their extensive workforce. The urban emphasis continued as the early industry gave way to the factory system, resulting in building types that contrasted with the rural distribution of the industry in Gloucestershire. As the industry adapted its processes to new products it became less dependent on water power, leading to the building of groups of steam-powered urban factories that were similar to those being built in some of the northern mill towns (Fig 1.5).

One of the country's largest textile industries of the 17th and 18th century developed in Devon and the adjoining parts of Somerset and Cornwall. This was a cottage industry specialising in the production of serge cloths, which used a combination of worsted for warp and woollen yarns for the weft. The international market for serge greatly expanded in the 17th century, when the other South West woollen industries were also adapting to new products. Its commercial centre was Exeter, from where the industry was controlled by a class of wealthy merchants. In the late 18th century the industry underwent a dramatic decline, almost disappearing over a few decades. A small number of businesses survived the collapse, however, and made a successful transition to the factory system, so the area retains a number of historically important early mill complexes, including the largest textile sites in the South West region.

A different type of medieval textile industry was established in the countryside of South Somerset and West Dorset. Hemp and flax were grown in this area and used for making twine, rope, sailcloth and netting from the 13th

Fig 1.3
The historic textile industries of the South West. [90m SRTM Topography data courtesy of the CGIAR, http://srtm.csi.cgiar.org]

Fig 1.4
The setting of Pitchcombe Mill, Gloucestershire, shows the typical position of a small water-powered mill close to the dam of the mill pond. The site also illustrates the development from a clothier's house, to the left of the pond, to an early factory.
[AP24970/044]

century; netting products are still manufactured at some of the historic mill sites today. The industry traditionally concentrated on products for the ship-building and fishing industries, and was an important supplier to the navy. Locally grown raw materials were supplemented with imports from the 18th century, enabling the move to factory production and the rejuvenation of an industry that was closely tied to the history of both towns and the countryside.

The silk industry in the South West developed later and was less geographically restricted than some of the early industries, with centres of production in towns and villages scattered across a large area of Gloucestershire, Wiltshire and Somerset. It was completely dependent on imported raw material, and was strongly influenced by developments in international trade and government legislation. Silk throwing, spinning and weaving became well established in some areas in the 18th century, frequently by manufacturers who were associated with silk merchants in London or Coventry. A small number of silk mills were purpose-built for the industry, including some of the earliest textile factories in the region, but the majority were re-used woollen or corn mills, mainly employing women and children for low wages.

The lace and hosiery industries in the South West were also strongly influenced by events outside the region, but in the early 19th century lace production developed into one of the country's most progressive textile industries, which was to have a dramatic impact on towns in Devon and Somerset. Up to the 18th century, handmade lace was a high-value product in several parts of the region, most notably Honiton in Devon. The traditional industry was undermined, however, by the migration of innovative machinery makers and factory builders from the East Midlands, led by John Heathcoat, one of the great pioneers of the factory system. The advanced new factories they built transformed the economies and the appearance of some Devon and Somerset towns, symbolising the beginning of the end of the handmade lace industry. The machinery in the factories was developed from hosiery-knitting machines, and the traditional hosiery industry in parts of the South West, notably Tewkesbury in Gloucestershire, was also altered by innovative manufacturers from the East Midlands.

Fig 1.5
Court Street area, Trowbridge, Wiltshire. Woollen mills, finishing works and workshops in the Court Street area of Trowbridge. Densely packed groups of steam-powered mills and housing characterised the urban development of the textile industries from the early 19th century.
[AP26128/039]

Historic buildings of the textile industries

The textile industries in the South West are associated with a remarkable variety of historic sites spanning a wide range of dates. The development of its buildings and landscapes has parallelled the history of the industries, with each of the main stages of growth being characterised by a particular range of sites and features. The mills and factories which still dominate some of the historic textile areas represent the dramatic changes of the 18th and 19th century, when the old, established industries adopted the new methods of the factory system. Before that important period of change, the textile industries underwent many generations of development, which created a great wealth of vernacular industrial buildings in the region's towns and countryside. This earlier form of industry, characterised by home-based workers rather than centralised factories, strongly influenced the development of the factory buildings which survive today. The earliest industries were the fine-woollen trade and the flax and hemp industry, whose origins have been traced to the 13th century, although no extant industrial buildings survive from that period. These medieval industries contrasted markedly with later periods, being restricted to the larger towns where they were controlled by guilds, such as those in Bristol, Exeter, Salisbury and Gloucester. The first tentative evidence of the organisation of the various trades around mills relates to the use of small water-powered fulling mills and dye houses close to some of the towns.

The locations of the main industries, and the origins of a large proportion of the extant sites, were established at a surprisingly early stage. From the 14th century to the 17th, the textile industry expanded from the medieval towns into rural areas where water power was available, close to a local supply of raw material. The earliest surviving buildings date from this long period, during which industry became a feature of rural life and the influence of the towns on its development was reduced. Surviving buildings date from the late 15th and early 16th century and include small fulling mills, warehouses and parts of some clothiers' houses. All are in vernacular materials and styles, with little evidence of the development of functional features specific to the textile industries (Fig 1.6).

The early factories, dating from between the mid-18th and the early 19th century, were a distinctive building type associated with new types of machinery and new forms of employment, but the origins of the factory system can be traced back to a reorganisation of production that began much earlier. The transition to the factory system was a prolonged process, in which the methods of production were gradually improved and organised more efficiently, and buildings in vernacular styles began to exhibit functional features that were suited to the textile industries. This transitional period largely determined the locations and the appearance of the early factory buildings, with the factories in different areas reflecting local variations in textile processes.

The main ancestors of the early factories were the wide variety of workshops that were built from around the mid-17th century, including house extensions, detached buildings and unpowered structures added to water-powered mills. Some of the characteristic features of early factories were previously seen on a smaller scale in vernacular workshops, such as the use of regular fenestration and fully open interiors to give good natural lighting. Other vernacular industrial buildings were intended for a more specific purpose, which can be deduced from the presence of functional features. Examples included dye houses and buildings for drying wool or cloth, which included ventilation features such as perforated brickwork or roof-top louvres.

Surviving examples of the first purpose-built factories, dating from the mid- to late 18th century, are now rare. They were distinct from the more familiar 19th-century factories by their architectural details, simpler methods of construction and their arrangement of processes. Some were entirely hand powered, with a close affinity to the earlier workshops, but most used a combination of hand and water power, borrowing vernacular details from both mills and workshops. With the introduction of steam power in the first years of the 19th century, large textile factories could be built away from water-power sites for the first time, leading to a new phase of urban industry characterised by the construction of closely packed groups of mills and terraced housing. In some rural areas, however, water power continued to be used in combination with steam power throughout the 19th century. The Victorian industrial townscapes of the South West were not unlike those in other regions, but close inspection of the mills reveals functional and architectural features that are distinctive to this region, reflecting the long early history of the local industry.

The development of factory architecture from the late 18th to the late 19th century, when most of the extant mill sites were built, continued at a much faster rate than the gradual adaptation of vernacular buildings in previous centuries. Factories were specifically designed to contain a wide range of textile machinery in the most efficient layout, and their architecture reflected the development of power systems and the principles of industrial design in the country as a whole. In the South West, many of the factories continued to use local building materials and traditional architectural details that were derived from the earlier vernacular mills and workshops. Most of the textile industries in the region saw the increased construction of large integrated mill complexes, which contained the full range of processes from raw material to the finished cloth (Fig 1.7). The functional features of the many buildings at these sites are often a clear indication of the processes they were originally built for. In the later 19th century, far fewer new mills were built than in the expanding textile industries in the north, but as the South West industry consolidated into a smaller number of progressive firms, it kept up with technical developments in other regions. The last generation of factories included architect-designed mills that utilised the latest approaches to layout of machinery, construction methods and power systems, with fashionable embellishment reflecting a pride in the long history of the industry.

Textile mills were widely associated with other types of development in both town and countryside, including the construction of housing, improvements to infrastructure and the growth of related industries, such as engineering. With some notable exceptions, such as the housing built for the lace factories of Tiverton, the construction of planned communities of factory-workers' housing was less

Fig 1.6 (opposite) Harnham Mill near Salisbury, Wiltshire, with decorative flintwork and drip moulds typical of a higher-status vernacular building of the 16th century. Like many early mills it was built for multiple uses, which included periods as a paper mill and a grist mill in addition to fulling. [DP025750]

OLD MILL HOTEL
& FREEHOUSE
OLD MILL
HOTEL
RESTAURANT
&
BAR FOOD
EN-SUITE
ACCOMMODATION

Fig 1.7
The exceptionally well-preserved Coldharbour Mill, now a working mill museum at Uffculme in Devon, has examples of the many functional building types associated with textile factories in the 19th century. The buildings of the water-power system are attached to the right end, those of the steam-power system to the left end.
[AP26637/037]

common than in other regions, reflecting the presence of a local industrial workforce before the factories were built. Factory housing was more commonly built by speculative developers, in some areas with domestic workshops for weaving and other specialist trades. As in other regions, handloom weaving thrived for a few decades after the construction of the first factories, partly due to the slow development of the power loom and partly because of the continued independence of the handloom weavers themselves.[1] The influence of the textile industries on the development of townscapes was considerable, and can be shown to have started several centuries before factory building. From the late 18th century it included the development of industrial suburbs in some areas, comprising factories, housing and a new street pattern, which could significantly expand the built-up area of a town. Contrasting examples can be seen in Bridport and Trowbridge.

Textile production was also part of the traditional way of life in much of the countryside of the South West, so that the buildings and other historic structures of the industry have become an essential part of the rural scene. Evidence of the landscape engineering of water-power systems is widespread in all the textile industry areas, with both intact and disused ponds and watercourses making an important contribution to the diversity of rural landscapes. Those areas which traditionally produced raw materials, such as wool and flax, often saw the development of a mixed rural economy, in which the textile trades were combined with seasonal work on the land. Factory building was also connected with the development of infrastructure in rural areas from the 18th century. Turnpike roads, canals and later railways could all be influenced by the distribution of mills, often because such schemes were part-funded by the mill owners.

The organisation of textile production

The traditional industries saw different approaches to the management of textile businesses and the organisation of production, and these influenced both the early mills, houses and workshops and the later buildings associated with the factory system. In some areas, notably Gloucestershire, the pre-factory industry was financed and organised by clothiers who endeavoured to control all the stages of production, often retaining ownership of the wool while it was processed by a succession of different outworkers. In contrast, the serge industry was largely financed by merchants who had little or no connection with spinning and weaving. In such cases, most stages of production were delegated to middlemen, who in turn employed master spinners and master weavers to organise the networks of outworkers. The flax and hemp industry was organised around merchant-manufacturers, who outsourced both the textile processes and the growing of the crops, in addition to purchasing imported raw materials. From the 18th century, the later industries such as silk, lace and cotton were increasingly controlled from outside the region, and often pioneered the introduction of factory methods. As will be seen in the following chapters, international trade was an important underlying factor in the history of all the South West textile industries. The origins and commercial development of the early vernacular industries were often closely related to fluctuations in foreign trade. From the late medieval period, most of the region's woollen goods that were intended for export were transported to the warehouses of Blackwell Hall in London, which served as both a trading market and as the centre of a national system of quality control for woollen exports (Fig 1.8). The later development of the textile industries was also closely linked to the growth of international trade. From the late 18th century, the much larger mills of the factory system were built to use large quantities of imported raw materials, and profits were dependent on the availability of overseas markets for their products.

Textile products

The South West industries have been associated with a notably wide range of products, with each constantly adapting its own raw materials and processes to suit changing markets. The early woollen industry, for example, was divided into areas specialising in dyed and undyed cloths, fine woollens, superfine woollens and cloths using different coloured yarns for the warp and weft. Flax and hemp were used for twines, ropes, sailcloths, netting, sackcloths and a wide range of products for the maritime industries. Serge was a development of the 17th century, comprising lighter-weight dyed cloths made from a woollen weft and a worsted warp. From the mid-18th century, the silk industry was using imported silks for the production of threads and high-quality fancy-woven fabrics. The lace and hosiery industries used a variety

Fig 1.8
Blackwell Hall, which formerly stood close to the Guildhall in London, was the initial destination of many of the woollen goods from the South West that were intended for export.
[Blackwell Hall, King Street, *1819, by Robert Blemmell Schnebbelie. © City of London, London Metropolitan Archives*]

of raw materials, including cotton, to manufacture great quantities of mainly domestic products in the 19th century. Throughout the histories of the different industries, changes in demand were one of the main influences on the organisation of production and the construction of industrial buildings. A high proportion of that demand came from foreign markets, even in the medieval industries. Fluctuations in the demand for exported goods, and the availability of imported raw materials, had major repercussions for the long-term development of the region's textile industries.

Textile processes

The ongoing improvement of manufacturing techniques was central to the history of all the textile industries and strongly influenced the development of mill buildings. Effective management of processes and operatives was of fundamental importance to the success of a textile business, enabling clothiers or manufacturers to control the quality of their products and to meet the changing demand for textile goods. Some processes were widespread, and were adapted for use by all the textile industries, while others were only used by one industry. Some required specific features in a building, but others simply needed space for the convenient layout of machinery and workers.

Processes were closely related to the establishment of the earliest industries in the region, such as the construction of large numbers of early fulling mills on the fast-flowing streams of Gloucestershire. They could also have a strong influence on the development of landscapes and townscapes, as was the case with the long history of twine spinning in the open walks of Bridport and the growing of hemp and flax in the surrounding countryside. In the 18th century, improvements to processes were closely related to the introduction of factory methods, involving both the widespread use of new types of machinery and the reorganisation of the workforce.

In addition to the ongoing improvement of processes and machinery, the history of the region's textile industries has largely concerned changes to the *organisation* of production, and this has also influenced the development of buildings. The characteristics of the final product were largely determined by the quality of the work that could be maintained throughout the full sequence of processes. Each stage of production depended on the output of the preceding stage. In the pre-factory industries most of the work was organised extensively, with processes carried out by skilled artisans scattered over a wide area, and this limited control of both the quality and quantity of production (Fig 1.9). Organisation was improved by the gradual integration of processes at the mill site, starting with those stages that were most critical to the finished quality of the product. Integrated working was achieved over a long period, involving a different chain of events in each industry, and greatly influenced the varied building types in different parts of the region.

The four main stages of production, common to each of the South West textile industries, were the preparation of the raw materials, the spinning of a yarn, weaving or net making and finishing. Additional processes were used with particular raw materials or to produce distinctive types of yarn or cloth, so each industry also developed specialised processes which were often concentrated in particular areas. The processes that were specific to particular industries are described in chapters 2 to 7, with further details in the Glossary.

Preparation

Preparation was a vital part of a textile business, often occupying large numbers of outworkers or a significant proportion of a mill, and was subdivided into many stages which varied greatly according to the nature of the raw material. In some industries the raw material was delivered to the mill in a partly prepared state, such as in the silk industry, but in others the useful fibre had to be mechanically separated from unwanted material before being cleaned and dried. Raw fibre from different sources might be blended at this stage to give a raw material with particular characteristics, as was common in the woollen industries. The flax and hemp industries involved initial stages that took place on the farm, often in the fields where the crop was grown, and the prepared fibre might be stored for many months prior to its use in the mill. The final stages of preparation usually involved processes in which the washed and dried fibres were aligned to make them suitable for spinning. For the wool and cotton industries this involved carding, in the worsted industry combing and in the hemp and flax industry heckling, all of which were distinctive and intricate processes requiring skilled labour that was dedicated to each industry.

Spinning

Various forms of spinning were used by all the textile industries, involving a sequence of processes to produce a great variety of yarn, twine, thread and rope. The number of stages in spinning varied with the different types of raw material, and each stage was further refined to suit the type of yarn required. The prepared fibre was initially formed into a loosely twisted cord, usually in a succession of stages, referred to as slubbing or roving in the woollen and cotton industries. In the pre-factory worsted industry the cord was produced by twisting the fibre together by hand. As in the other stages of textile production, the processes of manual spinning were improved over a long period before the use of machinery; in some industries local specialisation developed in particular processes before the introduction of factory methods, and influenced the pattern of factory building thereafter. Spinning normally referred to the final stage in the production of the yarn. When it was intended for weaving, up to the mid-18th century, yarn was spun on wheels; then on jennies, water frames, throstles or mules up to the early 19th century; and later on improved types of machines including ring frames (*see* Glossary for further information). Later stages of spinning involved the combining, or doubling, of yarns to make thread, twine or rope. The delicate processes of silk throwing and spinning were among the first to be successfully mechanised, involving highly distinctive machinery that was not used in the other industries. In the hemp and flax industry, yarn that was intended for use as twine or rope was spun by hand using a different method in a walk, a long open or covered plot; walks were also used for combining yarns into twine, and the laying of twines into rope.

Weaving, net braiding and lacemaking

Handloom weaving in cottage workshops was widespread throughout the South West textile industries, and was often combined with carding and spinning in rural households (Fig 1.10). By the 18th century, weavers were a numerous and relatively prosperous class of skilled artisans, who wielded considerable influence on the introduction of new machinery in different parts of the region. The most common type of handloom in the woollen industries was the broadloom, developed from the late medieval period to produce cloth to the widths required by legal statutes. A modified type was the drawloom, which enabled the weaving of patterned cloths from the 17th century. From the mid-18th century, the introduction of the flying shuttle increased the weavers' output, creating the demand for more yarn, which led to the introduction of new types of spinning machinery. Weavers in some parts of the region protested against the flying shuttle, however, and their opposition had a marked influence on some of the early factory builders. The so-called narrow looms, which could be operated by a single weaver, were used in some industries, notably for linens and sailcloth, and were more widely used in the woollen industries from the late 18th century; narrow looms were more easily accommodated in the loomshops that

a

b

c

Fig 1.9
Examples of textile processes in the 18th-century woollen industry, when production was often dispersed around workshops and cottages. The gradual concentration of processes at one site was one of the first signs of the transition to the factory system.

Fig 1.9a
Hand spinning and winding yarn into hanks. Published by Robins and Sons, Leeds, March 1st, 1814. [Reproduced courtesy of Milliken WSP. DP137626]

Fig 1.9b
*Raising the nap (*see *chapter 2). Published by Robins and Sons, Leeds, January 1st, 1814. [Reproduced courtesy of Milliken WSP. DP137628]*

Fig 1.9c
Cutting the nap, a widespread and highly skilled trade before the introduction of mechanical rotary cutters. Published by Robins and Sons, Leeds, September 1st 1813. [Reproduced courtesy of Milliken WSP. DP137624]

Fig 1.10
A disused handloom in a Wiltshire workshop, probably in Bradford-on-Avon, c 1890. Handloom weaving expanded following the introduction of powered spinning machinery, and such workshops remained widespread in the South West up to the mid-19th century. [Reproduced courtesy of Ken Rogers. © Alan Tegetmeier. DP137651]

Fig 1.11
Partridge Dye House, Bowbridge, Stroud *by Gerardin Delaplace. A rare contemporary illustration of a working dye works which was owned by several members of the Partridge family in the late 18th and early 19th century. Such cloth-finishing works often developed around much earlier fulling mills. [Reproduced courtesy of The Museum in the Park, Stroud CM_3979]*

were being built at that time. Important later developments included the Jacquard mechanism from the early 19th century, a system for controlling the weaving of patterned cloths, such as high-quality silks. Power looms were first successfully used in the 1830s, a decade or two later than in other regions, but handloom weaving continued in several parts of the South West until the late 19th century.

The making of industrial netting from hemp or flax twine, known as 'braiding', was also a long-established cottage industry by the 18th century. Machinery was introduced for manufacturing sheet netting in the late 19th century, but the hand production of specialist types of net has continued in some areas up to the present day. In other parts of the region, hosiery and lacemaking had developed as highly successful cottage industries by the late 18th century. The hosiery knitting trade was much more extensive in the East Midlands, where complex hand-operated stocking-frame knitting machines had been developed, and these were in use in the South West by the late 18th century. This type of machinery was greatly improved in the early 19th century, when it was developed into new types of 'bobbinet' machines, used for the manufacture of plain net lace. The machine-lace industry was the last major textile industry to be introduced to the South West, causing the decline of the traditional hand-lace industry and, for a few decades in the early 19th century, representing one of the most progressive textile industries in the country.

Finishing

The market value of textile products, and their suitability for particular uses, was largely dependent on such qualities as their weight, surface texture, colour, suppleness and durability. These characteristics were determined by a complex and varied range of processes that was subjected to continued development in each of the different industries. The early development of finishing processes was a significant factor in establishing the South West textile industries, as water-power sites were adopted for fulling and dyeing from the late medieval period (Fig 1.11). The clothiers began to increase their control of the finishing stages from an early date, concentrating such processes as raising, shearing and dyeing at their house or mill before the spinning and weaving processes were reorganised into workshops.

Fulling was perhaps the most influential process in the woollen industries. Water-powered wooden stocks were used to hammer the cloth, causing it to shrink and thicken. Combined with the processes of raising and shearing, this gave the cloth a smooth face in which the warp and weft were invisible (Fig 1.12; *see also* Figs 1.9b and 1.9c). Finishing techniques continued to influence the later development of the woollen and serge industries. Specialist dye and finishing works developed in some areas in which the processes were mechanised and further subdivided, resulting in factories that were quite distinct from other types of textile mill. Finishing was similarly important in the hemp and flax industry, where yarn bleaching was recognised as one of the key factors determining the durability of sailcloth. Other finishing processes included the sizing of twine for fishing nets and the tarring of rope for use in ships. Dyeing was particularly important in the silk industry, in which the delicate filaments required a different sequence of processes to the other industries. Some types of silk were spun in the South West, taken to London for dyeing, and then returned to the South West for the final spinning process.

Fig 1.12
The processes and tools associated with the hand raising and shearing of fulled cloth are carved into this 16th-century bench end at Spaxton Church, Somerset. A wide range of skilled textile trades were practiced across the region long before the introduction of factory working.
[DP139888]

2

The Gloucestershire woollen industry

The largest concentration of textile mills in the South West can be found in Gloucestershire, where the mills and other buildings of the fine-woollen industry exhibit a distinctive architecture that has developed over an exceptionally long period.[1] Many of the county's mill sites were occupied for three centuries before the construction of factory buildings began in the mid-18th century, so the surviving mills merely represent the last phase in the development of the industry and are closely connected with the history of the landscape. The Gloucestershire woollen trade was well established by the 16th century, expanded to its full extent in the 17th and 18th centuries and then consolidated into a smaller number of very large complexes by the end of the 19th century. The architecture of the woollen mills was strongly influenced by the equally distinctive vernacular buildings of the clothiers, with their houses, workshops and fulling mills. Physical evidence of the earlier generations of mills is scarce but of great interest, providing an insight into the scale and complex organisation of textile production before the Industrial Revolution. The early mills determined the extent of the industry and in many cases directly influenced the construction of the surviving factories. The Gloucestershire woollen industry has long been of great interest to historians, and some of the pioneering research into English industrial history was carried out in Gloucestershire in the 1960s and 1970s.[2] The aim of this chapter is to discuss the character of the mills in a national context, and to highlight their qualities as a class of historic buildings that document the area's exceptional industrial history.

Gloucestershire's industrial landscape

The history of the Gloucestershire woollen industry was closely related to the distinctive landscape in the north-western part of the Cotswold Hills (Fig 2.1). Centred on Stroud, and now mostly within Stroud District, the area comprises the main Stroud and Nailsworth Valleys, the towns of Dursley and Wotton-under-Edge to the west and a large number of smaller tributary valleys. This network of deep valleys was unusually well suited to the development of the early industry. The streams provided the essential water supply for power and processes, the level valley floors offered sites that were eminently suitable for mill building and the higher ground had a long tradition of sheep farming. These natural advantages were key factors in the distribution of the woollen industry, resulting in an unusually large concentration of late medieval fulling mills, and led to many early mill sites being continuously occupied as the industry later expanded. Between the 15th and the 17th centuries, woollen mills and associated buildings spread throughout the area, creating much of the present-day pattern of roads and settlements. In contrast to other industrial regions that were dominated by 19th-century factory building, the Gloucestershire industry had reached its maximum geographical extent by the end of the 18th century, before the construction of most of the extant factory buildings.

Throughout the development of the industry the landscape influenced both the distribution of the mill sites and the nature of the buildings themselves. The density of mill sites in Gloucestershire is relatively high but the woollen industry remained essentially rural in character, and was not associated with the growth of urban areas. From the late 18th century, new types of factory buildings were built on the sites of earlier mills and could employ a local community which had been connected with the woollen industry for generations; in other areas the early factories were often built alongside new housing for a relocated workforce. The most important factor in the overall pattern of early

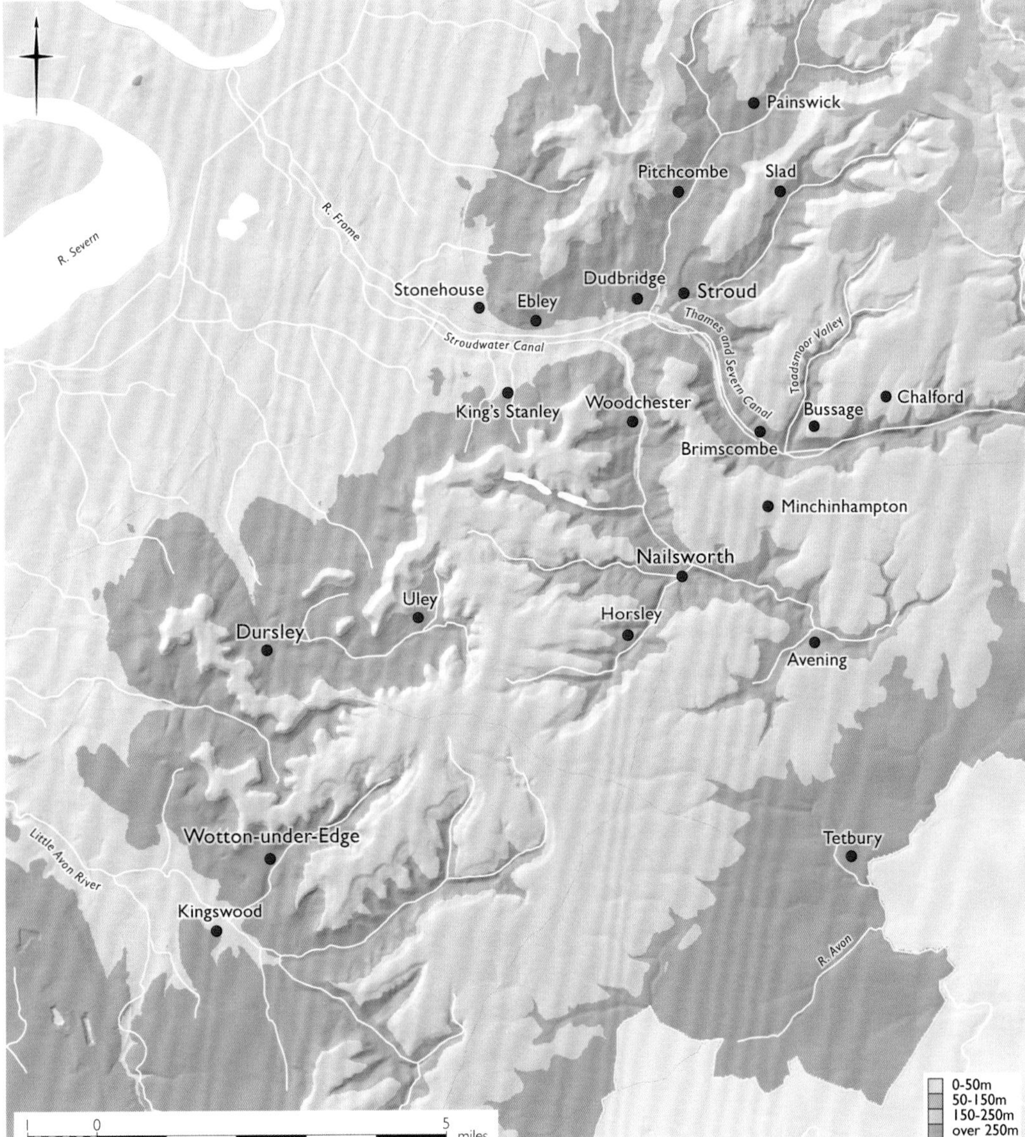

Fig 2.1
The Gloucestershire woollen industry was concentrated along the narrow valleys in the north-western part of the Cotswold Hills , which were suited to the early development of water power. [90m SRTM Topography data courtesy of the CGIAR, http://srtm.csi.cgiar.org]

mill building was the widespread availability of water-power sites, and water supplies continued to have a strong influence on the later development of the industry. The abundance of water power meant that when steam power was added in the 19th century it was used to supplement water power, rather than replacing it, so the ponds and other features associated with the older power systems were retained and became an intrinsic part of the countryside. Landscape also influenced processes inside the mills. Copious amounts of water were essential for textile processes, especially for preparation, finishing and dyeing, and enabled the development of the traditional dyed fine-woollen broadcloths that became Gloucestershire's most successful product.

By the end of the 18th century the valleys converging on the main towns had all acquired chains of mill sites, fully exploiting the potential of each stream for the development of water power. The distribution of textile mills was far from uniform, and different valleys became associated with mills of a particular size, period or function. In general, the earliest mills were built in the locations that were most suited to water power, often on the main streams in the middle and upper stretches of the valleys, where the topography suited the scale of post-medieval fulling mills.[3] These sites combined a reliable water supply with space to build a mill and a house; other desirable features were also largely determined by the topography, including space for later expansion, such as the construction of a pond or leat, and proximity to open ground for tentering the cloth (Fig 2.2). By the 18th century the more favourable sites were occupied by the wealthiest clothiers, and these firms had sufficient capital to successfully convert their mills to factory working in the 19th century. For this reason the largest surviving mill complexes, located in the main valleys, are also those which have seen the longest periods of continuous use. Mills in the more restricted side valleys and the remote sites saw less redevelopment, and were increasingly occupied by smaller, specialised firms or converted to non-textile uses. Ironically, the steep-sided valleys which suited the early development of water power in the area probably hindered the further expansion of the industry in the late 19th century, when new mill buildings needed to be much larger to compete with the industries in other areas.

Stroud: the hub of the Gloucestershire woollen industry

Stroud itself, benefiting from its location at the natural junction of the roads, rivers and, later, the canals and railways that connected the mill sites, grew into the main centre of the Gloucestershire woollen industry. In the 17th and 18th centuries the town saw development associated with some of the nearby mill sites, and the addition of streets of artisans' housing that was comparable to the suburban growth of industrial towns in Wiltshire and Somerset (*see* chapter 3). In the 19th century, however, it did not develop the commercial functions or the typical range of buildings that might be expected in an important industrial town. Its early development was also unusual, post-dating the establishment of the local woollen industry, so that Stroud was neither a typical

Fig 2.2
St Mary's Mill, Minchinhampton, was used by the clothier Francis Halliday by the early 16th century, although the extant mill was an addition of the early 19th century. The site occupies a constricted part of the Stroud Valley that was well suited to the small scale of the early fulling mills, with a flat valley floor that provided enough space for later development.
[DP025075]

late medieval wool town nor a typical 19th-century factory town. It was still a small hamlet when the local mill sites were being established in the 15th and 16th centuries. In contrast, the historic wool towns in the surrounding parishes originated before the development of the mills in the valleys, and were the main commercial centres for the area's pre-factory woollen industry. Some of the earliest woollen industry buildings are their historic market halls that were associated with trading wool and yarn, such as those in Tetbury (Fig 2.3) and Minchinhampton, while cloth halls survive in other towns, including Chipping Campden. Most of the development of Stroud took place from the 17th century as a consequence of the growth of the water-powered woollen industry, when the focus of the industry moved from the merchants in the market towns to the clothiers in the valleys. In the 19th century, Stroud lacked the warehousing and other commercial buildings that typically appeared during the later development of mill towns in other regions. The large factories of the 18th and 19th centuries were mostly spread along the surrounding valleys, and often included their own warehousing. Some were grouped around the larger villages, notably Nailsworth, but dependence on water power ensured that the factory buildings continued to be dispersed around the area. As a result, Stroud avoided most of the extensive rebuilding that was commonplace in 19th-century industrial towns. Many of its smaller historic buildings still retain the features of the 18th-century Cotswold vernacular architecture that pre-dated factory building.

The early woollen industry in Dursley and Wotton-under-Edge

A separate group of early woollen mills developed along the system of valleys flowing westwards from the Cotswolds, including those of the Little Avon, Ewelme and Cam Rivers, and was centred on the towns of Wotton-under-Edge, Dursley and Kingswood.[4] Wotton-under-Edge in particular was a well-

Fig 2.3
Several of the larger Gloucestershire market towns retain historic buildings connected with their roles as commercial centres for the pre-factory woollen industry. The extant Market House at Tetbury, built in 1655, was used as a yarn market in the early 18th century. [DP139651]

established market town in the formative stages of the industry, when it was a larger settlement than Stroud, and together with Dursley its townscape saw more emphasis on the construction of workshops, dye houses and clothiers' houses. Prior to the completion of the Stroudwater Navigation in 1779, this area probably benefited from more direct communications with Bristol and Wiltshire than was possible from other parts of Gloucestershire. The valleys upstream of the towns saw a similar linear pattern of early mill building to the wider Stroud and Nailsworth Valleys, but the narrow valley floors and insufficient water supply meant that fewer later mills were built in the area. A notable exception, however, was the valley of the River Ewelme above Dursley, where the landscape around the village of Uley was transformed by a variety of industrial sites by the late 19th century, including foundries in addition to woollen mills and dye works. The more open, lower-lying countryside to the west was more suited to the construction of larger woollen factories, several being built in the early 19th century on the sites of fulling mills (*see* New Mills and Charfield Mills, p 41 and p 42). In the 20th century the industry in the upper valleys saw a more dramatic decline than in other parts of Gloucestershire, with a higher rate of conversion or demolition of the mills, so the area is now of more rural character than the mixed landscapes in the valleys converging on Stroud.

The early woollen industry in this area was of comparable significance to that in the main Gloucestershire valleys, and local clothiers seem to have adopted a pioneering role in the introduction of lighter cloths in the early 17th century. One of the most widely produced was the so-called 'Spanish cloth', made in part using imported Spanish wool, which was first produced by Benedict Webb of Kingswood in *c* 1600. Webb learnt the improved methods needed to use this short-staple wool in France, and started producing the new dyed cloths in Taunton before expanding the business around Kingswood.[5] The use of Spanish wool to make the new cloths was widespread in the area by the mid-17th century, when it was also used in the Shepton Mallet and Bradford-on-Avon districts of Somerset and Wiltshire. Another notable clothier in the transformation of the late 17th-century woollen industry was John Eyles, who was reputedly the first to use Spanish wool in the parish of Uley.[6]

Products and processes

The main traditional product of the Gloucestershire woollen industry, up to the early 19th century, was a range of fine-woollen broadcloths. These thick, heavy cloths were high-quality products that were much in demand in the 16th and 17th centuries, and continued to be made in Gloucestershire well into the 19th century. They included a variety of specific types of cloth, some dyed locally and others sold undyed to be finished outside the area. The changing fortunes of the broadcloth trade were a major influence on the history of the pre-factory industry, and local clothiers and artisans gradually developed processes, machinery and building types that were suited to broadcloth production. When lighter-weight cloths became more fashionable from the mid-18th century, many of Gloucestershire's long-established firms were slow to adapt. Consequently the number of local working mills declined during the period when the textile industries elsewhere saw a dramatic expansion.

Fine-woollen broadcloths were extensively manufactured in late medieval England and developed into an important export trade. They included a wide variety of cloths produced in different regions, but all involved the use of short-staple wool to produce fulled cloths ranging from 60in to 100in (1.5–2.5m) wide.[7] Broadcloth of this width had to be woven by more than one operative because of the width of the loom; the so-called narrow cloths that became more common from the late 18th century could be produced by a single handloom weaver. Most of these medieval industries originated in areas that were suited to the rearing of appropriate breeds of sheep, but Gloucestershire had the additional benefit of a landscape suited to the development of water power. As a result, the broadcloth industry remained in the area after most of the medieval industries in other areas had declined, including the important early industries in Suffolk, Hampshire and the Welsh Borders. By the 17th century the Gloucestershire clothiers increasingly used imported wool and had earned an international reputation for what were termed 'superfine' broadcloths.

During the 17th century most parts of the English woollen industry were influenced by a widespread transition from the production of traditional heavy woollen cloths to lighter cloths that were made from longer-staple wools. The best-known examples were the 'New Draperies' of East Anglia and the serges of Devon and Somerset (*see* chapter 4), cloths which included long-staple worsteds and the combined use of short- and long-staple wools for the warp and weft.[8] Their introduction was marked by the greater use of imported wools, by the growth of some regional textile industries, particularly those which could develop a wider range of processes, and by the decline of others. Similar new cloths using Spanish wool were introduced in the Wotton-under-Edge area of Gloucestershire in the early 17th century (*see* p 18). The woollen industry across the whole of the west of England underwent a widespread transformation as clothiers responded to the increasing demand for the new types of cloth. In Gloucestershire, the industry saw significant growth in this period, benefiting from the well-established trade of its clothiers and the potential for the further development of water-power sites. The early development of cloth dyeing in the local valleys was another advantage, since the earlier trade in the export of undyed cloth was also in decline. The area's reputation for heavily fulled fine-woollens continued, but the later development of the industry was increasingly characterised by a diversification into lighter and mixed cloths. This trend continued into the early factory-building period and throughout the 19th century, as the capital of the clothiers and their understanding of textile processes enabled the introduction of the new cloths which suited factory production.

Processes in the traditional fine-woollen industry

The overall sequence of processes used in Gloucestershire was comparable to that in other woollen industries, but there was a local emphasis on the development of processes related to the fine-woollen broadcloth trade.[9] Broadloom weavers were more productive after the widespread introduction of the flying shuttle in the mid-18th century, which in turn placed greater demands on yarn spinners and on the carding and preparation stages. Most of the 18th-century improvements involved using new types of manual or partially powered machines in workshops. Fine-woollen broadcloth was seen as a specialised branch of the woollen industry by the late 18th century, when the industries in other regions, and many mills in Gloucestershire, were concentrating on lighter cloths woven with a combination of wool or worsted with other fibres. The traditional fine-woollen broadcloths were a high-quality product with a smooth face that required careful preparation of the raw wool, a long period of fulling and the skilled use of raising, shearing and drying processes to produce the best finish. The Stroud area was also well known for its dyed fine woollens from the 15th century,[10] which led to the development of specialised independent dye works by the mid-18th century.

Locally sourced wools were used in the early days of the industry, but by the 17th century English fine wool was being replaced by, or mixed with, a range of imported wools, notably from Spain.[11] The raw wool was thoroughly washed, or scoured, and then dried and oiled before carding. These were all manual processes that were put out to cottage workers until the mid-18th century, after which they were increasingly mechanised to prepare greater quantities of wool for spinning and weaving. A distinctive building type related to improvements in wool preparation in this period was the circular drying tower, in which the washed wool was spread on racks and dried with hot air from a stove.[12] After drying the wool was treated to improve its handling in the later processes. In the cottage industry, butter was often applied to the wool manually, but by the 18th century Gallipoli oil (a type of olive oil) was widely used, and is often specified in inventories of clothiers' goods.[13] From the late 18th century, oiling was achieved more efficiently by the use of scribbling machines, in which the wool was coated with oil by a system of rotating spikes. Carding was another widespread manual process that was mechanised from the late 18th century. Carding engines were heavy machines that were usually water or steam powered, and were associated with the increased use of workshops and small mills. In the small early factories, only part of the building was powered and used for the heavier machinery, normally the basement or ground floor, while hand-powered machinery continued to be used in other parts of the building (Fig 2.4).

Spinning and weaving were extensive cottage industries throughout the west of England woollen industry, with hand carding, spinning and sometimes preparation processes often carried out by other members of the hand-loom weaver's household. The most significant development in spinning was the introduction of the jenny from the late 18th century, a hand-

Fig 2.4
One of the few examples of a carding machine to remain in situ *at a Gloucestershire mill in the early 1990s, at Longfords Mills, Minchinhampton. [BB040450]*

powered machine with multiple spindles using similar technology to the traditional spinning wheels (*see* Fig 3.5). Jennies produced much more yarn but required more space, and were often located in unpowered early workshops and partly powered mills. A powered version of the jenny, known as the throstle, was introduced in the early 19th century, but the most suitable machine for fine-yarn spinning was the mule, which remained in use in Gloucestershire from the early 19th century to the 1990s (Fig 2.5). By the late 19th century mules with several hundred spindles achieved high output, but were large machines that had a significant influence on the layout and power systems of the later mills. In weaving, the machine which helped establish the pre-factory fine-woollen industry in Gloucestershire was the broadcloth handloom, and skilled handloom weavers were a highly influential class of artisans by the 18th century. This was probably a factor in the relatively slow adoption of power-loom weaving in Gloucestershire in the early 19th century, when handlooms continued to be widely used and several of the larger firms were investing in purpose-built workshops specifically for handloom weaving. By the time power looms were in more general use, the Gloucestershire industry had contracted to a small number of integrated mills, which combined the full range of processes at one site. The late 19th-century specialised weaving sheds that were seen in other regions were rarely built in Gloucestershire (Fig 2.6).

After weaving, a sequence of finishing and dyeing processes largely determined the quality and value of fine-woollen cloths. The most

Fig 2.5
A self-acting mule at Stanley Mill in 2010. These later, very long spinning machines had to be arranged longitudinally when installed in an earlier mill. The original machines were normally sited transversely, between the columns. [DP115120]

Fig 2.6
Power-loom weaving in a north-light shed with overhead line shafting at Longfords Mills, c 1912. In comparison with other regions, surprisingly few specialised weaving sheds were built for the Gloucestershire woollen industry.
[Reproduced courtesy of the Stroudwater Textile Trust. BB040981]

important process, and probably the one which most influenced Gloucestershire's early industry, was fulling. In combination with raising and shearing, fulling produced the fine, dense surface that was the defining characteristic of the cloth. In the medieval woollen trade fulling was a slow manual process, achieved by using wooden clubs or by 'walking' the pieces in vats, which greatly limited cloth production. Powered fulling enabled larger quantities of cloth to be finished, and for the duration of fulling itself to be extended, so the water-powered fulling mill occupied a key role at the centre of the fine-woollen clothier's out-working business (Fig 2.7).[14] Fulling mills were in common use from the medieval period but have not been widely studied as a building type. The few known surviving examples illustrate the development of fulling mills just before the process was superseded by other machines in the mid-19th century. A widespread feature of the early woollen factories in Gloucestershire, those built from the mid-18th to the early 19th century, appears to have been the installation of fulling stocks in the ground floor of the main building, close to the waterwheels or steam engine. From the 1830s the use of fulling stocks was superseded by milling machines, invented by John Dyer of Trowbridge in 1833, a more compact machine using a system of powered rollers which was more suited to installation in large factories (*see* chapter 3). Milling machines were often used alongside cloth-scouring machines in the later mills and finishing works (Fig 2.8; *see also* Fig 3.6).

Fulling or milling was followed by tentering, in which the cloth pieces were dried on racks to control the amount of shrinking. Tentering was also used after dyeing or bleaching. Open-

Fig 2.7
Fulling stocks were lifted by a tappet wheel driven by underfloor shafting, as seen in these well-preserved stocks at Cam Mills, Dursley, in 1964.
[Photograph courtesy of Lionel Walrond. DP139052]

Fig 2.8
From the 1830 fulling stocks were replaced by milling machines in which cloth pieces were stitched into a long loop that was repeatedly passed through wooden rollers under high pressure. Milling machines were used in combination with cloth-scouring machines, as was the case at Longfords Mills. [BB040947]

air tentering was the traditional method, with 'rack fields' commonly identified on tithe and estate maps (Fig 2.9). With the increased output of the early factories, dry houses enabled tentering to continue uninterrupted by the weather. Dry houses were distinctive long, narrow buildings which used a combination of natural ventilation and warm air heated by stoves.

After drying, the smooth face of fine-woollen cloth was produced using a combination of raising and shearing. The precise sequence of fulling, tentering, shearing and raising might be carefully adjusted or even repeated to

Fig 2.9
Vernacular buildings and landscapes of the pre-factory woollen industry at Wallbridge, Stroud, late 18th century. Woollen cloth is being dyed and rinsed in the open channel alongside the canal. Tenter racks supporting 'Stroud reds' and some undyed cloths can be seen on the surrounding hillsides. Artist and date unknown. [Reproduced courtesy of The Museum in the Park, Stroud. 1948_500]

achieve the desired finish. Raising the nap of the cloth was achieved manually by brushing it with teazles mounted on a board, but from the mid-16th century teazle gigs were commonly used to produce a more consistent finish.[15] The teazle gig comprised a large rotating drum covered with teazles against which the cloth piece was passed using rollers (Fig 2.10). The use of gig machines was opposed by handloom weavers in some areas in the late 18th and early 19th century, notably in Wiltshire, but gigs appear to have been widely used by the Gloucestershire clothiers.[16] Similar principles are used in the raising machines of modern woollen mills, usually with a wire brush instead of teazles. A mid-18th-century variation of these processes, which was confusingly referred to as 'knapping', was used at some Gloucestershire dye and finishing works to give the cloth a distinctive ribbed finish.[17]

The nap of the cloth was removed to produce its distinctive smooth surface using heavy iron shears, in another widespread and highly skilled craft that was replaced from the early 19th century, in spite of strong opposition by the shearmen themselves (*see* Fig 1.9c). The shearing process was greatly speeded up by the development of a rotary cutting machine by John Lewis of Brimscombe, patented in 1815, which seems to have been partly based

Fig 2.10
Teazle gigs were in use at clothiers' mills and workshops by the end of the 17th century in Gloucestershire, such as these at Longfords Mills, although their use in neighbouring Wiltshire and Somerset was strongly resisted until the early 19th century. Cloth pieces were stitched into a continuous loop that was passed through the machine on rollers. The nap of the cloth was raised by rows of teazles mounted on a rotating drum.
[BB040488]

on an earlier American cutting machine.[18] The Lewis machine was widely adopted, effectively bypassing the traditional craft of the hand shearers, and was improved further in 1830 when Lewis introduced a system for feeding long pieces continually through the machine (Figs 2.11 and 2.12).

Gloucestershire earned an early reputation for the production of dyed woollen cloths. The famous 'Stroud reds', for example, are shown prominently on tenter racks in 18th-century paintings (*see* Fig 2.9). Dyeing was normally carried out at the cloth-finishing stage, but from the 17th century the increased production of 'medleys', which used warp and weft of different colours, led to an increase in yarn dyeing.[19]

Fig 2.11 (top)
A well-preserved early example of a Lewis rotary cloth cutter, the machine used for cutting the nap of woollen cloth after it was raised on a teazle gig. On display at The Museum in the Park, Stroud.
[DP137218]

Fig 2.12 (bottom)
Detail of Lewis rotary cloth cutter.
[DP137220]

Traditional dyeing involved a series of manual processes using heated vats of liquor in small, well-ventilated buildings, usually sited close to a water supply for 'streaming', or washing-out the surplus dye. Dye houses were being added to fulling mills and clothiers' houses by the 18th century, along with workshops for spinning, weaving and teazle gigs, before the construction of factory buildings (for example at Pitchcombe Upper Mill and Egypt Mill, *see* p 31 and p 34). Specialised dye and finishing works had developed around some older fulling mills by the mid-18th century, earlier than most other textile areas, where the full range of cloth-finishing processes were carried out for clothiers from both Gloucestershire and the adjoining counties (Figs 2.13, 2.14 and 2.15; *see also* Fig 1.11).[20]

The pre-factory woollen industry

The Gloucestershire woollen industry had expanded to its maximum extent long before most of the surviving mills were built. The present-day distribution of mills, and in many cases the layout of mill sites, provides evidence of the long and complicated early history of the industry. The extant mills mostly date from a period of rebuilding, when vernacular mills were replaced with factories, between the mid-18th and the mid-19th centuries. Consequently, many Gloucestershire mill sites have exceptionally early origins, and although early structures rarely survive, their influence can often be seen in the extant buildings. Documentary references indicate that several fulling mills were in use as early as the 13th century and that mills had occupied most of the best water-power sites by the end of the 15th century.[21] The main period of geographical expansion was between the 15th and the early 18th century, significantly pre-dating the classic period of the Industrial Revolution in other regions. It included several phases of expansion interspersed with periods in which trade was depressed, and was marked by major changes in the organisation of textile businesses, the markets for their products and by the ongoing improvement of textile processes. Gloucestershire's extant woollen mills thus represent the last of many phases of successive development, and survived largely because of the continued importance of water for power and processes. This remarkable continuity of use of many sites is also reflected in their history of occupation; the first factories were frequently built by firms descended from clothier families

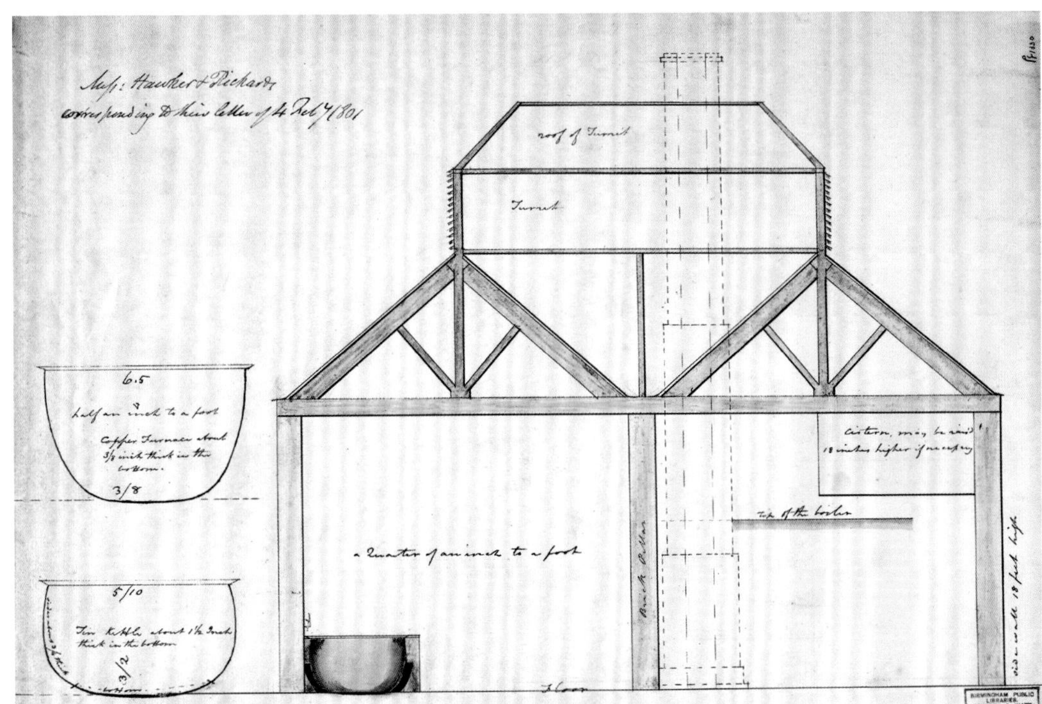

Fig 2.13
A rare example of early 19th-century drawings showing the arrangement of processes in part of the Dudbridge Dye Works. The drawings show the addition of a boiler and piping to heat the dye vats, with individual vats dedicated to particular colours. The main dye house was ventilated through opening slats in the rooftop louvre.
[Reproduced with the permission of Birmingham Archives & Libraries, Boulton and Watt Archive, Portfolio 1330. DP137102]

who had occupied earlier buildings at the same site.

During the post-medieval period the industry was organised quite differently to that in medieval towns, where all aspects of cloth production had been strictly controlled by guilds and the availability of sites for mill building was limited. In common with other rural textile-producing areas, the Gloucestershire industry was controlled by clothiers, merchants who traded in raw wool and facilitated the production of the cloth by cottage-based spinners and weavers. The absence of guild restrictions enabled the gradual improvement

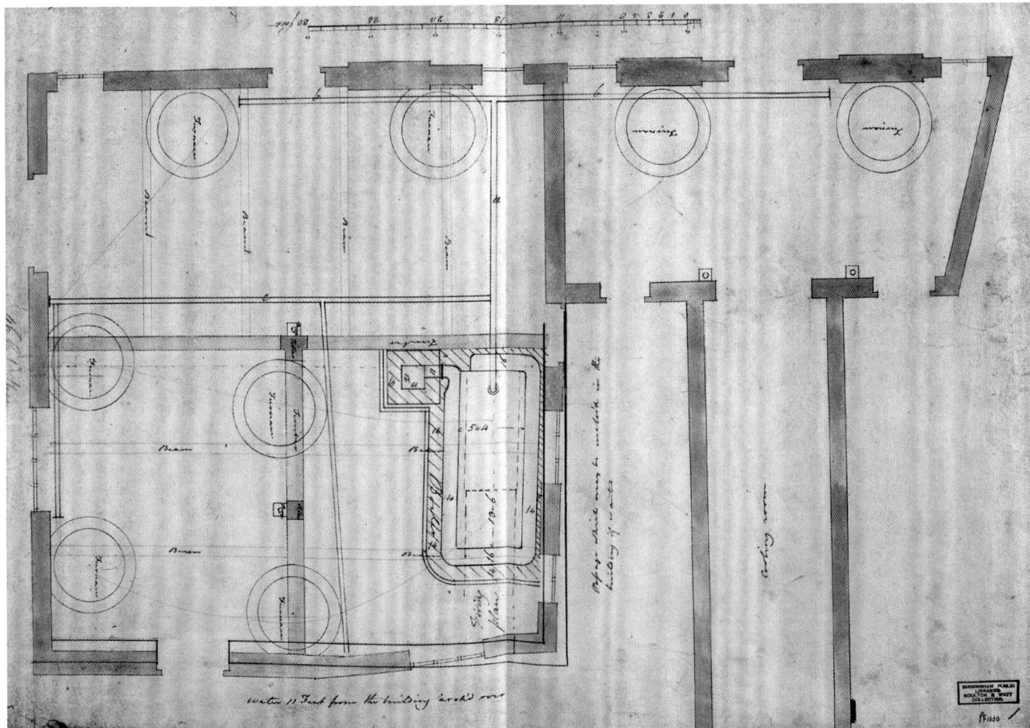

Fig 2.14
As in other Gloucestershire finishing works, the dye houses were added in many phases to an earlier water-powered fulling mill.
[Reproduced with the permission of Birmingham Archives & Libraries, Boulton and Watt Archive, Portfolio 1330. DP137101]

Fig 2.15
Interior of a dye house at Longfords Mills, photographed in c 1912, showing a similar arrangement of vats to those in the early 19th-century drawings of the Dudbridge Dye Works.
[Reproduced courtesy of the Stroudwater Textile Trust. BB040978]

of the methods of production, while the widespread availability of water-power sites allowed the dispersal of the industry throughout the area. It was this pre-factory phase that firmly established the woollen textile industry in Gloucestershire; the industry of the clothiers survived far longer than the factory system that followed it.

Significant variations developed in the roles of clothiers in the different pre-factory textile industries in the South West. Some industries, notably the serge industry in Devon, were often financed by merchants who had little or no direct connection with cloth production, while in other cases the commercial role was combined with the organisation and management of outworkers. In general, Gloucestershire's clothiers were involved with all aspects of the production and sale of fine-woollen cloths, and gradually increased their control of the processes which most determined the value of their products. The role of the clothiers in this area just prior to the period of factory building was aptly described in 1757:

One person, with a great stock and large credit, buys the wool, pays for the spinning, weaving, Milling, Drying, Shearing, Dressing, etc. That is, he is Master of the whole manufacture from first to last, and probably employs a thousand persons under him.[22]

The Gloucestershire clothiers retained ownership of the goods throughout all the stages of production, and so exercised more influence on commerce, organisation and production than those in other regions. The level of control they acquired was central to the long-term success of the superfine woollen industry in this area, and began the combination of processes that developed into the major feature of Gloucestershire's integrated factories in the 19th century.

The industry of the gentlemen clothiers

The clothiers' businesses varied greatly in size and longevity. Published research on the Stroud area, for example, indicates that by the late 15th century the clothiers included some wealthy landowners with property outside the local area and capital outside the textile industry, along with a range of smaller firms and artisan workers.[23] No intact mill buildings are known to survive from the early phase of the industry, although the functions and approximate locations of the mills can often be inferred from documentary evidence. From the late 16th century, when most of the main stream sites had been occupied, further mill building required more extensive use of leats and earthworks to manage the available water supply.[24] The main period for the establishment of new mill sites was from the late 16th to the end of the 17th century, which saw the industry expand along most of the lower valleys in the area and the development of a much more numerous middle class of rural clothiers.

From the 17th century, the rising class of clothiers acquired both property and political influence in Gloucestershire as a direct result of the growth of the industry.[25] The present-day distribution of textile mill sites largely reflects the success of these gentlemen clothiers. Clothiers' houses from this period survived long after most of their associated fulling mills were demolished or rebuilt. The expansion of the clothiers' industry was followed in the 18th century by a period of technical development and increasing competition, both within the local trade and with the newer textile industries emerging in other areas. As demand increased for new types of lighter woollens and mixed cloths, the more prosperous firms invested successfully in new machinery and factory buildings. As the traditional industry declined, however, many clothiers were forced into smaller mills in the more remote sites. For these clothiers the attempted move into factory methods was often short-lived, resulting in the demolition of mills or their conversion to non-textile uses.

Clothiers' houses

Gloucestershire's clothiers' houses, dating from the 16th to the 18th century, are the most widespread buildings of the area's pre-factory woollen industry.[26] They survived long after most of their associated fulling mills were demolished or rebuilt, and now form one of the most distinctive types of vernacular architecture in the South West region. Characterised by their use of local Cotswold stone with ashlar dressings, narrow plans, low stone-flagged roofs with dormers to the main elevations, mullioned windows and a variety of ornamental detailing, most were built overlooking a fulling mill site. They were extended with wings and architectural details that reflected both the wealth of the owner and, in many cases, the concentration of industrial processes close to the house. Far fewer of the contemporary mills survive, but physical and documentary evidence indicates that they were of similar materials, proportions and vernacular details to the clothiers' houses (Figs 2.16 and 2.17; *see also* Fig 2.9). The houses belonging to the most successful clothier families, such as the Gardners and the Winchcombes of Stratford House (now The Museum in the Park), the Clutterbucks of St Mary's Mill and the Pauls of Woodchester Mill, not surprisingly show the most evidence of extensions and improvements. Many of the larger houses were re-fronted and extended in the late 18th and early 19th century, reflecting the increasing prosperity of the early

Fig 2.16
One of the largest 17th-century clothiers' houses was built for Richard Webb of Egypt Mill, Nailsworth, in 1698.
[DP137152]

Fig 2.17
Clothiers' housing was often associated with workshops, rooms for sorting and storing wool and small industrial outbuildings. This example at Chestnut Hill, Nailsworth, dated 1726, included warehousing and workshops in the upper floors and loading doors for goods.
[DP137147]

factory builders. The Gloucestershire architect Anthony Keck was commissioned to update several of the larger clothiers' houses with fashionable Georgian façades and extensions.[27] Similar alterations were made to some of the early vernacular-style mills, disguising their industrial origins, including Upper Steanbridge Mill and the early part of Lodgemore Mills. The close proximity of clothiers' houses to the mill and other industrial buildings continued to be desirable into the early factory-building period, when the mill owners of other regions were increasingly building houses that were some distance away from their industrial sites. Perhaps the grandest example of the architectural development of a clothier's site was at New Mills, Stroud, where in 1766 Thomas Bayliss combined his woollen mill, workshops and adjoining house into a single long building of somewhat ostentatious Georgian style to create the appearance of a large country residence, complete with landscaped gardens (Fig 2.18).[28]

Early woollen mills

The location of the early fulling mills, and to a large extent the form of the buildings themselves, was largely determined by their use of water for power and processes. Landscape features associated with former water-supply systems survive throughout the area. Earthworks are amongst the most extensive historical evidence of the textile industry in Gloucestershire, and possibly the least studied. Leats, weirs, ponds and bypass channels of different dates can be detected in most of the valleys used for mill building, often extending for hundreds of metres beyond the mill sites, although the features associated with the earliest mills have generally been eroded or replaced. The development of the water-supply system mirrored the development of the mill itself, and many of the intact features date from the period when early mills were rebuilt as factories, from the mid-18th to the mid-19th century. Enlarged

Fig 2.18
The development of water-powered mills with workshops enabled some of the wealthiest 18th-century clothiers to indulge their interest in architectural fashions. New Mills near Stroud was clearly intended to evoke the style of a large country house and estate. [Engraving from Samuel Rudder, 1799, A New History of Gloucestershire. *DP149083]*

or rebuilt mills usually required more power, and were accompanied by modifications to the leats and ponds to raise the level of water at the headrace. Other alterations reflected the problems of distributing the available water supply amongst an increasing number of mills, such as the need for larger storage ponds.

A small number of Gloucestershire mills retain well-preserved early 19th-century waterwheels, although, in general, historic machinery of any kind rarely survives in textile mill buildings. Many more of the extant sites retain other types of physical evidence of the development of water power. A typical sequence of development included modifications to the waterwheel, sluice mechanism and the power transmission system, all of which left distinctive features in the building, and the eventual combination of water power with a steam engine. In most cases all the mechanical features have been removed, and any that remain are likely to date from the later phases of alterations.

Some of the early factory mills in Gloucestershire used water power on a very large scale, but by the late 18th century many local mills were using water-power systems that were less technically developed than those being installed in large new mills in other regions. Examples include the type and construction of the waterwheels, the power transmission systems and the locations of the wheel pits. In other areas, new types of suspension wheels were installed in segregated or external chambers, but Gloucestershire mills continued to be built with cast-iron or timber waterwheels that were fully exposed in the ground floor (Fig 2.19). This apparent conservatism in the development of water power seems to be a reflection of the long-established tradition of water-powered mill building in the area, and the fact that the good water supplies obviated the need for advanced types of wheels.

Fig 2.19
The first generation of large factories in Gloucestershire continued the tradition of locating the waterwheels in the main body of the mill, such as these at Ebley Mill photographed in 1935, often occupying most of the ground floor. Later water-powered mills sited the wheels in external wheel houses, enabling the ground floor to be used for textile machinery. [English Heritage Archive, George Watkins Collection, 28a. AL2386/004/01 (SER_28)]

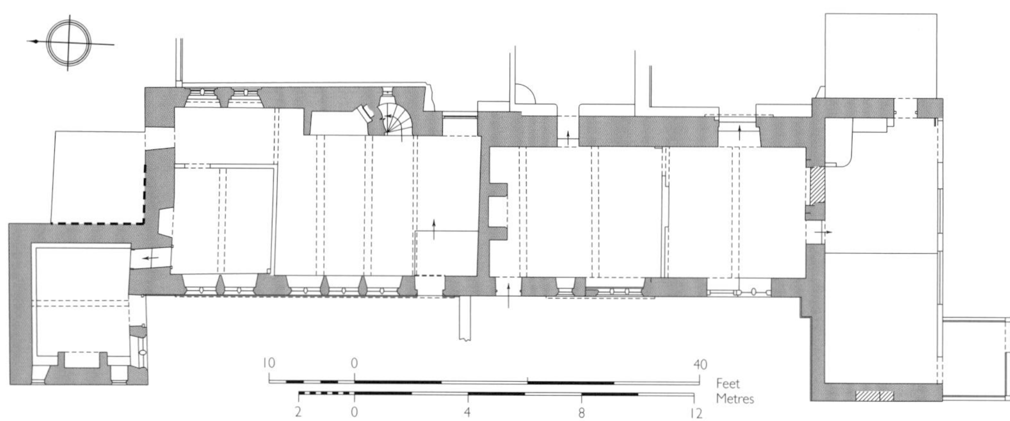

Fig 2.20
Upper Steanbridge Mill in the Slad Valley shows the narrow proportions of the early fulling mills, and a typical arrangement of house and mill in the same building. An external waterwheel was formerly located at the right end.

As stated earlier, any evidence relating to the development of Gloucestershire's pre-factory mills is of considerable historical interest. A consequence of the re-use of mill sites is that few early structures survive and these are often heavily altered. No intact mills survive dating from before the 18th century. In some cases, however, the partial remains of early mills have been incorporated into later buildings, and other examples were converted into houses. Together with documentary evidence this provides a general indication of the buildings that housed the pre-factory industry.

The early fulling mills were essentially small vernacular buildings, often combined with grist mills, which were built to narrow plans and usually sited at a right angle to a stream or leat. In many cases the mill adjoined the clothier's house. The few surviving fulling mills represent a late stage of development, being contemporary with the improvements to textile machinery in the first half of the 18th century. Previous generations of fulling mills were strongly influenced by local building traditions, with little or no resemblance to the surviving factory buildings, and were built with materials and architectural details similar to contemporary small houses or farm buildings. They were low in height, typically between one and two and a half storeys, and had steeply pitched stone roofs with gables to both the end and side elevations. Small ancillary buildings, such as gig houses or dye houses, also reflected the traditional local vernacular, but the workshops being added by the 18th century had some features that were also seen in the early factories, such as rectangular plans, open interiors and regular fenestration.

Upper Steanbridge Mill, Painswick

Although the site has been extensively altered, Upper Steanbridge Mill provides a good indication of the size and appearance of early Gloucestershire mills and also shows how industrial origins can be disguised by later conversion to domestic use (Fig 2.20). The building probably dates from the late 17th or early 18th century, with major 19th- and 20th-century alterations. It was bought as a fulling mill with two stocks and a gig in 1781, and was

Fig 2.21
The re-facing of vernacular houses and mills was common in Gloucestershire from the late 18th century, creating taller and more fashionable elevations. At Upper Steanbridge Mill the former gabled appearance of the front elevation can be discerned in the stonework of the top storey.
[DP137209]

reputed to be one of the first local mills to be equipped with spinning jennies.[29] Internally the building was divided by a central wall into a house in the northern half and a mill with an external waterwheel in the southern half. It was built to a narrow plan which is end-on to a tributary stream of the Slad Valley, and was the highest of a line of nine mills extending downstream towards Stroud.[30] The remains of a substantial pond and dam are located immediately upstream, their large size suggesting they may also have supplied some of the other mills. Joints in the front elevation indicate that it was formerly of two and a half storeys, and of typical vernacular appearance with four prominent gables (Fig 2.21). The alterations may date from the early 19th century, when more regular Georgian-style façades were being added to traditional houses in the Gloucestershire area, as elsewhere. In this case, however, the stone-mullioned windows with drip moulds were retained. The larger windows suggest that parts of the building were intended to provide workshop space, possibly for jennies, with fulling stocks in the ground floor.

Frogmarsh Mill, Woodchester

This is one of the best examples of the architectural development from the vernacular woollen industry to early factory buildings, and is one of over a dozen early sites along the Nailsworth Stream to the south of Stroud. A fulling mill was in use here by 1658, when it contained two fulling stocks, a gig and a dye house.[31] It was developed as a woollen mill during the transformation of the industry between the mid-18th and early 19th century, and was converted for use as a pin mill from the early 1850s.[32] The extant buildings span an unusually wide date range, including substantial parts of a 17th-century clothier's house with attached 18th-century workshops (Fig 2.22), good evidence of a 17th- or 18th-century fulling mill and several phases of additions and rebuilding in the 19th century. The clothier's house retains typical domestic features and decorative mouldings of the late 16th and 17th century, but was later extended with a long workshop range and converted to industrial use (Fig 2.23). The early fulling mill was also attached to the house. Surviving parts of its walls indicate that the mill was of two and a half storeys and of similar vernacular appearance to contemporary houses, with a series of gables to the side elevations. It was later raised and extended with another three-storeyed mill attached to its north side. Most of the fulling mill was finally replaced with the surviving factory building in the late 19th century, when the site was in use as a pin mill.

Inchbrook Mill and Egypt Mill

Two of the best-preserved fulling mills in the county survive in the upper Nailsworth Valley, illustrating the development of the later fulling mills in the 18th and early 19th centuries. Both are of comparable proportions with two main phases of building, and were owned by successful clothiers during the reorganisation of the industry that preceded factory building. In the early 18th century, Inchbrook Mill was in use for fulling by the clothier Richard Cambridge, who also owned St Mary's Mill (*see* p 48). Its later extension probably dates from a period of ownership by Playne and Smith of Dunkirk Mills (*see* p 42) a century later.[33] The extension included a large internal wheel chamber and a ground floor which originally had a door but no windows, suggesting it may have contained fulling stocks. Egypt Mill was owned by the clothier Richard Webb and his descendants

Fig 2.22
At Frogmarsh Mill at Woodchester, near Stroud, the 17th-century clothier's house in the foreground was extended with several phases of textile workshops by the early 19th century. [DP025977]

Fig 2.23
The main buildings at Frogmarsh Mill were rebuilt in the mid- and late 19th century on the footprint of the fulling mill that was attached to the clothier's house. Parts of the walls of the vernacular fulling mill were incorporated in the rebuilding.
[AP26009/005]

from the late 17th century (Fig 2.24). Webb probably built the nearby house, which bears a stone plaque inscribed 'RW 1698'. The house is lit by ovolo-moulded windows, fashionable in the late 17th century, but has a less typical square plan; its upper rooms were used as a wool loft. By the early 19th century the site was in use as a finishing and dye works, with buildings for scribbling, dyeing, bleaching and shearing, in addition to the fulling mill, warehouse and a nearby rack field.[34] The earlier phase of the mill includes large openings, now blocked, between the upper-floor windows; similar large openings have been seen in other fulling mills, suggesting that their upper floors may have been used as a ventilated drying area.

Cloth finishing: Brimscombe Upper Mill and Dudbridge Dye Works

Finishing and dye works became more significant in the mid-18th century, providing a range of essential services for clothiers before the local trade was dominated by fully integrated factories. Brimscombe Upper Mill operated as the successful finishing works of William Dalloway in the 1740s, although fulling mills were in use at the site by the mid-16th century.[35] The site retains a collection of small water- and steam-powered buildings and workshops, of late 18th to late 19th century date, built around a yard, typical of the piecemeal development seen at textile finishing works in other regions. Dalloway's well-preserved account books of the 1740s give details of a wide range of dyeing, fulling and knapping jobs for Gloucestershire clothiers and other customers from as far afield

Fig 2.24
The exceptionally well-preserved Egypt Mill and clothier's house at Nailsworth. The earlier fulling mill occupied the lower five bays at the left end. The extension retains late 19th-century corn milling machinery.
[DP137153]

as Bristol and Birmingham.[36] The accounts also provide a rare insight into the complex business relationships that characterised the outworking system in the 18th century, and the need to transport large quantities of cloth around the county. In addition to their cloth-finishing work the firm was letting out machinery for their customers to use and putting out some jobs to other nearby mills. Dalloway was also involved in foreign trade ventures and in the survey and promotion of the nearby Thames and Severn Canal, which was completed in 1785. Another important early dye and finishing works was the Dudbridge Dye Works of Richard Hawker, which does not survive. Fulling appears to have been located at the site since the 13th century.[37] In the early 19th century this works also included buildings for knapping. An 18th-century plan shows the complex and the nearby owner's house, which does survive, and early 19th-century drawings from the Boulton and Watt Collection give a rare detailed plan and section views of the dye house (Fig 2.25; *see also* Figs 2.13 and 2.14).[38]

The first factories

The Cotswold-stone mill buildings which are characteristic of a large part of the Gloucestershire countryside mostly date from a period of rebuilding between the mid-18th and the mid-19th century. In this period the traditional form of business of the clothiers, with their networks of skilled outworkers, was gradually superseded by the firms that adopted the principles of the factory system. From the mid-18th century the more progressive clothiers began to construct new types of mill buildings, mostly on the sites of earlier mills. The new mills were generally comparable in date and size to those being built in other regions, but their role in the history of the industry was quite different. In other areas, factory building marked a dramatic expansion of the textile industry, and was associated with new technologies, a new class of capitalist manufacturers and a new way of life for local people. In contrast, Gloucestershire's early factories resulted from the reorganisation and consolidation of a much older industry. They were not associated with urban development, the relocation of the workforce or the creation of completely new firms, and displayed architectural and technical features that reflected their continued ownership by long-established clothier families.

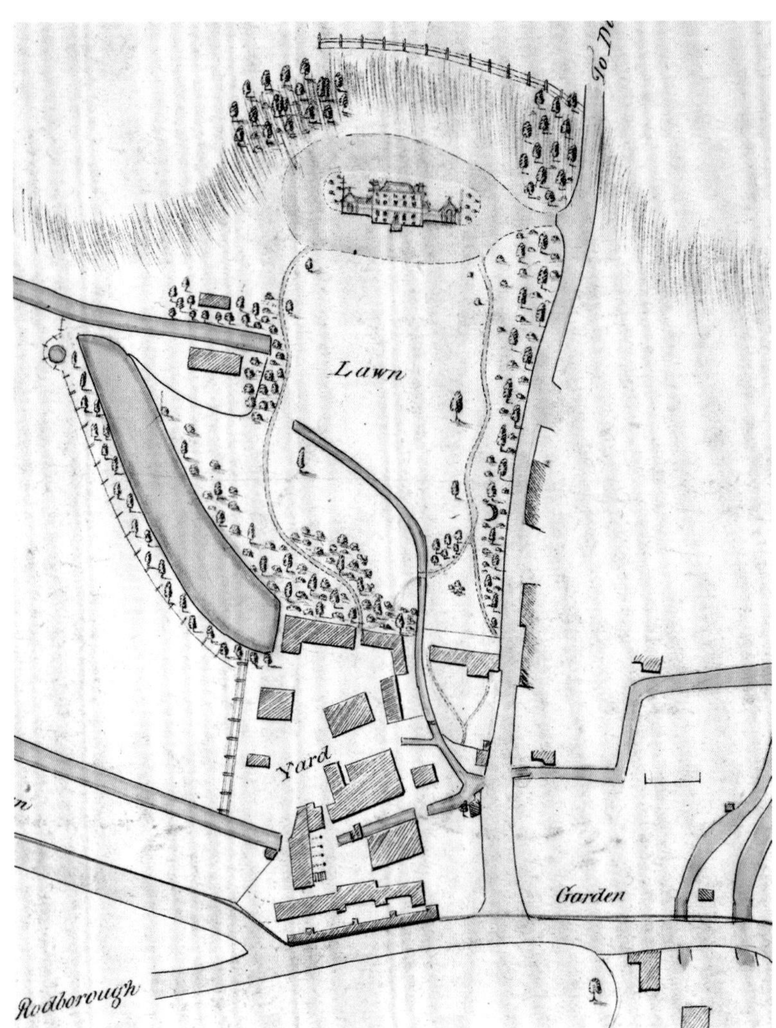

Fig 2.25
The former dye works of Richard Hawker at Dudbridge in c 1825. The works expanded around the site of a medieval fulling mill into a complex of small buildings with specific functions, typical of other cloth-finishing works but contrasting with the larger scale of contemporary spinning mills. The works was sited at the end of the gardens of the proprietor's residence, shown at the top of the plan.
[Reproduced courtesy of Gloucester Archives, TS/267/2. DP137425]

Factory buildings in the mid- to late 18th century

The early factories represented a pioneering and innovative approach to manufacturing, but are now an extremely rare building type. Traditional fulling mills were usually not large enough to accommodate the new types of machinery, but the early factories were larger and enabled a reorganisation of processes and workers to achieve increased output with better control of production. Improvements in machinery for spinning and weaving had already benefited outworking in domestic workshops, and similar types of machines could be used more efficiently in a factory setting. The stages of production that were previously put out were gradually brought into the mill, where a variety of new building types reflected the increased range of processes carried out at the site. The new types of mills were built with more storeys and provided a larger, open floor space with better lighting to enable groups of machines to be conveniently located. They were essentially large, multi-storeyed workshops built to accommodate hand-operated machines, with restricted use of powered machinery. The first factory builders appear to have been as concerned with achieving an efficient layout of processes, and closer supervision of the workers, as they were with the use of power to drive machinery.

Investigation of the few surviving examples of early factory buildings, and of contemporary documents, suggests that they were simple structures that were only partly powered, or not powered at all. Textile mills of this period were transitional buildings, combining the materials, construction methods and architectural features of the earlier vernacular mills with the larger, open interiors and regular fenestration that suited the new thinking of the factory system. Their functional details indicate that a transitional stage had also been reached in the internal arrangement of processes, with hand-powered machinery and warehousing in the upper floors and powered machines in the ground floor. Local Cotswold stone continued to be widely used, along with traditional types of mullioned windows, but larger plain roofs replaced the vernacular-style multiple-gabled roofs of the earlier mills. By the end of the 18th century both mills and workshops were being built with new types of larger square windows, similar to those used in factory buildings elsewhere. Workshop space was often combined with some form of warehousing, as indicated by the presence of domestic-type fireplaces for heating the workshops, with internal hoists, floor traps and large external doors for loading and unloading goods. Staircases were increasingly boxed in behind panelling or located outside the main rooms, to avoid interfering with machines. One of the defining features of the earliest transitional buildings was the absence of any specialised types of factory construction, such as the stronger or more fire-resistant floors, larger windows or wide-span roofs that were developed for factory building in the early 19th century. In the mid- to late 18th century, woollen industry buildings used traditional timber floors and heavy wooden roof trusses that were not significantly different to those seen in contemporary houses or farm buildings.

Old Mill, Longfords Mills

A building which epitomises the main characteristics of the early factories, Old Mill at the Longfords Mills complex, is situated in the Avening Valley to the east of Nailsworth. The site was used for fulling by the 14th century, but from 1759 to the mid-20th century it was developed by the firm of Thomas Playne and his descendents into one of the largest integrated mill complexes in Gloucestershire.[39] The four-storeyed Old Mill was one of the first additions made by Playne, originating in the early to mid-18th century but partially rebuilt following a fire in the late 1820s (Fig 2.26). Investigation of the structure has suggested that parts of the exterior were retained during the post-fire rebuilding.[40] The building represents the transition from the vernacular architecture of traditional workshops to the more formal design of the early factories (Fig 2.27). It combines similar architectural details and construction to those seen in traditional non-industrial buildings of the mid- to late 18th century with the fenestration of a large workshop and the open, rectangular plan and water-power system of an early factory. The most notable feature is probably the small, three-light stone-mullioned windows, clearly pre-dating the windows of the early 19th century mills. By the early 19th century, Old Mill was being absorbed by buildings associated with the development of integrated production at the site, with new mills and other buildings added for dyeing, tentering and teazle gigs. The ground floor still contained fulling stocks and machinery for grinding dyestuffs in the late 19th century.

Pitchcombe Upper Mill

A rare example of a small early mill that was newly built by one of the lesser known Gloucestershire clothiers, Pitchcombe Upper Mill avoided demolition by its conversion to other uses and is now a private house. The well-preserved rear elevation shows the typical fenestration of a small early factory (Fig 2.28). It was built between March and July 1792 by the clothier Jeremiah Cother, and was used until 1806 for most of the stages of woollen cloth manufacture.[41] The site illustrates how even the smaller firms in Gloucestershire were attempting to build factories for integrated production. It was built in an elevated position with a limited water supply, remote from the larger mills that were already established on the better

Fig 2.26
Old Mill, on the right, is the earliest mill at the Longfords site. It was built in the mid-18th century but partially rebuilt in the early 19th century. It retains the fenestration and vernacular construction of a partly powered 18th-century factory.
[DP137162]

water-power sites, and was attached to an earlier clothier's house and dye house.[42] The mill was powered by a narrow internal waterwheel, and despite its small size contained a wide range of machinery for preparation, weaving and dyeing, but no fulling stocks, suggesting that the cloth was sent to other mills for finishing.[43] It was only used in the woollen industry for 14 years. The business failed with Cother's bankruptcy in 1806,[44] after which new owners adapted the building for various non-textile uses including a saw mill, a malt house and a bakery.[45]

Lodgemore Mills, Stroud

Other evidence of the scale and proportions of the early factories can still be found, but is often disguised by later alterations and changes of use. Lodgemore Mills is the largest of a group of early woollen mill sites along the River Frome immediately downstream of Stroud. It has been occupied by the woollen industry under various owners from the 15th century, and saw development in the 18th, early 19th and late 19th century, and is still used for the manufacture of specialised woollen products (*see* p 51). The building now used as company offices in the centre of the site is probably the altered remains of an earlier house with an attached mill or workshop (Fig 2.29).[46] It appears to have been extended, raised and re-roofed, and

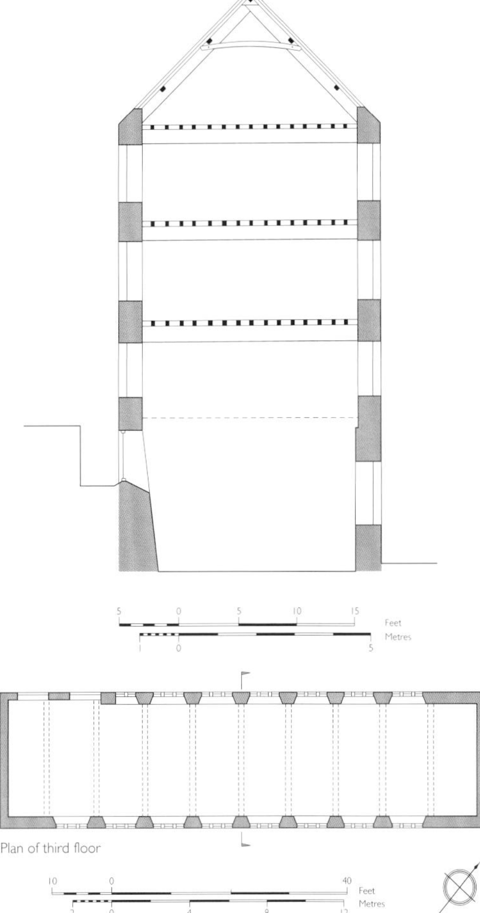

Fig 2.27
The tall, narrow proportions of Old Mill are similar to those of contemporary workshops, but on a larger scale.

Fig 2.28
Pitchcombe Upper Mill, built 1792, was an attempt by a local clothier to expand into factory working, but was converted to other uses after the business failed in 1806. By the 1790s, when all the water powered sites in the main valleys were occupied, smaller businesses were forced into mills on the more remote tributary streams. [DP139285]

Fig 2.29
The building currently used as offices at Lodgemore Mills probably originated as a house with an attached industrial building, probably a small mill, which was re-fronted to create a fashionable elevation. [DP137240]

then re-fronted in the style of a fashionable Georgian house. Early to mid-19th century workshops and warehouses, mostly with later alterations, are attached to the west and the north (Fig 2.30).

The development of integrated working

The development of mill sites from the late 18th to the mid-19th century was closely related to the further integration of processes. At an integrated mill the many different stages of production, from the preparation of the raw material to the dyeing of the cloth, were combined at one site, enabling greater control of the quality of the finished product. In other areas the new textile factories were often specialised buildings, intended to achieve a high output by concentrating on a narrow range of processes, such as those built for particular types of yarn spinning. In Gloucestershire the

Fig 2.30
Extensions for workshops or warehousing were added to the rear of the early Lodgemore Mills building.
[DP137231]

Fig 2.31
Longfords Mills in the 1950s. The large pond, latterly named Gatcombe Lake, was built as part of the expansion of the site with a water- and steam-powered integrated factory from 1806.
[BB04976]

early proponents of the factory system appear to have been more concerned with combining a wider range of processes under their direct control, so that the early factory mills developed alongside various types of related ancillary buildings.

The continued development of Longfords Mills in the early 19th century created an early example of a partly integrated factory, with most of the preparation stages and cloth finishing carried out at the site, and weaving put out to handloom weavers scattered across a wide area. In this case, the expansion of the site included the construction of a large new pond, providing water for both power and processes, along with a new water-powered mill, dye works, finishing works and dry house located immediately below the dam (Figs 2.31 and 2.32). At some sites, an early form of integrated working was achieved before the introduction of power looms by installing handlooms in purpose-built loomshops adjoining or close to the mill. Examples included the addition of unusually large loomshops to Dunkirk Mills (*see* p 42), and the construction of a detached loomshop close to Woodchester Mill (Fig 2.33).

The integration of processes was gradual, with some stages being brought into the mill

Fig 2.32
Longfords Mills, Minchinhampton:

A *Old Mill, mid-18th to early 19th century*
B *Loomshop, gig house, early 19th century*
C *Offices, warehouse, late 18th to early 19th century*
D *Lake Mill, c 1806–13*
E *Dry house, early 19th century*
F *Finishing and dye works, early 19th century*
G *Steam-powered spinning mill, 1858*
H *Weaving sheds, 1906*

site before others, and the extent to which it was adopted varied between the different textile industries. Gloucestershire clothiers had already brought a range of processes under

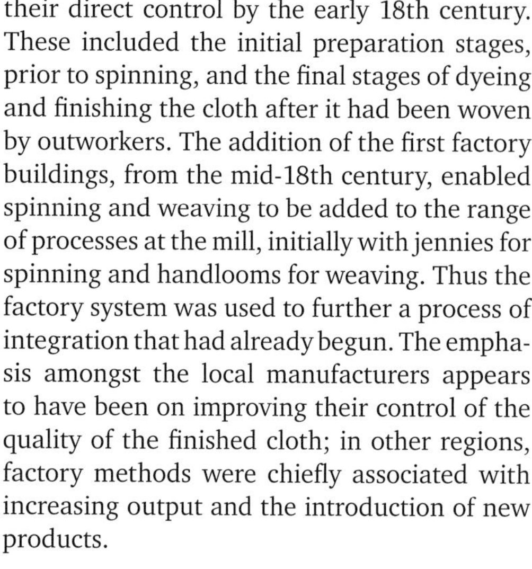

their direct control by the early 18th century. These included the initial preparation stages, prior to spinning, and the final stages of dyeing and finishing the cloth after it had been woven by outworkers. The addition of the first factory buildings, from the mid-18th century, enabled spinning and weaving to be added to the range of processes at the mill, initially with jennies for spinning and handlooms for weaving. Thus the factory system was used to further a process of integration that had already begun. The emphasis amongst the local manufacturers appears to have been on improving their control of the quality of the finished cloth; in other regions, factory methods were chiefly associated with increasing output and the introduction of new products.

The Gloucestershire woollen industry in the 19th century

The development of integrated working became a distinguishing feature of the Gloucestershire

Fig 2.33
Detached loomshops, such as this three-storeyed early 19th-century example in Woodchester, combined the fenestration and open interiors of factories with the scale and proportions of some contemporary houses. [DP115194]

woollen industry in the 19th century. In contrast with the expanding textile industries in other regions, the number of functioning woollen mills gradually decreased, as the industry consolidated from the widely dispersed clothier-owned mills of the late 18th century to a smaller number of integrated sites located in the main valleys. Significantly, all of the successful integrated complexes that were still in use at the end of the 19th century had developed on the sites of the earliest generation of Gloucestershire mills, those that had benefited for centuries from their occupation of the best water-power sites (Fig 2.34).

In the first decades of the century some non-integrated or partly integrated mills continued to be built in Gloucestershire, such as those built to carry out fulling and spinning for off-site weavers, but from the mid-19th century most of the new building took place at the large integrated sites. This was not the case in the expanding textile industries in other regions, such as the Yorkshire worsted industry and the Lancashire cotton industry, where firms concentrated more on maximising output and specialised working became more common. In some areas, notably south-east Lancashire, the textile industry became divided into towns dominated by either spinning mills or weaving mills, contrasting markedly with the continued emphasis on integrated production in Gloucestershire. By the late 19th century local differences were beginning to emerge in the economic structure of textile firms, and this probably influenced the construction of particular types of mills. Gloucestershire's woollen mills continued to be run by privately owned family firms, often descended from earlier clothier businesses, whereas the new specialised mills in other regions were increasingly set up as limited-liability joint-stock firms funded by shareholders.

In comparison with the northern textile industries, Gloucestershire was relatively slow to adopt power-loom weaving, with its characteristic north-light weaving sheds, which did not make significant inroads into the county until well into the mid-19th century. For the first three to four decades of the century local mills continued to build loomshops for handloom weaving. This combination of handloom weaving with powered spinning and cloth finishing represented a distinct phase in the development of the Gloucestershire woollen mill; in other textile industries the first major shift into integrated working came with the introduction of power looms from the late 1820s.

The further development of power systems and machinery was also related to the integration of processes. The integrated mills needed complex systems of powered shafting to drive the many types of machinery, and the logical development in Gloucestershire was to add steam power to the earlier water-power system.

Fig 2.34
The changing landscape of the woollen industry in the early 19th century. This rendition of Nailsworth shows several early water-powered factories, notably Day's Mill in the centre of the view, which contrast with the scale and vernacular style of the earlier woollen industry shown in Fig 2.9. [Reproduced courtesy of Gloucester Archives, D2424/19. DP137428]

Such combined power systems required a substantial investment in both the power plant and the system of shafting, gears and pulleys used to transmit power around the site. Steam power was initially used to supplement water power, but its importance to the development of the industry increased considerably during the 19th century. Steam engines could be installed where needed, permitting greater flexibility in the layout of buildings at the larger complexes. By the end of the 19th century the water-power systems that had been so important to the early success of the Gloucestershire industry were no longer an advantage, and steam had become the essential source of power for a viable woollen mill.[47]

The considerable amounts of capital needed to develop an integrated mill were reflected in the increasing dominance of a small number of very large businesses. Company mergers and takeovers of the smaller firms became more common in the late 19th century, and most of the new building took the form of additions to the integrated mills. The changes that were taking place in the textile industries in all areas favoured larger, highly capitalised firms that could produce higher output to sell at lower prices, and the smaller mills were increasingly abandoned or converted.

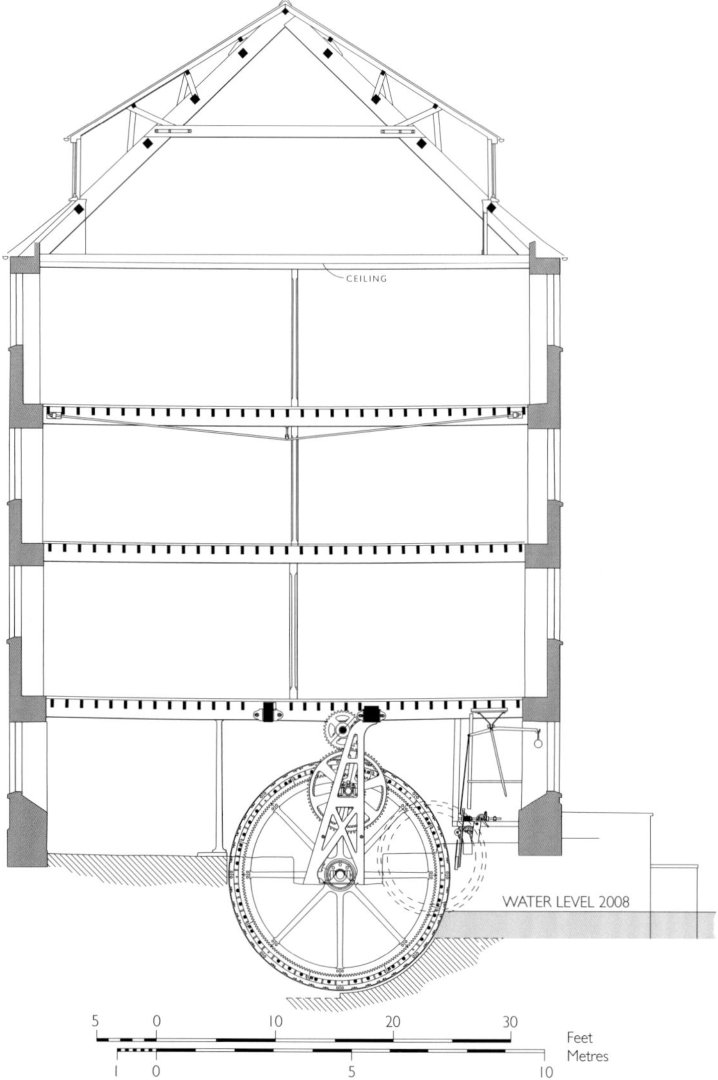

Fig 2.35
At St Mary's Mill, Minchinhampton, the internal waterwheels of the c *1819 mill were supplemented by an external beam engine by the 1830s, a development of power systems that was seen in many of the larger Gloucestershire mills.*

Gloucestershire woollen mills in the 19th century

The number of working woollen mills in Gloucestershire contracted in the 19th century, but the sites which remained in use saw the development of an industrial architectural style which is clearly distinguished from those of the other English textile industries. There was far less emphasis on the replacement of early 19th-century mills with new and larger buildings than was seen in the other textile areas. The long history of integrated working in Gloucestershire had already produced an unusual diversity of buildings at many mills, and its continuation in the 19th century meant that incremental additions were more commonplace than wholesale rebuilding. Consequently, one of the most distinctive features of the surviving sites is their combination of a wide variety of well-preserved functional building types spanning a wide date range. In other areas, the smaller specialised buildings found within a mill complex, such as dye houses and early workshops, were often replaced in the later development of the site. Of further interest was the widespread combination of water power with steam power in Gloucestershire, when steam was increasingly dominant in other areas; this also added to the range of building types while encouraging the preservation of ponds and watercourses (Fig 2.35).

In all branches of the English textile industry the technical development of mill buildings continued throughout the 19th century, and mills in many areas were seen to epitomise the dramatic progress of industrial design, engineering and architecture. In the early 19th century large water- and steam-powered mills were built in most of the textile regions, representing the national development of a new building type, but significant variations were seen between the different areas. By the late 19th century the principles of mill design and engineering had been greatly refined and mill buildings were becoming more standardised, with local variations limited to the use of a particular architectural style or material.[48]

Gloucestershire's early 19th-century factories initially paralleled the rapid developments seen in other areas, with the construction of new types of buildings that were of similar huge scale to those being built in parts of the north and the midlands. From the mid-19th century, however, the local industry did not follow the national trend for ever larger mill buildings designed to maximise economies of scale for a specific product. Integrated sites remained at the forefront of the Gloucestershire trade, with development restricted to the addition of new types of ancillary buildings. Most of the large multi-storeyed mills in the county were built before 1850. The dramatic expansion in mill building elsewhere had little impact in Gloucestershire, although there were some notable examples of rebuilding or extensions employing the latest styles of architecture and design (*see* p 52). Another distinctive feature of Gloucestershire's woollen mills was the relatively high proportion that were converted for use in another textile industry or for non-textile uses. Since re-use was an effective form of preservation, by the end of the century the number of intact mill buildings greatly exceeded the number of firms still working in the industry.

New Mills, Kingswood

In the early 19th century the industry in the Wotton-under-Edge area began to expand across the lower-lying countryside to the west of the hills, where several large mill complexes illustrated the progress of woollen mill design in that period. They were built for water-powered spinning and cloth finishing, in the period when weaving was still put out to cottage workers, and were later extended for steam-powered weaving. New Mills was built between 1806 and 1811, on the site of an 18th-century fulling and grist mill, by Humphrey Austin, a successful manufacturer who already owned several mills further upstream (Fig 2.36). One of the largest mill buildings in Gloucestershire, New Mills illustrated the recent fashions in Georgian factory architecture, with a symmetrical brick elevation that contrasted with the more piecemeal additions being made to other mills.

Fig 2.36
The very well-preserved New Mills, Kingswood, built 1806–11, shows some of the scale and grandeur of the larger Georgian industrial buildings. It represents a transition in factory design, the technology of its internal construction and water-power system being more typical of the smaller earlier factories.
[DP025240]

Its narrow plan, timber floors and water-power system represent some of the limits in mill design reached by traditional builders prior to the construction of the radically different Stanley Mill, in 1813 (*see* p 46). The site is now exceptionally well preserved, with new uses found for both the mill and the later north-light sheds and ancillary buildings (*see* chapter 8).

Charfield Mills

Close to New Mills, Charfield Mills is a complex of three smaller mills which show the development of power systems and the frequent alterations to mill buildings in the first half of the 19th century (Fig 2.37). The site was built by the successful firm of Samuel Long, who occupied a large house close to the site; his firm also ran New Mills in the 1860s and 1870s. The two earlier mills at the site were built for water power by *c* 1812, one being later adapted for combined water and steam power and the other converted to housing. The third, larger mill was purpose-built for steam power in 1825, its wider plan, internal engine house and attached boiler house all contrasting with more traditional mills in the area (Fig 2.38).[49] The attached north-light shed, added in the mid-19th century on the site of an earlier tenter field, was probably built to house power looms. It is one of the earliest examples in the county, of notably lower proportions and heavier construction to the more common later sheds.

Fig 2.37 (right)
The early 19th-century Charfield Mill site included separate buildings for water power, on the right, and the steam power, in the background.
[DP085607]

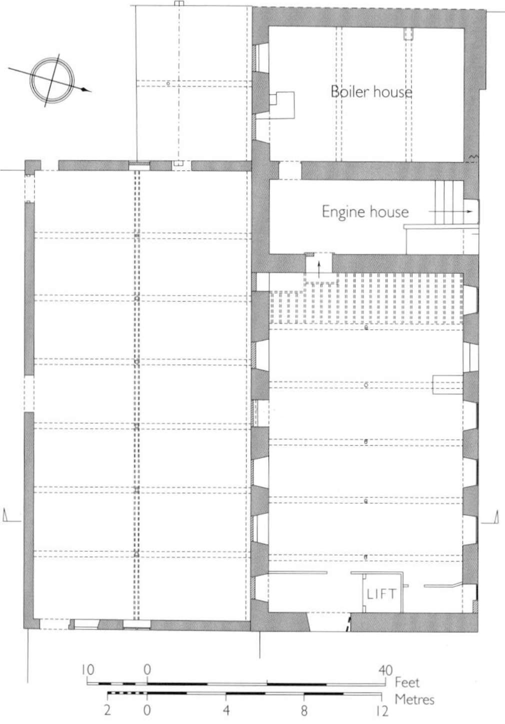

Fig 2.38 (far right)
The steam-powered mill had a typical layout of the 1820s, with an internal engine house, external boiler house and a wider plan in comparison with mills built a decade or so earlier.

Day's Mill and Dunkirk Mill, Nailsworth

A much greater number of mill sites acquired new buildings in the main Stroud and Nailsworth Valleys, producing the wide diversity of mill architecture that now largely defines the Gloucestershire textile mill. In the Nailsworth Valley, the variety of early factory building can be seen by comparing Day's Mill in Nailsworth and Dunkirk Mill, two miles downstream. Day's Mill was built in the first decade of the 19th century, incorporating parts of an earlier mill that was owned by the clothier Jeremiah Day by the 1780s (Fig 2.39).[50] The mill and its pond were built on the outskirts of the town but were absorbed by late 19th-century development. The narrow plan and proportions are similar to the 18th-century style of Old Mill at the Longfords site, but the segmental-headed windows are more typical of the early 19th century (Fig 2.40). Dunkirk Mill is a much larger site, one of the most impressive early multi-storeyed mills in Gloucestershire, which was built in at least six phases between 1798 and *c* 1914.[51] It was built close to the site of a mid-18th-century fulling mill, probably on the same watercourse, and was associated with a number of well-known clothiers and manufacturers, notably John Cooper in 1798 and the Playne family in the mid- to late 19th century (Fig 2.41). The main building was oriented along the valley, parallel to a raised leat, and by the mid-19th century included separate warehousing, dye houses, drying stoves and extensive ponds to supply water for power and processes. The south end of the mill comprises a five-storeyed loomshop, added in 1827, which is the largest building of its type in the South West (Fig 2.42). Of additional interest is the exceptionally well-preserved evidence of the water and steam power system, including three *in situ* waterwheels. A five-bay section of the mill added in 1818 included an external Boulton and Watt beam engine and retains two waterwheels in the original wheel pits; the wheels both show evidence of ongoing maintenance and alterations in the 19th century, as is expected for wheels that remained in use, but substantial parts of the north wheel are probably original to the building (Fig 2.43).[52]

To contemporary observers, a characteristic feature of the Gloucestershire woollen industry in the early 19th century would have been the very wide range in the scale of its buildings. At that time the area still retained large numbers of the small vernacular fulling mills, but some of the new factories such as Dunkirk Mill were a dramatically different scale of architecture,

Fig 2.39
Day's Mill, Nailsworth, shows the use of a developed type of mill window, contrasting with the smaller, three-light mullioned windows of earlier factories. The larger windows are combined with the narrow plan that was still common in the first decade of the 19th century.
[DP025296]

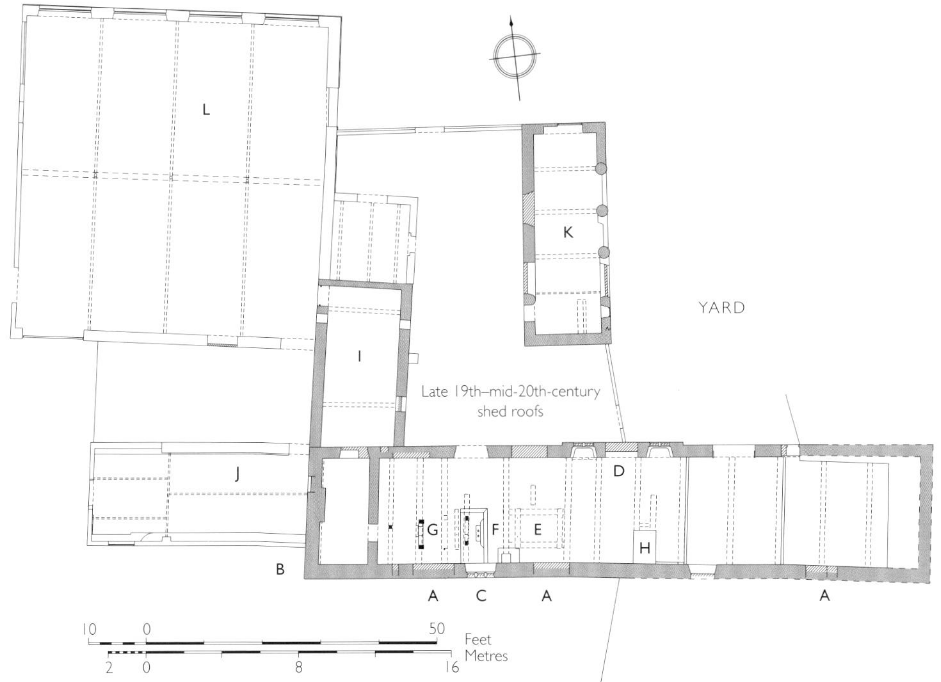

Fig 2.40
Day's Mill was built on the site of an 18th-century fulling mill, below the dam of the pond, which is now filled in. It was extended into a small town-centre complex, including an external engine house and north-light sheds, and was later used as a silk mill.
***A** Possible former headraces*
***B** Bypass channel (in use)*
***C** Early hollow-chamfered window*
***D** Early 19th-century entrance*
***E** Inserted trimmer beams*
***F** End-bearing for wheel shaft*
***G** Late 19th-century hurst frame*
***H** Hoist*
***I** Former engine house*
***J** Brick extension*
***K** Store or stable*
***L** Late 19th-century shed*

Fig 2.41
Dunkirk Mill is one of the largest early textile factories. It was built in at least seven phases alongside a headrace, including four water-powered mills, a supplementary external engine and a large hand-powered loomshop. Ancillary buildings filled the available space in the narrow valley floor, including warehousing and a dye house.
[AP26008/015]

Fig 2.42
The five-storeyed south end of Dunkirk Mill was built as a tall but very narrow loomshop. It was one of the largest and last examples of the construction of unpowered workshop space at a Gloucestershire mill before the introduction of power-loom weaving.
[DP085748]

comparable to the largest of the new factories being built in the north and the midlands. In other regions the huge factories were usually built by new firms employing a migrant workforce, whereas those in Gloucestershire, as stated previously, were built by established clothiers, representing the culmination of a centuries-long tradition of local cloth manufacture.

Ebley Mill, Cainscross

The largest of the Gloucestershire factories were built on the sites of late medieval fulling mills along the more open, lower stretch of the River Frome, downstream of Stroud. Ebley Mill was bought and rebuilt by the Clissold family from 1799, the extant main range, known as Long Mill, being added in 1818 (Fig 2.44). A mill of this size, powered by five internal waterwheels, was a massive investment, indicating a high level of confidence within the industry. By the 1830s John Figgins Marling had taken over the site and was producing kerseymeres, a relatively new type of fine-woollen cloth, woven on narrow looms, that was lighter than

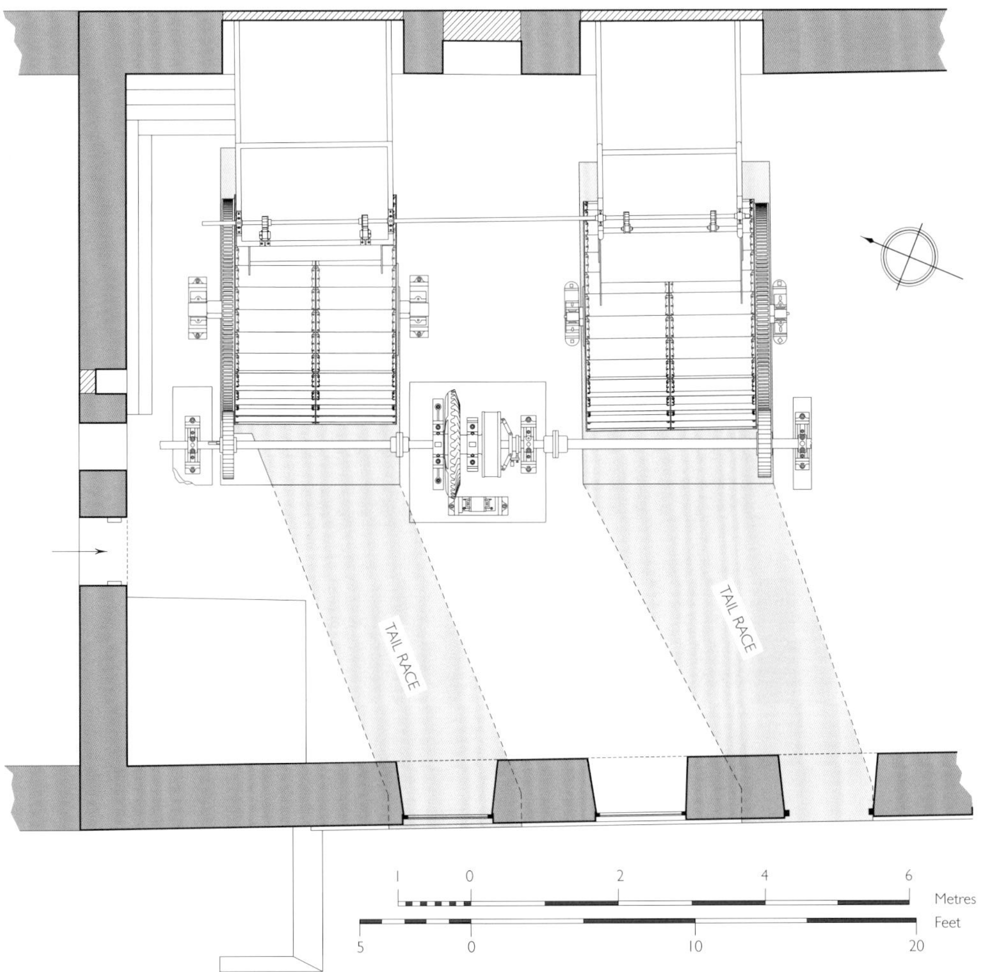

Fig 2.43
Two of the three well-preserved waterwheels at Dunkirk Mills are located in the 1818 mill. Both occupy the original wheel pits but, not surprisingly, were subjected to ongoing maintenance and alteration. The northern wheel retains good evidence of its former wooden shaft, shrouds and other early features.

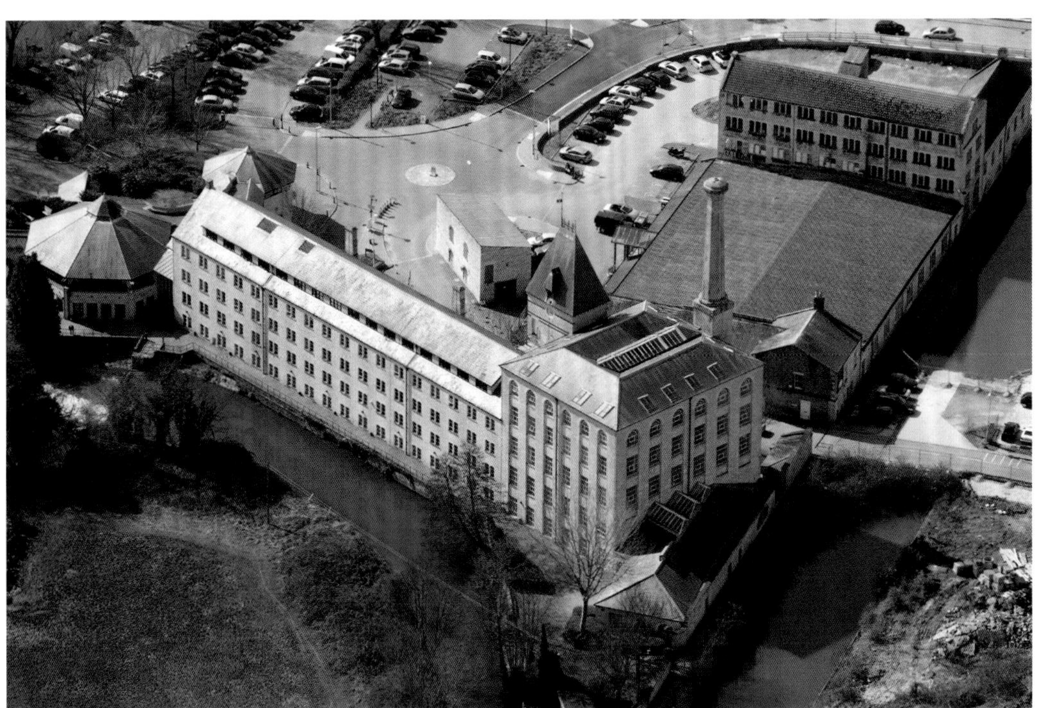

Fig 2.44
The long 1818 block of Ebley Mill was positioned so that the headraces to the wheels in the basement could be supplied directly from the River Frome. The single-storeyed building alongside the Stroudwater Canal is the partially rebuilt power-loom weaving shed that was added in the mid-19th century, converting the site into a fully integrated factory.
[AP24969/041]

Fig 2.45
Ebley Cloth Mills, Stroud, Gloucestershire, c *1850, by Alfred Newman Smith. This painting shows the appearance of the cross wing before it was rebuilt following a fire* c *1862. [Reproduced courtesy of The Museum in the Park, Stroud. 2194_501]*

the broadcloths and widely made from the late 18th century, notably in Wiltshire.[53] The Marlings were one of the most successful clothier dynasties in the Stroud area, acquiring several other large mills including Ham Mill (*see* p 54) and Stanley Mill (*see* below). At Ebley Mill, a major mid-19th-century addition was a detached weaving block, built to the west of the mill, which was one of the few examples of a purpose-built power-loom weaving mill in Gloucestershire. It was built in a similar layout to the numerous weaving mills in other areas, with a central north-light shed (now replaced by a modern shed roof) flanked by multi-storeyed ancillary buildings, which included a separate steam plant (Fig 2.45). Another large block which adjoined the north end of Long Mill was burnt down and replaced in *c* 1862, but retaining an earlier steam engine. The architect of the rebuild was G F Bodley, who incorporated details typical of 1860s mill architecture in other regions, including a wider plan, taller ceilings, large segmental-headed windows and an external fireproof stair tower.

Stanley Mill, King's Stanley

The greatest expression of Gloucestershire mill building stands a few miles downstream from Ebley Mill at King's Stanley. The site of Stanley Mill was acquired in 1811 by the firm of Harris, Maclean and Stephens and redeveloped over the following two decades into one of the most spectacular early factory sites in the country (Figs 2.46 and 2.47). The five-storeyed main buildings, dated 1813, comprise two wings of fireproof construction built in an L-shaped plan, with an attached full-height timber-floored wing. A two-storeyed fireproof dry house was added in 1817, and a Boulton and Watt beam engine and shafting in 1824 (Fig 2.48). The early 19th-century complex included many additional buildings to perform the full range of functions at an integrated mill, including a dye house, teazle-drying house, warehousing, offices and, later in the 19th century, north-light power-loom weaving sheds.

Stanley Mill has long been admired and studied, and is the subject of many publications and reports.[54] Attempts to identify a designer for the building have met with little success, although few early textile factories had a named architect, and no published research has revealed the original layout of the machinery that was the main purpose for constructing the mill. Its most outstanding feature is the unique and highly intricate internal framework of cast-iron beams and columns (Fig 2.49). This dates from a period when cast-iron structures were still being developed and represented the forefront of structural technology, with engineers in different parts of the country producing different solutions to common structural problems. This was the only example of an early fireproof mill in Gloucestershire, where new mill building declined as iron-framed mills were becoming more common in other areas. Fireproof construction was expensive and was more widely used in industries with a higher fire risk, notably cotton and flax. At Stanley Mill, the frame uses pairs of columns to create a central aisle along each floor, supporting both the transverse floor beams and pairs of deep, cambered longitudinal beams of open-web design. The visual impact of the structure is most impressive, especially in the ground floor which has higher ceilings and heavier framing to support the waterwheels and shafting.

Stanley Mill was originally powered by five internal waterwheels located in the two fireproof wings, which were claimed to produce 200 horse power, making it one of the most heavily powered buildings of the period.[55] The problems of accommodating the waterwheels and the horizontal and upright shafting throughout the building appear to have strongly influenced the design of the structural iron-

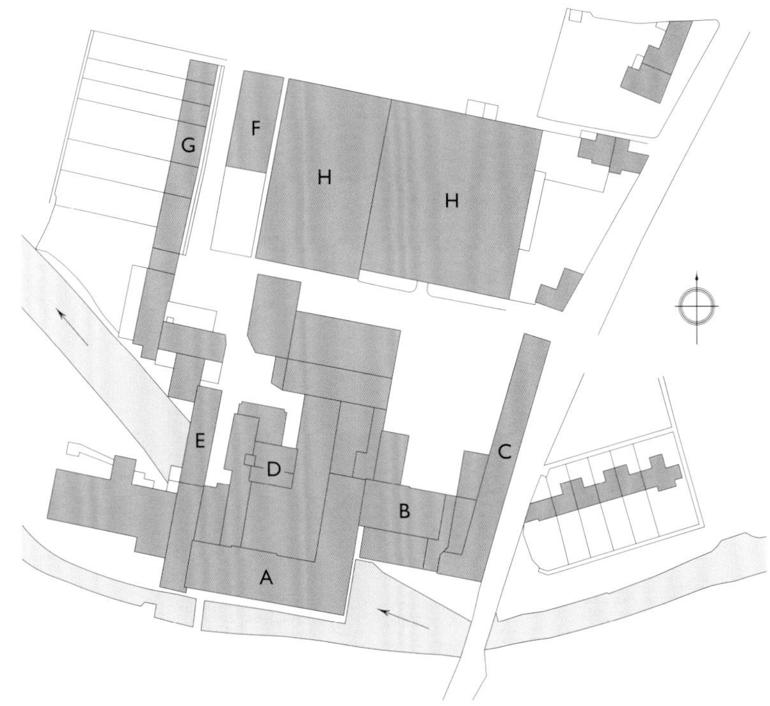

Fig 2.46
Stanley Mill, main buildings:

***A** Fireproof mill, 1813*
***B** Non-fireproof wing,* c *1813*
***C** Dry house, 1817*
***D** Beam-engine house, 1824*
***E** Pier and panel building, mid-19th century*
***F** Drying stove*
***G** Cottages*
***H** Mid-20th-century factory*

Fig 2.47
Stanley Mill, seen here in 2008, is arguably one the most important industrial sites of the early 19th century. Its intricate cast-iron frame was one of the most radical designs to appear during the early development of 'fireproof' factories.
[AP24969/016]

work. Its fireproof qualities, which were not replicated at other Gloucestershire mills, were probably less important than its ability to support the machinery and power system.

St Mary's Mill, Minchinhampton

More representative of Gloucestershire mill building in the early to mid-19th century are two well-preserved sites in the upper part of the Stroud Valley. St Mary's Mill occupies one of the best water-power sites in the area (Fig 2.50; *see also* Figs 2.2 and 2.35). It included a fulling mill by 1548, and a gig mill by the end of the 16th century, pre-dating the general expansion of the industry in the 17th century. It was owned by a succession of clothiers until the late 18th century, when workshops were added to a fulling mill. It was under the ownership of Samuel Clutterbuck from the early 19th century that much of the site was rebuilt into its present form. It developed into an integrated complex including two mills, a dry house, loomshop and a wool stove, all illustrated in a sale brochure of the 1830s (Fig 2.51). The main mill building was rebuilt in *c* 1819, and is now a very well-preserved example of a typical Gloucestershire

Fig 2.48
Steam power was added to the water-power system of Stanley Mill in 1824, comprising a Boulton and Watt beam engine in an external engine house with adjoining boiler house and chimney. This is one of the earliest free-standing mill chimneys in the country, pre-dating the development of the octagonal and circular chimneys that later became commonplace. Contemporary chimneys were normally built onto a corner of the mill itself. [DP115140]

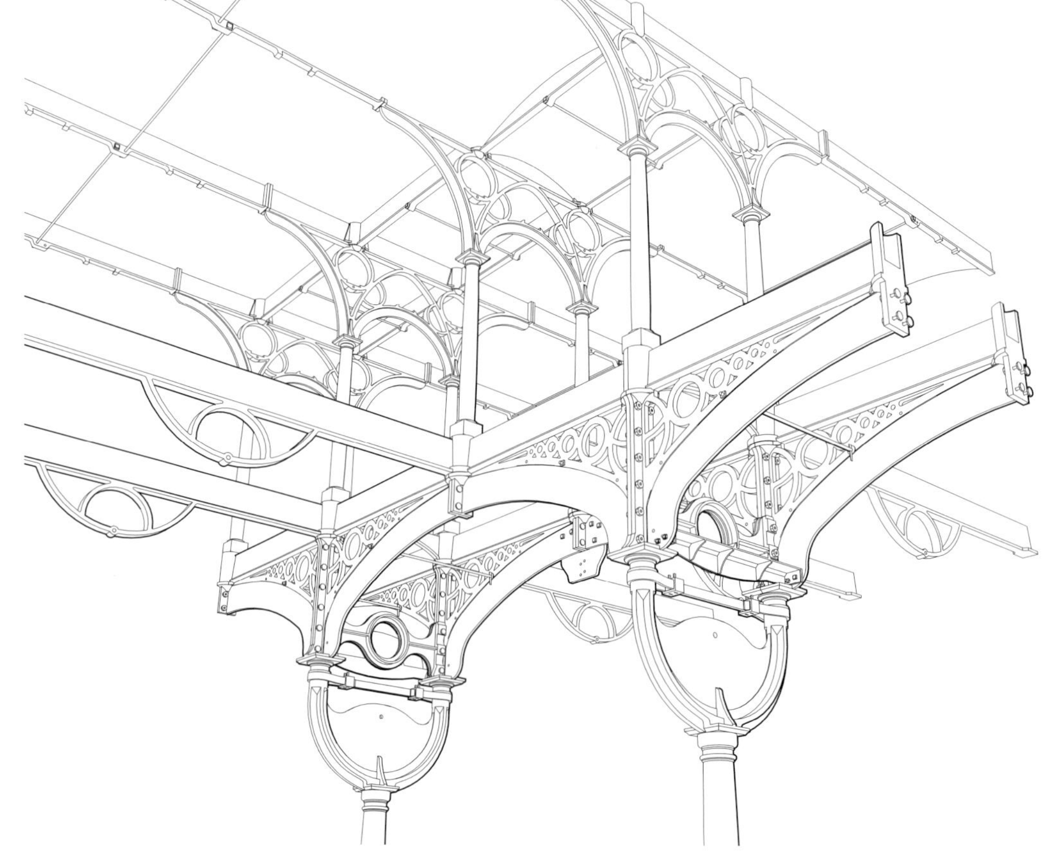

Fig 2.49
Detail of the complex framework in the ground and first floors of Stanley Mill. The mill dates from a period of rapid progress in the development of structural cast iron, but its designer is not known. Very few of the innovative early textile factories were attributed to named architects.

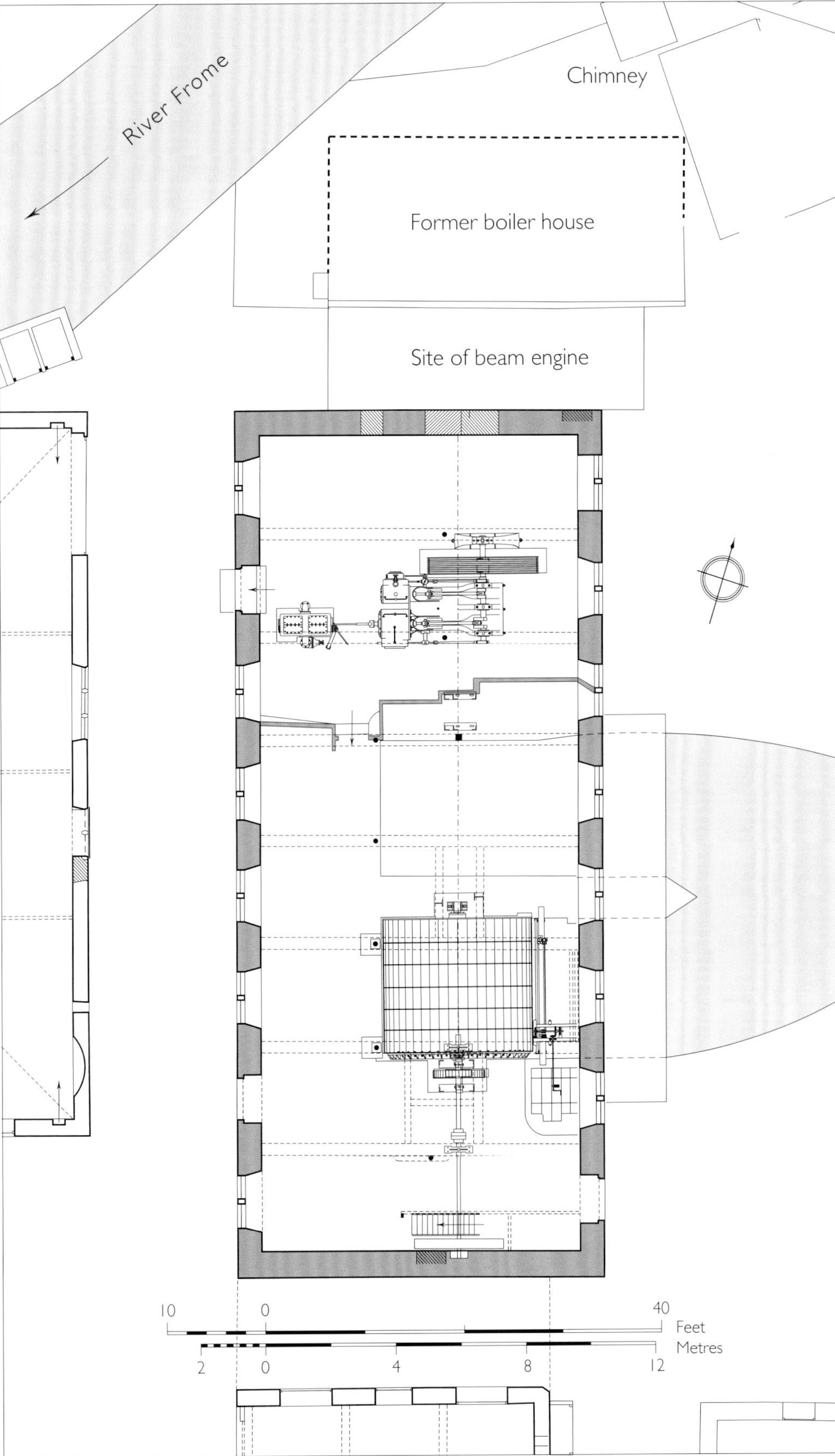

Fig 2.50
St Mary's Mill was built with side-by-side internal waterwheels, occupying most of the ground floor, one of which is in situ. *The steam engine in the north end room was installed when the mill was later used for manufacturing walking sticks.*

Fig 2.51
St Mary's Mill was developed from the late 18th century with the full range of building types prior to the introduction of power-loom weaving, including powered mills, a cloth-dry house and a loomshop. From undated sale notice, c 1830s. [Reproduced courtesy of Audrey Penrose. DP058061]

mill built during the peak years of the industry. The two-light windows are very similar to the 1818 building at Ebley Mill, as are the timber floor construction and the tall attic, lit by dormer windows. The ground floor contains two central wheel pits, one with an *in situ* early 19th-century waterwheel, with space alongside for fulling stocks. The wheel is now connected to a late 19th-century power transmission system, inserted when the mill was converted to other uses, including the manufacture of flock and walking sticks (Fig 2.52). A horizontal compound engine was installed in 1904, which, remarkably, survives completely intact in the north end of the mill.

Bourne Mill, Brimscombe

Bourne Mill is of similar proportions to St Mary's Mill but occupies an unusually congested site, its development being constrained

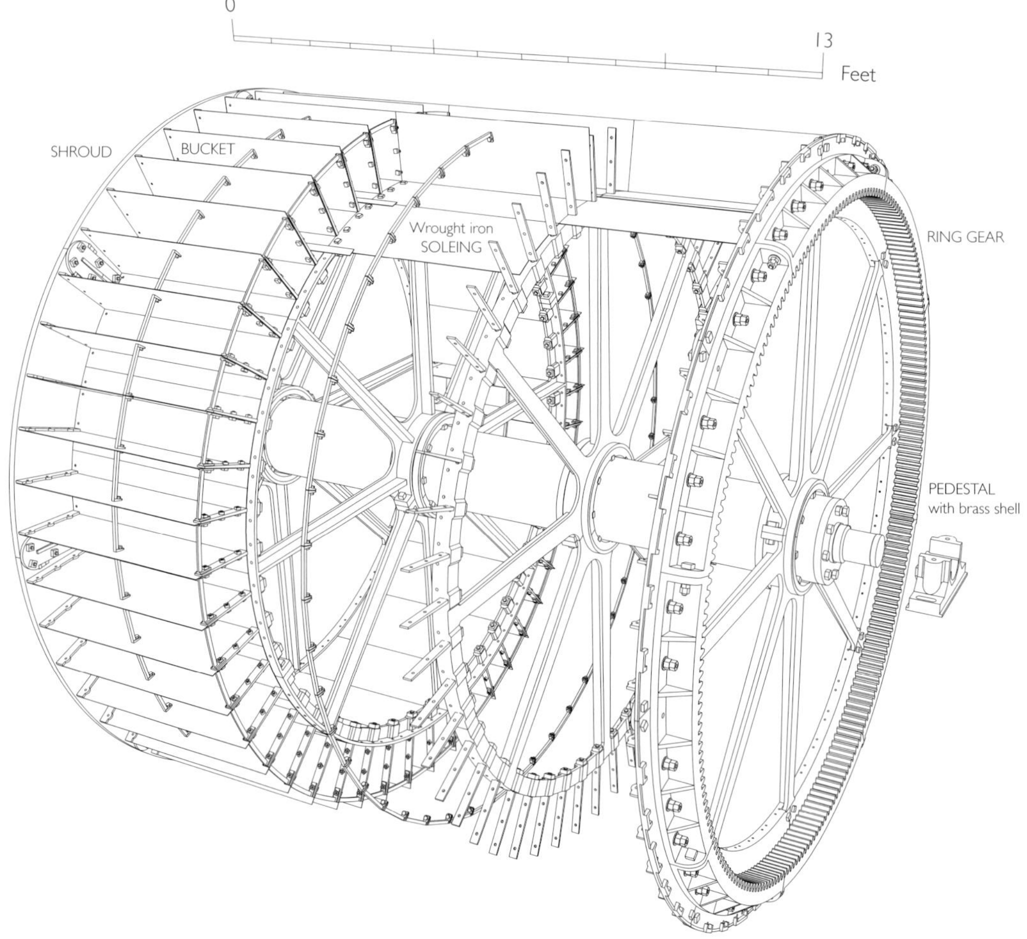

Fig 2.52
The exceptionally well-preserved in situ *waterwheel at St Mary's Mill, shown here in an exploded view. This wheel has the unusual combination of cast-iron arms and a tubular iron shaft, suggesting it dates from a period of rapid development in waterwheel construction. The ring gear was a later addition.*

Fig 2.53
Bourne Mill typifies the mixed industrial landscape of the Stroud Valley. The mill with its stove and workshops occupy a constricted site between the Thames and Severn Canal, the River Frome and the local branch of the Great Western Railway.
[DP085673]

at different times by the River Frome, forming its southern boundary, the Thames and Severn Canal immediately to the north and the brick viaduct of the local branch of the Great Western Railway. The viaduct actually spans some of the buildings attached to the south end of the mill, forming an unusually complex assemblage of industrial features for a rural site (Fig 2.53). The mill was probably in use from the 17th century, but in the early 19th century it was rebuilt and let out for other uses in addition to its main function as a woollen mill.[56] These included a saw mill, silk mill and walking-stick factory. It was owned by N S Marling of Ebley Mill by the 1850s, when it included buildings for wool preparation and cloth finishing, but no looms. The main block was apparently rebuilt at this time, but retains parts of two earlier wings at its south end, one of which has been demolished. Detached buildings include a four-storey workshop to the west of the mill and a very well-preserved wool stove, retaining most of its cast-iron floor, stairs and roof structure (Fig 2.54).

Lodgemore Mills, Stroud

No completely new mills were built in Gloucestershire in the second half of the 19th century, and the local industry was increasingly dominated by large firms who bought up the smaller sites as their owners went out of business. Several sites saw significant rebuilding, however, or the addition of new wings or ancillary buildings, and these show far greater architectural influence from outside the area than was the case with the earlier mills. The firm of J G Strachan bought Lodgemore Mill in 1865, in addition to owning other mills in the Stroud area. One of the two mills at the site was completely destroyed by fire in 1872, and was soon replaced by a new building by J R Ferrabee that

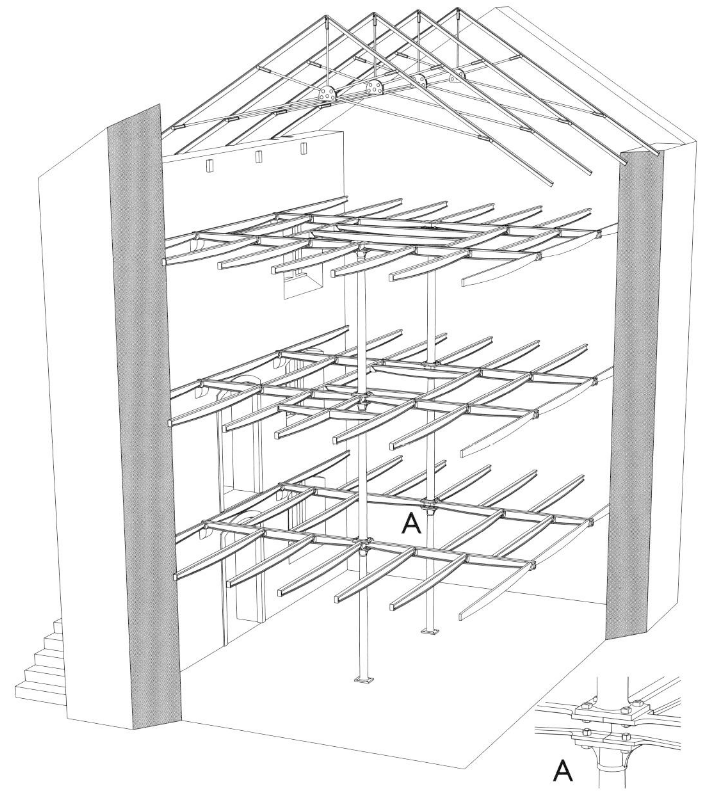

Fig 2.54
The rectangular wool-drying stove at Bourne Mill, part of a series of mid-19th century additions, was a development of the earlier types of circular or octagonal stoves. It was built with a grid of intersecting cast-iron floor beams to support a perforated floor, with an iron staircase and an iron roof.

Fig 2.55
In dramatic contrast with the tradition of Cotswold stone mill building in Gloucestershire, Lodgemore Mills was rebuilt in 1872 with pier and panel walls in red, blue and yellow brick with limestone details. [DP137237]

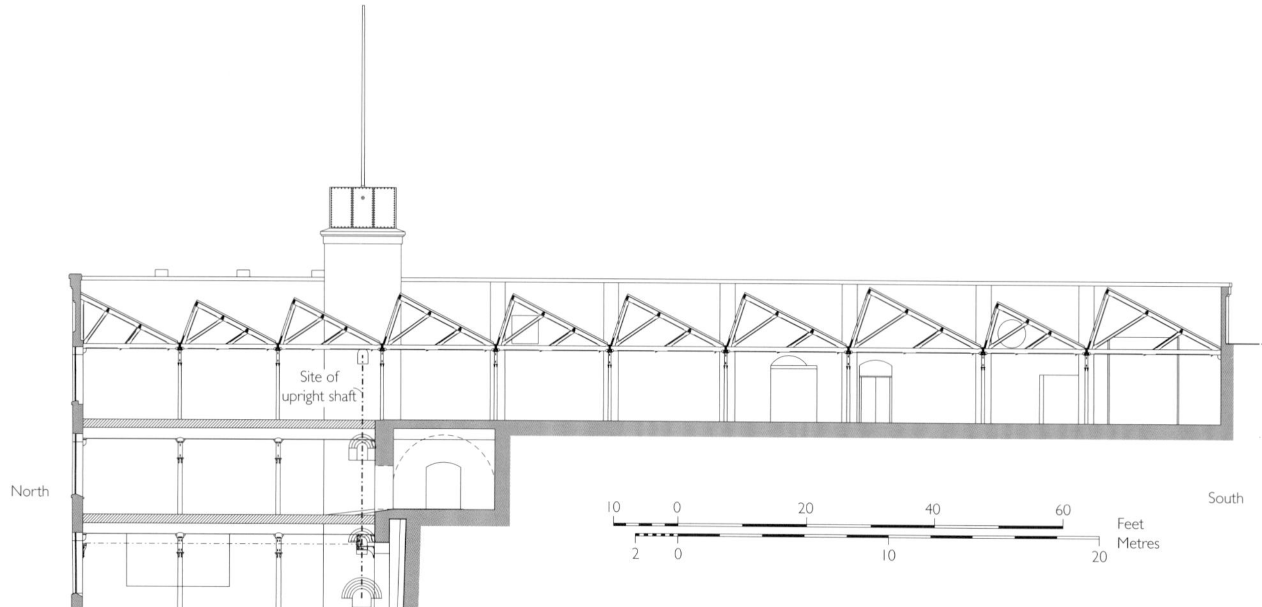

Fig 2.56
Lodgemore Mills was rebuilt to a modern layout, with a steam-powered shed extending from a fireproof three-storeyed block built on the site of the previous mill, which had been destroyed by fire. The tower supported the water tank of the sprinkler system and the massive main upright shaft driven from the attached engine house.

embodied the latest principles of textile mill engineering developed in other regions, along with a flamboyant embellishment in polychromatic brick that dramatically contrasts with the conservative Cotswold stone architecture of the earlier Gloucestershire mills (Fig 2.55). It was built on a sloping site, the top storey comprising a large north-light shed, of typical wide proportions for a shed mill, but with two lower storeys of fireproof construction at the lower end of the slope. The building presents a three-storeyed elevation to the downhill side, and a plain single-storeyed shed wall to the uphill side (Fig 2.56). External embellishment is to a high standard, reflecting the fashions of the 1870s, with polychromatic red, blue and cream brick used to good effect with recessed panels, pilasters and a corbelled parapet. The mill was entirely steam powered from an attached engine house built for a horizontal engine, with an upright shaft transmission system in a purpose-built shaft tower (Figs 2.57 and 2.58). The architectural treatment is continued into the engine house, boiler house and the shaft tower, with its iron water tank and flag pole. The top storey was probably used for power-loom weaving, the site having 157 looms in 1889, but the bottom storey contained scouring and milling machines powered directly from the steam engine.

In addition to these developments in the woollen industry, new industries emerged in the 19th century to become significant employers in the smaller mills that could not be readily adapted to integrated working. These included processing the by-products or waste obtained from the larger mills. A notable example in Gloucestershire was the processing of flock for use in the manufacture of wallpaper or as a stuffing for furniture. Flock mills were often set up at disused water-powered mills in the smaller tributary valleys, such as the Toadsmoor Valley, ensuring that some of the early mills survived without extensive conversion to new uses.

The fully integrated woollen factory

By the late 19th century the Gloucestershire woollen industry was dominated by large, integrated complexes located in the main valleys, and smaller mills were increasingly restricted to specialised functions, such as flock production, or were converted to non-textile uses. The integration of processes had been achieved gradually over a long period, starting with the attempts by clothiers to improve the quality of fine-woollen broadcloths in the 17th and 18th centuries. In the late 19th century, however, only the largest firms could afford to invest in the full range of powered machinery, specialised building types, a steam-power system and the larger workforce that was needed to

Fig 2.57
The engine house of Lodgemore Mills was built with wider proportions than the earlier beam-engine houses to accommodate a horizontal cross-compound engine.
[DP137423]

Fig 2.58
The interior of Lodgemore Mills in the late 19th century. The mill shafting was driven directly from the flywheel at the back of the room.
[Reproduced courtesy of Milliken WSP. DP137601]

compete with the textile industries of other areas. The large integrated complexes, with their wide variety of buildings and landscape features, therefore represent the end point of a long process of development that had started before the introduction of the factory system.

Integrated mills are identified by their large size and their wide variety of building types, many with functional features that were specific to a particular process. The long history of occupation of many of the sites means that many also retain buildings of an unusually wide date range, with each phase of building reflecting the addition of a new process or type of machinery. At Longfords Mills, for example, single-storeyed buildings for scouring and dyeing were added with two-storeyed dry houses in the early 19th century (Fig 2.59). A steam-powered mule-spinning mill was added in 1858, built to a wider plan than the earlier mills to accommodate the larger machines (*see* Fig 1.1). Later in the 19th and in the early 20th century, north-light sheds were added for power-loom weaving and additional mule spinning. The succession of building types at the integrated sites therefore parallels the history of processes in the industry. A similar development of buildings for particular types of machinery can be seen at most of the other large sites which remained in use into the late 19th century, including Stanley Mill, Ebley Mill, New Mill, Wotton-under-Edge, and Lodgemore Mills.

Ham Mill, Brimscombe and Thrupp

One of the best-preserved integrated mills in the main Stroud Valley, Ham Mill stands on the site of a 16th-century fulling mill and saw multiple phases of development, including the addition of dyeing, before the extant buildings were constructed between the early 19th and the early 20th century. It was associated with several prominent clothiers, including the Webb family from the mid-17th to the mid-18th century, and the Marlings from the early to mid-19th century.[57] The Marlings and later occupiers concentrated on spinning and cloth production, with steam power and power-loom weaving added by 1836. The earliest extant buildings are a three-storeyed water-powered mill, built across the valley floor and forming the dam of a pond, with an attached four-storeyed steam-powered wing. This arrangement provides a good illustration of how the position of earlier watercourses influenced the development of mills in the 19th century (Fig 2.60). The most extensive late 19th-century buildings are the north-light sheds, used for the extension of power-loom weaving and eventually for carpet production (Fig 2.61). The combination of multi-storeyed mills, usually used for spinning, with single-storeyed north-light sheds, usually for weaving, is a defining characteristic of the integrated textile mill. North-light sheds were an innovative building type, first introduced in other regions in the early 1830s, which

Fig 2.59
The development of integrated working at Longfords Mills saw the construction of an early 19th-century dye and finishing works immediately below the dam of the pond.
[BB040941]

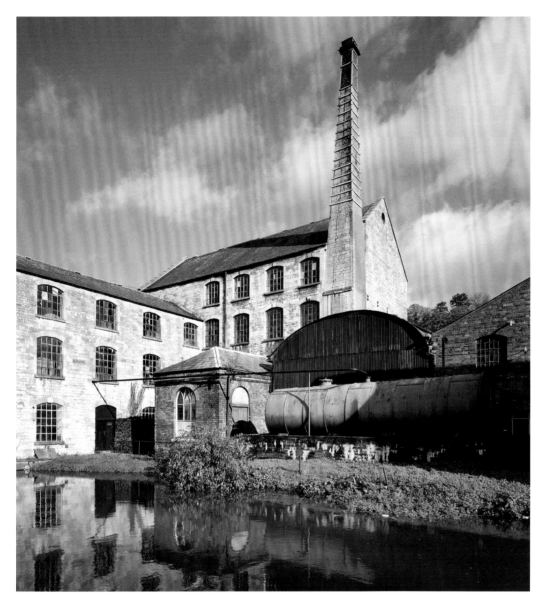

Fig 2.60
The layout of the water- and steam-powered buildings at Ham Mill was largely determined by the position of the earlier watercourse. The steam-powered wing retains a rare example of a well-preserved integral chimney, a type that was often later replaced by free-standing chimneys.
[AA017692]

Fig 2.61
Extensive north-light sheds were added to Ham Mill in the late 19th and early 20th century. The combination of single-storeyed sheds with multi-storeyed mills and the buildings of the steam-power system typified the 19th-century integrated mill.
[AA017702]

provided a wider, more adaptable floor space than a multi-storeyed mill with more flexibility for the location of powered shafting. They also provided exceptionally good natural lighting, and were later used for other processes, such as carding, spinning and cloth finishing. Ham Mill was one of the first Gloucestershire mills to install power looms, and its looms were originally located in the multi-storeyed buildings, an arrangement comparable to the earlier loom shops, before the addition of the sheds. In the 20th century, the site was adapted for carpet manufacture and remained in use until the late 1990s, thus preserving many of the functional features of the buildings.

Conclusion: The architectural vernacular of the Gloucestershire woollen industry

The architecture and design of the late 19th-century textile mill buildings in Gloucestershire reflect something of the unusual nature of the county's woollen industry in that period. In general, the second half of the 19th century saw the renewed growth of the mainstream English textile industries, with the construction of new and ever-larger types of mill buildings that confidently displayed embellishment in the latest architectural fashions, including Italianate, Egyptian and Baroque. The Gloucestershire industry was far smaller than the northern industries by the late 19th century,[58] however, and in contrast to the national trends the later additions to its woollen mills show less evidence of the development of construction methods or the use of new styles of architecture. With a few notable exceptions, there was also less evidence of the work of the new breed of specialised mill architects that was to have a major influence on mill building in the north.[59] The exceptions included some undoubtedly modern designs, however, such as the rebuilt wing and tower of Ebley Mill, by G F Bodley in *c* 1862, and the rebuilding of Lodgemore Mills by the architect John Ferrabee, dated 1872. The Gloucestershire industry was increasingly controlled by a small number of well-established local firms in the 19th century, mostly descended from 18th-century clothiers, and the influence of these industrial dynasties can be seen in the architecture of the buildings. Many of the later mills showed a preference for traditional design features at a time when new approaches to mill building were being adopted in other regions by completely new firms funded by shareholders. The continued use of locally sourced stone and brick in factory buildings, together with a preference for the re-use of some vernacular features, such as mullioned windows, suggests that Gloucestershire's 19th-century mill builders wanted to express their proud association with an exceptionally long tradition of woollen manufacture.

The 20th century saw a continuation of the slow decline of the local textile industry, in which only the largest integrated sites survived as profitable businesses. In a marked contrast with other textile industries, the contraction of the Gloucestershire woollen industry was not accompanied by the widespread dereliction or complete removal of disused mill buildings. The local economy was diverse, and hence more resilient, than in areas which were dominated by textile industries, with the result that a far higher proportion of Gloucestershire's mills remained intact. The buildings and landscapes of the traditional textile industry were preserved after the industry declined because of their early adaptation for non-textile uses that were compatible with the existing buildings. The new occupiers of the mills, frequently several firms at each site, were mainly small businesses involved with a variety of light industries that could be accommodated in both the mill and its smaller ancillary buildings. The re-use of textile mills was unusual in a period of industrial decline, but can be seen to have pioneered the conversions of historic mills that were to become a feature of many former industrial areas by the 20th century.

3

The Wiltshire and Somerset woollen industry

Wiltshire and Somerset contain the most extensive section of the historic fine-woollen industry that had developed across the west of England by the 17th century. The overall range of processes in the area was similar to that in the Gloucestershire woollen trade, and in parts of Hampshire and Oxfordshire, and the industry had similar early origins in all these neighbouring counties. From an early date, however, local variations developed within the west of England industry which eventually influenced the types and the locations of textile mill sites. By the 17th century, when the demand for textiles was shifting towards a wider variety of lighter cloths, the clothiers of Wiltshire and northern Somerset had begun to emphasise different products to those in Gloucestershire, requiring subtle differences in processes and in the organisation of the industry. With less emphasis on heavily fulled and dyed cloths, and the use of water for power and processes, the clothiers in this part of the industry were increasingly based in market towns. From the early 18th century, the workshops and other buildings associated with new machinery were more frequently built in the towns, often close to the clothiers' houses, in a period when the Gloucestershire industry continued to develop at rural sites with adequate water supplies. The differences between the two areas became more apparent in the early 19th century, when Wiltshire and Somerset saw a strong emphasis on the construction of steam-powered factories in urban settings. Factories of this type were notably similar to those being built in the north of England, but were almost completely absent in Gloucestershire. Research into the long history of the Wiltshire and Somerset woollen industry has paralleled the development of industrial archaeology for several decades, and a wide range of previous publications provide the basis for this appraisal of the industry's historic buildings.[1]

Landscapes and townscapes of the Wiltshire and Somerset woollen industry

A notable feature of the fine-woollen industry in Wiltshire and Somerset was the distinction between its rural and urban development. By the 18th century the extensive outworking businesses of the clothiers resulted in the construction of vernacular domestic and industrial buildings throughout the countryside, but the larger businesses showed a preference for locating near the wool towns with their markets and wool fairs. This contrast with the Gloucestershire industry was partly due to the topographies of the two areas and differences in the organisation of the industry, but was also influenced by statutory factors (*see* p 62). The later development of the industry, characterised by periods dominated by large water-powered factories and then by factories that were entirely steam powered, saw it becoming even more concentrated in the towns. In the 19th century, the later types of steam-powered factories, which were comparable to those being built in other regions, were central features of urban development, with the main towns acquiring densely packed suburbs of steam-powered mills and related housing.

Buildings associated with the industry are widespread throughout the area, extending from the open countryside and water meadows of south Wiltshire, through the numerous scattered market towns in the centre and north of the county, and westwards into a region of deeper valleys of the Rivers Frome and Avon in northern Somerset (Fig 3.1). The earliest evidence of the industry relates to the cloth trade in the major medieval towns, such as Salisbury and Bath, and to smaller market towns that were particularly suited to the construction of fulling mills, such as Bradford-on-Avon and Malmesbury. The regionally important industry

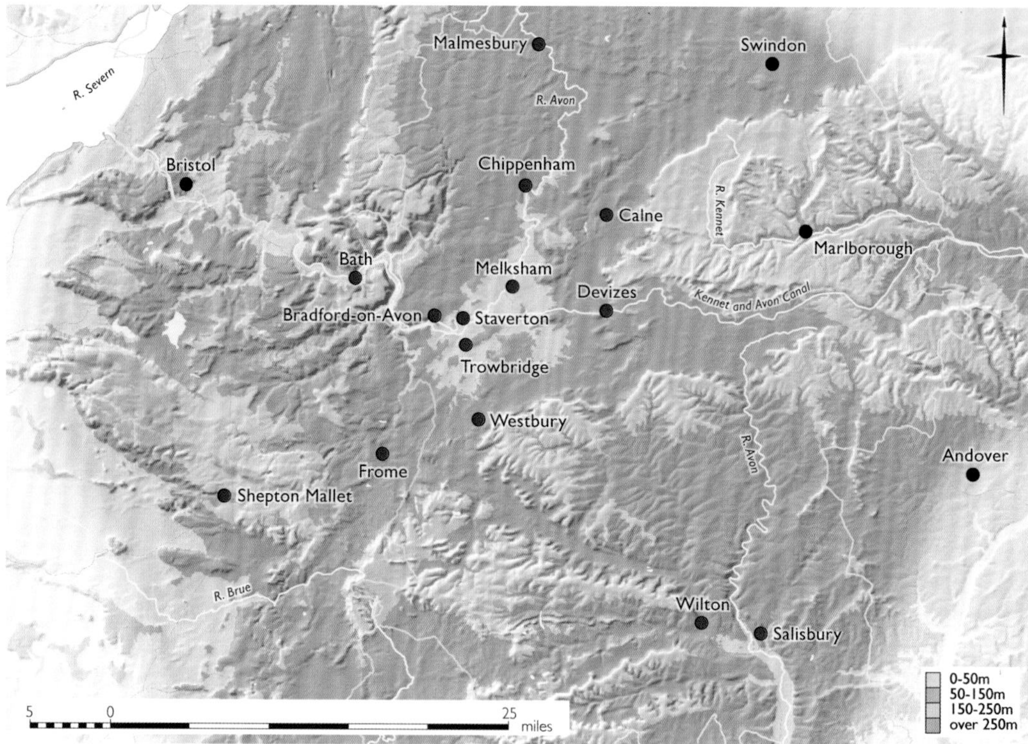

Fig 3.1
The Wiltshire and Somerset woollen industry was scattered across a wide area, but was concentrated in the larger market towns by the 18th century.
[90m SRTM Topography data courtesy of the CGIAR, http://srtm.csi.cgiar.org]

that laid the foundations of later factory building became more extensively established in the 16th and 17th centuries. Wiltshire and northern Somerset contained the earliest main centres of the industry, and saw most of the later mill building, but by the 18th century the woollen trade was well established across a wider area that extended further into Somerset and adjoining parts of Dorset.[2]

The outworking industry of the Wiltshire and Somerset clothiers developed at roughly the same time as that in Gloucestershire, but emphasised different products and was less constrained to the floors of narrow river valleys. The surviving clothiers' townhouses often display urban characteristics, contrasting with the rural vernacular of the clothiers' houses in the Gloucestershire valleys. Wiltshire and Somerset saw less emphasis on the production of superfine woollen cloths, and consequently were less dependent on the widespread use of fulling mills than in Gloucestershire. This was reflected by the mid-18th century in the development of a larger number of independent cloth-finishing works, which carried out the fulling and other processes as contract work for the clothiers.[3]

In the late 18th century, the industry of the clothiers and their workshops continued to develop towards factory working throughout most of the area, but the contemporary factories could only be built on sites that were suited to the development of water power on a large scale. Thus for a short period most of the early factories were built near the main rivers, sometimes in rural locations, with initially less emphasis on new factory building in the market towns of central and southern Wiltshire (Fig 3.2). Many of the early factories were built in the north and west of the area, along the valleys of the Wiltshire Avon and its main tributaries, with notable examples at Bradford-on-Avon, Frome, Bath and Malmesbury, all of which had sites that were ideal for the larger water-powered factories in addition to the earlier fulling mills.

The steam-powered mills of the early 19th century could be built in a wider range of locations, enabling industrial development in and around more of the traditional wool towns. Trowbridge, Melksham and Chippenham, for example, all saw the construction of large steam-powered factories in the early 19th century. The supply of coal was improved by the opening of the Chippenham branch of the Wiltshire and Berkshire Canal in 1810. Many of the earlier water-powered factories saw the addition of steam power in this period, but a distinctive feature of this part of the South West was the high proportion of new mills that were built solely for steam power. A small stream or

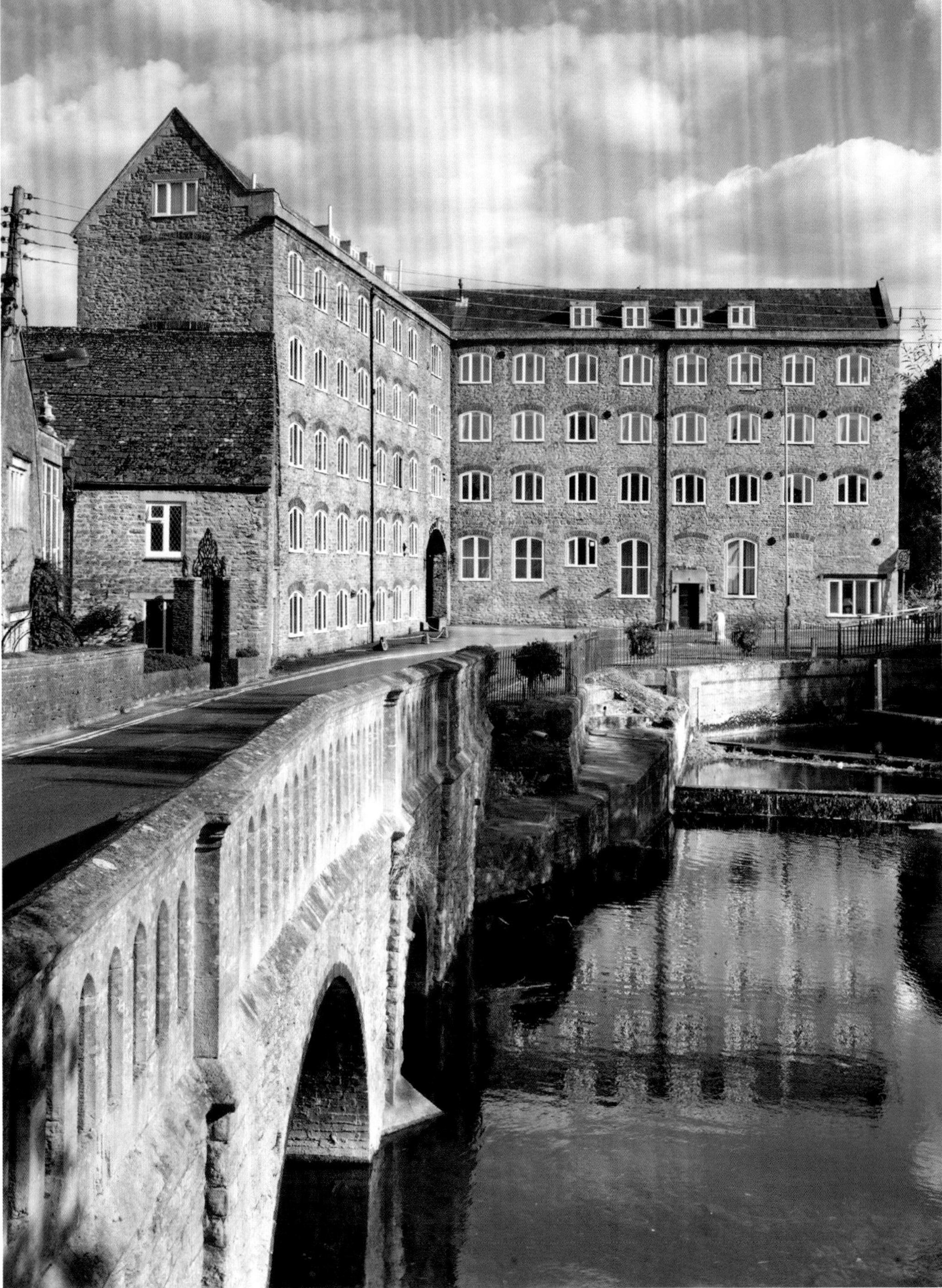

Fig 3.2
Many of the first generation of factories were built at sites that were suitable for large-scale water power in rural areas or on the outskirts of towns, such as Avon Mills at Malmesbury, built from 1791.
[DP137186]

leat was still needed to supply water for steam plant and textile processes, but many of the steam-powered factories were built in locations that were not suited to large-scale water power. In some cases, notably Trowbridge, factories were built in groups accompanied by new streets and related development, creating early industrial suburbs not dissimilar to those of industrial towns in other regions. Steam power was more extendible than water power, and enabled the further development of these industrial districts in the second half of the 19th century, long after the Gloucestershire woollen industry had ceased to expand. From the 1840s, the opening of railways connecting the central Wiltshire towns enabled further industrial development, but had more influence on engineering and other non-textile industries.

Products and processes

The overall range of woollen industry processes, as described in chapters 1 and 2, was similar throughout the traditional west of England broadcloth industry, which extended across Wiltshire, Somerset, Gloucestershire and parts of Oxfordshire and Hampshire. By the 17th century, however, local variations in processes had begun to differentiate the Wiltshire and Somerset industry from that in Gloucestershire. From the late medieval period Wiltshire and Somerset emphasised the production of undyed cloths, whereas the Gloucestershire industry, especially in the Stroud area, became known for its superfine dyed cloths.[4] Further changes in the demand for textile goods in the 17th century, in particular the move away from heavy woollens to lighter cloths made from coarser wools, were to have a profound impact on the history of the English textile industry, leading to the greater use of imported wool, the development of processes and to regional differences in the organisation of production, all of which influenced the later pattern of mill building.

In the 17th century English wool was notably coarser than imported wool, and more suited to worsted-type cloths, leading to the greater use of imported wool for fine cloths. In Gloucestershire, the production of fine woollens continued to develop alongside the new coarser cloths, but in Wiltshire and Somerset the clothiers gave more emphasis to new products and the use of imported wool. The clothiers of Shepton Mallet and Bradford-on-Avon, for example, were noted pioneers in the use of Spanish wool in the early 17th century.[5] In some cases the 'Spanish cloth' they produced was woven entirely from Spanish wool, but it was common to blend the expensive imported fibre with English wools. One of the distinctive features of the new cloths was their greater range of colours, achieved by the use of different coloured yarns that were dyed in the wool, producing cloths usually referred to as 'medleys'. They also required less fulling than the traditional heavy woollens, and different dyeing and finishing processes to those used in Gloucestershire. In other parts of the South West the production of serges, a type of the new lighter cloths that used a combination of worsted for warp and wool for weft, was greatly expanded in the late 17th and 18th centuries (*see* chapter 4).

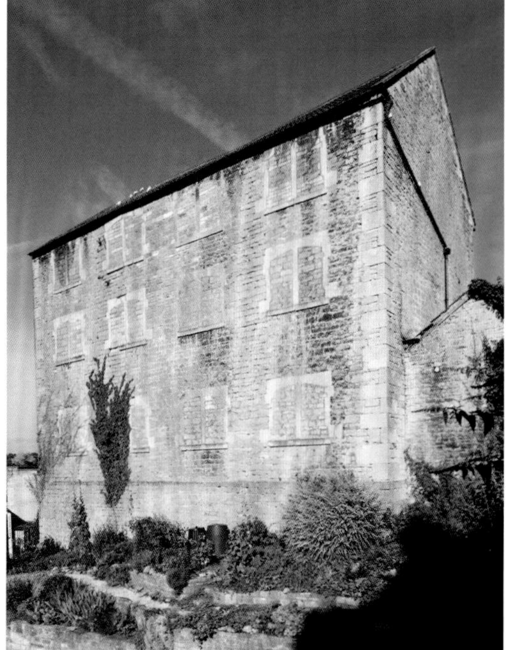

Fig 3.3
Textile workshops formed an important part the growth of market towns in the 17th and 18th century, such as these at Coppice Hill in Bradford-on-Avon, Wiltshire. Workshops continued to be built after the introduction of factories, however, in particular for handloom weaving and related trades.
[DP137130]

In Wiltshire and Somerset, additional new cloths were introduced in the 18th century that were better suited to production in loomshops and the early factories (Fig 3.3). The traditional broadloom was thought to be unsuited to installation in loomshops, so the new cloths were woven using narrow looms (Fig 3.4).[6] A

Fig 3.4
From the mid-18th century, new types of cloth were introduced for weaving on narrower looms, which were more easily set up in loomshops than the traditional broadloom.
[Reproduced courtesy of Trowbridge Museum. DP137748]

particularly successful new cloth was cassimere, patented by Francis Yerbury of Bradford-on-Avon in 1766,[7] which was commonly made on narrow looms throughout the west of England in the early 19th century. Narrow looms could be installed in loomshops and in domestic workshops, and the production of cassimeres has been associated with the increased building of cottages with workshops in Trowbridge, Chippenham and other Wiltshire towns in the early 19th century.[8]

From the late 18th century, other textile processes, in addition to weaving, were being developed to suit the floor space and power systems of the factories. As in Gloucestershire, hand-powered jennies were widely used for spinning in both workshops and partly powered mills by the late 18th century (Fig 3.5). There was more resistance to the introduction of machinery than in Gloucestershire, however, leading to several widely reported examples of machine breaking and rioting. The teazle gig, for example, was widely used by Gloucestershire clothiers by the mid-18th century, but its introduction in 1766 at a mill in Horningsham, Wiltshire, led to serious unrest.[9] The use of narrow handlooms enabled loomshops to be added to factories in Wiltshire, Somerset and Gloucestershire by the mid-19th century, eventually bypassing the independent handloom weavers and undermining their former influence on the progress of the industry. Shearmen were another trade of influential and skilled cloth workers who strongly resisted any challenge to their traditional livelihood, both in Wiltshire and in other regions.

The increased construction of domestic workshops in towns such as Trowbridge has been recognised as evidence of the continued independence of the handloom weavers into the mid-19th century.[10] The narrow handlooms paved the way for the introduction of power looms at steam-powered mills from the 1830s, which were initially used for the production of similar types of cloth to the loomshops.[11] The preparation and finishing stages were also developed to match the increased output of the workshops and factories. Wool-drying stoves and dry houses, or tenter houses, were used as widely here as in Gloucestershire from the late 18th to the mid-19th century. Local variations included octagonal wool stoves and the use of cloth drying rooms in the upper floors of some early factories (*see* p 69). One of the most important developments in cloth-finishing techniques was invented in Wiltshire in 1833, when John Dyer of Trowbridge patented the rotary fulling, or milling, machine, which was to have a marked influence on later mill building (Fig 3.6).[12] Although it was soon improved by Dyer, and by James Ferrabee of Stroud in the 1850s, the milling machine finally severed the centuries-old dependence on fulling mills, enabling mills and cloth-finishing works with much greater output to be located away from

Fig 3.5
The hand-powered spinning jenny was widely used in both workshops and the partly powered early factories in most of the regional textile industries. [Reproduced courtesy of Trowbridge Museum. DP137741]

Fig 3.6
The fulling or milling machine, patented by John Dyer of Trowbridge in 1833, was one of the most significant developments in the woollen industry, increasing the output of the finishing processes in factories and marking the demise of the traditional fulling mill. [Reproduced courtesy of Trowbridge Museum. DP137747].

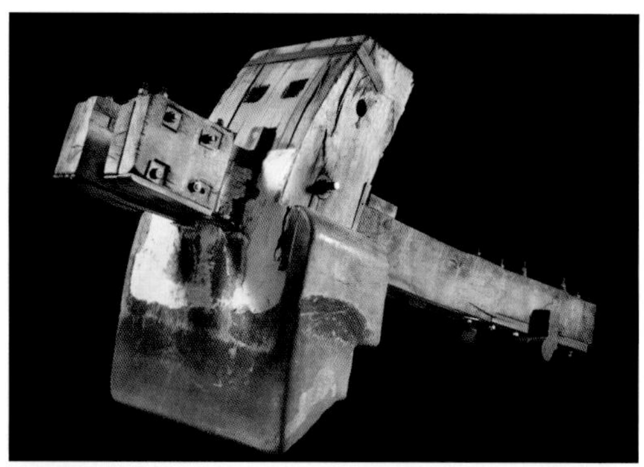

Fig 3.7
Traditional fulling stocks continued to be used at smaller sites and for specialised products. This fulling stock, which is 2.78m long, was formerly used at a felt works in Wilton. [Reproduced courtesy of Trowbridge Museum. DP137738]

Fig 3.8
Carpet manufacture developed into a specialised and prestigious textile industry in Wilton and Axminster from the mid-18th century. The Royal Wilton Carpet Factory site retains several well-preserved early workshops and factory buildings. [DP025871]

water-power sites. Its introduction was gradual, however, and initially limited to the larger, steam-powered sites. Fulling stocks continued to be used at smaller mills and for specialised products, such as felt, until well into the late 19th century (Fig 3.7).

The increased emphasis on the combination of processes can be seen in the range of buildings at many of the larger sites in the late 18th and early 19th centuries, but before the factory-building period there were fewer signs of the early development of integrated working than was the case in the Gloucestershire industry. In Wiltshire and Somerset dye houses were associated with clothiers' houses, and specialist dye works became more common in the 18th century. This reflected the area's growing production of the lighter dyed cloths, which were dyed at the wool preparation stage, as opposed to the piece dyeing and open-air tentering associated with the older heavily fulled woollens.

A small but significant branch of the Wiltshire woollen industry was the manufacture of carpets, notably at Wilton near Salisbury, where the famous Royal Wilton Carpet Factory is still in production (Fig 3.8; *see* p 72). In the early 18th century, a local cottage industry was probably making 'Brussels' carpets in the area, in which the warp threads were manually extended into loops to form the pile of the carpet, but the trade was rejuvenated by the patronage and support of the Earl of Pembroke, of nearby Wilton House. In *c* 1741 the earl is said to have arranged for the migration of two skilled French carpet weavers, who started manufacturing 'Wilton' pile carpet by applying techniques that were already used to make high-quality French carpets.[13] Wilton carpet was a development of the Brussels type, made by cutting the loops to form a dense and resilient pile. The technique employed the use of a new type of carpet loom, and was granted an English patent in 1741.[14] The cut-pile carpet was successfully manufactured by at least two firms at Wilton and, from the late 18th century, was developed by the rapidly expanding carpet industry at Kidderminster in Worcestershire. Another significant type of early carpet was introduced at Axminster, east Devon, by Thomas Whitty in 1755. Described as similar to traditional Turkish carpets, this involved the hand knotting of tufts of woollen thread to form the pile, requiring from 50 to 100 tufts per square inch. The Axminster factory was initially successful but was bought by the main Wilton firm in 1835, which then manufactured both types of carpet.[15]

The early woollen industry in Wiltshire and Somerset

The varied development of the west of England woollen industry across Wiltshire, Somerset and Gloucestershire was in part a reflection of the region's topography, but was also influenced from an early date by medieval taxation and statutory controls. In the 13th century English wool was an important export and was a valuable source of income for the Crown. Wool was the first commodity to be systematically taxed. From the 14th century, however, the lower taxation of cloth, together with fluctuations in the production of cloth abroad, provided great encouragement for cloth making in England. Wool merchants became more interested in cloth production, leading to the rise of the clothiers and effectively marking the beginning of the English woollen-cloth industry.[16] A statutory system for controlling the dimensions and quality of broadcloth, known as the ullnage, operated from the 14th century and was periodically updated to reflect changes in the types of cloth being produced. By the second half of the 14th century wool and cloth together accounted for half of all export revenue.[17] The cloth trade continued to expand thereafter, but wool exports decreased. Cloth production benefited from later changes in taxation and, in the late 15th century, by legal restrictions on wool exports which channelled English wool into the English cloth industry.[18]

Throughout the late medieval period the further growth of the industry was influenced by ongoing changes to taxation and to the statutory controls on production, both national and local, including attempts by clothiers, merchants or trade guilds in some areas to protect their businesses from increasing competition. The regulations reflected the distribution of the early industry, and may have encouraged its development in the towns of some areas and the countryside of others. An Act of 1557, for example, stated that all woollen cloth production was to be limited to the market towns where the trade was already established, except in specified rural areas which already had significant industries. In the South West, Cornwall and the Stroud Valleys of Gloucestershire were identified as rural areas where the industry could continue to develop, but its growth in Wiltshire and Somerset appears to have been restricted to the market towns.[19]

By the 14th century, woollen industries existed in towns such as Bristol, Salisbury and Winchester, but very few of its buildings survive. In this early period fulling mills were not a widespread building type, wool being a more important product than cloth, and were mostly associated with the guild-controlled industries in the towns.[20] The surviving stone-built wool warehouses in Southampton, dating from *c* 1400, and in Poole, dating from the 15th century, are amongst the earliest intact buildings associated with the South West woollen industry (Figs 3.9 and 3.10). The growth of the early industry around Salisbury (and in neighbouring parts of Hampshire) is indicated by broadcloth exports from Southampton, which increased from around 500 pieces per year in the mid-14th century to almost 10,000 pieces by the end of the century.[21] As cloth production increased, fulling expanded rapidly into favourable water-power areas outside the towns, the largest concentration being in the valleys of Gloucestershire, and thereby established the basic geography of the industry that was retained for the next six centuries.

The earliest extant mill in the region which was connected with late medieval fulling is Harnham Mill, Salisbury (Fig 3.11). This picturesque and very well-preserved building dates

Fig 3.9 (below)
Late medieval shipping warehouses are some of the earliest buildings of the woollen industry – this one at Poole, Dorset, is now a local studies library.
[DP137197]

Fig 3.10 (bottom)
Late medieval wool warehouse at Southampton, converted into a maritime museum.
[DP140121]

Fig 3.11
The extant building at Harnham Mill, Salisbury, probably dating from the early 16th century, is one of the earliest intact fulling mills in the region, although it was also used as a paper mill, corn mill and spinning mill. Many fulling mills were used for more than one function.
[DP139290]

from *c* 1500, but a mill has stood at the site from the late 13th century. It is distinguished by the use of high-quality stonework, with hollow-chamfered mouldings to windows, doors and fireplaces. The ground floor and gable-end walls feature the use of knapped and squared flint in a chequerboard pattern with ashlar blocks. This is an unusually ornate form of construction for a small industrial building, and almost certainly reflects the status of the owner as well as local building tradition. Three water channels remain intact beneath the ground floor, suggesting the former presence of one or two waterwheels and a bypass channel. It has been used as a grist mill and a paper mill in addition to fulling. The evidence of more than one wheel suggests that the mill may have been built or adapted to serve a dual function, as was common with late medieval watermills.

The woollen industry of the clothiers

The late medieval trade in fine-woollen broadcloths endured for longer than any of the later stages in the history of the industry, spanning the 14th to the late 16th centuries. The late medieval industry was chiefly financed by merchants, but as cloth production expanded it increasingly came under the control of clothiers, who combined the trading of wool and cloth with the management of the spinning, weaving and finishing processes. The clothiers' industry was organised along similar lines to that in Gloucestershire, but with local variations in different types of cloth in Wiltshire and Somerset. The greater concentration of clothiers in the market towns is reflected in the architecture of their fine houses (Figs 3.12 and 3.13). By the late 16th century, the most

Fig 3.12
Clothiers built some of the finest houses in the market towns of Wiltshire and Somerset. This example, one of several on Fore Street, Trowbridge, was built for the clothier Thomas Cooper in the early 18th century. [DP137274]

successful clothiers had become influential figures in Wiltshire and Somerset towns. Little survives, however, of the buildings that were actually used for cloth production in this period, when most processes were located in cottages or very small workshops. An unusual exception was the use of Malmesbury Abbey for weaving in the mid-16th century, by the clothier William Stumpe, which in effect utilised parts of the site as an early loomshop.[22] Stumpe was a prominent landowner who became established in the woollen industry by acquiring monastic estates after the Dissolution. The house he built in the abbey grounds, later extended by his descendents, is one of the largest clothiers' houses in the county (Fig 3.14).

The transition to the production of new types of cloth from the early 17th century was seen throughout the west of England woollen industry, but the clothiers of Wiltshire and Somerset began to emphasise different processes to those in Gloucestershire. Fulling mills continued to be used in Wiltshire and Somerset and saw less rebuilding and demolition than other areas, since later factory building often took place at different sites in the towns. Archive photographs and other documents suggest that they developed similar proportions to the later fulling mills in Gloucestershire, larger than the few surviving late medieval mills but without the more rational and larger designs of the early factories. An intact example is Iford Mill, which

Fig 3.13
Westcroft House, on British Row, Trowbridge, was built by the clothier John Waldron in 1784. In common with many of the 18th-century clothiers' houses, textile workshops were formerly attached to the rear. [DP137261]

Fig 3.14
One of the largest early clothiers' houses in Wiltshire is Abbey House at Malmesbury, built by William Stumpe and his descendents in the 16th and 17th century. Parts of the adjoining Malmesbury Abbey were used as textile workshops.
[BB91/19484]

Fig 3.15
Fulling mills were perhaps the most important early building type in the west of England woollen industry, but intact examples are now rare. Iford Mill at Hinton Charterhouse, Somerset, now a house, is probably representative of the size and proportions of rural fulling mills before the factory building period.
[DP139951]

originated as one of the mills of Hinton Priory but was used for fulling by clothiers from the mid-16th century (Fig 3.15). The larger fulling mill at West Lavington, though still a traditional vernacular building, is of comparable size to the late fulling mills in Gloucestershire, such as Egypt Mill (*see* chapter 2), with tentative evidence of the provision of ventilation in the upper storey (Fig 3.16). One of the last purpose-built fulling mills, built in *c* 1800, was later converted into the Whitchurch Silk Mill, now a working museum in Hampshire. Although its floors and windows were significantly altered in the conversion, the original proportions of the brick exterior were retained and are clearly more influenced by the symmetrical designs of the early factories than the smaller vernacular fulling mills (Fig 3.17).

By the 18th century the outworking system of the clothiers was a well-established feature in both the landscapes and the society of the area. A vivid description of the industry in the 1720s was provided by Daniel Defoe, who listed 17 market towns in Wiltshire and Somerset where the principal trade was the production of 'fine medley or mixed cloths, such as are worn in England by the better sort of people'.[23] Clearly impressed by the extent of the industry, Defoe's description points to an early stage in the concentration of production, 70 years before the first local factories were built, in which spinning was still located in the many smaller villages, and weaving was based closer to the clothiers themselves in the towns. Cirencester, Gloucestershire, was noted as a major centre for the trading of wool brought from across the south and east of England, while Trowbridge, Bradford-on-Avon, Frome and Shepton Mallet were amongst the most successful cloth-producing towns. The organisation of the clothiers' business was described with no mention of the wide range of dyeing and finishing processes, implying that those stages were already developing as specialised activities in separate locations:

> Generally speaking, the spinning work of all this Manufacture is performed by the poor people; the Master-Clothiers, who generally live in the greater Towns, sending out the Wool weekly to their Houses, by their Servants and Horses; and at the same time, bringing back the yarn that they have spun and finished, which is then fitted for the loom.[24]

Defoe noted that dyeing and finishing were more widespread along the River Avon and its tributaries, where clothiers in towns such as Bradford and Trowbridge had become wealthy by concentrating on the production of the dyed 'Spanish' and mixed cloths.[25] As stated in chapter 2, the clothiers of Shepton Mallet had been recognised from the early 17th century as amongst the pioneers in the production of lighter cloths using imported fine Spanish wool. Most of the industry's output was taken overland to London for sale at the Blackwell Hall cloth market.[26]

The larger market towns retain historic market halls and other commercial buildings dating from this prosperous period in the pre-factory woollen industry. In some cases the buildings were used solely for textiles, but in others the

Fig 3.16
West Lavington Mill, Wiltshire, on the left, shows the larger scale of fulling mills during the expansion of the pre-factory industry in the 17th and 18th centuries. Photograph not dated.
[Reproduced courtesy of Wiltshire & Swindon History Centre, WILTM:7074. DP136792]

Fig 3.17
Whitchurch Silk Mill, Hampshire, was also built as a fulling mill, and still retains the proportions of an early 19th-century factory. Fulling mills by this period represented the last stage in the long development of fulling with stocks, prior to the spread of the milling machine from the 1830s.
[DP140111]

Fig 3.18
Both Bradford-on-Avon and Trowbridge saw the development of new suburbs for the cottage-based textile industry in the late 17th century, such as this artisans' housing at Newtown in Bradford-on-Avon. The use of workshops preceded factory building, and actually increased as the first factories created a demand for processes that were not yet fully mechanised.
[DP137129]

industry shared market facilities with other trades and the sale of general produce. Wool halls and markets in the area were used for trading both wool and yarn in the early 18th century. This suggests that the spinners retained some financial independence from the clothiers, contrasting with the situation in Gloucestershire where the clothiers tended to control all the stages of production themselves (*see* chapter 2). Tetbury was one of the oldest-established wool towns, which like Cirencester was positioned to serve both the Wiltshire and Gloucestershire areas of the industry, and it acquired separate market buildings for wool and general produce (*see* Fig 2.3). Another notable building used for the wool trade was The George at Norton St Philip, a well-preserved coaching inn that originated in the 14th and 15th centuries. The inn included rear buildings around a small courtyard that were used for storing wool and cloth that was traded at the local wool fair.[27]

Several of the Wiltshire and Somerset wool towns saw the addition of distinctive areas of vernacular artisans' housing from the late 17th to the late 18th century, often built in rows along newly created streets, which included workshops and other small woollen-industry buildings. These developments survive as evidence of the prosperity of the domestic industry of the clothiers in the period leading up to the construction of the first factories, although domestic workshops continued to be built for some processes for several decades after factory building started. Well-preserved examples can be seen in Bradford-on-Avon and Trowbridge,[28] both of which include 'New Town' areas of artisans' housing dating from this period (Fig 3.18), and in Shepton Mallet. This type of early industrial housing reflected the growing concentration of the Wiltshire and Somerset industry in towns, and distinguished it further from the architecture of the Gloucestershire industry, which saw far less emphasis on artisans' housing in urban areas.

One of the most significant examples of housing and workshops in the pre-factory period is in the Trinity area of Frome, where the town was extended with a new suburban development built to accommodate a range of artisans in the 17th and 18th century (Fig 3.19). Defoe also visited Frome on his travels, commenting that the town had undergone rapid growth from the 1680s to the 1720s, acquiring a similar-sized population to Bath and Salisbury, and stated that 'its trade is wholly clothing'.[29] This was perhaps an exaggeration, but population statistics compiled in the late 18th and early 19th centuries indicate that about half the population was by then working in textiles, and the Trinity area still provides a remarkably well-preserved illustration of the type of development that Defoe had encountered. The woollen industry was the largest source of employment when the area was originally built, the local community including spinners, weavers, scribblers, shearmen and clothiers.[30] The area contains a distinctive variety of house types, contrasting with the uniformity of later factory housing, which reflects their construction by different builders during a period of prosperity. Investigation of the housing in the 1970s revealed a range of different types of domestic workshops and workshop extensions, most of which had been altered during the later development of the area. The textile industry in Frome declined in the early 19th century, when the focus of development shifted to the steam-powered factories in towns such as Trowbridge, and much of the original housing was subdivided into smaller dwellings, with additional small houses inserted into yards and alleys.[31]

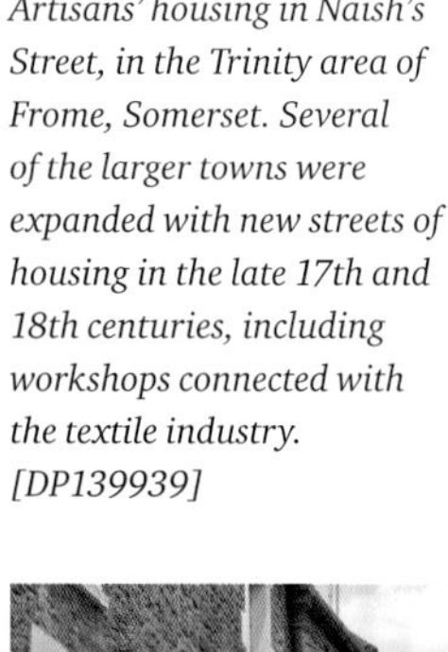

Fig 3.19
Artisans' housing in Naish's Street, in the Trinity area of Frome, Somerset. Several of the larger towns were expanded with new streets of housing in the late 17th and 18th centuries, including workshops connected with the textile industry.
[DP139939]

The earliest indication of the transition to the factory system in Wiltshire and Somerset was an increase in the use of independent workshops and loomshops in the early to mid-18th century, mainly in towns and villages, which occurred well before the construction of new types of factory buildings. Clothiers gradually abandoned the traditional outworking system, and made more use of workshops to concentrate the new types of hand-powered machinery and reorganise workers.[32] Jennies in workshops began to replace the use of spinning wheels in cottages, and narrow handlooms, for the weaving of cassimeres and other narrow cloths, were more easily located in loomshops and domestic workshops than the traditional broadlooms. In some other regions, notably the Yorkshire Pennines and the East Midlands, traditional buildings include good functional evidence of former cottage industries, but such features are less common in the vernacular architecture of Wiltshire and Somerset. Eighteenth-century workshops were often similar in scale, materials and architectural details to contemporary housing. Many have been demolished or incorporated into dwellings, disguising their industrial origins, but small workshops are of interest because they represent an early stage in the transition to factory working. Workshops in general are utility buildings which can be adapted to a wide variety of uses, but features such as external loading doors and openings for ventilation can indicate a former use in the textile industry. Some types of domestic workshops continued to be built in the early 19th century, especially those used for handloom weaving before the addition of power looms to the factories.[33] These later domestic workshops are more clearly defined by their wide workshop windows, which are of similar proportions to those seen in other regions.

As in Gloucestershire, a range of other building types were associated with this period of increasing production in the fine-woollen industry, which preceded the construction of the first factories. A particularly distinctive building type, also found in Gloucestershire, was the drying stove, used for the warm-air drying of washed raw wool.[34] These were circular or octagonal in plan, typically of about 16ft (4.88m) internal diameter, of two storeys and with a conical roof. They contained an iron heating stove and central flue, surrounded by racks for spreading out the wool. Stoves were commonly added to clothiers' houses in the 18th and early 19th century, a clear indication that the pre-factory industry was having to adapt to prepare greater quantities of raw material. Good examples survive in Melksham, Bradford-on-Avon and Frome (Figs 3.20 and 3.21).

Fore Street, Trowbridge

The addition of workshops for hand-powered machinery to clothiers' houses seems to have been widespread in the Wiltshire towns for a prolonged period, and well-preserved examples now form a distinctive townscape which

Fig 3.20
Circular or octagonal drying stoves, built for the drying of washed raw wool, are one of the most distinctive features in the vernacular architecture of Wiltshire, northern Somerset and Gloucestershire. This former drying stove is now the Frome Tourist Information Centre.
[DP139940]

Fig 3.21
Church Street, Melksham. Another example of a converted drying stove.
[DP137191]

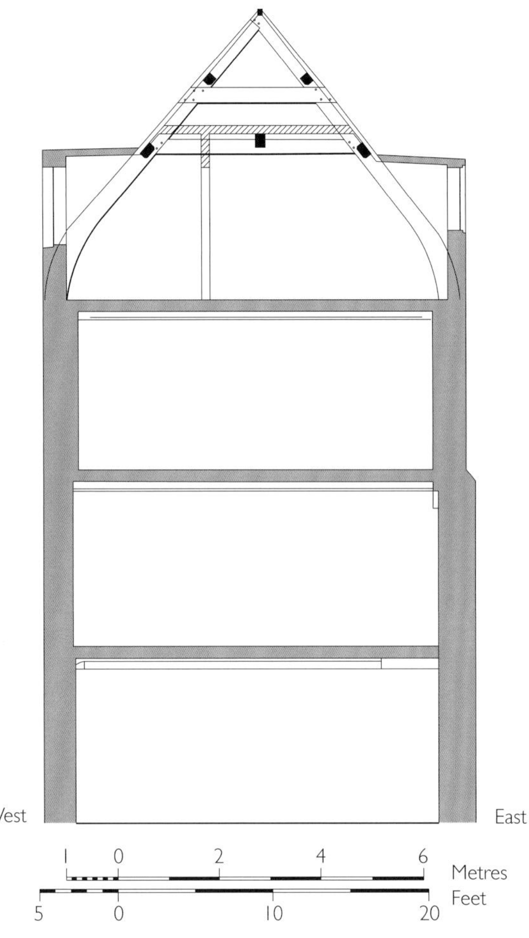

Fig 3.22
The largest of workshops added to the rear of 2 Fore Street, probably dating from the mid-18th century, is distinguished by a tall attic with jointed-cruck roof trusses. Textile workshops often combined vernacular construction with elements of early factory design.

illustrates the small-scale nature of industrial building before factories.

The Fore Street area of Trowbridge contains several good examples of the gradual addition of successive workshops to the backs of 16th- to 18th-century houses, creating long groups of small industrial buildings overlooking the yards and alleys that separate the properties. The front building of 2 Fore Street, for example, retains parts of the internal structure of the 16th-century house, including floor beams and a wind-braced roof, but most of the architectural details, and the front elevation, were altered in later conversions to shops and offices. The site was owned by the clothier John Mortimer and his sons from the early 18th century, and sold to another clothier in the early 19th century.[35] Workshop extensions were added in several phases, starting with a 17th-century wing which was raised to four storeys in the mid-18th century. This has a distinctive tall attic, supported by jointed-cruck trusses and lit by wide workshop windows (Fig 3.22). Additional two- and three-storeyed workshops were attached to the rear in the early 19th century, one of which may have contained a small steam engine (Fig 3.23).[36]

Fig 3.23
The two- and three-storeyed workshops added in several phases to the rear of clothiers' houses on Fore Street, Trowbridge.
[DP137736]

Anstie's Factory, Devizes

The largest of the late 18th-century workshops in Wiltshire was built at Devizes in 1784 by the clothier John Anstie. This was a huge four-storeyed building on New Park Street, dwarfing most of the contemporary powered mills, and is still one of the largest historic buildings in the town (Figs 3.24 and 3.25). It included two rear wings, the whole site being built to contain the full range of jennies, handlooms and other hand-powered machinery used for the manufacture of cassimeres.[37] The scale and architectural treatment of the building, which is one of the largest 18th-century workshops in the country, were exceptional. The site indicates the ambitious scale of Anstie's business, which included about ten sites in the Devizes area. It was located well away from any source of water power, and illustrates the upper limit reached by the hand-powered workshops in north Wiltshire shortly before the construction of the first water-powered factories.

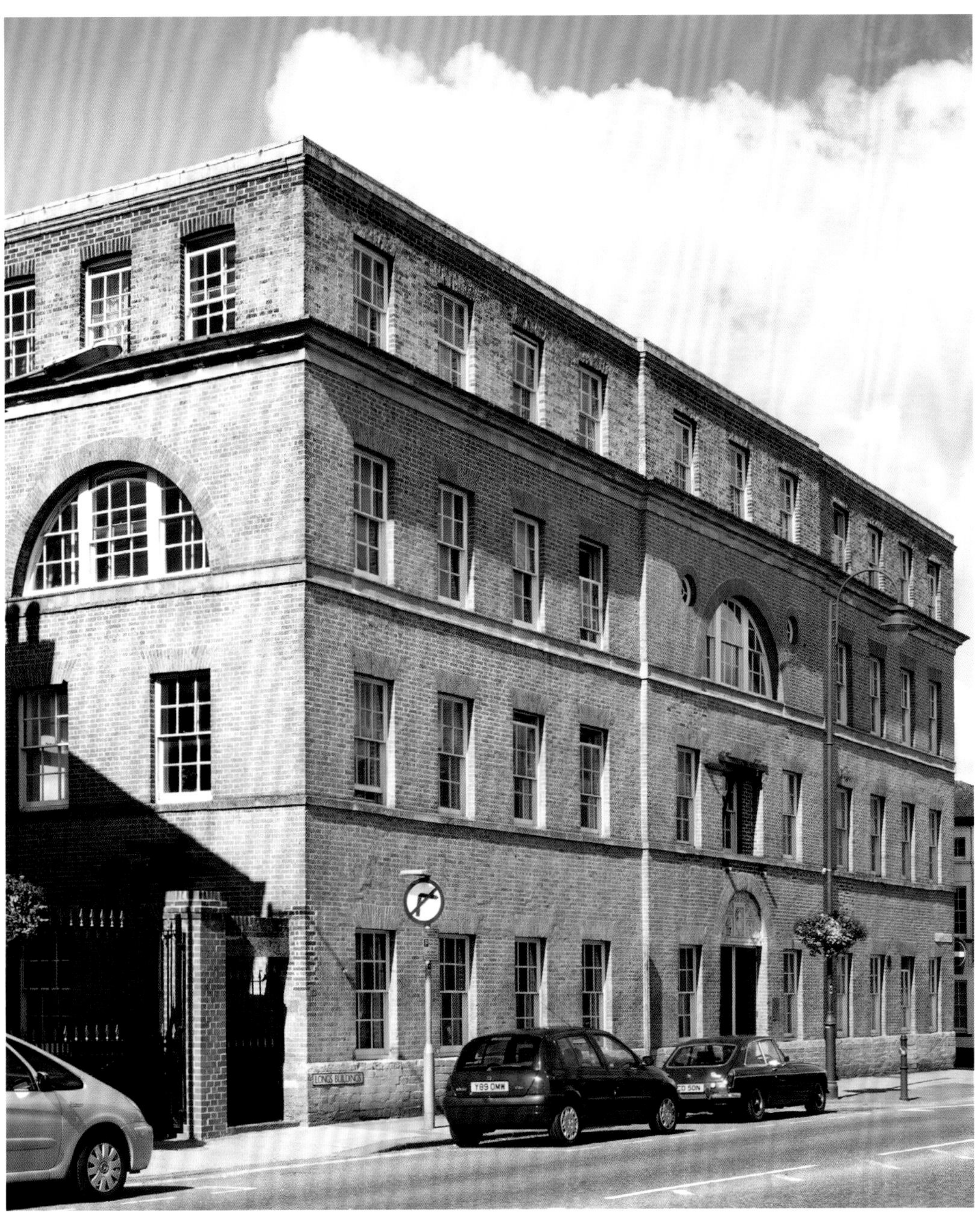

Fig 3.24
The largest textile workshop in north Wiltshire, built by John Anstie of Devizes in 1784, was really a proto-factory that was of similar scale to the largest of the contemporary powered mills. It is defined as a workshop by the absence of an original power system, although the Georgian style of the exterior was highly unusual.
[DP137144]

Fig 3.25
In common with many 18th century manufacturers, John Anstie's house was located very close to his Devizes factory.
[DP137142]

Royal Wilton Carpet Factory

The earliest surviving buildings at the Royal Wilton Carpet Factory site comprise well-preserved workshops, warehousing and ancillary buildings dating from the successful growth of the business up to the early 19th century (Fig 3.26). Its later development was curtailed after 1815 because of increased foreign competition following the end of the Napoleonic wars. Wilton had developed a broadcloth-weaving industry by the 17th century, mainly employed in supplying the merchants of Salisbury. As stated above, a local carpet-weaving industry was established by the 1740s with the support of the Earl of Pembroke. The original carpet factory was destroyed by fire in 1769,[38] and most of the buildings at the extant site date from its development under a succession of proprietors from the early to late 19th century, notably Stevens,

Fig 3.26
Perhaps the best-preserved textile workshop in Wiltshire is this late 18th-century building at the Royal Wilton Carpet Factory (left of tower), which uses traditional materials and construction with similar windows to contemporary domestic workshops.
[DP025861]

Blackmore and Sons in the early 19th century and Yates and Wills from 1871 to 1904.[39] The three-storeyed range on the south side of the main yard has avoided extensive conversion and is now one of the best-preserved textile workshops in the county. It includes a re-set 1655 date stone, but probably dates from the very late 18th or early 19th century, the period of transition from unpowered workshops to the early powered factories. It is distinguished by a narrow plan and tall mansard roof, neither of which were characteristics of the later factories, and by unusually well-preserved, widely spaced three-light wooden casement windows that are of similar proportions to those in contemporary domestic workshops.

The buildings of the early factory system

The first generation of factory mills had notable similarities to the earlier workshops, but incorporated new design principles that later developed into the characteristic features of the 19th-century textile mill. They were initially used for a limited range of processes, mainly spinning. Weaving and other skilled processes, all essential to the success of a textile business, continued to be based in various kinds of workshops until well into the 19th century. Early examples of factories, dating from *c* 1790 to *c* 1820, were built with locally available materials and often included traditional vernacular details, such as mullioned windows. They were built to long, narrow plans, typically of four to six storeys, and of similar proportions to loomshops but significantly larger. The main functional difference was the provision of power to drive the carefully arranged groups of machinery, enabling higher output and closer supervision of the work. Most of the early factories in Wiltshire and Somerset were originally water powered, and therefore had to be built in locations with a good water supply, but supplementary steam power was being added a decade or so later. Mills designed specifically for steam power, which could be located in towns without a large river, began to be built in the early 19th century, and pioneered the construction of steam-powered factories in the South West. Structural details in the early factories also showed similarities with workshops and vernacular buildings. Floors were mostly of joisted timber, of lighter construction than those of later mills, with no intermediate supports, or simply supported by timber or cast-iron props under the beams. Roof construction was also adapted from other building types. Most were of plain gabled form, sometimes hipped, with a covering of stone or locally sourced tiles. Trusses, purlins and rafters were similar to those used on warehouses or larger farm buildings, with much use of traditional carpentry methods and pegged construction.

Water-powered factories

Avon Mills, Malmesbury

Avon Mills at Malmesbury, the first purpose-built water-powered textile factory in Wiltshire, clearly shows the much larger scale of building associated with the early factory system, although its internal structure was simpler than those of factories built just a few decades later (Figs 3.27 and 3.28). It was built in *c* 1791 for Francis Hill, a clothier of Bradford-on-Avon, and equipped with a full complement of machinery for spinning, finishing and weaving, including fulling stocks.[40] Parts of the site contained large numbers of spring looms (the local term for handlooms that used the flying shuttle), in spite of widespread opposition to their introduction in Wiltshire and Somerset. The factory may have been built in Malmesbury to avoid the unrest in Bradford-on-Avon as weavers and shearers protested about the introduction of machinery. Steam power was added by the 1830s, probably in an extension of the original mill. The site was used by a succession of woollen manufacturers up to *c* 1851, and was then used as a silk mill until the mid-20th century. The five-storeyed original block was of comparable size and narrow proportions to the largest contemporary factories in Gloucestershire. It was extended later in the 1790s with a full-height wing, and in the 1830s a separate five-storeyed mill was added to the north. The two late 18th-century buildings illustrate how the early factories often combined large size with unsophisticated internal construction. Despite their height, both are extremely narrow, with internal widths of around 16ft (4.88m), and have lightly built upper floors, suggesting that powered machinery may have originally been limited to the lower storeys.[41] The floor structure, wooden hinged-casement windows and thin walls are all more typical of large 18th-century workshops than powered factories. The detached mill to the north was

Fig 3.27
The 1790s phases of Avon Mills, Malmesbury, represent the first phase of water-powered factory building in Wiltshire. Its narrow proportions and simple internal structure were comparable to those of contemporary workshops and loomshops.
[DP137177]

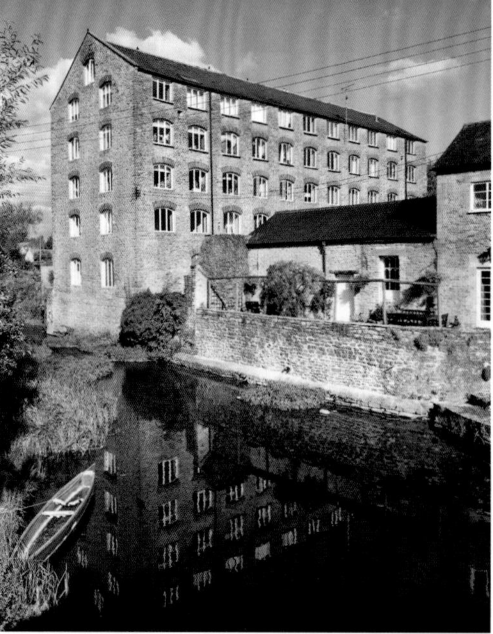

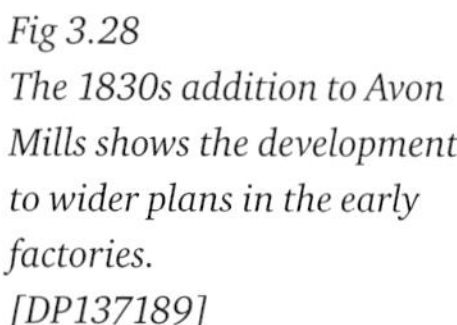

Fig 3.28
The 1830s addition to Avon Mills shows the development to wider plans in the early factories.
[DP137189]

built three decades later, and shows some of the development of factory construction in the early 19th century. It was built to a wider plan with floor beams that were supported by cast-iron columns, the walls decreased in thickness in the upper floors and the original windows were fixed casements, more typical of factory buildings.

Staverton Factory and Kingston Mill, Bradford-on-Avon

Two of the most notable examples of water-powered factories, which clearly showed the grand scale of the early factory system in Wiltshire, were built at Staverton and Bradford-on-Avon, but unfortunately do not survive. Archive illustrations show the considerable attention to architectural detail seen in the larger early factories, which borrowed fashionable details from other building types in the period before factories had acquired their own architectural style. Symmetrical fenestration, parapets, angled pediments, ashlar string courses and window details and prominent bell cupolas all expressed the confidence of the manufacturers' business, although the internal construction of their factories was not significantly developed from that of workshops. Staverton Factory was probably the largest water-powered mill in the region when it was completed by John Jones in 1800, requiring a spectacular level of investment which may have limited the success of the business.[42] It was equipped with the full range of modern machinery and powered by three suspension wheels, which it was claimed could produce up to 200 horse power (Fig 3.29). Its construction was met with violent opposition from local shearmen and weavers, however, including a riot quelled by armed dragoons in 1802. Under new owners, it was completely rebuilt following a fire in 1824, and was then used by a succession of woollen industry firms until the end of the 19th century. Another outstanding example of early factory architecture was Kingston Mill at Bradford-on-Avon, built *c* 1807 by Thomas Divett, the owner of the nearby Kingston Hall (Fig 3.30). It was built on the site of one of three fulling mills along the local stretch of the River Avon. The new factory was used by Thomas Divett and various other clothiers until 1848, after which it formed part of the pioneering rubber factory established by Stephen Moulton and later occupied by the Avon Rubber Company.[43] The building

Fig 3.29
Staverton Mill as rebuilt c *1825 was another impressive example of the dramatic increase in scale achieved in some of the early factories. Photograph dated 1897.*
[Reproduced courtesy of Wiltshire & Swindon History Centre WILTM:P8022. DP136793]

Fig 3.30
Kingston Mill, Bradford-on-Avon, seen at the rear in this view, featured the mullioned windows, string courses, cupola and attic dormers that became the hallmarks of Wiltshire's early factory architecture. Most of these building were demolished in the 1970s.
[BB71/03025]

Fig 3.31
The main building at Kingston Mill included the rare survival of a water-powered main upright shaft, with its bevel gearing and supporting columns.
[BB72/03032]

survived until it was demolished in 1972, when it retained a rare example of an *in situ* main upright shaft and bevel gearing (Fig 3.31).

Greenland Upper Mill, Bradford-on-Avon

Greenland Upper Mill was built in the first decade of the 19th century a short distance upstream of Kingston Mill, on the site of another fulling mill. When recorded in 1994 it retained most of the features that characterised the first generation of water-powered factories, but it has since been extensively rebuilt following fire damage and converted to flats (Fig 3.32).[44] It originally comprised a five-storeyed mill with an internal wheel chamber built for an 18ft (5.49m)-diameter breast-shot waterwheel. A pond to supply the wheel was dammed against the upstream side of the mill and was fed directly from the river, without a weir. The tailrace was an open channel cut across lower ground on the downstream side (Fig 3.33). Power was transmitted to machinery in the four lower storeys by a free-standing upright shaft, driven directly from the waterwheel shaft and supported by bearings bolted to the floor beams. The main rooms were heated from small fireplaces in the end walls; a common feature of early factories was their use of stoves and flues to circulate warm air around the building. Architectural features were similar to those shown in illustrations of other contemporary mills which do not survive. The segmental-headed mullioned windows had ashlar jambs and heads, and a parapet stood above a moulded stone cornice. The staircase and main entrance were in an external tower attached to the end wall, which included a goods hoist with floor traps. The roof structure was also intact, including original dormer windows to both sides. Long dormers

Fig 3.32
Greenland Upper Mill, Bradford-on-Avon, shown here in 1994, was notably similar to Kingston Mill in its architectural treatment and internal water-power system. Steam power was added later in the building in the foreground. The mill was largely demolished and rebuilt as apartments following a fire in the late 1990s.
[BB94/05688]

were widely used in early textile factories, but were not common after the mid-19th century. Before the introduction of north-light sheds, attics with long dormers probably offered the best form of natural lighting at factory sites. In most cases the attics were not powered, suggesting they were used for manual processes that needed good lighting, such as inspecting the finished cloth.

Twerton and Weston factories

To the west of Bath, Twerton and Weston saw the construction of four of the largest early factory complexes from the late 18th to the mid-19th century, none of which survive. The mills were built at the opposite ends of two weirs on the River Avon, and accompanied by related workers' housing. They originated as a group of small water-powered mills used for fulling, grist and leather working, but from the 1790s three of the sites were extended by clothiers into water-powered woollen factories. Gigs and other machines appear to have been used successfully in the factories when they were still met with violent opposition elsewhere in Wiltshire. Twerton Upper Mill and Lower Mill, on the south bank of the river, were further developed by the firm of Charles Wilkins in the early 19th century, claiming to be the largest woollen factories in the west of England by the 1830s, with 800 factory workers and 200–300 outworkers, all producing broadcloth (Fig 3.34).[45]

Buildings related to the early factories

The early factories increased the production of yarn, which created a need for more workshop buildings for processes that were still hand powered. The continued use of workshops for skilled processes was widespread in the early to mid-19th century, resulting in the piecemeal addition of large numbers of small utility buildings that contrasted dramatically with the scale of the main factory buildings they augmented. Small early ancillary buildings rarely survive at early factory sites, and their original functional features would be altered as textile processes were improved, or removed if the building was adapted to a completely new use. Until the introduction of cloth tentering machines in the late 19th century, dry houses, using both heated and natural air drying, were built alongside factories and, in some cases, incorporated into factory buildings (Fig 3.35). Another distinctive early building type was the teazle-drying house, or handle house.[46] These small air-drying houses, typically built with perforated brick walls or hinged wooden louvres, contained racks for drying the wet teazles. Large quantities of teazles, mounted on gigs, were used at the factories for raising the nap of the fulled cloth, which was damp, and constantly needed to be dried (Fig 3.36).

The delayed introduction of power-loom weaving resulted in the continued building of loomshops and domestic workshops in parallel with the development of the early factories. The delay was caused by a combination of the technical problems of mechanising weaving and, especially in Wiltshire and northern Somerset,

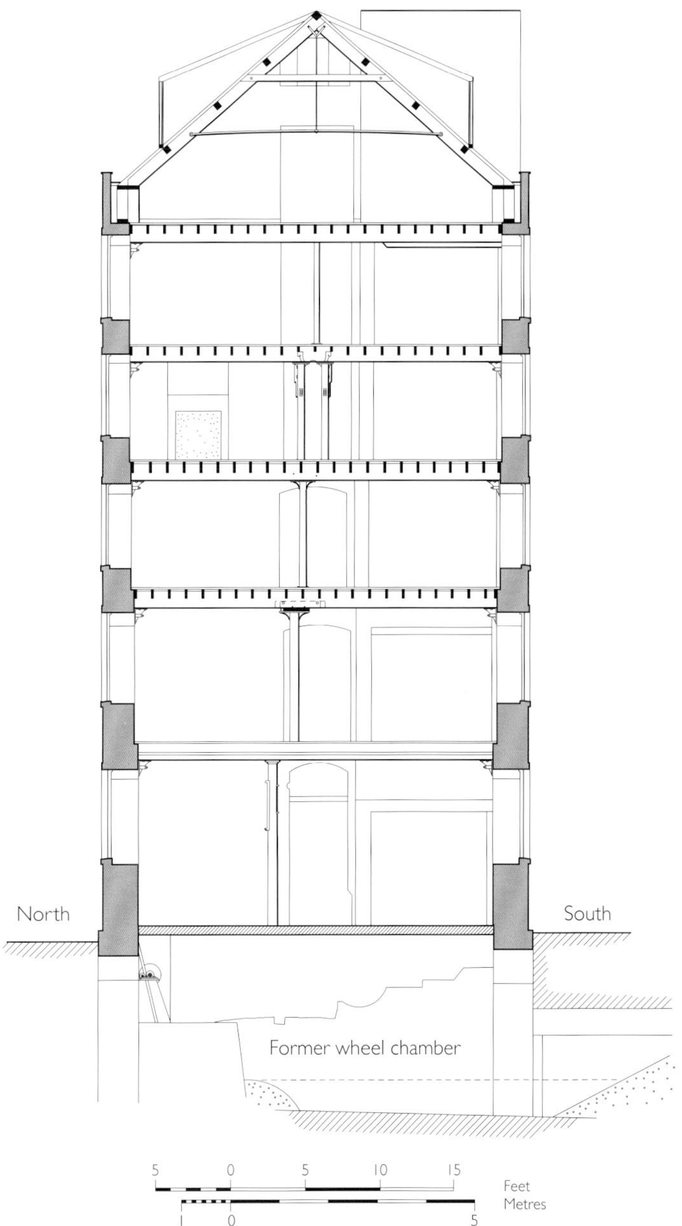

Fig 3.33
Early factories such as Greenland Upper Mill were characterised by their tall, narrow proportions and internal wheel chambers. The attic dormer windows were an original feature, but were less common in later mills with wider plans.

Fig 3.34 (above)
Twerton developed into an industrial suburb of Bath in the early 19th century, centred on four water- and steam-powered mill complexes built on opposite banks of the River Avon, none of which survive. Twerton Upper Mill was one of the largest woollen factories in the region in the 1830s. Photograph dated 1903.
[© Bath Through Time. 26950]

Fig 3.35 (right)
Bitham Mill, Westbury. Rooms for drying cloth or wool were sometimes incorporated into early factories, ventilated either by opening louvres or, as in this case, by panels of perforated brickwork. Engraving dated 1849.
[Reproduced courtesy of Wiltshire & Swindon History Centre, 2271/1. DP136795]

by the opposition to mechanisation from hand-loom weavers; power looms were not widely used for four decades after the first use of powered spinning machines. Loomshop space was sometimes included in an unpowered room of the main factory building, in an attached wing or in a separate building. Workshop space was also widely incorporated into workers' housing in the first half of the 19th century. The expanding factory towns in north and central Wiltshire saw the construction of numerous long rows of cottages with distinctive workshop windows; these domestic workshops provided a flexible space that could be used for both textiles and other local industries (Fig 3.37).

The addition of steam power to water-powered factories

Steam was being used as supplementary power at the water-powered factories within a few decades of their construction. The engines

Fig 3.36
The Handle House of the former Bridge Mills in Trowbridge, was built across the River Biss for drying the teazles used in raising the nap of woollen cloth. The walls are entirely composed of ventilated brickwork. The late 18th-century clothier's workshop adjoining Bridge House can be seen on the right. The late 19th-century Studley Mill is to the rear. [AA009640]

themselves were usually smaller than those installed in purpose-built steam-powered mills, suggesting that water remained the preferred source of power. In this period they were usually single-cylinder beam engines installed in attached buildings or sometimes a dedicated engine house, and required the addition of a boiler house and chimney close to the mill's water supply. The additional power was often associated with the extension of the mill building, and the power transmission system would be altered to enable steam-powered shafting to be connected to the earlier shafting.

Steam power was also associated with the addition of completely new buildings to water-powered sites. In the mid- and late 19th century, one of the most common types of steam-powered addition was the power-loom weaving shed, although there were also some early examples of power looms being installed in multi-storeyed mills. Sheds contained extensive line-shafting systems, mounted on the columns supporting the roof, which required the use of large steam engines or a combination of water- and steam-power. Weaving sheds, along with sheds used for carding, spinning and cloth finishing, became a characteristic feature of late 19th-century mill towns in most of the textile areas (Fig 3.38). Early examples had roofs of symmetrical ridges, as was the case in the first weaving sheds to be added to Greenland Upper Mill in the mid-19th century, but the asymmetrical north-light roof soon became the standard form. The steeper slopes of the roof were fully glazed and arranged to be north-facing whenever possible, which created a well-lit interior without shadows.

Fig 3.37
Domestic workshops were a widespread feature of Trowbridge houses in the late 18th and early 19th century, as seen here on Yerbury Street. They were built to accommodate weaving and other processes that were put out by the early factories. [DP137250]

Fig 3.38
The former north-light sheds adjoining Studley Mill, Trowbridge. Power-loom weaving sheds were added to spinning mills in many of the textile regions from the late 1820s. In the South West, they often indicate the addition of steam power to an earlier water-powered factory. Photograph dated 1873.
[Reproduced courtesy of Wiltshire & Swindon History Centre, WILTM:P7988. DP136791]

Steam-powered woollen mills in Wiltshire and Somerset

Woollen factories built solely for steam power represented a distinct phase in the development of the Wiltshire and Somerset industry. Early examples were built in the first decade of the 19th century in towns such as Westbury, Bradford-on-Avon and Trowbridge.[47] Their construction indicates that the industry in this area was undergoing similar changes to most of the textile industries in the north of England, where steam gradually supplemented water as the essential power source for large factories in the 19th century. In the South West, Wiltshire and Somerset were at the forefront of the adoption of steam power in the woollen industry, with more steam-powered mills built in the 19th century than in the adjoining counties. The increasing use of steam in the area was marked by a shift in the distribution of the industry towards the larger towns, particularly those of north Wiltshire and adjoining parts of Somerset, which benefited from more direct road, canal and railway connections with coal fields and the major cities. Those areas and market towns which were less suited to the construction of large, steam-powered factories saw a relative decline. Salisbury, Frome and Shepton Mallet are all examples of towns with important early woollen industries that fared badly in competition with the expanding steam-powered mills that were being built elsewhere.

Angel Mill, Westbury

The first steam-powered factory in Wiltshire, Angel Mill was built in Westbury between 1806 and 1809 for the firm of Matravers and Overbury.[48] Like many of the early 19th-century factories in the Westbury–Trowbridge area it was built in red brick with stone used for window surrounds and embellishment (Fig 3.39); Bath stone continued to be the main building material for most factories in northern Somerset. Angel Mill retains its original angled pediment, its embellishment perhaps reflecting the greater level of investment required by even the smaller steam-powered factories. The firm was successful up to the 1840s, controlling several mills around Westbury. In the 1860s the mill was extended into an integrated factory under new owners with the addition of a power-loom weaving shed. It was powered by a Boulton and Watt beam engine from *c* 1817, but since the mill was not built on a water-power site it probably had an earlier engine.[49]

Fig 3.39
Angel Mill, Westbury, built by 1809, was the first purpose-built steam-powered factory in Wiltshire. The power-loom weaving shed was added in the 1860s.
[DP137280]

Abbey Mill, Bradford-on-Avon

Steam power was introduced on an even larger scale at the Abbey Mill site in Bradford-on-Avon. The late 19th-century mill which still dominates the river frontage was a rebuilding of an earlier steam-powered mill, built in *c* 1807 for the firm of Saunders, Fanner and Co. Archive photographs indicate that this was a huge mill of six storeys and two wings, and may have been powered by up to three steam engines.[50] It was built on the site of the house and workshop of John Saunders, and was associated with other nearby loomshops and the adjoining Church Street Mills to the west. In *c* 1875 the site was completely rebuilt as a spinning mill for the firm of Harper, Taylor and Little to the designs of Richard Gane, a London-based architect and son of an earlier Richard Gane who built several of the early 19th-century woollen mills in Trowbridge (Fig 3.40).[51] The rebuilt Abbey Mill is arguably one of the finest examples of late 19th-century industrial architecture in the South West region. The younger Richard Gane employed Gothic details throughout the exterior; the Gothic influence was fashionable, but far from typical of the architect-designed mills in other areas. Together with the use of local stone, it produced a modern building that complemented the older parts of the town (Figs 3.41 and 3.42). This was unusual in a period when industrial architecture generally represented a dramatic contrast with the style of traditional buildings. The functional aspects of the design are well documented, indicating that its construction, power system and machinery were comparable to the latest types of textile mills in other areas. The mill was powered by a 300-horsepower engine by

Fig 3.40
Abbey Mill, as it was rebuilt in c *1875, with part of Church Street Mill on the right. By this period the steam-powered woollen mills and their associated buildings dominated parts of the historic centre of Bradford-on-Avon, creating a distinctive townscape that combined traditional vernacular with new industrial architecture. From* The Textile Manufacturer, *15 Sept 1876, p 251.*
[Reproduced by courtesy of the University Librarian and Director, The University of Manchester Library.]

Fig 3.41
Abbey Mill, architectural detail.
[DP137116]

Fig 3.42
The Gothic features used at Abbey Mill by the architect Richard Gane were fashionable but not typical of this building type, contrasting with the Italianate or Classical details seen on late 19th-century textile mills in other regions.
[DP137125]

G K Stothert and Co of Bristol, and a full complement of machinery was purchased from Platt and Co of Oldham, one of the largest of the Lancashire machinery makers. The original machinery layout was conservative, however, and may have been more similar to that used in early 19th-century Wiltshire mills. Spinning mules and carding engines were located side-by-side in the upper floors, with gigs and milling machines in the ground floor. In other areas, late 19th-century mills were adopting a more efficient vertical arrangement of processes, with all of the carding machines on the ground floor and the upper floors used mainly for spinning. Weaving at Abbey Mill was more typically located in power-loom sheds, formerly located alongside the nearby Church Street Mill, which was also owned by the firm.

The townscapes of the woollen industry

In the 19th century the geography of the west of England woollen industry was divided into two distinctive areas, with the northern parts of Wiltshire and Somerset characterised by the architecture of urban factories, workshops and artisans' houses, while the traditional semi-rural nature of the industry persisted in Gloucestershire. In the woollen industry of Wiltshire and Somerset the emphasis was firmly on steam-powered factories by the early 19th century. The resulting industrial townscapes were unusual in the South West but notably similar to the mill towns appearing in other regions. This urbanisation of industry was also related to national demographic changes, such as the growth of urban populations, and to the changing structure of employment in the factory towns. The steam-powered textile factories were associated with the growth of related industries, including foundries, engineering, infrastructure and house building, and other industries expanded to provide foodstuffs for the growing population. They were accompanied by a variety of related industrial development, along with new types of housing suited to the factory workers. The new building types included the homes of the rising class of factory owners, who could afford more luxurious accommodation outside the industrialised environment of the town centres.

In Wiltshire and Somerset the urbanisation of the woollen industry can be seen as a gradual process, beginning with the increased use of workshops well before the introduction of steam power, which has produced two distinct types of townscape. In the first, the factories were the latest and largest of a series of industrial buildings added in many phases to former clothiers' houses. The earlier extensions, usually a combination of workshops and warehousing, represented the gradual development of the business in the pre-factory era. This kind of informal development contrasted markedly with the uniformity and larger scale of later industrial architecture. It produced a highly distinctive townscape, characterised by the successive addition of small workshops and related buildings. Factories were not added in all cases, since some of the early businesses in workshops did not successfully convert to the factory system. At sites such as Fore Street in Trowbridge, however, the gradual addition of workshops paralleled the development of the industry, with the later workshops being contemporary with the first generation of factories. In some cases factories that were added later took the form of extensions to the earlier buildings, while in others they were built separately on a nearby open plot.

The second type of development comprised the expansion of a town with the construction of industrial buildings, residential streets and other infrastructure in a new industrial suburb. This was a characteristic type of early 19th-century industrial development, and was also seen in different forms in other regions. Well-preserved examples are now rare, since the early suburbs were often absorbed in the later redevelopment of town centres. A common feature of industrial suburbs is a regular street pattern, laid out with separate areas allocated to factory building and housing, contrasting with the piecemeal development of industry in the more congested older parts of the town.

Early factory building in Trowbridge

At Trowbridge, an almost continuous line of early steam-powered factories was built in an industrial corridor along the course of the River Biss, around the western and southern peripheries of the historic town centre (Fig 3.43). The north of this area, around Town Bridge, was characterised by early to mid-19th-century factories that were built close to, or adjoining, earlier workshops attached to clothiers' houses. In spite of much redevelopment, substantial parts of these houses, workshops and factories survive, representing the development of woollen-industry buildings from the late 16th to the mid-19th century. In comparison with the other textile regions of England, this was a quite exceptional chronological range for industrial buildings in a town centre.

The River Biss was utilised by several small 18th-century mills to the north of the town, along with the first textile mills in the industrial corridor. It was too small to support the construction of a group of large water-powered factories, but provided enough water for early boilers and steam engines.

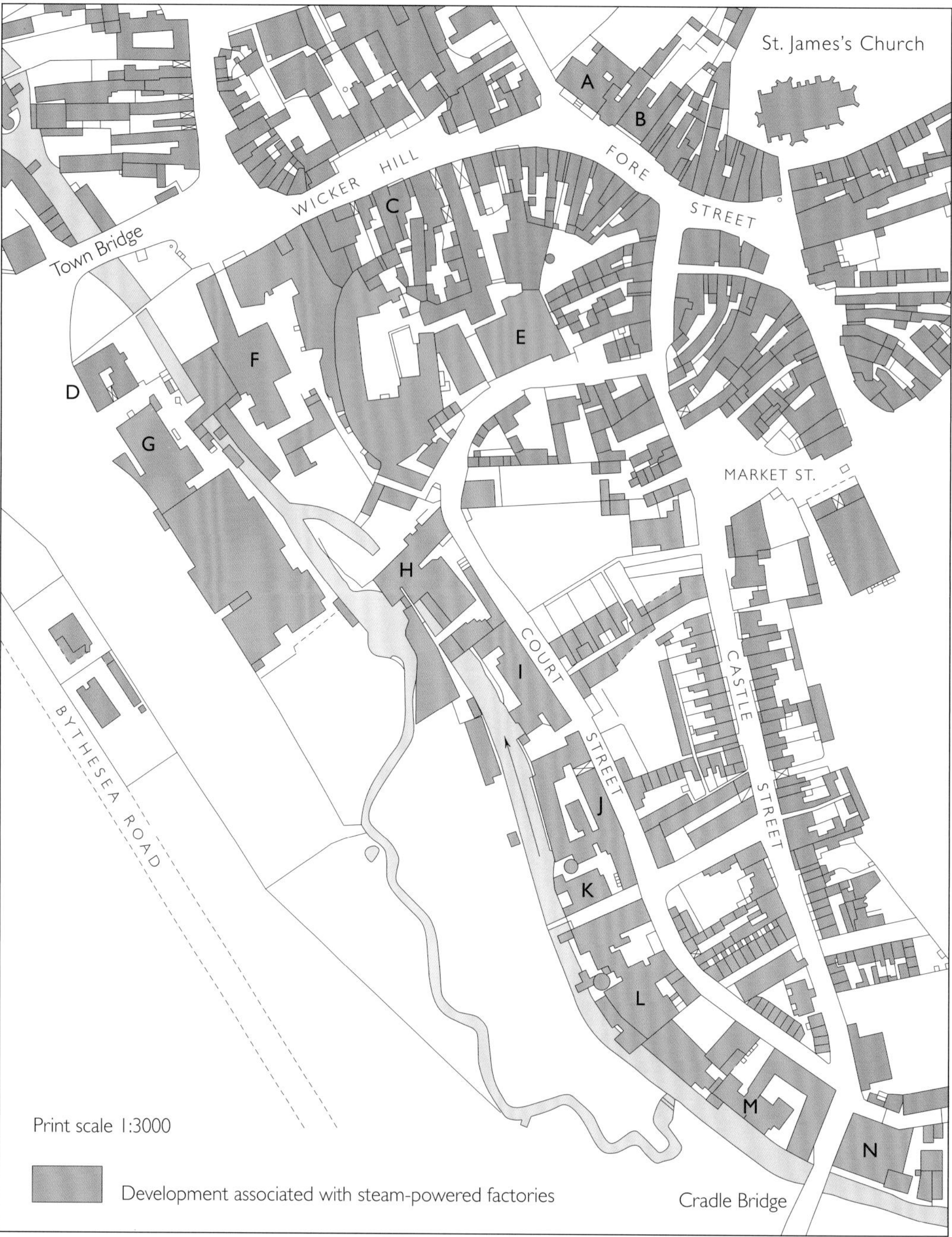

Fig 3.43
Early 19th-century steam-powered factories and associated buildings created a new industrial suburb alongside the houses and workshops in the older parts of Trowbridge.

A *Late 18th-century clothier's house*
B *Late 18th-century clothier's house*
C *17th-century clothier's house, with later rear workshops*
D *Bridge House, early 18th-century clothier's house*
E *Home Mills*
F *Bridge Mills*
G *Studley Mills*
H *Stone Mill*
I *Brick Mill*
J *Castle Mill*
K *Castle Court Factory*
L *Site of dye works*
M *Site of Cradle Bridge Mill*
N *Site of Victoria Mill*

Bridge Mill

The earliest site in the group, which was demolished in the late 1960s, was probably Bridge Mill, which was located just south of the Town Bridge.[52] This was the site of dye houses from the mid-15th century to *c* 1811, when a factory complex was built that included buildings for fulling, jennies, dyeing and cloth drying, and was powered by one of the first steam engines in the area (Fig 3.44). The only substantial water-powered mill along this section of the river was located further south, at the downstream end of a long leat.

Stone Mill

Stone Mill was built close to the site of an ancient mill associated with Trowbridge Castle, but the extant building comprises two phases built in the late 18th century and *c* 1817, when steam power was added in an extension. The earlier water-powered part of the mill was built across the leat, and this leat was the key factor that enabled the construction of the group of steam-powered mills and dye works to the south in the 19th century (Fig 3.45).

The rest of the industrial corridor extended from Stone Mill to beyond Cradle Bridge in the south east, in a densely packed group which contained a further eight factory complexes, all woollen mills and dye works. In spite of the inevitable demolition of some industrial buildings following the decline of the woollen industry, this remains a classic example of an early 19th-century industrial suburb, comparable to similar developments in factory towns in other regions but with functional and architectural features specific to the South West (Fig 3.46). None of the factories had ponds, suggesting that the Stone Mill leat provided

Fig 3.44
Bridge Mill, photographed in 1873, epitomised the range of building types that developed at Trowbridge mill sites in the first half of the 19th century. Only the Handle House remains extant (gabled structure right of centre; see *Fig 3.36).*
[Reproduced courtesy of Wiltshire & Swindon History Centre, WILTM:P394. DP136796]

Fig 3.45
Stone Mill, Trowbridge, originally water powered, was built in the late 18th century on a long leat supplied by the River Biss, and stood close to the site of a much earlier mill associated with Trowbridge Castle. The leat provided the water for a group of 19th-century steam-powered mills that dominated this part of the town.
[DP137264]

sufficient water for the steam plant and thus enabled the factories to be built so close together. The factories were all built along the west side of Court Street, which ran parallel with the leat, while side streets to the east saw the construction of factory-workers' housing and detached workshops. Additional rows of houses with domestic workshops still stand on the nearby Castle Street (*see* Fig 3.43).

Castle Mill

Castle Mill, the largest extant mill in the group, is unusually well preserved, retaining all the main features of an early steam-powered textile mill together with the distinctive architectural details that characterised early factories in the Trowbridge area (Fig 3.47). It was built, and probably designed, in 1828 by the firm of Charles and Richard Gane for the manufacturer John Stancomb.[53] It was the first mill built on the site, its construction marking the expansion of manufacturing outside the old parts of the town with their clothiers' houses and workshops. The five-storeyed front block along

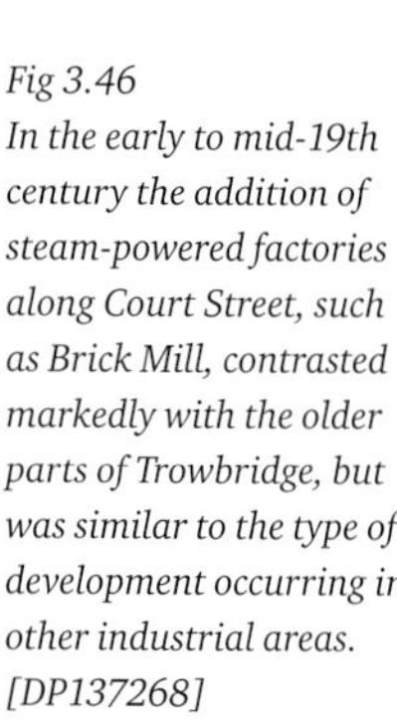

Fig 3.46
In the early to mid-19th century the addition of steam-powered factories along Court Street, such as Brick Mill, contrasted markedly with the older parts of Trowbridge, but was similar to the type of development occurring in other industrial areas.
[DP137268]

Fig 3.47
Castle Mill, Trowbridge, was typical of the closely packed layout of urban steam-powered mills in the early 19th century, comprising three tall buildings grouped around a narrow yard. [DP137270]

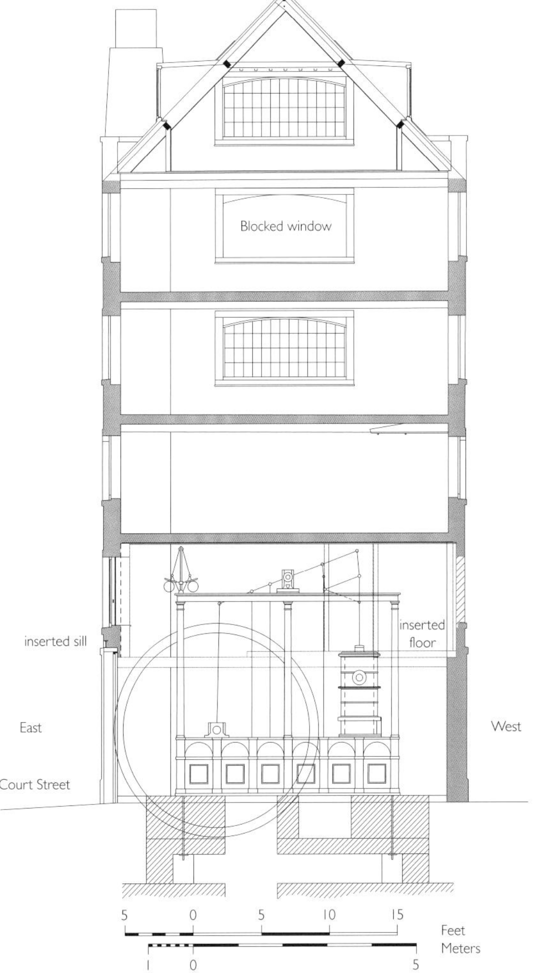

Fig 3.48
The steam-power system of Castle Mill was notably similar to those seen in other regions, with an internal engine house containing a Boulton and Watt beam engine, an internal boiler house and an integral chimney.

Court Street has main elevations of Flemish-bond red brick and a half-hipped roof, lit by three long dormers on each side, behind a low parapet. Ashlar was used for window heads and jambs throughout the site, those in the front block projecting forwards of the brickwork, and the end walls are lit by wide segmental-headed windows with similar details. In the early to mid-19th century a parallel unpowered block was added to the rear, which together with a connecting wing formed a secure private yard, a feature that was also found in early factories in other urban areas.

The steam-power system was located in the south end of the front block, with the internal boiler house in the two end bays and the internal engine house, which contained a Boulton and Watt beam engine, in the third bay (Fig 3.48).[54] The engine house retains its arched windows and coved mouldings to the ceiling, and the boilers were accessed through a wide opening in the rear wall. Mills of this period pre-dated the development of the free-standing chimney, and had integral chimneys attached to a side wall or corner. In this case the original stack remains built into the south-east corner of the boiler house, part of its square upper section projecting above the parapet.

In the mid- and late 19th century, the architecture of steam-powered mills and related buildings continued to make a significant contribution to the development of the industrial areas around the centre of Trowbridge. The increased use of various forms of architectural embellishment was a feature of all the industrial regions in the later 19th century.

Studley Mill

The main block of Studley Mill, which was rebuilt by the firm of J and T Clark in the late 1850s, has the typical wide plan and larger windows that characterised mid-19th-century mills, which were designed to accommodate larger machines in well-lit interiors, but is distinguished by two centred windows that are distinctive to the area (Fig 3.49). Gothic influences can be seen throughout the building, including narrow lancet windows and blind arcading to the external stair tower; mill architects in other regions were beginning to favour Italianate embellishment in this period. It was designed by the firm of Charles and Richard Gane, who were also responsible for Castle Mill and Abbey Mill, Bradford-on-Avon. Greater use of embellishment can be seen in the nearby late

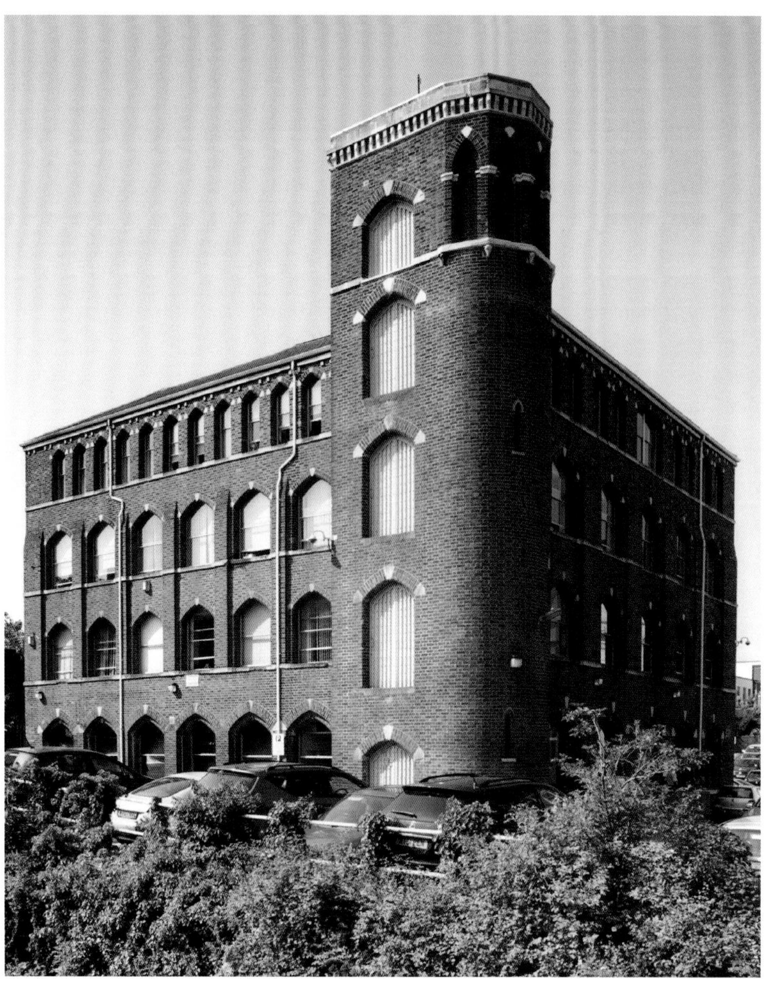

19th-century warehouses and showrooms on Stallard Street, a rare example of commercial warehousing associated with a textile mill in the South West (Fig 3.50).[55] Another building type that was widely added to Trowbridge mills in the late 19th century was the north-light shed, most of which were built to accommodate power looms following the decline of handloom weaving in domestic workshops. Extensive weaving sheds were added to the south side of Studley Mill in 1865, later demolished, with others of various sizes filling the spaces between the mills in the Court Street group (*see* Fig 3.38).

Ashton Mill

The last newly built mill in the town was Ashton Mill, built in 1860 as a modern integrated steam-powered factory with a connected spinning mill and north-light weaving sheds, that was notably similar in its layout and power system to contemporary mills being built in the Yorkshire and Lancashire industries (Fig 3.51).

Housing associated with the early factories

The most widespread building type associated with steam-powered mills in Trowbridge was the housing for the workforce. As stated earlier, a consequence of early factory building was

Fig 3.49 (above)
*Studley Mill, Trowbridge, was rebuilt in the late 1850s, by which time most of the thriving woollen industry firms in Wiltshire were located at urban sites. Another design by the firm of Richard Gane, it features a similar use of Gothic detailing to Abbey Mill, Bradford-on-Avon (*see *Figures 3.40–3.42). [DP137256]*

Fig 3.50 (right)
The later 19th-century development of the industry in Trowbridge included a range of related building types, such these warehouses, shops and offices close to Studley Mill. [DP157994]

Fig 3.51
Ashton Mill, built on the outskirts of Trowbridge in 1860, was a modern, steam-powered, integrated woollen mill. Avoiding the constrictions of a town-centre site, the power-loom weaving shed could be the largest building. This combination of north-light sheds with a multi-storeyed spinning mill and a steam-power system was a typical layout of the late 19th-century integrated factory.
[AP26128/008]

an increased demand for handloom weaving, since the factories built before the 1830s were used primarily for spinning and cloth finishing, with the other stages of production put out to cottage workers. In Wiltshire's industrial towns, large numbers of existing workshops continued to be used for manual processes in the early 19th century, including handloom weaving and shearing, but a noted feature of the factory system was the construction of new rows of artisans' cottages that incorporated domestic workshops (Fig 3.52).[56] This distinctive type of urban housing dates from the period after the construction of the first factories, but before steam power was applied to the full range of processes. It was often built close to the factories, but was also sited in residential suburbs that were expanding around the towns. In common with urban textile industries in other areas, the housing was not generally built by the mill owners, as occurred at many rural factories, but by speculative builders. Later in

Fig 3.52
The early factories led to the construction of new streets of housing with domestic workshops around Trowbridge, such as these along Newtown, which can be contrasted with the earlier artisans' housing in Bradford-on-Avon (see Figure 3.18).
[DP137252]

the 19th century, when the full range of processes had been brought into the factories, more conventional workers' housing was built, comprising terraces of smaller cottages which did not include space for industrial processes. The construction of regular streets of such factory-workers' housing was a characteristic feature of 19th-century industrial townscapes throughout the country. In older industrial towns, such as Trowbridge, the construction of workers' housing without workshops was contemporary with the appearance of north-light weaving sheds at the factories, marking the end of the economic independence of the handloom weavers.

Conclusion: The historical significance of the Wiltshire and Somerset woollen industry

The Wiltshire and Somerset woollen industry has an exceptionally long history, and this is reflected in the great variety of its historic buildings and landscapes. From its earliest origins in the wool trade of the medieval towns, to the extensive outworking industry of the clothiers, and later the new technologies and regimented lifestyle of the factory system, the evidence of cloth production in this area can be said to represent all the main stages in the development of the English textile industry.

The medieval fine-woollen industry was widely established in Wiltshire and Somerset, but from the 14th century the streams in neighbouring Gloucestershire saw a more concentrated development of fulling mills. Thereafter, the varied landscapes of the west of England continued to influence the local development of the woollen industry, with merchants and clothiers congregating in the market towns of Wiltshire and Somerset. They shared the market-town facilities with many other trades, but undoubtedly became the main industry in the rural economy from an early date. Many such towns are still known locally as historic wool towns, centuries after the industry relocated to other places.

A fortunate consequence of the changing geography of the industry is that good evidence survives of the generations of buildings that preceded the factories in the main towns. As the industry moved on to new locations, with new types of buildings, the older sites avoided the threat of large-scale rebuilding, and workshops and smaller mills became available for new uses. This contrasted with areas in which the industry remained rooted to its original sites, where the later mills tended to replace the earlier buildings. In the market towns which did not see factory building in the 19th century, traditional vernacular architecture survives that was closely associated with the woollen trade, including clothiers' houses, wool stores, workshops, drying stoves and the market halls themselves. The industrial origins of these vernacular buildings, particularly workshops and warehouses attached to clothiers' houses, are often disguised by their later conversion for domestic use.

The early factories used water power on a large scale and were located at suitable rural sites, but the later steam-powered factories were often built close to clothiers' houses in the towns, sometimes attached to the workshops which had contained previous generations of textile machinery. The architecture and technology of the 19th-century mills, together with their association with industrial suburbs, defined a radically new building type that was directly comparable with contemporary developments in the textile industries of other regions; parts of Trowbridge were actually referred to as the 'Manchester of the West' in the early 19th century.[57] In contrast with most of these other regions, however, the defining characteristic of the Wiltshire and Somerset mills is their strong connections with the long history of vernacular industry that preceded the factories.

4

The serge industry of Devon, Somerset and Cornwall

The countryside, market towns and ports of Devon, Somerset and east Cornwall have strong historical connections with the textile industries, and at different times were noted for the manufacture of wool, worsted, flax, hemp and silk. The most extensive industry to develop in this area was the production of serges, cloths that combined a worsted warp and a woollen weft, both of which were originally obtained from local farms but later imported. Different methods were used to prepare and spin the two fibres, so the industry involved a wider range of processes than the woollen industries of Gloucestershire and Wiltshire. The most dramatic evidence of this industry is a number of huge integrated mill complexes, including the largest textile sites in the region, which now seem out of place in what has remained a largely rural area. These integrated factories were built by businesses that emerged from the decline of one of England's most successful pre-factory textile industries. In the 17th and 18th centuries, serge making had developed into an extensive cottage industry, with spinning and weaving often combined with farming. A degree of local specialisation developed at an early date, along with variations in the system of outworking; some areas became noted for the cottage spinning of worsted yarn (Fig 4.1), and facilities for cloth finishing were established around Exeter. These variations later influenced the development of the extant mills, although few of the early firms successfully adapted to the factory system. The largest

Fig 4.1
Serge was a mainly rural industry, often supplementing other forms of income in the countryside and market towns. Some of the markets reflected a local emphasis on particular products, as was the case at the Dunster yarn market in Somerset. Late 19th-century photograph by F T S Houghton.
[AA42/06791]

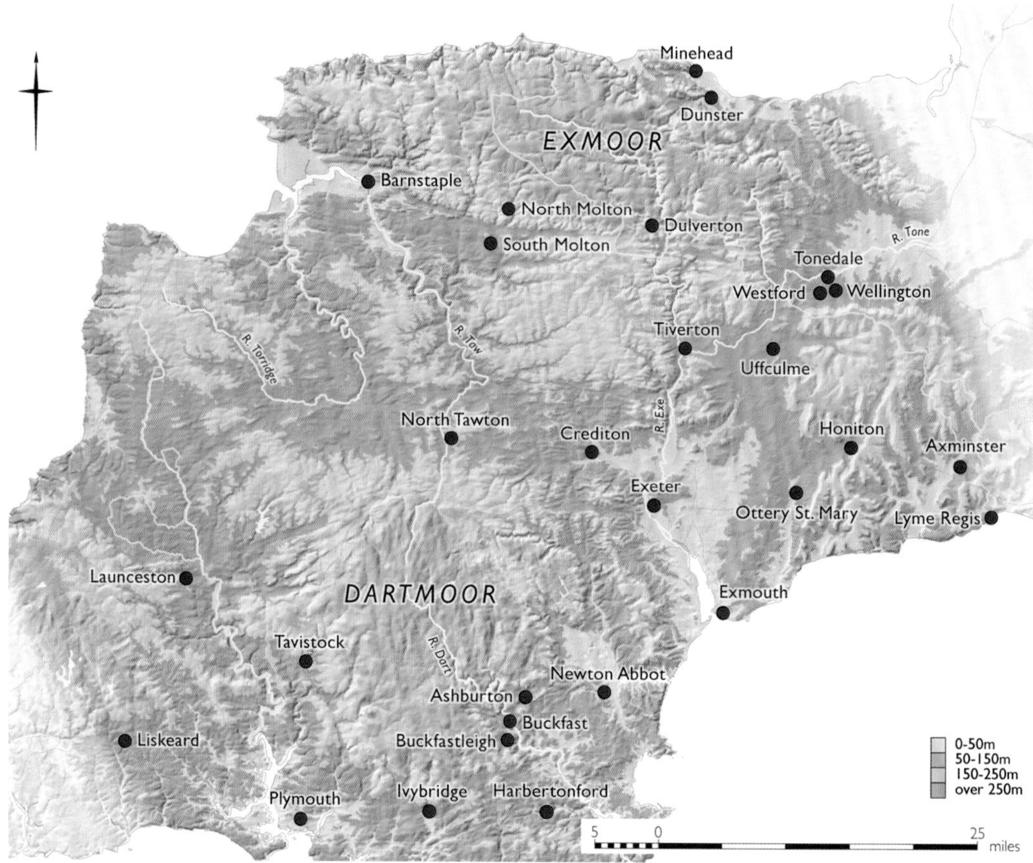

Fig 4.2
The South West serge industry.
[90m SRTM Topography data courtesy of the CGIAR, http://srtm.csi.cgiar.org]

centre was Tiverton in Devon, but the production of serge was organised around local wool markets throughout the area. The main commercial hub of the industry was the port of Exeter, which in the 17th century was one of the most important cloth-trading cities in England.

By the 17th century the production of yarn and cloth was widely distributed in towns, villages and countryside (Fig 4.2). The industry extended from Wellington and Uffculme in the north-east to beyond Tavistock in the south-west, including coastal sites in both north and south Devon and the valleys adjoining Dartmoor and Exmoor. In comparison with the vernacular architecture of other regions, however, relatively little physical evidence of the industry survives in the area's pre-19th-century buildings. Most of the spinning and weaving was carried out as a part-time activity, often in combination with farming, with less emphasis on the construction of specialised textile workshops. Another reason for the absence of pre-factory buildings was the dramatic decline of the serge industry in the late 18th century, the period when workshops were being built in the other textile industries. Significantly, the traditional industry had been organised differently to the fine-woollen industry to the east, with a prosperous class of merchants in Exeter and the main market towns having a strong influence on its development. Clothiers and manufacturers had less overall control of production, reflecting the separation of the industry into specialist trades, and often lacked the resources to invest in new factories. Only one section of the industry, in south Devon, saw a gradual conversion to the factory system in the early 19th century. In other areas, however, the few firms that did adopt factory methods benefited from an absence of local competition, which in part explains the large size of the surviving sites.

Products and processes

Serges were lighter than the traditional woollen cloths, often woven with a diagonal twill weave, and their production was favoured by a general decline in the demand for the heavily fulled fine woollens. The South West serge industry initially benefited from the local availability of both worsted and woollen fibre, but in the 17th and 18th centuries its development was also linked to its use of wools from other parts of England and foreign wools imported via the local ports.[1] In the 19th century the pioneers of the factory system further refined the processes used for serge production. Thomas Fox of Wellington, for example, greatly refined the techniques for the manufacture and finishing of a range of serges and lighter flannel cloths from the early 19th century, which led to the long-term success of the firm (Fig 4.3). Modern versions of these lightweight, high-quality flannels are still produced by Fox Brothers and Company in Wellington today.

The preparation, spinning and weaving of worsteds involved skilled processes that were more specialised than those used in the fine-woollen industry, and this may have contributed to the greater separation of worsted production into independent trades in the 17th century. The full sequence of preparation and spinning processes was not successfully mechanised until the 1830s, several decades after it had been achieved in the fine-woollen and cotton industries and post-dating the collapse of the cottage industry in Devon and Somerset. The most distinctive stage was the preparation of the fibre for spinning, which involved combing instead of the carding used for shorter-staple wools. The process of manual combing used in the 17th and 18th centuries was laborious and highly skilled, and was dominated by a class of specialised workers. After the initial washing, sorting and oiling of the raw wool, a pair of heavy combs with metal teeth was used in a delicate procedure to separate and extract the long worsted fibre (Fig 4.4). This was then combined by hand into a loose, continuous sliver, known as a 'top', which was used for spinning the yarn. The combing processes were repeated in successive stages, each extracting shorter-staple fibres. The metal combs, and the fleece itself, were heated by a stove in the comber's workshop, which helped reduce breakages of the long worsted fibres.

Spinning and weaving were both specialist trades carried out independently of the combers. Hand spinners and handloom weavers used similar tools to those in other textile industries but both had to develop specific techniques, either to spin the strong, hard worsted yarns or to weave the mixed twill fabrics. In the 17th century, clothiers appear to have exercised less

Fig 4.3
Samples of serge, wool and worsted manufactured by Fox Brothers at Tonedale Mills and Tone Works, Wellington. From the late 19th century, large integrated firms continued the local tradition of using different types of wool in producing a wide variety of cloths.
[BB96/06884]

Fig 4.4
A pair of heavy iron wool combs, used for manually separating and extracting the valuable longer fibres used for spinning the warp of serge cloths. The use of combs in workshops was not replaced by machines in factories until the mid-19th century.
[Reproduced courtesy of Ashburton Museum. DP148450]

control over the various stages of production than in the fine-woollen producing areas, such as Gloucestershire, and were mainly concerned with trading the cloth that they purchased from the weavers. Finishing processes used for mixed cloths were similar to those used in other industries, involving a combination of scouring, dyeing and fulling, along with raising and shearing for some cloths, and it is likely that the clothiers were more widely involved with cloth finishing than with the earlier stages. Mixed worsted-woollen cloths were fulled so the availability of water-powered fulling mills influenced the distribution of the serge industry, as it did the fine-woollen industry elsewhere. Fulling mills and dye works were a noted feature of the Exeter area in the 17th and 18th centuries, built to finish the serges that had been purchased for export by the local clothiers.

The finishing processes in the serge industry were described in some detail by the traveller Celia Fiennes during a visit to Exeter in 1698.[2] Large quantities of cloth were carried to the city by packhorse, where it was described as unfinished and still oiled, giving it 'noe pleasing perfume'. The cloth was soaked in urine, followed by soap; it was then fulled until it attained the required thickness, and scoured in water. The author was impressed by the 'great violence' of the fulling stocks, described as 'huge notched timbers like great teeth'. After scouring the cloths were tentered on closely spaced racks in fields around the town. When dried, the cloth was burled (inspected) to remove the unwanted knots and defects, then folded and pressed using heated iron plates. Some was dyed but most was sent to London undyed.

Fiennes's widely quoted description of cloth dyeing in Exeter provides a rare and evocative insight into the nature of the textile industry a century before the transformations of the factory system:

> I saw several fatts they were dying in, of black, yellow, blew, and green – which two last coullours are dipp'd in the same fatt, that which makes it differ is what they were dipp'd in before, which makes them either green or blew; they hang the serges on a great beame or great pole on the top of the fatt and so keep turning it from one to another, as one turns it off into the fatt the other rowles it out of it; soe they do it backwards and forwards till its tinged deep enough of the coullour; their furnace that keepes their dye panns boyling is all under that roome, made of coale fires; there was in a roome by it self a fatt for the scarlet, that being a very chargeable dye noe waste must be allow'd in that; indeed I think they make as fine a coullour as their Bow dies are in London; these rolers I spake off; two men does continually role on and off the pieces of serges till dipp'd enough, the length of these pieces are or should hold out 26 yards [23.77m].

The factory sites that emerged from the decline of the traditional serge industry in the 19th century showed a progressive approach to developing the methods of production, using new machinery and techniques that were comparable to the worsted industries of other regions. In contrast to the fragmented nature of the earlier industry, the successful firms adopted an integrated approach to production. This eventually enabled full control of each process from the sorting and combing of the raw wool to the dyeing and finishing of the cloth; in the largest sites a system of parallel integration was achieved, with separate processes for woollen and worsted production. The emphasis on integration seems to have been far greater than

Fig 4.5
A Noble combing machine in the restored combing shed at Coldharbour Mill Museum, Uffculme.
[AA024573]

Fig 4.6
Power-loom weaving in north-light sheds began at Tonedale Mills, Wellington in the mid-19th century, and continued without interruption until Fox Brothers ceased working at the site in the late 1990s.
[BB96/06856]

Fig 4.7
Scouring and milling machines were efficiently laid out when Tone Works was rebuilt in the 1890s, replacing the fulling stocks used in earlier finishing works. The machinery layout in this 1912 view was retained up to the 1990s (see Fig 4.48). [Courtesy Fox Brothers & Co archive. AA95/06574]

in other worsted-producing regions, where the earlier division of the industry into separate trades was continued with the construction of specialist mills later in the 19th century.[3] Combing was one of the last textile processes to be successfully mechanised, but from the middle of the 19th century hand combing was finally replaced by new types of machines with vastly increased output (Fig 4.5).[4] Powered worsted spinning was achieved with similar machinery to that used in the cotton and woollen industries, initially water frames or mules, and ring-frame machines from the late 19th century. Power-loom weaving was adopted from the middle of the 19th century (Fig 4.6), while powered scouring machines and milling machines were introduced to replace the earlier fulling stocks. This complex range of manufacturing and finishing processes has continued to be developed for the production of traditional cloths in Somerset up to the present day, resulting in the exceptional preservation of some sites (Fig 4.7; *see* Tone Works, p 121).

The early history of the serge industry

The use of long-staple worsted for serges was a defining feature of the Devon and Somerset cloth industry, but prior to the 17th century the industry had become established in the area by developing a successful trade in less specialised cloths. Between the 14th and the 16th centuries it produced a range of coarse woollens known as kerseys, similar to those that were then produced in many other parts of England.[5] By the 1590s this local woollen industry appears to have been in difficulty,[6] but cloth making had become rooted in the rural economy and laid the foundations for the great expansion of the serge industry in the 17th century. Fulling mills had been built on the streams adjacent to the upland areas by the 14th century, representing the first powered textile mills in the area, including those at Dunster, North Molton and Dulverton.[7] The early industry began the trading of wool, yarn and cloth at local weekly markets, with notable examples at Crediton, Dunster, Tiverton and Ashburton (Fig 4.8). Importantly, the local supply of both long and short wools established the range of skills that were needed by the serge industry.

The development of the serge industry reflected a national trend towards the production of lighter cloths from the late 16th century, but by the late 17th century it had expanded beyond most of the competing areas to become one of the largest textile industries in the country. The lighter cloths were the so-called 'New Draperies' that were replacing the older types of heavily fulled cloths in most of the traditional woollen industry areas. Devon, Somerset

Fig 4.8
The Shambles *by Warwick N. Mann. Prior to the factory system, the serge industry was organised around weekly wool, yarn and cloth markets in the main towns, such as those held at the former market hall in Ashburton, seen here. [Reproduced courtesy of Ashburton Museum, AQ1869. DP148453]*

and Cornwall were well placed to adapt to the new trade. The later growth of the industry outstripped the local supply of wool, however, and depended on the increased use of imports from Ireland and other counties of England.[8] In this respect the industry also benefited from its local port facilities, which saw significant expansion as a result of the serge trade.

Prior to the 17th century most of the woollen and worsted cloths produced in the South West had been taken to London for sale at the Blackwell Hall market. The fine-woollen industries of Gloucestershire and Wiltshire appear to have retained their overland trade with London in the 17th century, but in Devon and Somerset the serge industry increasingly exported via the regional ports, including Exeter, Barnstaple, Minehead and Lyme Regis. New harbours and warehousing were added to thc local ports in the 18th century, reflecting a general growth in the regional economy, but other facilities were added specifically for the cloth trade. These included cloth-finishing works and the extension of yarn and cloth markets. The development of a pre-factory textile industry around a regional port was unusual in itself, but the organisation of the Exeter trade also differed from the other early industries. Merchants financed much of the serge industry, but while they were often part-owners of fulling mills they were not closely involved with the other stages of manufacture, which were delegated to master spinners and weavers who organised the outworkers in the surrounding area.[9]

Contemporary descriptions provide an indication of the huge size of the industry by the 17th century, although its full extent is difficult to assess because of the lack of statistical information. One source suggests that the Devon and Somerset industry was significantly larger than those of Gloucestershire and Wiltshire, and probably exceeded the combined output of Lancashire and Yorkshire.[10] The scale of the cloth trade at Exeter in the 17th and 18th centuries was such that three large cloth and yarn markets could not accommodate all of the goods for sale.[11] The city's mid-18th-century cloth trade was described as being second only to that of Leeds, and annual cloth exports via Exeter reached 330,414 pieces in 1768.[12]

The merchants of Exeter and Tiverton were the main driving force behind the growth of the serge industry. Their wealth and influence had increased as the industry imported more raw wool and exported more of the finished goods. They were capitalists who consolidated their businesses by investing in the production of the cloth, using manufacturers, or clothiers, as middlemen to organise the networks of outworkers. Thus the cottage-based industry in the countryside operated as part of an extensive system of international trade, and was not concerned with producing goods for local consumption. By the 18th century some Exeter merchants had added workshops to their town houses, and most leased fulling mills for cloth finishing, but in general the merchant classes remained separated from both the manufacturing processes and the dyeing of the cloth. By the late 18th century, when the demand for serges began to decline and factory-based industries were emerging in other regions, this detached role of the merchants was a disadvantage, and most of the clothiers had insufficient capital to invest in the new factory methods. Significantly, from the late 18th century the most successful of the factory builders were descended from clothiers whose businesses were not controlled by independent merchants.

Significant local variations developed in the serge industry, both in processes and in the organisation of outworkers, which later influenced the construction of building types associated with 19th-century factories. Areas with good access to the ports and the main towns made greater use of imported raw materials and saw more direct control of outworkers, concentrating on weaving and the finishing of cloth prior to export. Tiverton had been established as a hub of the Devon woollen trade by the late 16th century, with a class of wealthy merchants and manufacturers providing employment for outworkers over a large area of the surrounding countryside. Substantial merchants' houses remain an impressive feature of the town centre, notably the 'Great House' of George Slee (*c* 1555–1613) on St Peter Street (Fig 4.9). The merchant John Greenway (*c* 1460–1529) added his own chapel to the parish church of St Peter, together with a south porch decorated with ships and other details reflecting the importance of the wool trade (Figs 4.10a–4.10c). The town prospered in the 17th century by concentrating on serge production, with numerous clothiers, fullers and serge makers. It contained around 1,500 looms and 700 specialist combers by the early 18th century.[13] The industry was in decline in Tiverton by the middle of the 18th century, however, in part because the influential combers resisted the introduction of new machinery and the importing of Irish yarn, both of which were benefiting the textile industries of other regions.

Fig 4.9
Tiverton retains parts of several of the grand houses built by prosperous wool merchants between the 16th and 18th centuries. The earliest intact example is the early 17th-century Great House of George Slee, now an exceptionally well-preserved example of a provincial merchant's town house.
[DP144046]

a

b

c

Fig 4.10a–c
The decoration and monuments of St Peter's Church, Tiverton, reflect the influence of the town's prosperous wool merchants. John Greenway added the ornate chapel and porch in the early 16th century, embellished with carvings depicting international trade, the tools of the woollen industry and his own wool mark. [DP139642, DP139628, DP139632]

Areas close to the higher ground of south Devon and east Cornwall made greater use of locally sourced worsted, with continued separation into specialist trades and more emphasis on independent combing and spinning. This system of outworking differed considerably from that in other regions, where the clothiers had more direct influence over the whole range of processes. It was summarised by Westcote in 1630, during the period of expansion of the Devon serge industry:

> First the gentleman farmer, or husbandman, sells his wool to the market, which is bought either by the comber or spinster, and they, the next week, bring it thither again in yarn, which the weaver buys; and the market following brings that thither again in cloth; where it is sold either to the clothier, (who sells it to London,) or to the merchant who (after it hath passed the fuller's mill, and sometimes the dyer's vat,) transports it. The large quantities whereof cannot be well guessed at, but best known to the customs-book, whereunto it yields no small quantity. And this is continued all the year throughout.[14]

Westcote was describing an approach to business that contrasted with the increasing control of textile processes which was being sought by the clothiers in the fine-woollen industries.[15] There was no overall control of the separate stages of production, and the members of each specialist trade only needed to meet on market days to exchange goods. The industry appears to have remained unchanged in south Devon until the late 18th century, when clothiers introduced crucial changes to the outworking system which enabled the local industry to convert to factory working (*see* p 102).

The main reasons for the decline of the serge industry were changes in the demand for cloth and the increasing competition from the factory-based industries in other regions, notably the Yorkshire worsted industry. The maximum output of the pre-factory industry was achieved in the mid- to late 18th century, when most of the production was of serge cloths for export by the East India Company. Ironically, the East India Company may have contributed to the eventual decline of the industry by discouraging the development of new products or creation of new firms, both of which were important factors in the growth of competing industries. The East India Company's dominant position was certainly perceived at the time to be limiting the growth of factory-based firms. Thomas Fox of Wellington, Somerset, founder of the highly successful firm of Fox Brothers and Company, succeeded in forcing the company to trade directly with the manufacturers, thereby cutting out its own factors and merchants.[16] This suggests that the waning influence of the East India Company was directly related to the early successes of the factory builders who emerged from the decline of the traditional industry.

Exeter's role as the hub of the serge industry

The port facilities at Exeter, the commerce of its merchants and the development of an early cloth-finishing industry around the city, were all key factors in the emergence of a regional textile industry that was largely independent of London. Other South West ports were also used by the serge industry, for both imports and exports, but handled far less of the trade than Exeter (Fig 4.11). The merchants of Exeter and Tiverton also influenced the organisation of outworking in the countryside, where they employed middlemen to put out the production of yarn and cloth. They were less influential from the late 18th century, when the demand for serge exports declined; thereafter, the traditional outworking methods of the serge industry were replaced by the integrated factories built by a new generation of industrialists.

The importance of Exeter to the serge industry in the 17th and 18th centuries is indicated by the quantities of goods exported. At the beginning of the 18th century the port handled about one-sixth of England's wool exports, valued at about half a million pounds per annum.[17] This was the period of maximum prosperity for the serge industry, about a century before the introduction of the factory system, when serge was the largest sector of the wool export trade and the other regional industries were achieving a far lower output. The value of serge exports fluctuated after the 1720s, although the quantity exported reached a peak of over 330,000 pieces per year in the late 18th century.[18] By the mid-18th century the industry was being affected by competition from other emerging textile industries, notably in East Anglia and Yorkshire. While the factory-based industries were developing elsewhere, the traditional serge industry in the South West resisted the introduction of new methods and the creation of new firms, both of which contributed to the collapse of the export trade by 1800.[19] From the late 18th century, serge production in the region was supported by the East India Company, but much of this cloth was taken overland to London for finishing, dyeing and export, bypassing Exeter's merchants and dyers. Most of the East India Company's serges were exported to China, a trade in which most of the profit was made from the importing of tea and other goods on the return trip.[20]

The bustling nature of Exeter's cloth markets at the height of the industry, in 1698, and the extent of the trade in the surrounding countryside, was described by Celia Fiennes:

> The large Market house set on stone pillars which runs a great length on which they lay their packs of serges, just by it is another walke within pillars which is for the yarne; the whole town and country is employ'd for at least 20 mile round in spinning, weaveing, dressing, and scouring, fulling and drying of the serges, it turns the most money in a weeke of anything in England, one week with another there is 10000 pound paid in ready money, sometimes 15000 pound; the weavers brings in their serges and must have their money which they employ to provide them yarne to goe to work againe.[21]

The export of serge was greatly facilitated by the development of an important finishing and dyeing industry around Exeter by the late 17th century. Medieval documents indicate

Fig 4.11
Exeter Quay drawn from nature *by C F Williams; on stone by W Gauci,* c *1835. The quays and port facilities at Exeter were developed from the late 17th century, operating in conjunction with the quays at Topsham, which were linked to the city by a canal. Exeter's coastal and international trade was an important factor in the success of the South West serge industry. [Reproduced courtesy of Exeter Local Studies Library. SC0748]*

the early presence of fulling mills, and by the 13th century a series of leats had been built on the floodplain of the River Exe, to the west of the city walls, to power mills for both corn and fulling (Fig 4.12).[22] Cloth merchants leased the fulling mills from the City Chamber, but put out cloth dyeing to independent dye houses. By the early 18th century the leats were providing the power for an industrial district containing at least eight mills, used for corn, fulling and metal working, along with related serge-industry sites including dye houses, extensive tenter fields and a dry house. Parts of the leats remain extant but most of the early industrial buildings have been replaced. The best-preserved site developed around Cricklepit Mill, a corn mill built on the higher leat close to its confluence with the River Exe (Fig 4.13). The mill was established by the 13th century but saw many phases of rebuilding. It included fulling stocks by the late 15th century, and three separate fulling mills had been added on the leat nearby by the late 17th century. A purpose-built dry house was added in 1731, supplementing the tenter racks in the adjoining fields which are shown on early 18th century maps.[23] The modified remains of the corn mill, the dry house and parts of the fulling mills have been retained in the conservation of Exeter Quays, illustrating the vernacular scale of the city's post-medieval finishing industry.

The urban development of Exeter in the 19th century, together with the alterations to the Quay and its associated warehousing, has removed much of the built evidence of the serge trade. The three markets that were used for trading wool, yarn and cloth do not survive, although the Guildhall was partly used as a wool market in the 16th century. Tucker's Hall on Fore Street, dating from the late 15th century but with later alterations, is still used for meetings of the Company of Weavers, Tuckers and Shearmen (Fig 4.14).[24] Surprisingly few intact merchant's houses remain in Exeter. These include parts of Larkbeare House, the home of John Baring in the mid-18th century,[25]

Fig 4.12
Extract from John Hooker's 1587 map of Exeter, surveyed c 1584–5. The low-lying area between the city walls and the river was occupied by fulling mills by the 13th century, developing into an industrial district for dyeing and cloth finishing by the 16th century. The map shows leats, mills and cloth tenter racks.
[Reproduced courtesy of Devon Record Office. DRO 4292A/BS1]

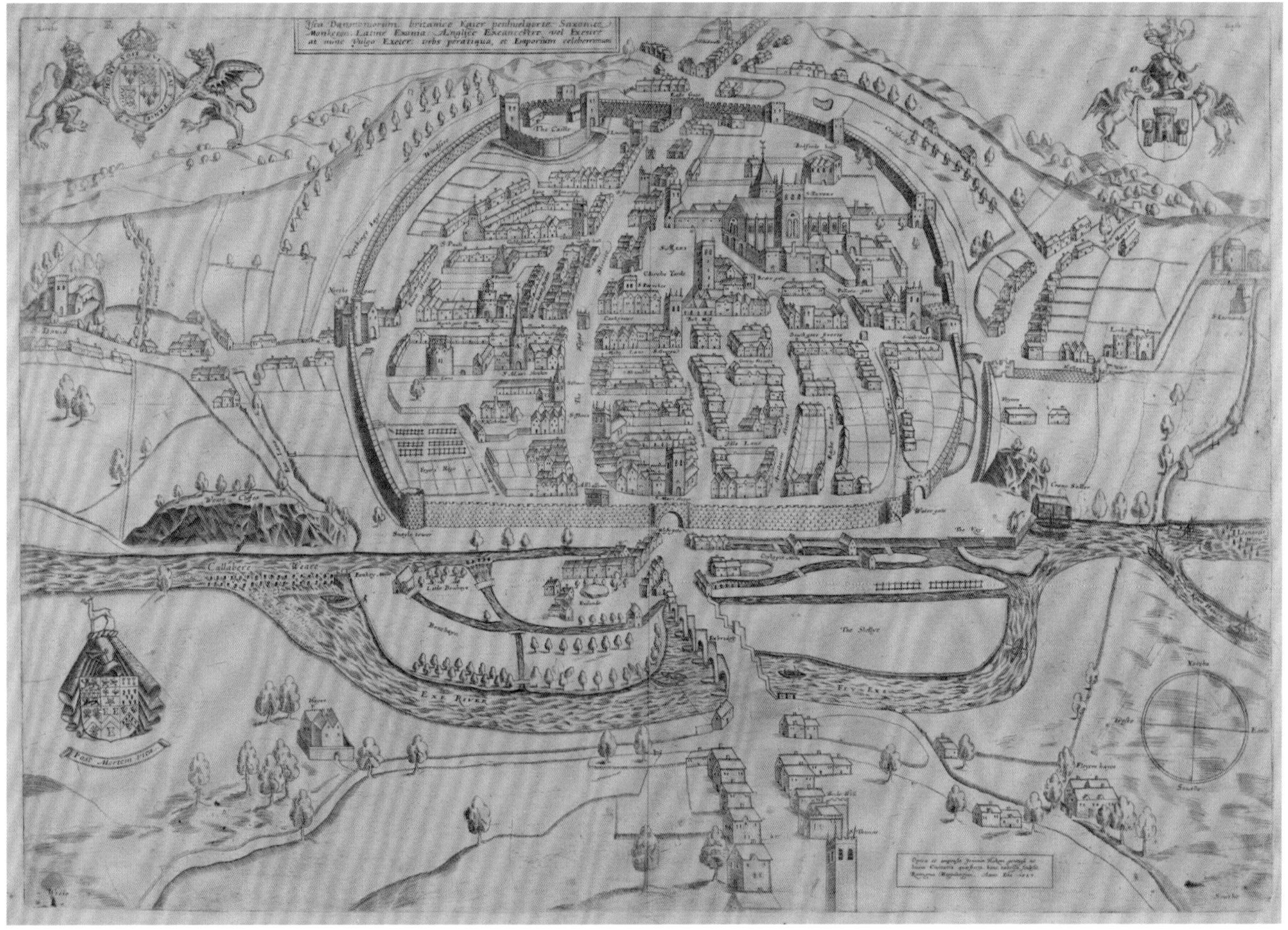

Fig 4.13
Cricklepit Mill was used for both corn milling and fulling. Located on one of the main leats outside Exeter city walls, the site had acquired three small mills and a dry house (on the left), built on the site of a former drying ground, by the mid-18th century.
[DP139548]

and Pinbrook House on Beacon Lane, dated 1679, which is said to have been built by the cloth merchant John Elwill. John Baring was a prominent merchant and serge manufacturer whose descendents included the founder of Barings Bank and a director of the East India Company.[26]

Fig 4.14
One of the earliest monuments to Exeter's important role in the woollen textile industries is Tuckers Hall, dating from the late 15th century and still used by the Company of Weavers, Tuckers and Shearmen.
[DP139881]

Early textile factories in the serge industry

In most parts of the serge industry early factory building differed significantly from that elsewhere in the South West. In comparison with the Gloucestershire woollen industry, for example, the relatively small number of new factories meant that there was far less continuity of occupation of industrial sites. A notable exception was the local serge industry in south Devon, which successfully adapted to factory working in the period when the rest of the industry was in decline. Elsewhere in the serge industry little evidence has been found of the early development of workshops, so outside south Devon the serge factories represented a distinct break from the earlier industry. Another distinction was that Devon and Somerset factories were often built in rural areas, contrasting with the 19th-century urban development of the Wiltshire industry. Rural sites provided the ample space that was needed for the large integrated factories that came to dominate the Devon and Somerset trade.

The transition to factory working in south Devon

In contrast to the widespread collapse of the serge industry from the late 18th century, the towns of Ashburton, Buckfast and Buckfastleigh saw a reorganisation of the old outworking system leading to the greater use of existing mills and eventually the building of integrated factories. In this area mills had developed along a series of tributary streams of the River Dart, flowing from the adjoining uplands of Dartmoor to the west and north, and the woollen industry had traditionally been a part-time activity combined with farming. The local supply of high-quality worsted ensured that the local clothiers were less dependent on the use of wool or yarn imported by the merchants of Exeter, and encouraged the development of worsted combing and spinning as independent trades. From the mid-17th century combers and spinners in a large area of south Devon and east Cornwall traded goods at the weekly market in Ashburton, ensuring a supply of yarn for the local serge weavers.[27] In the late 18th century, clothiers took greater control of yarn production, eventually putting the independent spinners out of business. Jennies were set up in small mills[28] and the preparation stages for both worsteds and woollens were sited in distinctive weatherboarded dry lofts and combing shops. The changes were comparable to those taking place in other regions, in which hand processes were concentrated in workshops before the introduction of powered factories, but involved a range of processes that was distinctive to the local serge industry.

Fig 4.15
The dry lofts on these cottages on Chapel Street, Buckfastleigh, include external taking-in doors. [DP139767]

Fig 4.16
Dry lofts were also included in some mill sites, such as this example attached to Belford Mill, north of Ashburton. [DP139768]

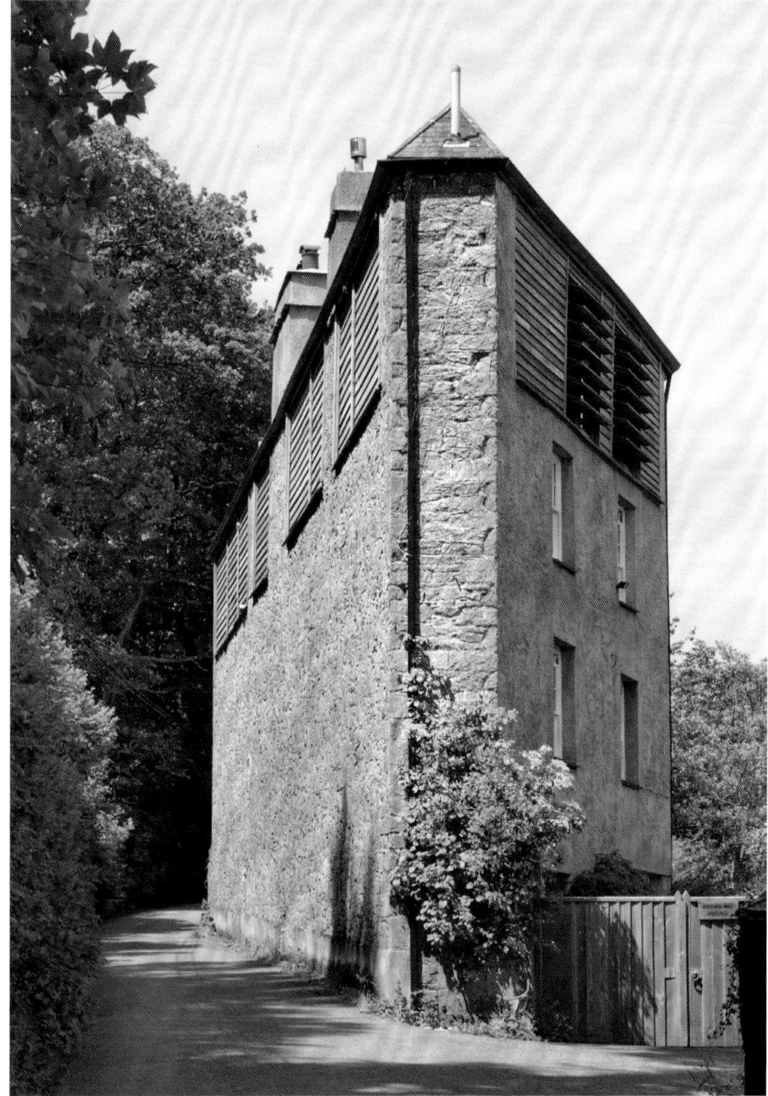

Wool lofts

The wool lofts were built to reorganise the outworkers engaged in the preparation of wool and worsted, in the period before the various processes were mechanised in powered factories. The use of spinning machines in mills and workshops meant that the preparation stages, comprising washing, drying, sorting, carding and combing, were a constraint on the output of the industry. The washing and combing of worsted in particular was a time-consuming, skilled craft that was not mechanised until well into the 19th century. Timber-clad lofts associated with drying and combing can be found in Ashburton, Buckfast, Buckfastleigh and the surrounding area, where they form distinctive features of workshops, warehouses and cottages (Figs 4.15–4.17). They are of similar scale and materials to local vernacular buildings dating from the late 18th and early 19th centuries. Some remained in use until the mid-19th century and possibly later, but all have since been converted to new uses. The lofts are now typically weatherboarded, some with taking-in doors, but most were originally ventilated with opening louvres. They are lightly built, with slate roofs supported by timber posts mounted on rubble ground-floor walls, and gable ends that have been re-clad in brick or corrugated iron.

Fig 4.17
Dry lofts associated with wool combing are a distinctive feature of the early 19th-century vernacular architecture in the Ashburton and Buckfastleigh area. This example on a workshop off Kingsbridge Lane, Ashburton, was used for wool combing and storage in the early 19th century. [DP139590]

One of the largest examples is a two-storeyed loft attached to the rear of an early 19th-century house in Kingsbridge Lane, Ashburton (*see* Fig 4.17). In 1840 the house and rear buildings were occupied by Peter Sparke, a prominent serge manufacturer, who used the rear buildings for air drying, wool and worsted washing, warehousing and combing; the pots (stoves) for heating the combs were located in the ground floor beneath the loft. The firm also used other lofts and workshops in Ashburton for the same purposes, including one which partly survives on St Lawrence Lane.[29] At Buckfastleigh a row of four late 18th- or early 19th-century cottages on Chapel Street is topped by another tall weatherboarded loft forming a continuous third storey. Other lofts were incorporated into industrial buildings at mill sites, with surviving examples at Higher Mill, Buckfast and Belford Mill, Ashburton.

The construction of the lofts was related to the increased use of the local woollen mills, including the addition of new buildings and machinery. At Buckfast, two earlier fulling mills were developed in the mid- and late 19th century under the ownership of Sparkes and Tozer, the firm occupying some of the Ashburton lofts mentioned earlier.

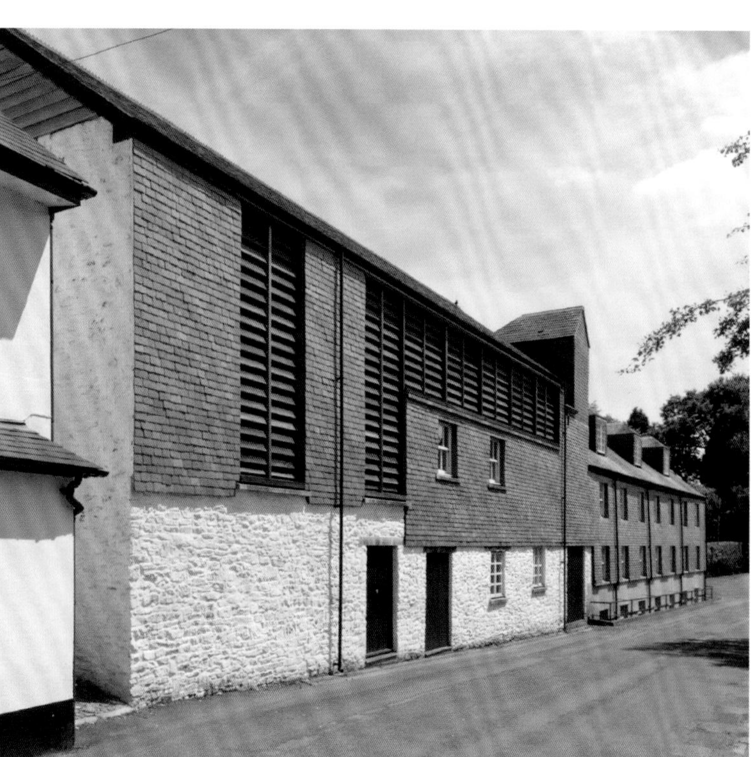

Fig 4.18
The restored former cottages adjoining Buckfast Higher Mill included ventilation louvres in the top storey and adjoining workshop. [DP139778]

Buckfast Higher Mill

The recently restored Buckfast Higher Mill comprised a single block of three storeys in the 1830s that only contained machinery for preparation and finishing processes, suggesting that spinning and weaving were done by outworkers or at another mill (Fig 4.18).[30] By the late 1840s the mill was acquired by the Hamlyn brothers, who later became highly successful serge manufacturers at Buckfastleigh. By this date the mill contained a much wider range of machinery, including 31 looms and 2 mules for spinning. Combing lofts were located in a row of cottages adjoining the mill.[31]

Buckfast Lower Mill

The nearby Buckfast Lower Mill, adjoining Buckfast Abbey, was also occupied by Sparkes and Tozer in the 1830s, when it contained a wider range of machines for the preparation and spinning of wool and worsted, along with stocks for fulling the cloth, but excluding combing and weaving.[32] Parts of the early mills and watercourses were retained as this site was extended in the late 19th century, with the addition of several phases of steam-powered sheds and mills.

Local mill sites continued to be extended as serge manufacture was added to powered spinning, but the earlier businesses that emerged from the reorganisation of the clothiers were consolidated into just two dominant firms. Buckfast Lower Mill was extended after *c* 1850 by the serge and blanket manufacturers John Berry and Sons, who had earlier owned a mill in Ashburton. Much of the site was rebuilt after a fire in 1877, but continued under the same owners until *c* 1950 when it was sold to the Buckfast Spinning Company for carpet yarn spinning,[33] which continues on the site today. Both cloth manufacture and yarn spinning used wool collected from the local farms.

Town Mill

The other major firm in the later 19th century was Hamlyn Brothers of Buckfastleigh. The firm started as fellmongers in 1806, later adding worsted combing, and buying Town Mill, near the centre of Buckfastleigh, in 1846.[34] Town Mill was extended into a huge factory complex, which by the end of the century included six multi-storeyed mills, some with dry lofts, and a central steam plant. This firm also continued to use local wool to manufacture serge and blankets. Their mills completely dominated the town but most have since been demolished. The two surviving buildings were amongst the last to be added, built in coursed rubble with red-brick dressings in a style of factory architecture that is clearly distinguished from the use of local materials in the earlier mills (Fig 4.19). By the late 19th century the local firms were exchanging goods with textile industries in other regions. The high-quality long wools produced by the local farms had helped retain the independence of the local clothiers in the 18th century, but were later thought to be too valuable for use in serge. In the late 19th century a trade developed with the Yorkshire industry, in which local worsted was sent north for use in the manufacture of fine cloths, while lower-grade worsted was brought back for use in the local serge industry.[35]

The Ottery St Mary Worsted Factory

Other areas of the serge industry also saw attempts to convert to the factory system in the late 18th century, some with less success than the clothiers of south Devon. At Ottery St Mary in east Devon, a huge water-powered worsted spinning mill was built in 1788–9, apparently in an attempt to revive the local industry by introducing factory methods on a large scale.[36] The imposing building contrasted with the gradual extension of older mills and workshops in south Devon, and was architecturally similar to contemporary worsted mills and cotton mills in other regions (Fig 4.20). It is now one of the best-preserved early worsted factories in the country. It was built by Sir John Duntze, a wealthy Exeter wool merchant and MP for Tiverton, in partnership with Sir George Yonge, a colonial governor and MP for Honiton.[37] It represented the latest type of mill building and machinery, but does not appear to have been commercially successful. The business was sold at a considerable loss in 1794[38] to a Devon serge maker, and the mill was converted into a silk mill by the 1840s.

The factory was built to specialise in worsted spinning, with no combing, weaving or cloth finishing, presumably to give work to the struggling cottage spinners in the Ottery St Mary

Fig 4.19
The surviving parts of Town Mill, still the largest buildings in Buckfastleigh, display a typical style of late 19th-century steam-powered factory architecture that contrasts dramatically with the preceding generation of workshops and lofts. [DP139762]

Fig 4.20
Ottery St Mary Worsted Factory, built in the late 1780s, is one of the best-preserved early factories in the country. It combined the use of powered spinning machinery on a very large scale with the internal construction and water-power system that were more typical of the pre-factory era.
[DP025370]

area.[39] In 1794 powered spinning frames were located in the second and third storeys, with roving in the fourth storey.[40] Preparation and combing must have been put out, although there is no surviving evidence of combing workshops or dry lofts in the nearby town. The mill was powered by an 18ft (5.49m) wheel with a full-height upright shaft geared to shafting in the machinery rooms. None of the machinery survives, but there is good evidence of the original power system. A rare contemporary illustration of similar machinery and shafting is shown in a painting of a worsted mill in Warwickshire (Fig 4.21).[41] At the Ottery St Mary factory worsted spinning continued under new owners in the early 19th century, when it was operated in conjunction with the woollen mill at Harbertonford by the serge maker Thomas Windeatt (*see* Fig 4.25).[42] Between *c* 1843 and *c* 1883 it was in use as a silk factory employing about 400 workers, and in 1882 contained the full range of silk preparation, throwing and weaving machinery.[43] It later remained in use for a variety of other industries, notably an electrical engineering works from the 1950s, which helped preserve the original structure. Mid-20th-century factory buildings remain attached to the south and east elevations.

The Ottery St Mary factory is probably the earliest surviving textile factory building in the South West. The red-brick walls and regular fenestration bear little resemblance to the local vernacular architecture of the period, but have notable similarities with contemporary textile factories in the midlands and the north. Although the mill has the appearance of an up-to-date textile factory of the late 18th or early 19th century, internally the original parts of its floor structure and power system seem more

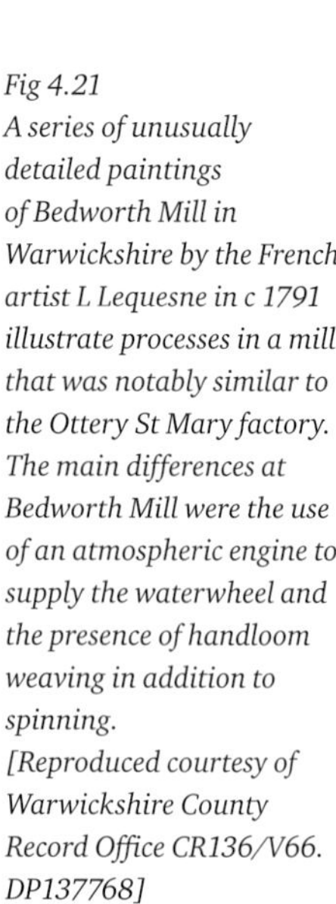

Fig 4.21
A series of unusually detailed paintings of Bedworth Mill in Warwickshire by the French artist L Lequesne in c 1791 illustrate processes in a mill that was notably similar to the Ottery St Mary factory. The main differences at Bedworth Mill were the use of an atmospheric engine to supply the waterwheel and the presence of handloom weaving in addition to spinning.
[Reproduced courtesy of Warwickshire County Record Office CR136/V66. DP137768]

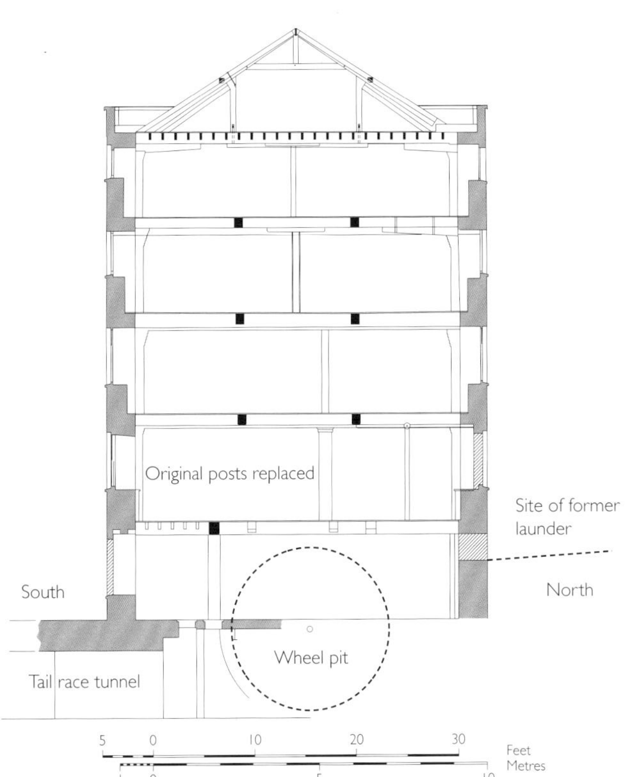

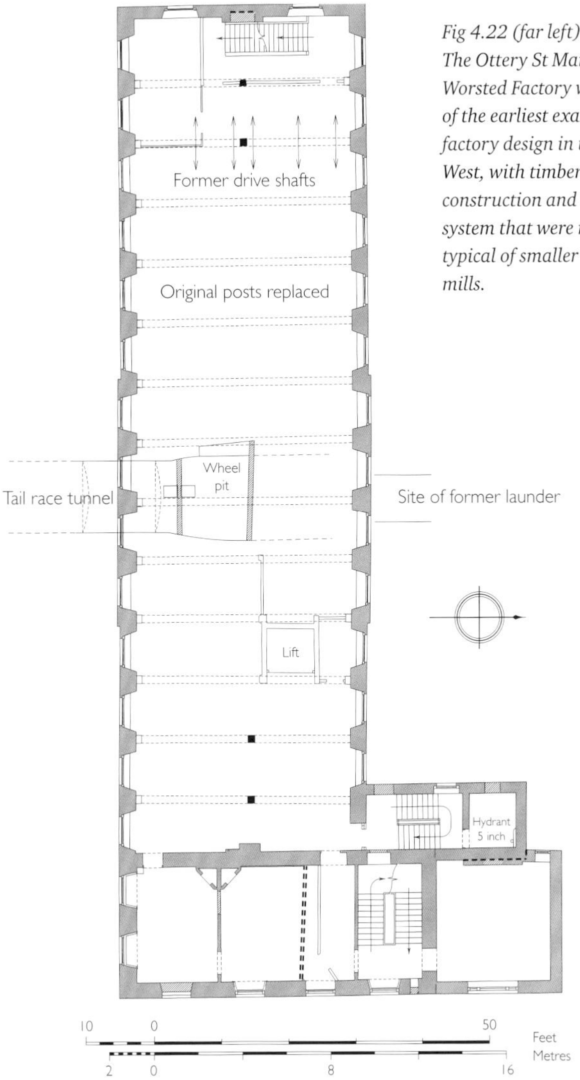

Fig 4.22 (far left)
The Ottery St Mary Worsted Factory was one of the earliest examples of factory design in the South West, with timber internal construction and a power system that were more typical of smaller vernacular mills.

Fig 4.23 (above right)
Ottery St Mary Factory. The overall size and narrow plan are comparable to the large early factories being built in the midlands and the north in the late 18th century. The end bay and projecting wing were used as a well-appointed manager's house in the late 19th century.

typical of the technology of a traditional corn mill (Figs 4.22 and 4.23). It is built to a long narrow plan of 16 bays with a full-height wing, originally containing offices, projecting from the west end. A stair tower providing access to the working floors is located in the angle between the wing and the mill, and a wider staircase in the wing gave separate access to the offices. Unusually, in the 1882 sale the wing was offered as a 'capital family residence', and still retains fireplaces, shutters, panelling and other details that are typical of an early to mid-19th-century town house.

The construction of the main floors of the mill pre-dates many of the developments seen in later factories, with joisted floors supported by deep beams and chamfered timber props. In the attic, the pegged queen-post roof trusses are similar to those used in 18th-century warehouses.

The water-power system was supplied from a leat alongside the River Otter that also supplied the nearby Town Mill. The leat terminates in an unusual circular weir feeding the culverted bypass channel (Fig 4.24). The mill's headrace comprised an overhead launder which passed across the road and yard adjoining the north side. A blocked opening in the north wall indicates where the launder entered the mill. The former wheel pit is partially intact beneath a later concrete ground floor. It retains a section of curved brickwork, confirming the diameter of the waterwheel, and the brick-arched tailrace tunnel. In the upper floors of the mill,

Fig 4.24 (left)
The internal waterwheel of the Ottery St Mary Worsted Factory was fed by an overhead launder at the end of a leat, located to the right of Town Mill shown in this view. The unusual circular weir in the leat served as an overflow to the River Otter. [DP025798]

additional heavy floor beams above the position of the wheel pit originally supported the main upright shaft and the gearing to the machinery shafts.

The development of the integrated factories

The factory-based industry that emerged from the upheavals of the 18th century was dominated by a small number of businesses that were each based at large integrated complexes. Their sites were characterised by a wide variety of building types, often including examples of most stages in the development of the textile factory, and reflected the need to continually improve manufacturing processes. Serges remained a major part of the industry, as they had been from the 17th century, and their production saw further technical development alongside a range of woollens. Local wool was used when it was practical to do so, but the largest firms increasingly imported raw materials, while British overseas interests ensured a strong demand for exports. In the late 19th century the South West contained fewer serge or worsted manufacturers than other textile regions but still exerted a significant influence on the industry. A process of mergers and takeovers saw the largest firms controlling mills throughout the South West and in other regions, eventually constructing some of the largest textile mill sites in the country.

Integration in the 19th-century serge mill

The region's most successful textile manufacturer in the 19th and 20th centuries was Fox Brothers of Wellington, whose exceptionally large mill sites are described later, but locally important factories were also established by other firms dispersed around the traditional serge-producing area. Nineteenth-century textile mills thus became a feature of the Devon and Somerset countryside. Most were built by serge manufacturers for powered spinning, in the period when weaving was still put out to handloom weavers. They were initially water powered, usually built on the sites of earlier mills. As the integration of processes increased this was later supplemented with steam power, so that complicated combined power systems became a feature of the industry. Power-loom weaving sheds were added in the second half of the 19th century, later than in other regions because the early power looms were not favoured for serge weaving.[44]

Harbertonford Mill

The four-storeyed factory at Harbertonford was the largest textile mill to the south of the Ashburton area (Fig 4.25). The slate-hung mill building included an attached manager's house and detached workshops, and was water powered from a long leat extending from the

Fig 4.25
Harbertonford Mill was operated by the same firm as the Ottery St Mary Worsted Factory in the early 19th century. Records of the machinery suggest that this site concentrated on water-powered spinning of weft yarns, while Ottery St Mary produced the warp.
[AP26224/038]

Harbourne River. It was reputedly built in the late 18th century and by 1815 it was leased to Thomas Windeatt, the serge manufacturer who also occupied the Ottery St Mary Factory. The site was used for spinning woollen yarns, containing powered machinery for preparation and carding and 62 jennies.[45] This serge business was therefore using the Ottery factory to make the worsted warp of the cloth and the Harbertonford Mill to make the woollen weft. By *c* 1850, however, the site had been converted into a corn and starch factory.

North Tawton Mill and Westford Mills

Two other early factories were extended for integrated cloth production in the late 19th century. At North Tawton, a serge and woollen mill was built in the early 19th century close to the site of a fulling mill, probably by the established woollen manufacturer John Fulford (Fig 4.26).[46] It was expanded by later occupiers into a fully integrated complex including powered weaving, cloth finishing and extensive facilities for cloth drying. The site was initially water powered, with a system of horizontal shafting driven by a suspension wheel in a detached wheel house. A large beam-engine house was added in the late 19th century to power several ranges of adjoining north-light sheds. One of the ancillary buildings has an unusual roof structure comprising single-piece cast-iron trusses, the only known example of this distinctive type of fireproof roof in the South West (Fig 4.27). Amongst the earliest buildings are a long range of three-storeyed workshops or warehouses with ventilated cloth-drying rooms in the top floor. Cloth-drying houses of various types were common features of the serge factories from the early 19th century, indicating that the mill sites were finishing large quantities of cloth when weaving was still being done on hand looms.

Another site showing a complex development of power systems was Westford Mills near Wellington, most of which was demolished for redevelopment in 2008 (Fig 4.28). It was established as a worsted mill by Thomas Elworthy in 1780, and remained in use by Elworthy Brothers until 1934. It comprised an early 19th-century four-storeyed mill with a large wheel chamber, and a mid-19th-century extension powered by a beam engine. Both buildings showed evidence of rebuilding and frequent alterations. The earlier mill retained much of its original wooden floor structure, with the beams supported by thick timber props, but the mid-19th-century wing was partly of fireproof construction, with a brick-vaulted ground-floor ceiling supported by cast-iron beams. The wing had been partly rebuilt in the late 19th century with a new north-light roof, suggesting that the attic was

Fig 4.26 (below)
Like most of the 19th-century serge factories, North Tawton Woollen Mill developed into a large complex despite its isolation from the main centres of industry. Its integrated mills and sheds were powered by a complex system of horizontal shafting driven by a large waterwheel and a beam engine.
[DP139706]

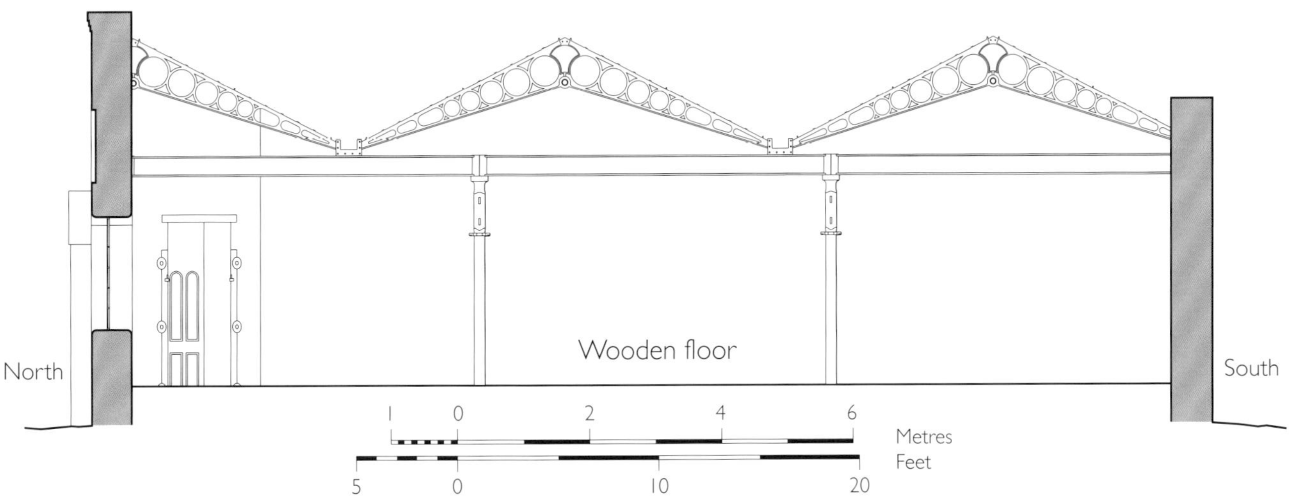

Fig 4.27 (bottom)
Cast-iron roof trusses in one of the ancillary sheds at North Tawton Woollen Mill.

Fig 4.28
Westford Mills near Wellington, which was mostly demolished in 2008, was centred on a well-preserved early 19th-century worsted mill which had been continuously extended by Elworthy Brothers until the 1930s. The building was notably wider than the late 18th-century factories, but still used timber props to support the floor beams.

used for power loom weaving. The later development of processes at the site included the addition of a large dye house in 1877, supplied with water from the leat (Fig 4.29).[47]

Fig 4.29
Westford Mills. The wider wing had a combined power system, comprising a large wheel chamber in the left end and an external engine house at the right end. The dye house at the top of this view was added in the 1870s.
[AP23057/006]

Fox Brothers of Wellington

The business managed by Thomas Fox from 1796 was one of the most successful and long lasting in the history of the industry, remaining under the control of the Fox family at Wellington, Somerset, until 2000. Under the leadership of Thomas Fox and his descendents it expanded almost continually up to the early 20th century to become the largest textile manufacturer in the South West, and one of the largest in the country. Its first factory, built in the late 1790s, was Coldharbour Mill at Uffculme in Devon, but the firm's headquarters was at Tonedale Mills, north of Wellington, with cloth dyeing and finishing at the nearby Tone Works. All three sites remained in use until the late 20th century, the last survivors of the South West serge industry.

The company originated in the pre-factory industry. It began as the 17th-century clothier business of the Were family, who were well established as serge makers in the Wellington area. Thomas Fox (1747–1821), the son of Anna Were, joined the business in 1768. He became sole proprietor in 1796, renaming the business and introducing the FOX cloth mark.[48] Under the management of Thomas Fox the firm acquired the resources to make the successful move to factory production. He negotiated improved business arrangements with the East India Company which enabled his firm to supply high-quality serge at a better price.[49] Large quantities of serge were delivered to the company in the 1790s, amounting to 300 pieces a week in 1794 and double that by 1799.[50] Fox invested heavily in powered factories to supply the yarns for the large number of handloom weavers, while developing Tone Works as a central facility for dyeing and finishing the cloth. The combination of factories with outworking enabled the firm to achieve an impressive output in the period when other areas of the serge industry were in decline. By 1804 Thomas Fox estimated that the firm supplied one-ninth of the cloth sold to the East India Company.[51]

In the 19th century the mills established by Thomas Fox were expanded with a range of building types that reflected the development of processes and the importance of controlling all the stages of production. As in Gloucestershire, the combination of processes began before the introduction of the full range of powered machinery, and continued as the early sites were extended into fully integrated factories. The company built on its heritage in the serge industry by continuing to introduce new types of woollens and worsteds, eventually supplying an exceptionally wide range of cloth. Its development of the finishing stages was of particular importance, enabling the production of lighter-weight flannels from the early 19th century. It had taken control of cloth dying by the late 18th century, and the expansion of Tone Works later included one of the largest dye houses in the region.[52] In the late 19th century Fox Brothers and Company increasingly obtained large orders from government departments. From the 1880s the company was closely involved in the development of khaki dyes and supplied large quantities of khaki serge for military uniforms. In the mid-1890s a new product line was the manufacture of knitted puttees, which were in demand for country wear and military uniforms. By the early 20th century the firm had expanded into the largest textile manufacturer in the region, taking over additional mills in Somerset, Devon and Oxfordshire (Fig 4.30). The size of the business is indicated by its output during the First World War, which included 12 million pairs of puttees and four and a half million yards of khaki serge.[53]

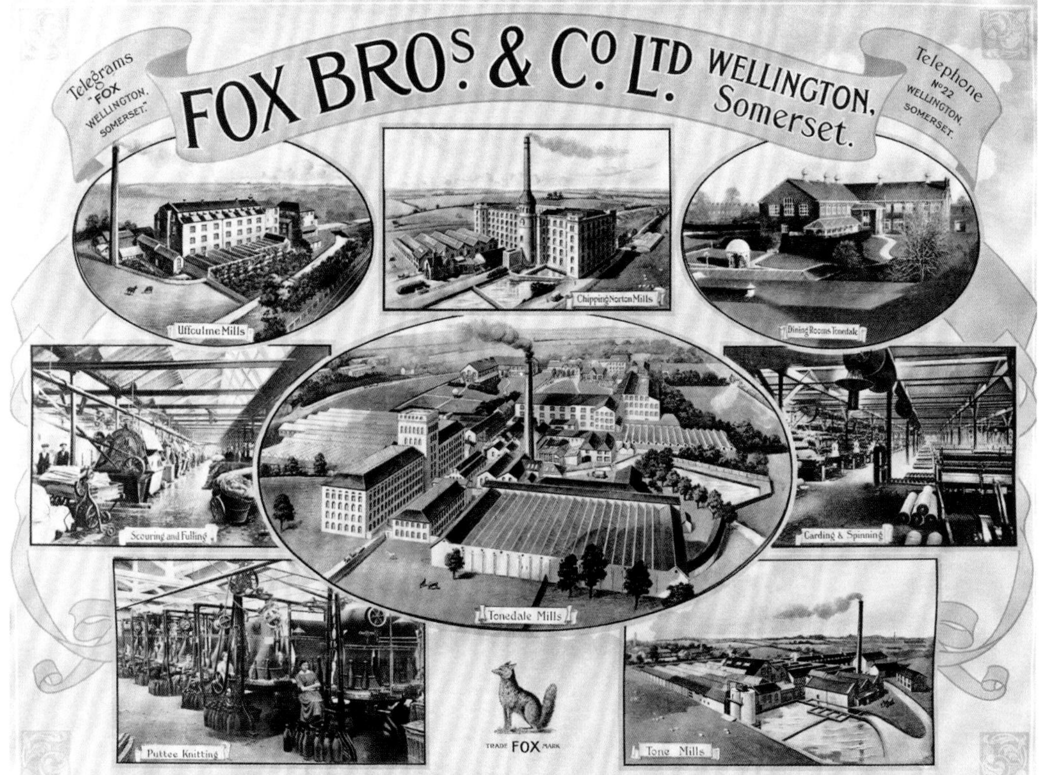

Fig 4.30
Fox Brothers developed from an 18th-century clothier's business into the largest textile firm in the South West region by the early 20th century.
[Courtesy Fox Brothers & Co archive. AA95/06574]

Fig 4.31
Coldharbour Mill was built by Thomas Fox in c *1800, the company's first textile factory. The building on the left includes parts of an earlier corn mill.* *[AA024521]*

Fig 4.32
Coldharbour Mill was preserved as a museum after Fox Brothers left the site in c *1970. It retains a full set of preparation, combing and spinning machinery.* *[AA024556]*

Coldharbour Mill

Built between 1799 and 1800 at Uffculme in Devon, this was the first of the new factories to be built by Thomas Fox. It remained in use by the firm until the early 1970s, after which the buildings, machinery and power systems were preserved as a working mill museum (Fig 4.31). The mill was built on the extended leat of a small grist mill, which the firm had occupied since 1797. Thomas Fox took a keen interest in the construction of the new mill, which was designed to initially contain 12 jennies alongside a set of preparation machines on each of three floors. The continued use of the mill for worsted spinning thereafter resulted in the ongoing improvement of machinery, power systems and buildings. The mill retains much of the combing and spinning machinery that was still in use in the late 20th century (Fig 4.32). Of particular interest are the exceptionally well-preserved features of the water- and steam-power system. In the early 19th century the mill was water powered from a suspension wheel (recently rebuilt) in an external wheel house attached to the east end, but a succession of three steam engines were later added to the west end. The last phase of steam power was a horizontal cross-compound engine installed in 1910, which is now preserved as the last example of an original textile mill steam engine in the South West (Fig 4.33). At about this time the mill's original upright shaft power transmission, driven by the waterwheel, was replaced by the surviving gear-drive system adjoining the wheel chamber, and was supplemented by a rope drive from the horizontal engine house attached to the west-end wall (Fig 4.34).

As with many historic textile mills, changes to the textile machinery had a direct influence on the development of the buildings. Unusually, the site retains most of its smaller ancillary buildings, including an engineer's workshop, the boiler house and economiser house (both containing steam plant) and the exceptionally rare survival of a gas retort house (Fig 4.35). Gas was widely used for lighting the larger textile mills in the 19th century, and often produced on-site independently of a mains supply, but its buildings and equipment were normally removed when electric lighting was introduced towards the end of the 19th century. The main mill building was of similar timber-floored construction to the other early factories in Devon and Somerset, with beams supported by timber props, but the beams were later reinforced to carry the additional weight of new machinery. It was lit by an unusual arrangement of large windows positioned in alternate bays, the blind bays being narrower, which seems to be a characteristic of the early Fox mills. Extensions were later added along both sides, a common modification to spinning mills which needed larger preparation areas to supply the later types of spinning machines. The north-light shed added to the south side in the late 19th century was built to contain powered combing machines (*see* Fig 4.5). The original roof was also replaced at this time with a tall well-lit attic that could also accommodate additional machinery.

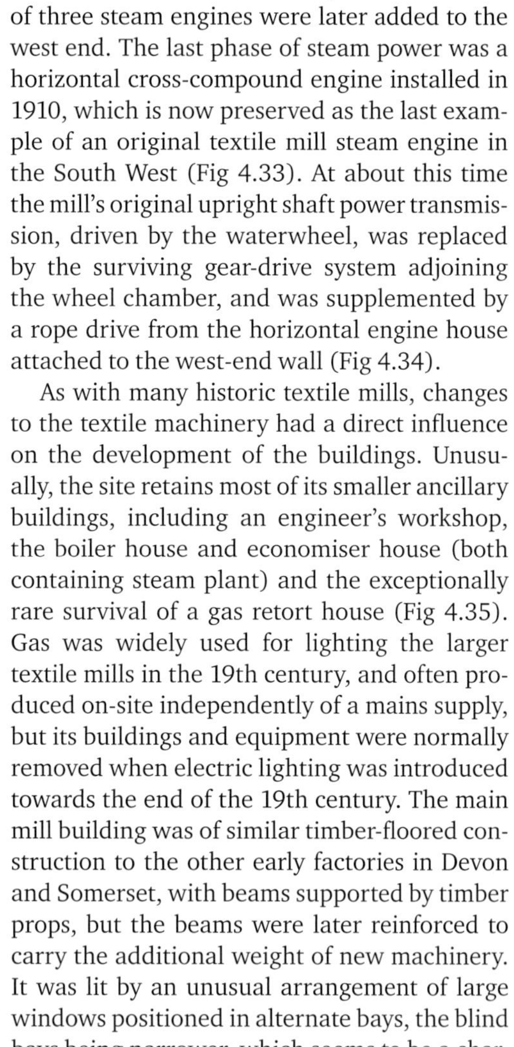

Fig 4.33
The working horizontal cross-compound engine at Coldharbour Mill, an addition of 1910, includes an external rope-drive system attached to the end of the mill. Line shafting could be powered from the steam engine at one end of the mill, or the waterwheel at the other end.
[DP139877]

Fig 4.34
Steam power was added to Coldharbour Mill in three phases, the first two of which were represented by narrow engine houses attached to the west end. Unusually, the mill retains a complete sequence of engine houses with boilers, economiser, chimney and rope race.
[DP139872]

Tonedale Mills

Tonedale Mills in Wellington was developed by Thomas Fox from the late 1790s as the company's headquarters, its main manufacturing site and the family home. At the end of the 20th century this was one of the largest textile mill complexes in the country, still owned and partly occupied by Fox Brothers and distinguished by both its size and the extraordinary preservation of its historic details. In addition to over 50 buildings, the site included working machinery, steam- and early electric-power plant, an engineering works, a fire station and a range of

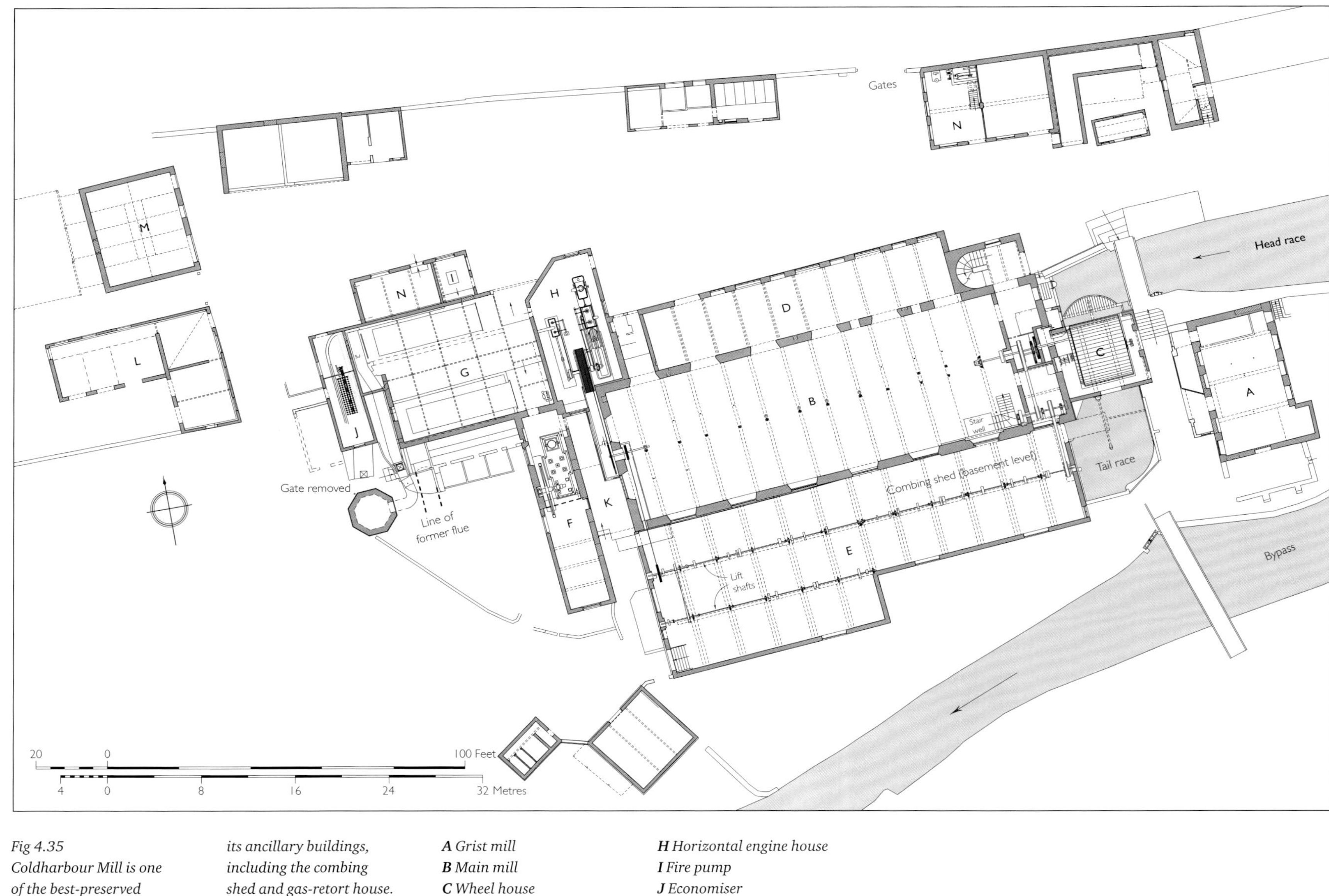

Fig 4.35
Coldharbour Mill is one of the best-preserved textile mill complexes in the country, retaining intact water- and steam-power systems and all of its ancillary buildings, including the combing shed and gas-retort house. The working museum contains a full set of worsted spinning machinery and line shafting.

***A** Grist mill*
***B** Main mill*
***C** Wheel house*
***D** North extension*
***E** Combing shed*
***F** Beam engine house*
***G** Boiler house*
***H** Horizontal engine house*
***I** Fire pump*
***J** Economiser*
***K** Rope race*
***L** Stables*
***M** Gas retort house*
***N** Workshops*

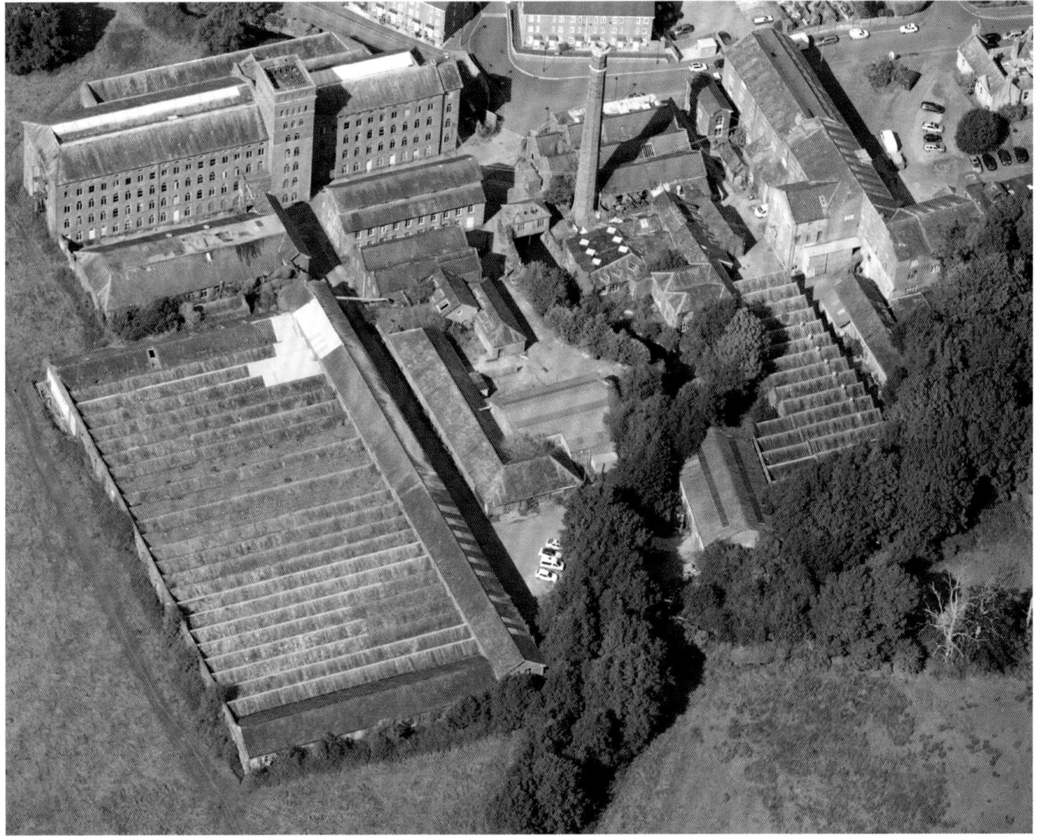

Fig 4.36
The headquarters of Fox Brothers at Tonedale Mills, Wellington, the largest textile mill complex in the South West. The recent housing at the top of this view replaced a large group of weaving sheds, a loomshop and three engine houses.
[AP24721/009]

Edwardian offices containing the company's private archive (Figs 4.36 and 4.37). In recent years, after the company was re-launched at another site, large parts of the complex have been demolished or neglected, although many of its principal historic buildings remain intact.

The factory erected by Thomas Fox is located at the east end of the site, comprising two ranges of mills and warehouses built to an L-plan adjoining Tonedale House, the villa built and occupied by Fox in 1807 (Fig 4.38). The three-storeyed warehouses were accessible from the house, and included fireproof and non-fireproof areas for the storage, unpacking and sorting of the raw wool. The adjoining range of mills includes the site of the original Town Mill that was purchased by Fox in 1796.[54] It was rebuilt as a water-powered textile factory in 1801–3, with similar large windows in alternate bays to those at Coldharbour Mill, but was badly damaged by fire in 1820. It was then rebuilt as the extant fireproof mill which remains attached to the warehouses, with a cast-iron floor and roof structure inserted within the walls of the earlier mill (Fig 4.39). A full-height extension was added to the north end shortly after the rebuilding, doubling the size of the mill and powered from a detached beam-engine house.

In the mid- and late 19th century the site was extended to the west and north with the

Fig 4.37
Tonedale Mills. The former corn mill purchased by Thomas Fox in the 1790s was rebuilt and expanded into one of the largest integrated textile mills in the country.
***A** Early 19th-century mills, with Old Mill to the south*
***B** Early 19th-century warehouses*
***C** Early 19th-century loomshop*
***D** Mid-19th- to early 20th-century weaving sheds*
***E** 1863–73 spinning mill*
***F** Late 19th-century boilers, workshops, wool scouring and DC electric plant*
***G** 1880s mills*
***H** Spinning and weaving shed, early 20th century*
***I** Offices, boardroom, warehouse, cloth inspection, early 19th to early 20th century*
***J** Canteen, mid-20th century*

Fig 4.38
The earliest mill at Tonedale, on the right in this view, was built on the site of Town Mill, a grist mill, by Thomas Fox in c *1800. After a destructive fire in* c *1820, it was lowered to its present height and internally rebuilt with fireproof floors and a fireproof roof. It was later renamed Old Mill.* *[BB94/21129]*

addition of a loomshop, weaving sheds, spinning mills and the large number of ancillary buildings needed to service an integrated factory. North-light sheds were added for power-loom weaving in several phases, initially powered by beam engines and later by the 'Iron Duke', a large tandem compound engine. The largest structure at the site is the five-storeyed spinning mill built in two phases in 1863 and 1873 around a central double beam-engine house (Fig 4.40). This was of comparable scale and architectural treatment to the largest mills being built in other regions, and was the largest spinning mill in the South West. In the 1890s the steam-power system of the whole site was reconfigured with the construction of a new central boiler house with an attached engineering workshop and fire station (Fig 4.41). A DC-electric power plant was added

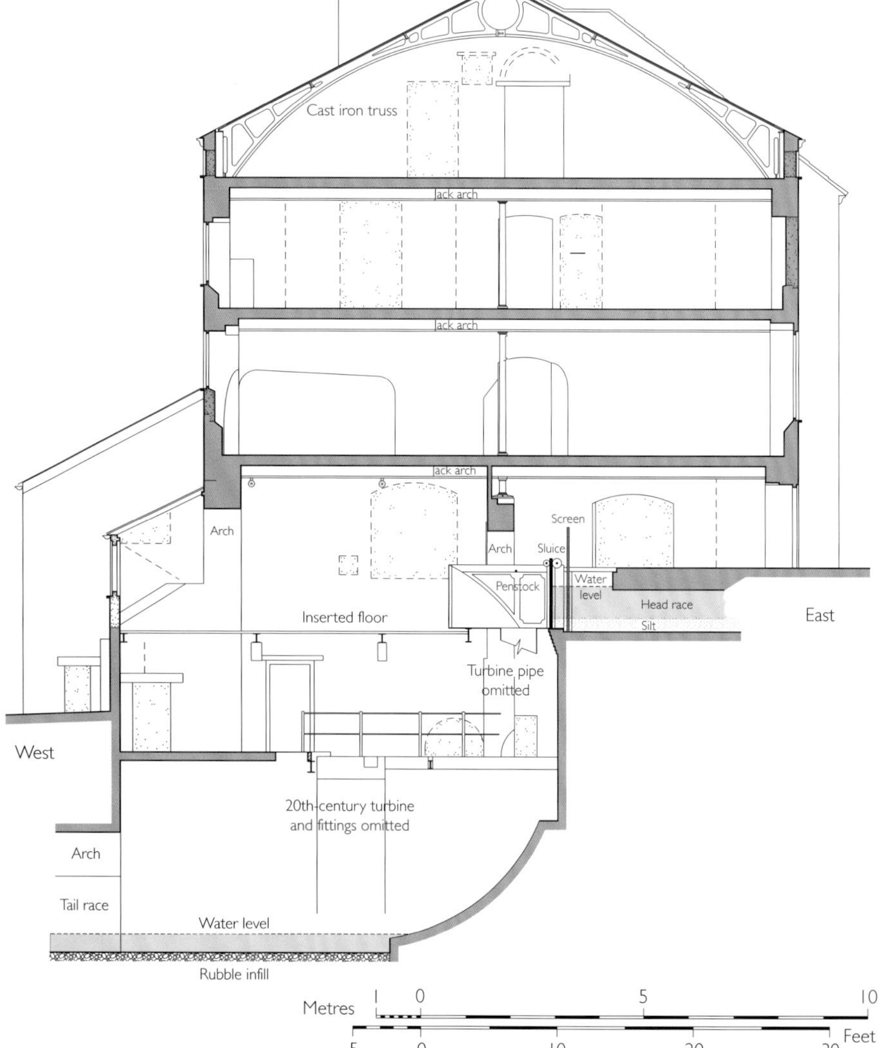

Fig 4.39
Old Mill at Tonedale, as rebuilt with a fireproof structure. The internal wheel house contained a suspension wheel, which was replaced by a turbine in c *1904.*

Fig 4.40 (above left) Tonedale was greatly extended from the mid-19th century. The new spinning mill was built in two phases in 1863 and 1873, and was powered by a double beam engine in a central engine house, located behind the sprinkler tower. [BB96/08577]

Fig 4.41 (above right) An industrial complex of the size of Tonedale Mills required a wide variety of ancillary buildings, which by the end of the 19th century included engineering facilities, a centralised steam plant and even an early fire-alarm system. DC electricity plant was added shortly after, including the steam-turbine-generator on the left. [AA96/03956]

by the early 20th century, including generators driven by diesel and a steam turbine. One of the last additions to the site was an early 20th-century shed mill, built for electrically powered carding and spinning in 1916,[55] which reflected the contemporary fashion for the construction of single-storeyed factories.

Tone Works

Tone Works was developed at Wellington from the late 18th century to provide a complete range of facilities for finishing the serge and other cloths produced by Fox Brothers on a large scale.[56] It was built around an earlier fulling mill owned by the Were family, proprietors of an extensive outworking business, and later extended by Thomas Fox and his successors into the largest cloth-finishing works in the region. The cloth itself was initially obtained from outworkers using handlooms, but by the mid-19th century it was manufactured in-house in extensive power-loom sheds built at Tonedale Mills. The great importance of cloth-finishing processes was recognised by Thomas Fox and remained central to the later development of the firm. Tone Works enabled the firm to produce serges of the consistent quality that was required by the East India Company, and later to meet the increasing demand for new types of cloths. It remained in use for two centuries, helping to preserve an exceptional collection of textile machinery and buildings. Processes, machinery, buildings, the power system and the water-supply system were all developed continuously from the early 19th to the mid-20th century (Figs 4.42 and 4.43).

In the early 21st century Tone Works still retains most of the recently disused equipment for the traditional finishing of worsted, woollen and combined cloths, and in spite of its derelict condition was probably the best-preserved finishing works in the country. Most of the machines were of early to mid-20th-century date, many having been repaired or rebuilt *in situ* during the course of normal maintenance, but research has indicated that they were identical to the range of machinery that developed at the site in the 19th century. The overall range of processes was similar to that used for cloth finishing in the early 19th century, but the main stages had been gradually subdivided and refined to give greater control of the appearance and feel of the cloth.

In the late 19th century the site was reorganised, following flood damage, into separate areas for scouring, milling, tentering, raising,

Fig 4.42
Tone Works, Wellington, located a short distance from Tonedale, was developed by Thomas Fox from the early 19th century to finish the serge cloths that were then still being woven by outworkers. It remained in use with traditional machinery until 1999, and is remarkably well preserved.
[AP24720/007]

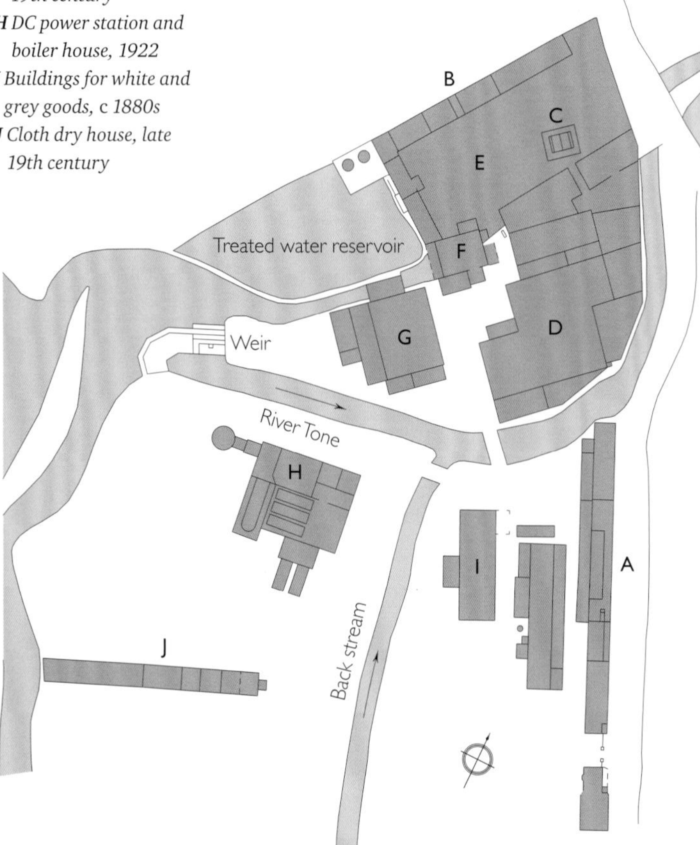

Fig 4.43
Tone Works site plan.
***A** Cloth dry house, early 19th century*
***B** Cloth dry house, early 19th century*
***C** Wheel chamber, early 19th century*
***D** Dye works, early to late 19th century*
***E** Finishing works, rebuilt 1890s*
***F** Streaming house, early 19th century*
***G** Boiler house, late 19th century*
***H** DC power station and boiler house, 1922*
***I** Buildings for white and grey goods, c 1880s*
***J** Cloth dry house, late 19th century*

shearing and dyeing. The arrangement of machinery reflected the company's emphasis on quality control, with segregated areas for 'wet' and 'dry' processes, and the separation of dyeing into different buildings for light and dark colours (Figs 4.44 and 4.45). Each of these stages could be adjusted and the overall sequence repeated if necessary to achieve a wide variety of cloth finishes. Separate groups of scouring and milling machines replaced fulling stocks from the mid-19th century, enabling more precise control of the washing, shrinking and felting of the cloth (Fig 4.46). In 1894, the 'wet' stages were reorganised and segregated from dry processes and dyeing in a rebuilt finishing works in the centre of the site. After scouring and milling, tentering involved drying the long pieces on racks while controlling the amount of shrinkage. At different times this was located outside the works on tenter racks in the nearby fields, or inside one of three large dry houses. The 'dry' stages of cloth finishing were increasingly mechanised in the 20th century. In the 1920s the dry houses were replaced by tentering machines. Raising the nap of the cloth involved the use of either wire or teazle gig machines, depending on the type of finish required, and shearing was achieved with rotary cutting machines.

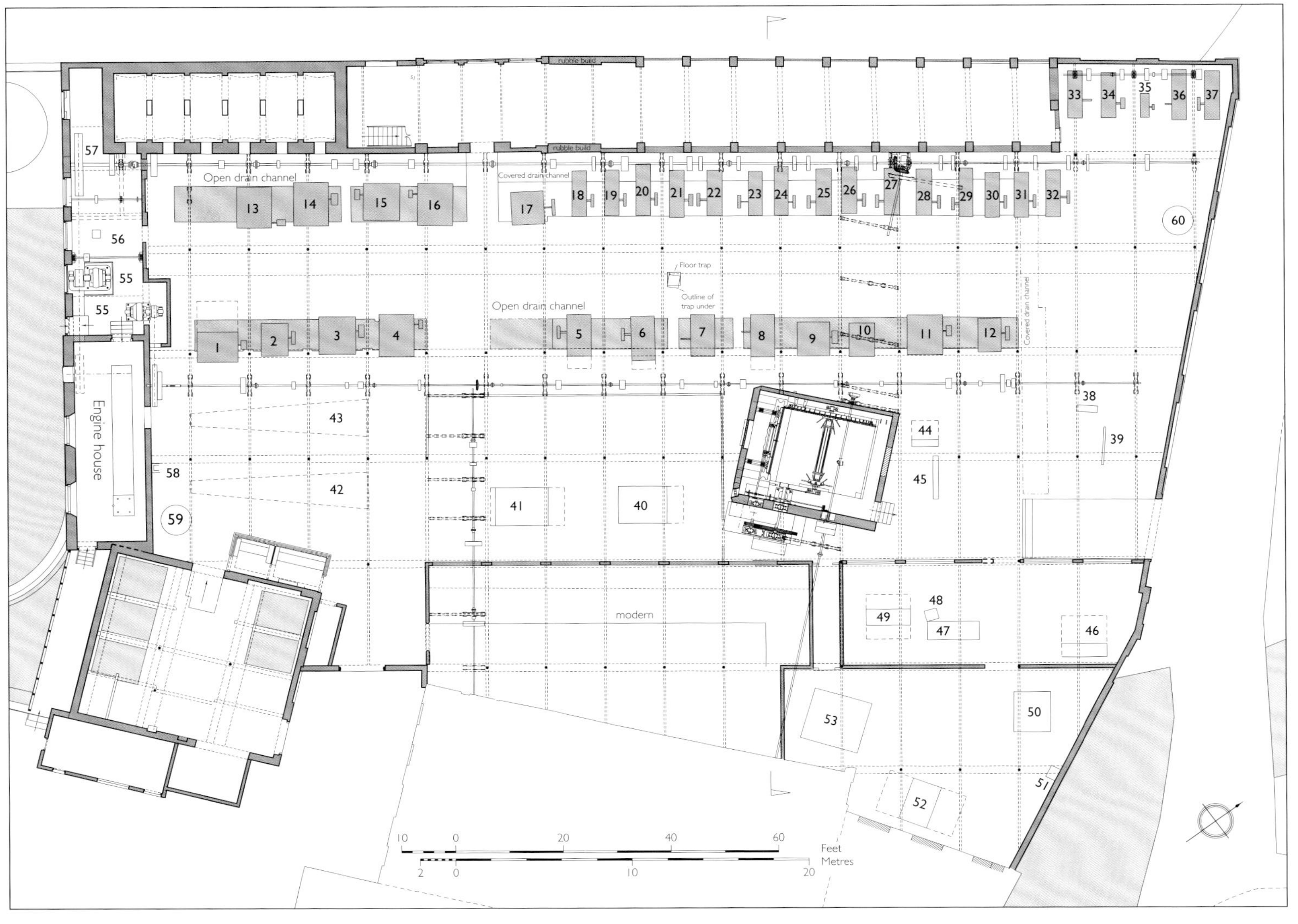

Fig 4.44
The finishing works was completely reorganised within a new north-light shed in 1894, and remained in use until the late 1990s. The line shafting could be driven by steam, water or DC electric power.

1–12 *Scouring machines*
18–37 *Milling machines*
42, 43 *Overhead stretching frames*
46, 53 *Raising gigs*
55 *DC electric motors*
57 *Main belt-drive pulley*
59, 60 *Centrifugal extractors*

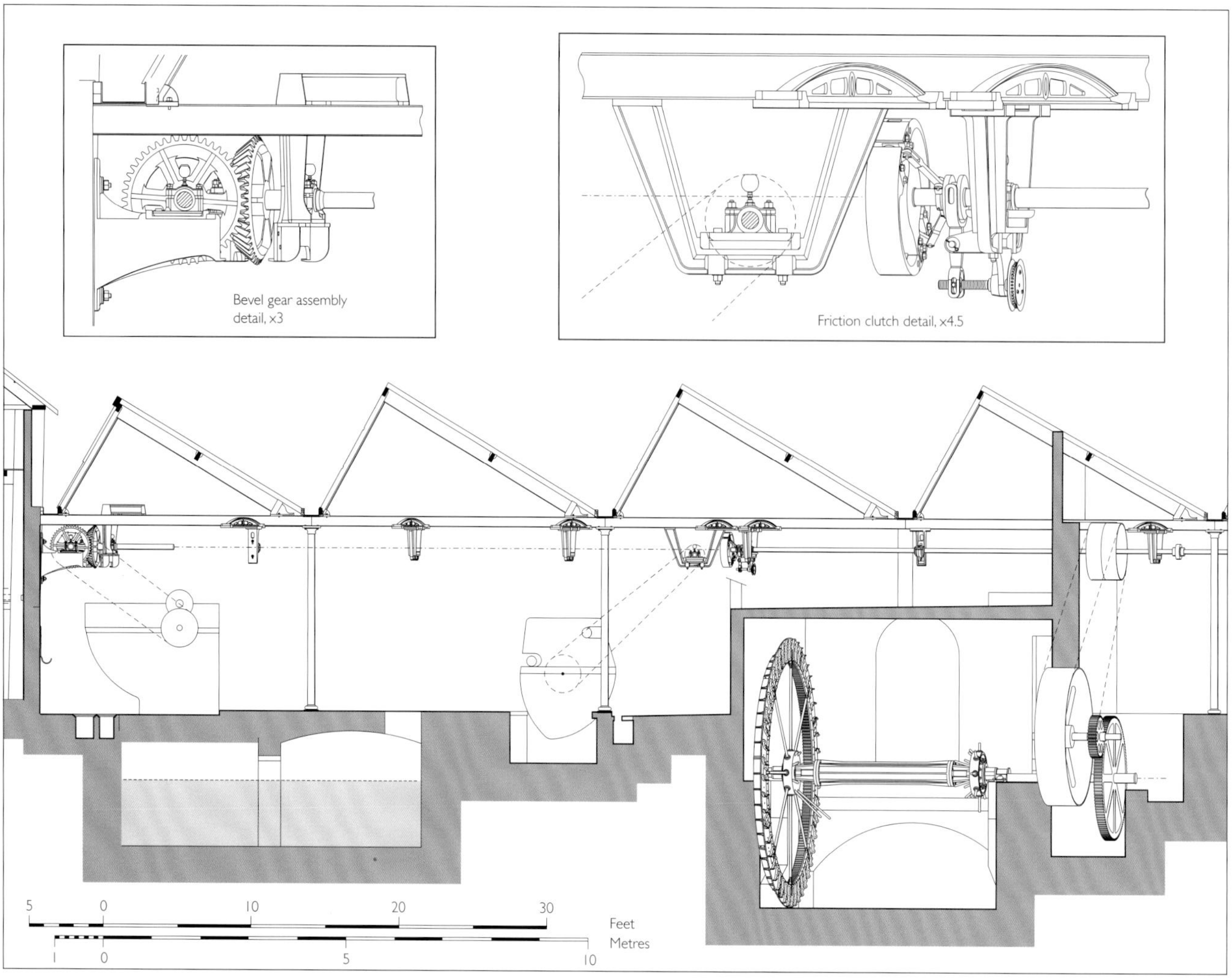

Bevel gear assembly detail, x3

Friction clutch detail, x4.5

5 0 10 20 30 Feet

1 0 5 10 Metres

Fig 4.45 (above)
The early 19th-century wheel chamber was incorporated into the rebuilding of part of the site as the new finishing works in the 1890s. Clutches enabled the water-powered shafting to be combined with steam-powered shafting driven from an external engine house.

Fig 4.46 (right)
Tone Works was still in use for finishing serges and light flannels in the mid-1990s. The scouring machines in this view are in the same positions as those in the 1912 photograph of the works (see Fig 4.7). [BB96/01681]

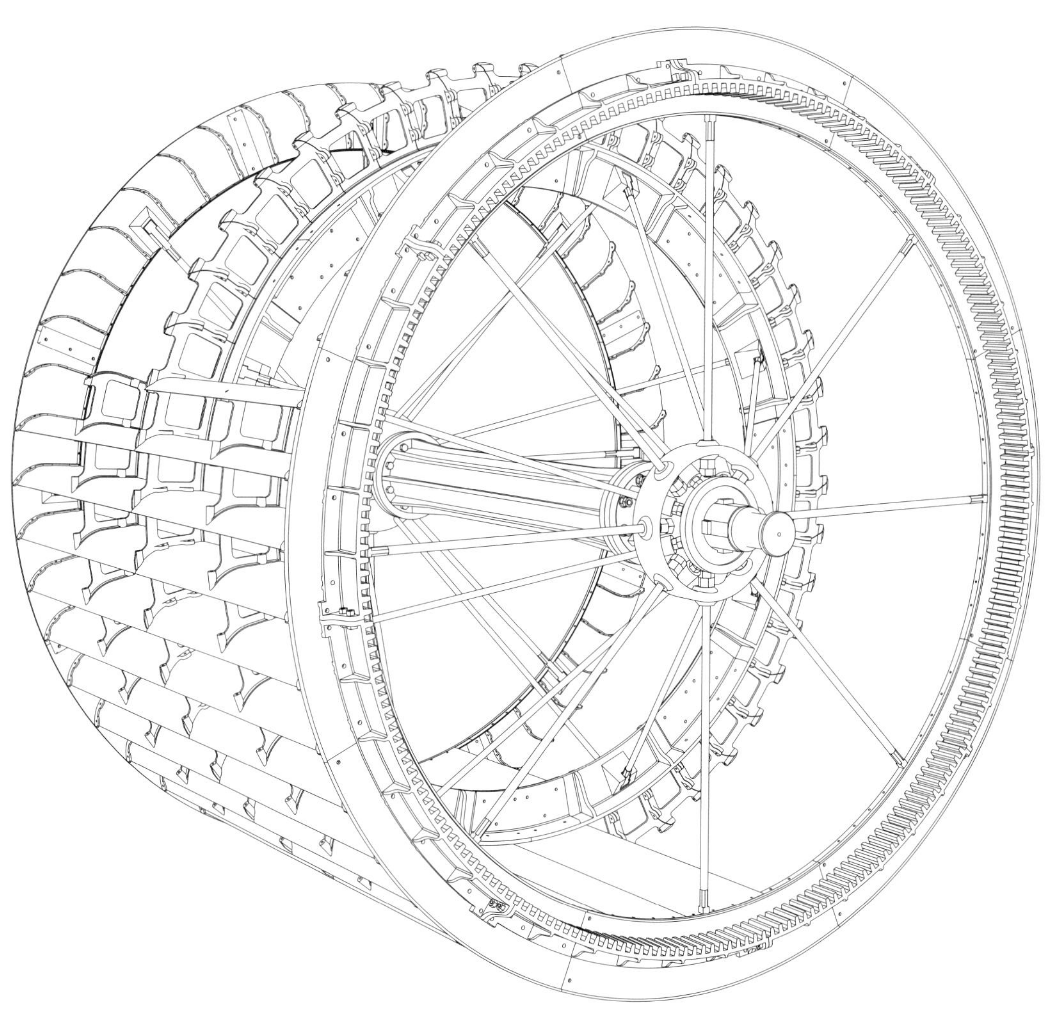

Fig 4.47
The Tone Works suspension wheel, reconstructed from surviving fragments found in the wheel chamber.

Fig 4.48
The combined water- and steam-power system, including most of the late 19th-century line shafting, is another remarkable survival at Tone Works. [DP139292]

The complex development of processes at Tone Works was reflected in the wide variety of functional building types, and also the unusually well-preserved evidence of the combined steam- and water-power system and the process-water system. In the 1894 finishing works, the machinery was belt-driven from line shafting that was steam-powered from an attached engine house, but could also be water-powered from an earlier wheel chamber (*see* Fig 4.44). The wheel chamber was retained from the early 19th-century building replaced by the new finishing works, and still contains parts of the dismantled suspension wheel (Fig 4.47). The wheel was connected to the late 19th-century line shafting via a set of large gear wheels and a system of clutches, enabling the works to be powered by a combination of water and steam. In the early 20th century the shafting could also be driven from a pair of large electric motors, supplied with DC current from the site's own generating station. In a remarkable survival, the main parts of this complex power system all remain *in situ*, including the line shafting, clutches, bevel gearing, electric motors and the belt drives to the machinery (Fig 4.48).

Conclusion: The hidden origins of the serge industry

In the early to mid-18th century, serge was arguably the most extensive of the South West textile industries, covering a larger area than the west of England fine-woollen trade in Gloucestershire, Wiltshire and northern Somerset. Geographically separated from both the other South West textile industries and from London, its historical development was highly distinctive. It was largely financed by wealthy merchants in the main towns and ports who were not directly involved with manufacturing. The various stages of production were delegated to local masters and clothiers, who themselves dealt with the large number of skilled artisans scattered across the countryside. With the later involvement of the East India Company, however, which required large quantities of cheap cloth to support its trade with the Far East, the traditional structure of the industry was retained during the critical period when the early factory system was being established in other parts of the South West and in Yorkshire. The consequent failure to modernise is reflected in the relatively low number of transitional-period workshops and early factories, and this was clearly linked to the dramatic collapse of most of the industry by the early 19th century. A notable exception was the serge industry in south Devon, which used its local supplies of high-quality wool to offset the dominance of the merchants, and was thus able to follow a transition to factory working that was more comparable to that in other areas.

The rest of the serge industry did not disappear, however, and the relatively small number of isolated factories that emerged from the early 19th century succeeded by adapting the traditional mixed-fibre cloths into new products. The absence of local competition, and the geographical separation from other textile industries, enabled the integrated factories to expand enormously; the Fox Brothers mills at Wellington were amongst the largest textile factories in the country by the early 20th century. Perhaps learning from the failure of the pre-factory industry, these firms adopted a progressive and innovative approach to the organisation of production, resulting in unusually complex factories that competed effectively with the woollen and worsted industries in the north.

5

The flax and hemp industry

The flax and hemp industry of Somerset and west Dorset is one of the oldest textile industries in England to remain in its original location. Documentary evidence of local rope, twine and cloth making dates back to the 13th century, and netting products are still being made in the area, mostly from synthetic fibres, in the early 21st century. Throughout its long history the industry has influenced the development of towns, the countryside and the adjoining coastal areas. Flax and hemp were widely grown, so the industry has traditionally provided employment in the cultivation and preparation of the fibre, as well as the spinning of yarn, twine and rope, weaving, net braiding, and the manufacture of a wide range of netting products. The local fishing and boat-building industry ensured a steady demand, but this was supplemented by the production of large quantities of sailcloth and ropes for the navy. From the mid-18th century the industry expanded considerably as a result of the increased business from international trade. The introduction of factory methods occurred slightly later than in the flax industry in other areas and resulted in different types of factory buildings, but nevertheless led to a renewed period of prosperity for the main centres of production. In the South West the factories did not completely replace the traditional methods, however, and had the unusual effect of preserving some of the older structures associated with the pre-factory industry.

Rope, netting and sailcloth were traditionally made for local use in fishing and ship building in many parts of the country, and several

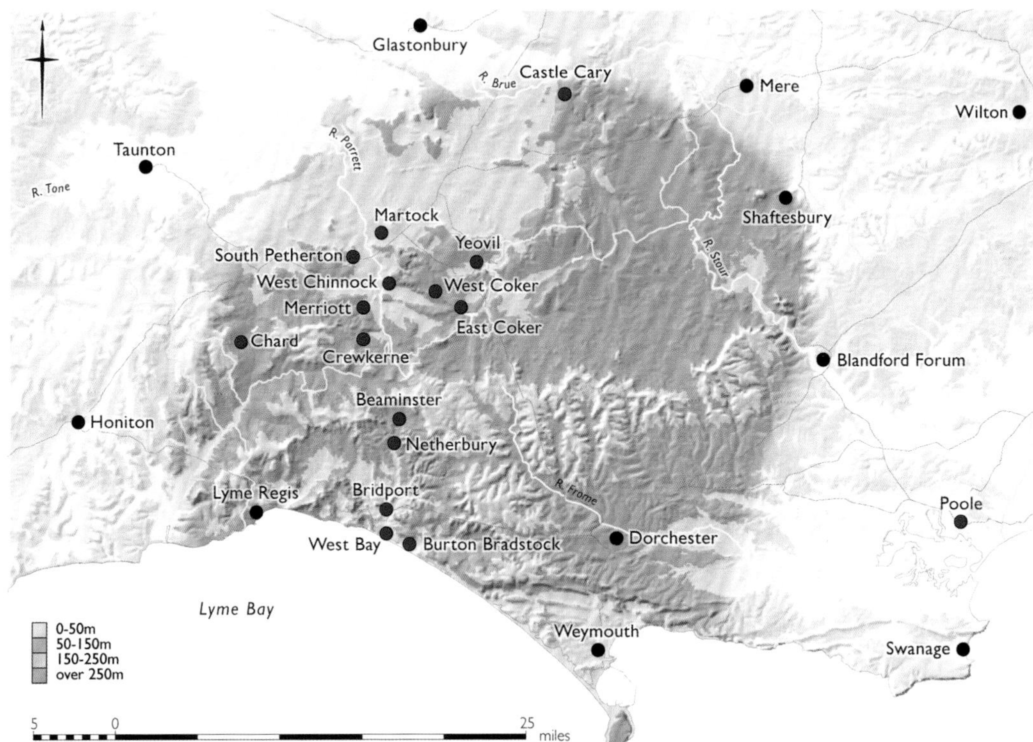

Fig 5.1
Flax and hemp were part of the traditional rural economy across a large area, with factories and related development mainly in the towns and villages to the north of Lyme Bay.
[90m SRTM Topography data courtesy of the CGIAR, http://srtm.csi.cgiar.org]

notable early flax factories were built in the midlands and the north, but few other areas developed industries that were as extensive or as long lasting as that in the South West. The main advantage of Somerset and west Dorset was the suitability of the area for growing flax and hemp, combined with its proximity to the region's ports and fishing industries. A variety of imported raw materials were also used, and were essential to the growth of the industry from the late 17th century, but the distribution of the industry largely reflected the general pattern of farming that had been established by the late medieval period. Flax and hemp both require a suitable climate with fertile, well-drained soils, and suitable conditions were found in the countryside to the north of Lyme Bay and south of the Somerset Levels (Fig 5.1). The main manufacturing centres were the towns of Bridport in west Dorset and Crewkerne in south Somerset, but significant industry and cultivation took place over a large area including Chard in the west, and Castle Cary in the north-east. The parishes surrounding Yeovil were extensively used for growing flax and hemp, with Yeovil itself retaining a flax market until the late 19th century. The villages between Yeovil and Crewkerne had acquired an international reputation for the production of sailcloth by the late 18th century, notably West and East Coker. The south of the flax and hemp area, centred on Bridport, acquired an early reputation for the production of rope and twine, and later specialised in the lighter types of cordage and net making. Throughout the area, by the 19th century, mills, workshops and cottages were used for processing the crops and preparing the fibre for spinning, with buildings associated with the industry often sited close to farms and villages, in addition to the main towns.

The early history of the flax and hemp industry

The flax and hemp industry was established in the South West at a very early date. The earliest available documentary evidence, referenced in many publications, refers to the production of rope and hempen cloth in the Bridport area in the early to mid-13th century. This included a large order for the navy from King John, which suggests that a significant industry was already present in the area.[1] Other research suggests that the crops were grown extensively in Dorset and Somerset from the 12th to the 15th century, and that rope and sailcloth remained important products thereafter.[2] Bridport was still an important centre of production for the navy in the 16th century, leading to statutory protection for the industry.[3] Dorset and Somerset benefited from the growth of the navy and the extension of international trade in the 17th century.[4] From the end of the century rope and cordage for the navy was made in the Royal Naval Dockyards using imported hemp,[5] but the local twine industry was sustained by an export trade that continued to develop until well into the 19th century. Sailcloth was not manufactured in the dockyards and was contracted out by the Navy Board; large quantities were supplied from the Coker area of Somerset from the 17th to the early 19th century.[6]

In the late 18th century the introduction of factory methods, combined with the development of local harbours, fuelled a dramatic resurgence of the industry throughout the area. By this period imported raw materials were widely used, but the government subsidised local flax production by providing bounties to growers from the 1780s.[7] A distinctive feature of the resurgent industry, which was strongly reflected in its extant buildings, was that the new factories did not replace the old methods but largely complemented the established firms, leading to the preservation of some of the industry's oldest sites. The new firms also supported the rural economy around the towns, both by providing a demand for locally grown crops and by outsourcing work to spinners, net makers and weavers in the surrounding villages.

The most notable sector of the export trade was the supply of nets, cordage and tackle to the Newfoundland fishing industry.[8] From the mid-18th century to the early 19th century, exports benefited from a series of improvements to Bridport Harbour, which was ideally sited to serve a large part of the hemp and flax-producing area. The growth in the production of rope and twine goods enabled the industry to prosper while the market for traditional sailcloth contracted. The reliance on skilled and specialised outworkers continued after the introduction of factories in the early 19th century, enabling the local merchants to supply a wider range of products, and smaller orders, than an integrated factory. In Bridport, merchants put out twine and rope making to small businesses in the many open walks located in the town, and net braiding to cottage workers in the surrounding villages. By the late 18th century the most successful Bridport merchant-manufacturers were directly involved with the export trade, even to the point of having ships built at the nearby harbour, in addition to outsourcing both textile production and the growing of the raw material (Fig 5.2).

Outworking was extensive throughout the hemp and flax area for centuries prior to the introduction of factory working, involving the full range of textile processes in addition to the farmwork associated with the growing and preparation of the raw fibre (Fig 5.3). Large quantities of sailcloth were produced in Somerset for the navy in the 17th century, for example, and, as stated above, from the mid-18th century the parishes of East and West Coker were well known as a source of good quality sailcloth, all of which was produced by cottage spinners and weavers.[9] Employment in the industry was often part-time, however, combined with another source of income. Part-time work enabled manufacturers to supply a wider range of specialised products than was typical for firms that were completely reliant on factory production. An unusual feature of the industry was that outworking continued for some specialised processes, such as the hand braiding of irregular-sized netting, long after the introduction of factories. Much of the hemp and flax growing that was recorded in the late 18th century was also combined with other work, being carried out by tenant labourers renting one field at a time, and not by major landowners.[10] The initial processing of flax and hemp crops was traditionally a winter occupation for farm labourers.[11] The seasonal nature of the pre-factory industry may have contributed to the general absence of industrial features in small vernacular buildings.

In comparison with other textile industries, there is also less historical evidence of a widespread and dominant class of clothiers or manufacturers to organise the outworkers. Much of the work seems to have been put out by middlemen working under contract for merchants located in the main towns or outside the hemp- and flax-producing area. Some of the merchants appear to have had little direct connection with the industry, but others were more closely involved in organising the growers and outworkers.[12] The businesses with more direct control of outworking, which acquired a practical understanding of the many stages

Fig 5.2
International trade fuelled the resurgence of the flax and hemp industry from the mid-18th century. The largest Bridport manufacturers, such as the Hounsell family of North Mills, had vessels built at Bridport harbour for the trans-Atlantic trade, although their second ship, the Mary Hounsell, *shown here, was built in Newfoundland. Artist and date unknown. [Reproduced courtesy of Bridport Museum. BRPMG 2182. DP137134]*

Fig 5.3
Hand spinning and weaving in a textile workshop, as depicted by Francis Newbery in a mural at Bridport Town Hall, 1924. Outworking in both towns and countryside persisted long after the construction of powered factories. [DP004864]

of production, were better placed to benefit from the introduction of factory methods, and had more influence on the development of the industry in the 19th century. Examples of early factory firms that combined the roles of merchant and manufacturer included Richard Roberts and Richard Hayward, and several of the most successful Bridport firms. In many cases these firms continued to put out work to net makers or twine spinners well into the 19th century.

Flax and hemp products

Flax and hemp have been adapted for a notably wide range of uses, including clothing, sailcloth, webbing, rope, twine and netting, and the history of the industry has been closely related to changes in the demand for its products. Both fibres have a very long history of cultivation, and both have been used for making different types of yarn and cloth. Flax was traditionally more suited to linen cloths and twine, and hemp to heavy cloths, stronger twines and a wide variety of ropes. Of particular importance in the South West was the demand for the great variety of cordage and cloth used in the ship-building and fishing industries, both locally and for exports.

Fig 5.4
Diversification into a great variety of new products, combined with amalgamations of many of the smaller firms, ensured the survival of the industry into the second half of the 20th century.
[Reproduced courtesy of the Museum of Net Manufacture, Uploders. DP004872]

The production of ropes and sailcloth for the navy was a key factor in the long-term success of the industry. Linen cloths made from flax were also produced for clothing, but following the rise of other textile industries, particularly cotton, the region's flax industry increasingly concentrated on other types of products. By the late 18th century the national production of linens for domestic use was dominated by a new generation of advanced textile mills being built in the north and the midlands, with the South West flax weavers concentrating on the production of sailcloth.

The demand for cloth and cordage used in sailing ships was influenced by the growth of foreign trade, particularly with overseas colonies, the wars of the 17th and 18th centuries and the expansion of the Royal Navy. The fortunes of the industry changed significantly when the navy began to manufacture its own ropes and other items for ships at the Royal Dockyards from the late 17th century, although the Navy Board continued to contract out the production of sailcloth. Sailcloth weaving employed large numbers of cottage workers, but from the mid-19th century the industry declined as sail was replaced by steam. By the 1880s steam was the dominant source of power for shipping, but some enterprising local manufacturers adapted to the more specialised market in sails for leisure craft.

The traditional South West fishing industries ensured a steady demand for twine and netting, but from the late 18th century the industry expanded to meet a considerable demand from foreign fisheries, notably those in parts of North America. In particular, the supply of netting and cordage to Newfoundland was central to a resurgence of the industry around Bridport, including the extension of local harbour facilities and the addition of new industrial areas to the town. In the late 19th and 20th centuries the industry adapted yet again to changing markets with a range of new products, including sports nets, horticultural netting and cargo-restraint nets (Fig 5.4). This reflected the national development of the flax industry in the 19th century, with most of the greatly increased output being sold for exports and a heavy reliance on the use of imported raw materials.[13] In this period flax and hemp were still grown in small quantities in the South West, but the growth of the industry from the mid-18th century was closely linked to the increased use of imported flax and hemp, much of it obtained from central Europe or from Russia. By the end of the 19th century sailcloth production was greatly reduced and other fibres were being used for twine, netting and specialised types of cloths, including manila, cotton and jute. The cultivation and processing of flax and hemp was revived by government support during both world wars, temporarily sustaining the smaller manufacturers outside the main centres. By the mid-20th century man-made fibre had largely replaced natural materials, but netting products remained an important part of the local economy.

Processes in the flax and hemp industry

The manufacture of twine, cloth and ropes has a long-standing connection with the countryside of Somerset and Dorset, and the development of the industry can be seen to have influenced the rural economy, the pattern of land use and the traditional way of life of rural communities. The cultivation of the crops likewise influenced the organisation and development of the textile industry. The proportion of imported raw materials increased from the 17th century, and enabled the growth in factory working in the 19th century, but the cultivation of English flax and hemp continued and was encouraged by government support when wars made imports unobtainable. A range of factors influenced the quantity and quality of both crops. The seasonal growing conditions, for example, could influence the proportion of line and tow obtained from flax.[14] Variations in the purchase price of new crops and the value of stored materials could significantly influence the profitability of a business, hence the need for merchants and manufacturers to build up reserve stocks in warehouses. In addition to flax and hemp fibre, seed was also imported and used for growing. Imports were mainly obtained from Europe and Russia, but with the wars of the late 18th and early 19th century, Russia became the main source. The Baltic port of Riga was the largest exporter of flax and hemp in the 19th century, most of it being sold to Britain, and seed from Riga was widely used by flax growers in the South West.[15]

At the beginning of the 19th century flax and hemp were therefore still widely produced and used in combination with imports by the local factories. Hemp was grown in nine parishes of Dorset in 1812, for example, and a further 23 parishes in the Yeovil area of Somerset.[16] Both crops involved labour-intensive farming methods, which increased their cost in comparison with imports.[17] The soil needed careful preparation and flax and hemp had to be rotated with other crops, usually over a period of between three and seven years.[18] They were sown and pulled by hand, and the removal of leaves, seeds and initial drying were also manual processes. The crops were dried in the field by being arranged into stooks for several days (Fig 5.5).

Further preparation of both flax and hemp also took place close to the area where the crops were grown, either in the fields, in local mills or in specialised farm buildings. Both plants have a hard stem which has to be removed to extract the useful fibre. The first stage involved softening the plant by retting, either by spreading the crop on the ground for several weeks, allowing it to rot, or by soaking in water-filled pits or tanks (Fig 5.6). Extracting the useful

Fig 5.5
Cut flax being dried in stooks, Bridport area c 1940. Cultivation of flax and hemp required careful preparation of the land and a range of skilled agricultural work before the crop was ready for use in the mill.
[Reproduced courtesy of the Museum of Net Manufacture, Uploders. DP000632]

Fig 5.6
Retting flax, Bridport area, c 1945. Retting involved the controlled soaking of the dried crop to soften and help remove the woody outer parts of the stem from the useful fibre. Traditionally, it was achieved either by spreading the crop in the fields, by stacking it in tanks or a combination of both. [Reproduced courtesy of the Museum of Net Manufacture, Uploders. DP000639]

fibre and preparing it for spinning involved a sequence of processes not found in the other textile industries, which in the flax trade were referred to as flax dressing. The hard parts of the stem were first broken by beating manually or, from the early 19th century in the South West, by using powered machines with rollers (Fig 5.7). After the initial breaking, the woody parts were removed from the useful fibre by scutching, either manually or by inserting the fibres between sets of rotating wooden blades in a powered machine.[19] The mechanised scutching processes were also referred to as 'swingling' in the South West. Water-powered flax swingling was probably first introduced into the area in 1803 by Richard Roberts at Grove Mill, Burton Bradstock, in West Dorset.[20] Hemp was a taller plant which required additional mechanical softening in a 'balling' mill; water-powered balling mills were in use around Bridport by the late 18th century.[21] At this point the fibre could be stored in a barn or warehouse and sold as a commodity. The final stage was heckling, a process that was broadly similar to combing in the worsted industry (Fig 5.8). Bundles of fibre were drawn through rows of fixed metal spikes, in an arduous procedure that was not widely mechanised until the mid-19th century. This laid the fibres parallel, removing any knots and separating the long fibres, known as line, from the shorter fibres, known as tow; the two types of fibre were then used for different products.

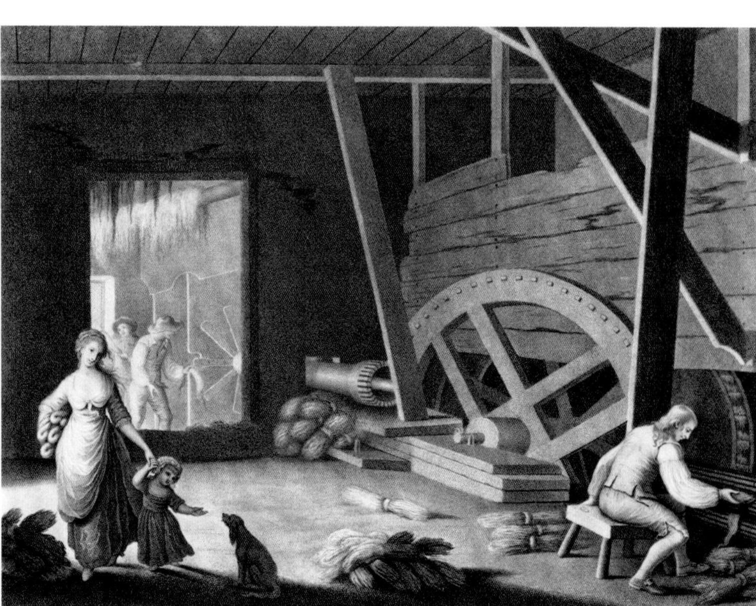

Fig 5.7
Powered scutching machines were used to break and separate the woody parts of the stem, as shown here in a 1783 illustration from Ireland. From William Hinckes, The Irish Linen Industry, *1783. [© The British Library Board. KTOP LII, 46.e]*

The spinning of yarns to be used for cloth involved processes and machines that were quite different to those used to make yarns for twine or rope. Flax yarn intended for weaving was spun on wheels, normally by women, in an extensive cottage industry. Hand spinning was not superseded by machinery in mills until the early 19th century, later than in most of

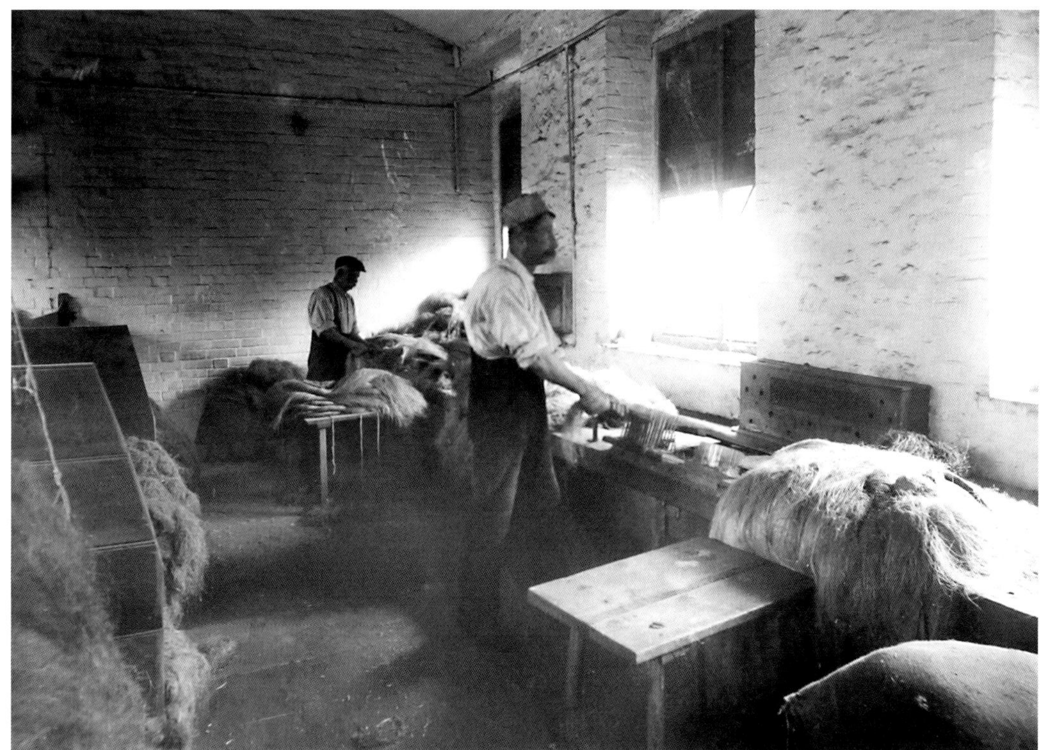

Fig 5.8
Heckling was originally a demanding manual process that involved drawing bundles of the fibre through metal spikes fixed to a bench. The shorter fibre was extracted and used for different products. The initial stage of heckling, seen here at Court Mills, Bridport, c 1910, remained a manual process after the introduction of heckling machinery.
[Reproduced courtesy of the Museum of Net Manufacture, Uploders. DP000564]

the other textile industries.[22] In contrast, the production of twine was carried out in a walk, typically a long, narrow plot adjoining a house, which enabled spinning in lengths of up to 100yds (91.44m).[23] The initial stage produced a yarn; yarns were then combined to form twine; and twine was combined to form rope (Fig 5.9). A spinner would carry a bundle of prepared fibre along the walk while manually extracting a continuous sliver that was kept off the ground on horizontal supports, known as 'skirders'. The sliver was attached to a revolving hook on a machine called a jack at the end of the walk; the jack was cranked by an assistant, rotating the hook and applying the desired amount of twist. A similar process using jacks with multiple hooks was used to combine yarns into twine and twine into rope. A variety of finishing processes, including bleaching, sizing and tarring, were used for cordage that was intended for particular applications, such as fishing nets or rigging.

Machinery for spinning flax was in use in Yorkshire by the early 1790s, leading to the construction of several very large early factories, but in general the introduction of machinery for both flax and hemp lagged behind the cotton and woollen industries.[24] In the South West, factory machinery was introduced on a smaller scale from the early 19th century, but complemented the continued use of walks and handlooms. In that period, manual processes were better suited to the twines, ropes and sailcloth which were the main products of the South West industry.

Sailcloth weaving was a successful part of the pre-factory industry, with large numbers of cottage-based handloom weavers located in villages throughout the area. By the late 18th century some districts were well known for the

Fig 5.9
Turning a jack to apply twist in the laying of a short length of three-strand rope at Higher Flax Mills, Castle Cary c 1970. Similar techniques were used in walks for making twine and rope in lengths of up to 100yds (91.44m).
[Reproduced courtesy of the Museum of Net Manufacture, Uploders. DP000602]

Fig 5.10
By the 19th century the hand production of netting was a well-established rural industry, especially in the countryside around Bridport, where villages specialised in the production of different types of net. Balloon Cottage, Eype, Bridport, 1913. [Reproduced courtesy of Bridport Museum TA 131. DP137136]

Fig 5.11
The jumper loom, named with reference to its foot-operated mechanism, was installed in factories in the second half of the 19th century, replacing cottage workers for the production of plain netting. This example was manufactured in Bridport c 1860. [Reproduced courtesy of the Museum of Net Manufacture, Uploders. DP000561]

weaving of good-quality sailcloth, notably the villages between Crewkerne and Yeovil such as East and West Coker. The cloth was woven to pre-determined weights and dimensions on narrow looms, typically from 24 to 36in (0.6–0.91m) wide. The bleaching of the raw fibre and the woven cloth was recognised as an important stage in the production of quality yarn and sailcloth, and 'bucking' houses for boiling the liquor were often sited close to mills and walks.[25] After the bleaching processes, yarn was air dried on racks or poles, with

yarn drying being a common sight in the fields adjoining mills and twine walks.[26] In most textile industries power-loom weaving became significant from the 1830s, but by this time the demand for sailcloth was already in decline. The earliest known reference to sailcloth weaving with power looms in the South West is at Priory Mills, Bridport, in 1831.[27] One of the last cloth mills in the area, the Coker Sail Cloth Works of Richard Hayward at Crewkerne, was using power looms for sailcloth weaving until the 1940s.[28]

Net making was a similarly extensive industry, mainly carried out by women, especially in the twine-producing areas around Bridport (Fig 5.10). The hand braiding of specialist types of nets by outworkers has continued to the present day. Machine-made netting, such as that produced on jumper looms, became significant from the late 19th century, when steam-powered shed mills for net making were added to some of the larger Bridport factories (Fig 5.11). The decline of sailcloth production in the late 19th century saw the industry diversify into new markets, with greater emphasis on twine and webbing products. Sheet netting produced on machines was used for making drift nets and trawl nets in the larger Bridport factories up to the mid-20th century. Other new products included horticultural netting, while sports nets, camouflage nets and aircraft cargo-restraint nets are still manufactured in Bridport today. A notable example of diversification in the Somerset flax and hemp industry was the weaving of horsehair fabrics in Castle Cary, which benefited from the local invention of a specialised type of power loom in 1871 (*see* p 139).

Buildings and landscapes of the flax and hemp industry

Evidence of the flax and hemp industry is widespread in the buildings, towns and rural landscapes of the area. The industry's influence is found in such diverse building types as vernacular cottages and mills in rural areas, farm buildings and flax barns, a wide range of factory buildings, the townscapes of the twine spinners and net makers and the shipping warehouses at Bridport Harbour. The extant industrial buildings range in date from the mid-18th to the mid-20th century, but the use of rope and twine walks up to the 20th century has also helped preserve the outlines of some of the earlier property boundaries. In Bridport, this has produced a distinctive townscape in which 19th-century factories are combined with artisans' housing and workshops of the pre-factory era, set within the narrow outlines of the former medieval burgage plots. In rural areas, integrated factories developed in the 19th century, but these were also distinctive in comparison with other textile industries, combining water- and steam-powered buildings with twine walks and unusually large amounts of warehousing.

The rural flax and hemp industry

The flax and hemp industry was a traditional feature of the Dorset and Somerset countryside that influenced the history of farming, vernacular buildings, the rural economy and the working life of rural communities. Industrial buildings in the countryside included 19th-century mill complexes, which reflect the developments in factory buildings seen in other textile industries, along with features specific to hemp and flax, and an earlier generation of smaller mills built for processing the locally grown crops. Historical research in many publications indicates that cottage weaving and net making were widespread in both counties,[29] but, as in some other parts of the South West, the surviving vernacular buildings do not show the clear evidence of industrial use that can be seen in other regions (Fig 5.12). There are also fewer early workshops dating from the

Fig 5.12
Outworking for the Bridport firms remained an important part of rural life in West Dorset until the mid-20th century, as seen here at Loders in c 1948. In contrast to the rural industries of other areas, however, the vernacular architecture of local cottages did not include obvious functional features, such as workshop windows. [Reproduced courtesy of the Museum of Net Manufacture, Uploders. DP000550]

transition to factory working. This is largely a reflection of the nature of the processes carried out in the industry, such as sailcloth weaving on narrow handlooms and the hand braiding of netting, which could be accommodated in the small rooms of a cottage. Throughout much of the history of the industry, locally grown flax and hemp were used in combination with imports, both of prepared fibre and of seed. Together with the seasonal nature of the industry, this required the use of larger storage facilities than were typical in other textile industries, with warehousing space of similar size or larger than the mills themselves.

Rural mills

Water-powered mills for the initial processing of flax and hemp were being built in the South West by the late 18th century. These were small vernacular buildings, often combined with corn mills, with materials and features that clearly pre-date the factory architecture that was introduced from the early 19th century.

The first swingling or scutching mill, used for the preparation of locally grown flax, was reputedly Grove Mill at Burton Bradstock, West Dorset, built by Richard Roberts in 1803 and used in conjunction with two other nearby flax mills.[30] Roberts was a pioneering flax manufacturer who used powered mills for preparation and spinning, put out weaving to around 200 handloom weavers and grew from 50 to 200 acres (20.23–80.94ha) of flax per year, in addition to purchasing large quantities of imported Riga flax.[31] Many of the small early mills combined the preparation of flax or hemp with corn milling. At least six small water-powered mills were being used at Bridport for softening hemp, in a process known as balling, from the late 18th century,[32] although most do not appear to retain their original buildings. In contrast, an exceptionally well-preserved dual-use site is Mangerton Mill, located two miles north-east of Bridport, which in the early to mid-19th century combined water-powered corn milling and flax processing, housed in separate areas to either side of a central wheel chamber (Fig 5.13).

Flax warehouses

As stated earlier, a considerable amount of warehousing space was needed for the more productive outworking businesses that were established from the late 18th century, and for the factories that were built in both rural and urban areas from the early 19th century. The relatively large warehouses at flax and hemp mills reflected the seasonal supply of the raw materials and frequent changes in their quality and value. Examples can be seen throughout the area. One of the few sailcloth weavers to successfully make the transition to the factory system was Richard Hayward (1769–1852), who established a sailcloth weaving business in West Chinnock in the 1790s and expanded to a new site at Tail Mill, Merriott, Somerset, in the early 19th century (*see* below).[33] The earliest buildings at the Merriott site are a large three-

Fig 5.13
Mangerton Mill, near Bridport, was built for both corn milling, located to the left of the brick wheel chamber, and for the preparation of locally grown flax, in the two bays at the right end.
[DP004834]

storeyed warehouse and a smaller two-storeyed mill, both dating from the period when weaving was still being put out to home-based workers. Other examples of large warehouses at flax mills can be seen at Pymore Mills and North Mill, to the north of Bridport, and at Higher Flax Mill, Castle Cary (Figs 5.14–5.16). In all these cases the warehouses occupied more floor space than the nearby mills themselves, but were of similar construction, materials and architectural details. The main physical evidence for their use as warehouses is the presence of loading doors and hoists, and the absence of any form of power system.

As in other textile industries, the early development of factory working involved the gradual concentration of processes that were previously put out, but differences occurred in the way in which factory work and outwork were combined. The sailcloth producing areas of Somerset and Dorset saw a steady decline due to the growth of steam shipping, but factory complexes showed a comparable type of development to those in other regions. The first buildings at the factory site were warehouses and small powered mills used for the preparation of the raw material, and in some cases buildings associated with finishing the yarn or cloth. Powered spinning was added later, followed by weaving on handlooms and, lastly, by powered weaving in purpose-built sheds. In these areas the factories replaced outworking, putting handloom weavers and other trades out of work. In contrast, areas concentrating on twine and netting, such as Bridport, showed a different type of development in which the factories led to an expansion of outworking (*see* p 143).

Tail Mill, Merriott

The integration of processes at mill sites had a direct bearing on the development of building types and power systems. The Tail Mill site of Richard Hayward, mentioned earlier, shows a typical sequence of building, ranging from its origins as the centre of an outworking business to its mid- and late 19th-century expansion into an integrated spinning and weaving factory (Figs 5.17 and 5.18).[34] The two-storeyed mill added in 1836 was built on the site of an earlier grist mill and combined the use of water and steam power in one building. Two internal waterwheels and an internal beam engine were supplemented by a third external waterwheel, a large amount of power for a small mill

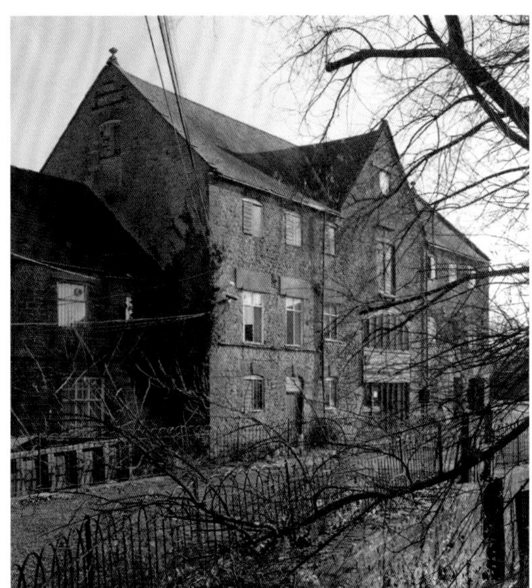

Fig 5.14
The seasonal nature of flax production, and frequent variations in its market price, led to the construction of unusually large warehouses at the South West flax factories. In several cases, such as Tail Mill, Merriott, the warehouse was the earliest and the largest building at the site.
[BB99/10374]

Fig 5.15
At Higher Flax Mills, Castle Cary, a row of mid- to late 19th-century warehouses was added close to the earlier water-powered mill.
[AA009497]

Fig 5.16
One of the two large flax warehouses at Pymore Mills, north of Bridport.
[DP000796]

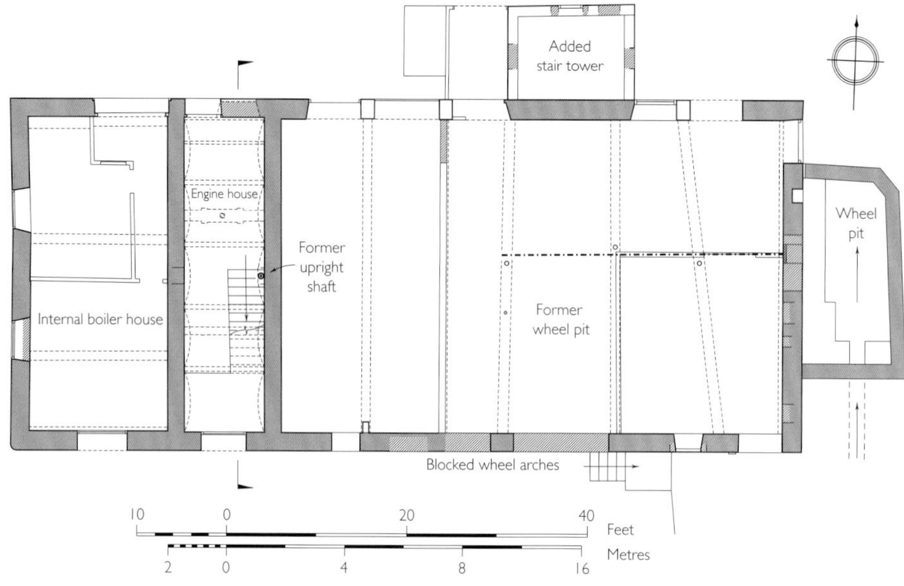

Fig 5.17
The expansion of manufacturing at Tail Mill, Merriott, led to the addition of a small but heavily powered mill to the earlier warehouse, incorporating both an internal engine house and internal waterwheels.

Fig 5.18
The beam-engine house is intact, having been preserved as a stair hall, retaining its fireproof ceiling and the wall fixtures which supported the engine's entablature beam.

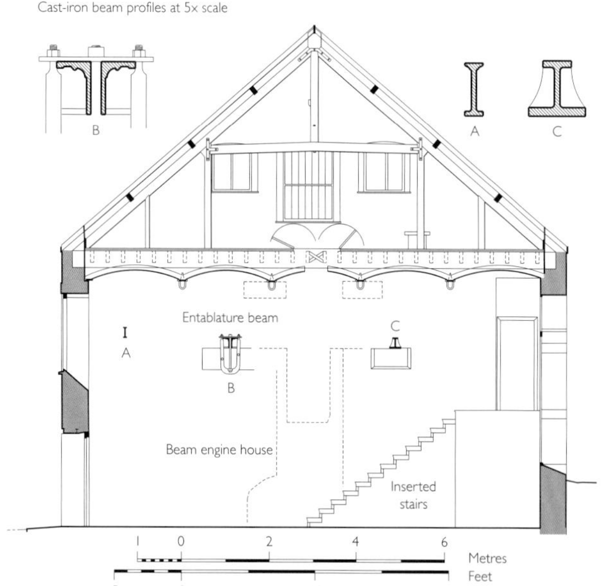

and a clear indication of the firm's intention to develop beyond the use of hand-powered machines (Fig 5.19). By the 1850s it contained spinning and carding machinery, the latter suggesting that it was mainly used for spinning tow.[35] North-light sheds were added for power-loom weaving in the mid-19th century, along with other buildings for heckling.

Coker Sail Cloth Works, West Coker

The firm of Richard Hayward continued under his descendents, but was split into two independent weaving businesses in 1868. At this time a second mill to the north of Crewkerne was purchased and developed for power-loom weaving under the title of Richard Hayward and Company, when it was known as the Coker Sail Cloth Works (Fig 5.20). The mill buildings

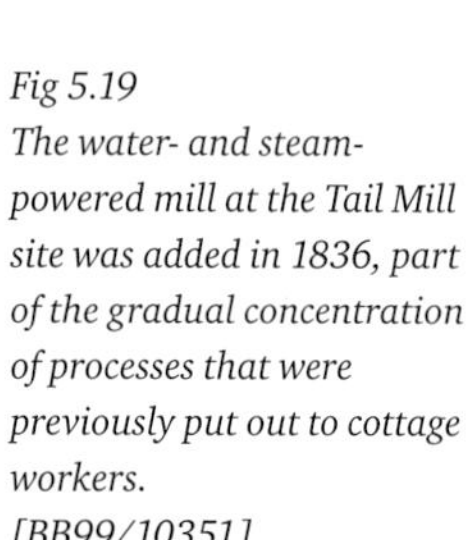

Fig 5.19
The water- and steam-powered mill at the Tail Mill site was added in 1836, part of the gradual concentration of processes that were previously put out to cottage workers.
[BB99/10351]

Fig 5. 20
The former Coker Sail Cloth Works, also known as North Street Mill, illustrated the typical development of an early water-powered mill, with a steam-powered extension and the addition of north-light sheds for power-loom weaving. Photograph dated c 1870. [Reproduced courtesy of Somerset Heritage Centre DD/X/LIV/11. DP140079]

are not extant, but comprised a water-powered flax spinning mill with three added ranges of steam-powered weaving sheds, a later example of the same sequence of development as Tail Mill. From the late 19th to the mid-20th centuries this site specialised in a new branch of the sailcloth industry, the weaving of cloths specifically for yachts and leisure craft. In developing this trade, the firm supplied sailcloth to the specifications of the historic sail-making firm of Ratsey and Lapthorne of Cowes, who negotiated the exclusive use of Hayward's cloth for the manufacture of sails for yachts; Hayward's had been supplying sailcloth to G R Ratsey from the early 19th century.[36]

Higher Flax Mills, Castle Cary

The late 19th-century development of a flax mill for spinning can be seen at Higher Flax Mills, Castle Cary, Somerset, an area with a long association with the growing and manufacture of flax and hemp (Fig 5.21).[37] In this case the range of building types reflects the development of the site as a specialised factory for the powered preparation of flax combined with the spinning of rope and twine in open walks (Fig 5.22). It was part of a group of five flax mills built along a small stream to the west of the town. An early mill and house were purchased by the firm of Thomas Donne in *c* 1848 and rebuilt into its present form in *c* 1870. The site comprised a three-storeyed water- and steam-powered mill built across the valley floor, with extensive areas of open walks laid out on levelled ground both upstream and downstream of the mill (Fig 5.23). Three large warehouses, plus ancillary buildings and offices, were built along the north side of the open walks, reflecting the firm's role as both manufacturers and flax and tow merchants in the 1870s. The walks downstream of the mill remained in use to the mid-20th century, being covered with distinctive cambered-roof sheds in the 1940s. The sheds still retain the original stone buildings that protected the machinery at the ends of the former open walks. T S Donne merged with another historic local firm, John Boyd, in the 1970s, and twine and webbing manufacture ceased in the early 1980s. The site

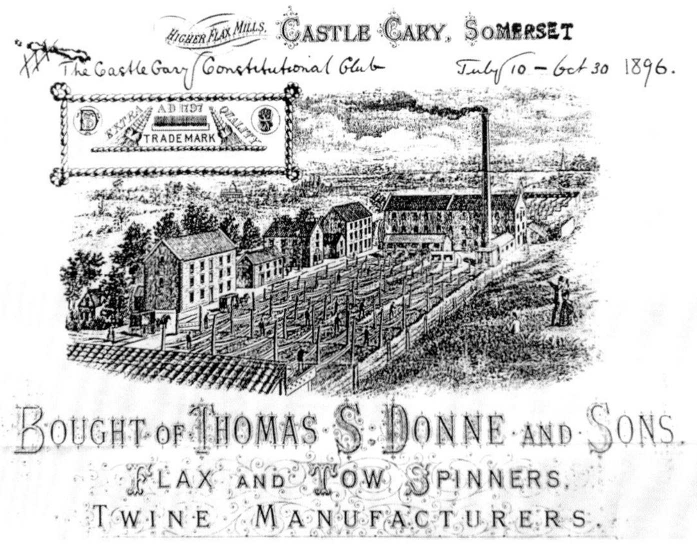

Fig 5.21
At Higher Flax Mills, Castle Cary, a steam-powered extension was added to a water-powered mill and flanked by two groups of open walks, three large warehouses, workshops and offices. This view from 1896 also shows the open-sided buildings that were often sited at the ends of open walks. [Reproduced courtesy of Somerset Heritage Centre DD/X/LIV/12. DP140089]

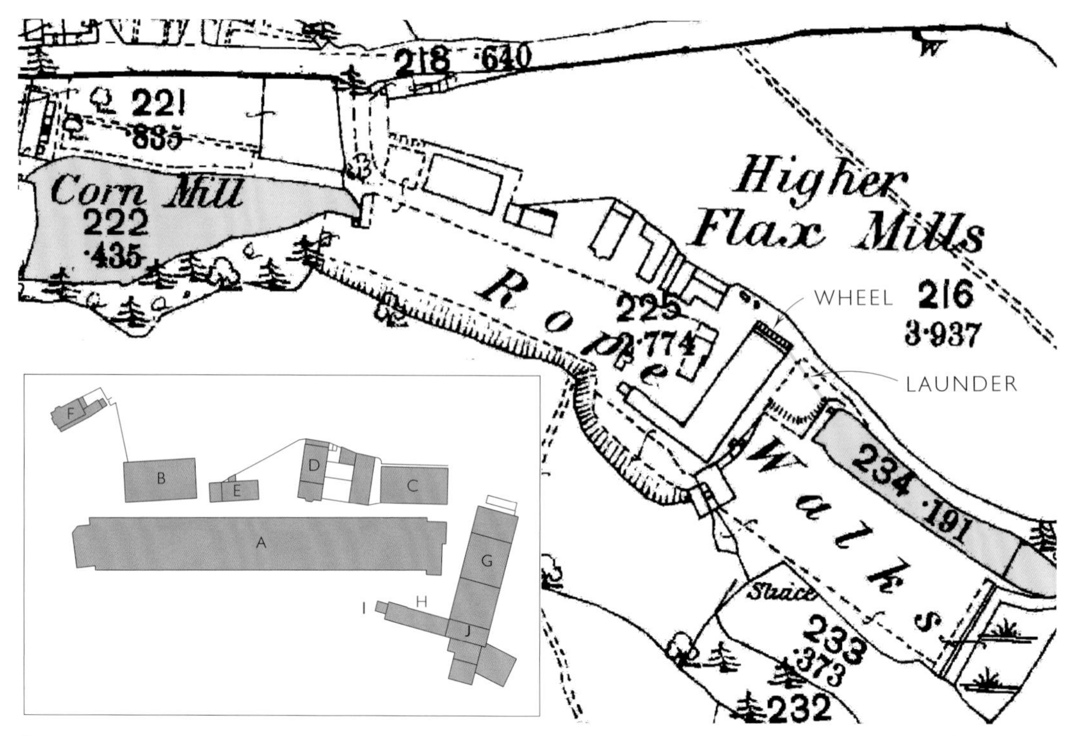

Fig 5.22
Higher Flax Mills, Castle Cary, developed along a valley floor to specialise in twine spinning in two groups of open walks, supported by a powered mill for preparation and a range of flax warehouses. Based on OS 1:2500, Somerset, published 1886.
***A** Former open walks*
***B** Warehouse*
***C** Warehouse*
***D** Warehouses and offices*
***E** Unpowered workshop*
***F** Entrance lodge*
***G** Powered mill*
***H** Site of boiler house*
***I** Site of chimney*
***J** Engine house*

Fig 5.23
Higher Flax Mills illustrates the use of local materials in the building types typical of an integrated flax factory. Open walks were sited on both sides of the powered mill, at the rear. The brick building on the right dates from the covering of open walks in the early 1940s. [AA009493]

is still occupied by John Boyd Textiles Limited for the weaving of horsehair cloth (*see* p 139).

Parrett Works, Martock

A contrast with the use of traditional building methods and local materials at Higher Flax Mills is the flamboyant Italianate architecture and fireproof construction used at the Parrett Works, near Martock, Somerset (Figs 5.24 and 5.25). This was an unusual example in the South West of a new textile business created in the mid-19th century as a joint stock

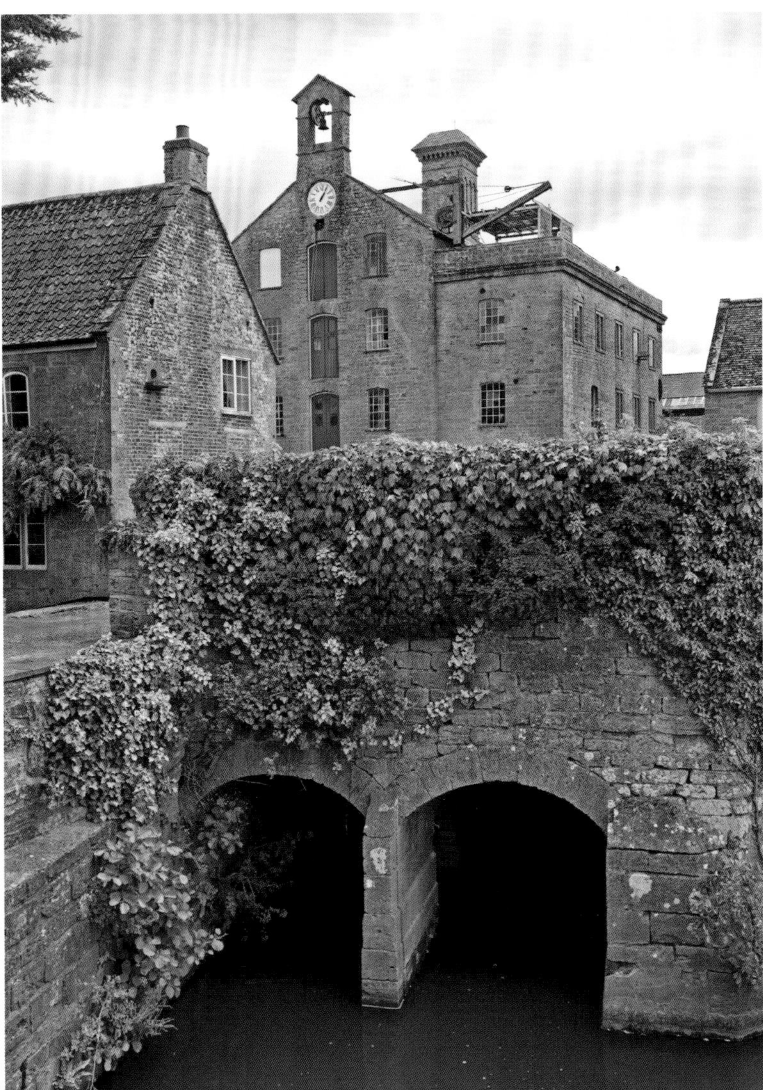

company, by the enterprising farmer and engineer George Parsons.[38] A large complex of multi-storeyed mills, warehouses, rope walks and weaving sheds was built on the site of an earlier mill, alongside a contemporary engineering works run by the same firm. The wide range of functions, and a combined water- and steam-power system, was reflected in the great variety of building types. The business was launched as the West of England Engineering and Coker Canvas Company in 1865. The combination of engineering and cloth production at one factory was unusual, however, and the business was not successful, being wound up in 1868. The architecture of the site is perhaps most notable for its four-storeyed fireproof warehouse and adjoining campanile-style chimney, a unique industrial monument in the South West.

Twine walks, West Coker

Nationally, one of the rarest industrial building types to survive intact is the purpose-built rope or twine walk, but two well-preserved examples survive in the village of West Coker, Somerset (Figs 5.26 and 5.27). Dawe's Twine Walk was built in the late 1880s close to the west end of the village. The site was previously associated with the Rendell family, one of the largest hemp and flax growers in the 18th century and a supplier of yarns to the Pymore Mill near Bridport in the 1820s.[39] Covered walks clearly illustrate the relationship between form and function in industrial buildings (Figs 5.28 and 5.29). The main building is a lightly built timber-framed structure of 30 bays, approximately 100yds (91.4m) long, in which twine spinning was located in the attic. The twine was sized

Fig 5.24 (above left)
The fashionable Italianate architecture of Parrett Works, Martock, reflected the ambitious level of investment at the site in the 1860s, which combined an integrated flax mill with an engineering works.
[BB97/06373]

Fig 5.25 (above right)
The main warehouse at Parrett Works, Martock, was entirely of fireproof construction, including brick-vaulted floors and an iron roof. The firm was one of the few public joint stock companies in the South West, but was not successful.
[DP139952]

Fig 5.26
Dawe's Twine Walk, West Coker, is a completely intact late 19th-century covered walk, along with a full complement of machinery. The open-sided ground floor was a ventilated area used for sizing the twine. [BB97/00166]

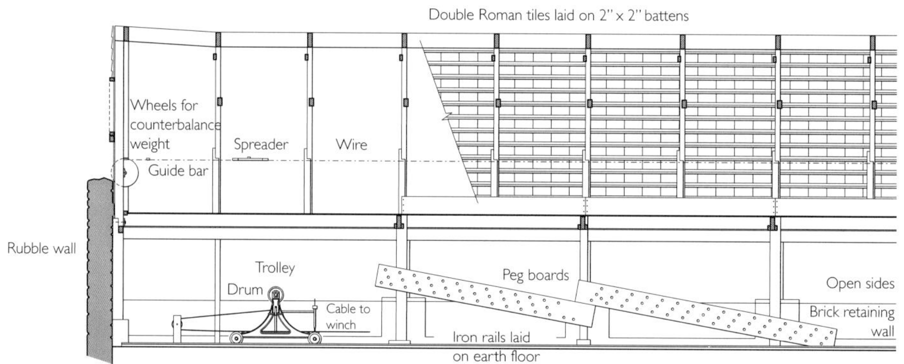

Part long section of west end of twine walk

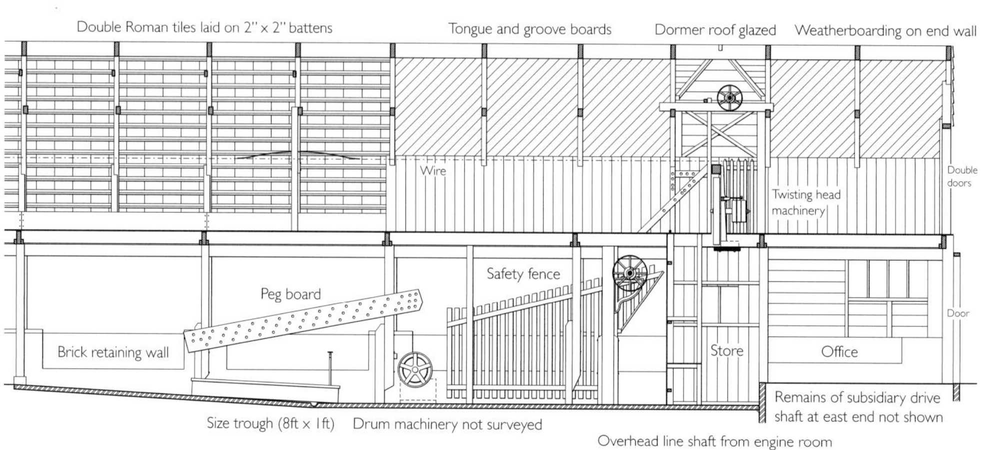

Part long section of east end of twine walk

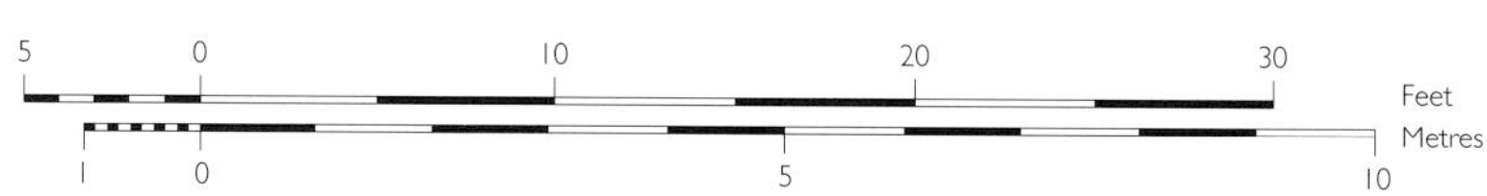

Fig 5.27
Dawe's Twine Walk is exceptionally well preserved, retaining all the machinery and fixtures used for spinning and finishing twine.

and dried in the ground floor, which was partly open sided for ventilation. The ground floor was also used for making heavier ropes. Unusually, the works remained in use until 1968 and was then used for storage, preserving almost all of the equipment and machinery *in situ*. Closer to the centre of the village is another brick-built late 19th-century walk of similar proportions, which was formerly used by the twine maker Job Gould (Fig 5.30).

The horsehair industry in Castle Cary

A notable example of the diversification of the flax industry, and the development of a related specialised industry, was the weaving of horsehair cloth, which became concentrated in the Castle Cary area of Somerset in the 19th century. These hard-wearing fabrics, typically used for high-quality furniture covering, used horsehair for the weft with a warp that was traditionally of flax, and latterly of cotton.

Ansford Factory and Higher Flax Mills

The local horsehair industry was established by Thomas Matthews in the early 19th century, and in 1851 was expanded with the building of a specialised horsehair factory on the outskirts of the town by John Boyd.[40] The Ansford Factory was originally a large three-storeyed hand-powered loomshop, one of the last to be built in the region, which enabled horsehair-cloth weaving on a larger scale than was possible by the cottage weavers (Fig 5.31). In 1871 John Boyd patented a new type of power loom for weaving horsehair, adding a north-light weaving shed and steam power plant to the factory. This innovative updating of a relatively specialised industry was highly successful, enabling the firm to weather the

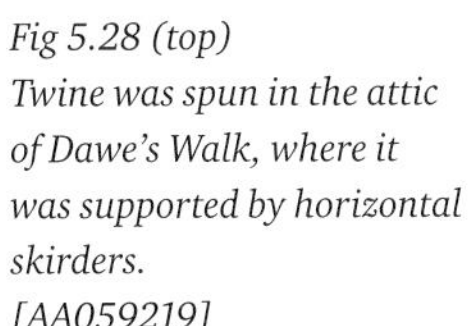

Fig 5.28 (top)
Twine was spun in the attic of Dawe's Walk, where it was supported by horizontal skirders.
[AA059219]

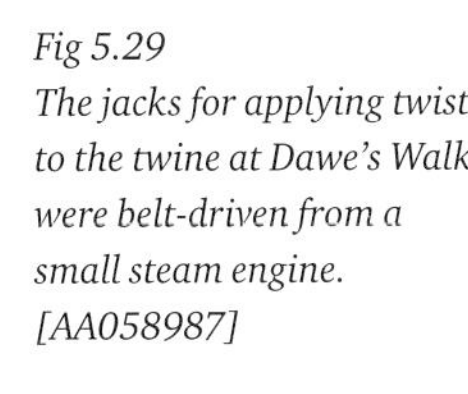

Fig 5.29
The jacks for applying twist to the twine at Dawe's Walk were belt-driven from a small steam engine.
[AA058987]

Fig 5.30 (left)
The survival of two sites with intact lightly built covered walks in West Coker is highly unusual. Gould's Twine Walk illustrates the extremely long proportions of a traditional walk.
[AP26126/011]

Fig 5.31
The three-storeyed range at John Boyd's Ansford Factory, Castle Cary, was actually built as a large loomshop for horsehair weaving using handlooms. A north-light shed was added in the 1870s to house a patented type of power loom. The business later transferred to the nearby Higher Flax Mills.
[BB015823]

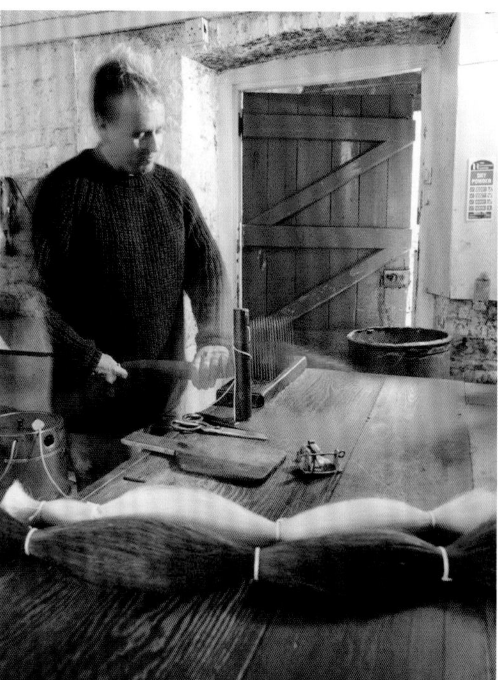

Fig 5.32 (right)
One of the original looms patented by John Boyd in 1872, still in use at Higher Flax Mills, Castle Cary. Individual horse hairs are extracted by a picker mechanism at the side of the loom, and inserted into the cotton or flax warp by a rapier in place of the normal shuttle.
[AA009445]

Fig 5.33 (far right)
John Boyd Textiles is a specialist manufacturer of high-quality horsehair fabrics using a full range of traditional processes. The imported horsehair is initially dyed and then heckled prior to weaving.
[AA009474]

decline of the larger industries by concentrating on niche products. In the late 20th century the firm relocated to Higher Flax Mills, merging with T S Donne before becoming the sole occupiers in the 1970s. The former warehouses were adapted with line shafting to drive the historic horsehair looms. John Boyd Textiles Limited still produces horsehair cloths at the site today, using the original patented looms, and is now the last known power-loom manufacturer of traditional horsehair cloths (Figs 5.32 and 5.33).

The flax and hemp industry in Crewkerne and Bridport

The two main centres of the flax and hemp industry saw a different type of development in comparison with the rural areas, their industrial districts acquiring an urban character that is quite different to the traditional vernacular architecture of the other local market towns and villages. Crewkerne was located close to a sailcloth-weaving area, and in the 19th century developed a typical mill-town architecture, comprising sailcloth and webbing factories with rows of workers' housing. Bridport saw the addition of 19th-century factories to its ancient rope and twine industry, giving the town a distinctive range of open walks, workshops, factory buildings and related artisans' housing that was not found in the other industrial regions.

Crewkerne had several late 18th-century flax- and hemp-processing mills, but did not see the extensive development of rope and twine walks that took place in Bridport. From the early 19th century the cottage weaving of sailcloth in the area was increasingly organised by early factory firms such as those of the

Fig 5.34
Viney Bridge Mills was the largest of Crewkerne's webbing factories. The site developed gradually, from small-scale vernacular to steam-powered factory buildings, along both sides of a narrow yard.
[DP139900]

Hayward family at Tail Mills and the Coker Sail Cloth Works, mentioned earlier. The site of the Coker works was used for sailcloth weaving by the 1840s, and the buildings extended with power-loom weaving sheds in the late 19th century.[41] Webbing production grew in importance in Crewkerne as the traditional sailcloth industry declined.

Viney Bridge Mills, Crewkerne

The largest local factory was Viney Bridge Mills, the early parts of which probably originated as part of the webbing business of Sparks and Gidley in the 1790s (Fig 5.34). Larger factory buildings were added under the ownership of Arthur Hart Webbing from the late 19th to the late 20th centuries. The site is well preserved, comprising many phases of building that illustrate the development from vernacular industry to steam-powered factory working in the 19th century, with steel-framed north-light sheds used for webbing looms added in the mid-20th century (Fig 5.35). It also included several nearby terraces of early to mid-19th-century factory-workers' housing, notably smaller than earlier artisans' cottages. One row of housing was later converted to form an extension of the factory (Fig 5.36).

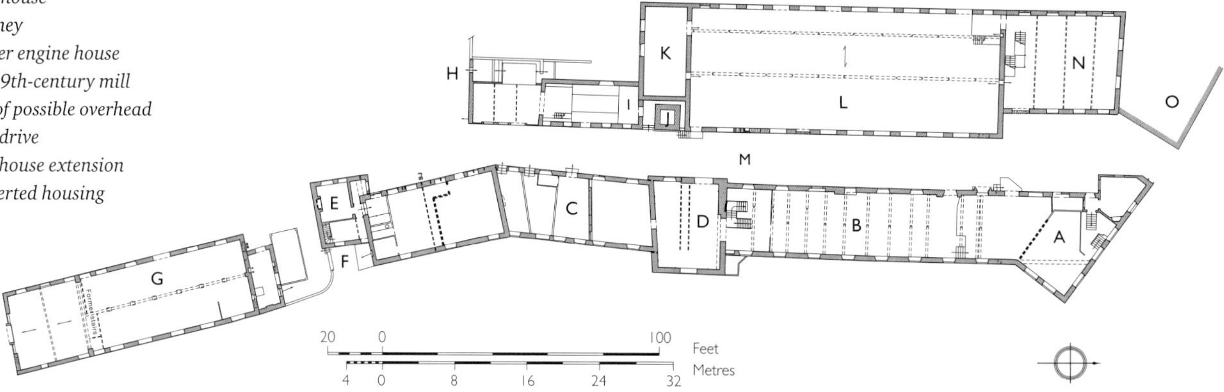

Fig 5.35
Viney Bridge Mills is a good illustration of the linear development of a succession of workshops, warehouses and powered mill buildings behind a street front.
A *Office*
B *Old mill, mid-19th century*
C *Old mill, early to mid-19th century*
D *Former engine house*
E *Cottage*
F *Site of aerial shaft*
G *East shed*
H *Site of rope race and aerial shaft*
I *Boiler house*
J *Chimney*
K *Former engine house*
L *Late 19th-century mill*
M *Site of possible overhead rope drive*
N *Warehouse extension*
O *Converted housing*

Fig 5.36
Viney Bridge Mills included workers' cottages, notably smaller than contemporary artisans' houses with domestic workshops. Those to the rear of this view were later converted into industrial buildings for the expanding factory.
[DP139897]

Bridport

In Bridport, by the 18th century, twine and rope making still took place in open walks located in and around the town, many of which were sited in the long, narrow gardens behind the cottages fronting the main streets.[42] In the older parts of the town the gardens marked the outlines of medieval burgage plots, and their continued use as walks ensured that the plots were not subdivided or built over (Fig 5.37). Burgage plots of sufficient length were ideally suited to rope and twine making, and were probably used for the same purpose before the 18th century. The open part of the walk contained rows of posts or trees to keep the twine off the ground, and awnings or small sheds were built at the ends to protect machinery and provide storage. The best-preserved examples of open walks can be found in the parallel gardens to

Fig 5.37
Many of the long, narrow gardens behind the cottages in East Street, Bridport, were formerly used as twine walks.
[SY 4692/78 NMR 18369/04 10/06/1999]

the south side of East Street, an area of late medieval burgage plots, while a group of later walks survives behind the rows of late 18th- to early 19th-century cottages on the west side of the town in West Allington. The surviving walks, workshops and adjoining twine-makers' cottages now form a highly distinctive early industrial landscape, contrasting with the workshops that were added to houses in the woollen industry areas.

The addition of factories to Bridport's traditional industry gave the town an unusual mix of industrial architecture, in which the new factories developed alongside the continued use of the buildings and open spaces associated with the older walks. This is best illustrated in the large area of former walks to the west of St Michael's Lane, which was developed from the late 18th century, with the adjoining factory sites of Priory Mills to the south and Court Mills to the north (Fig 5.38). In the early 19th century, factories were mostly built in the outskirts of the town, forming industrial suburbs that were comparable to those associated with factory building in other regions. In this case, however, the building within the industrial suburb was specific to the needs of the local industry. The factories were accompanied by the laying out of large areas of new open walks, most of which were of similar long and narrow proportions to the existing walks in the older parts of the town. The machinery at the ends of the walks

Fig 5.38
To the south-west of Bridport, a new industrial suburb was added from the late 18th century, seen here in c 1950, comprising a highly distinctive townscape of walks, workers' cottages, warehousing and a variety of ancillary buildings for making twine and netting. [Reproduced by permission of Museum of Net Manufacture, Uploders. DP000614]

was protected by small, open-sided buildings, and other adjoining buildings were used for processes such as bleaching, tarring and warehousing. In the late 19th and 20th centuries, many of these walks remained in use, some being extended while others were gradually covered with long, gabled roofs. The long history of the flax and hemp industry in Bridport has thus created one of the most distinctive industrial townscapes of the South West, in which factory building was combined with the continued use of the old methods of spinning in walks. It can be contrasted with the equally distinctive townscapes of Trowbridge, where workshops and mills were gradually added in piecemeal fashion to the clothiers' houses, and Tiverton, where the formal laying out of factory housing and community buildings was a prelude to the urban planning of the 20th century.

The housing associated with Bridport's flax and hemp industry is more varied than that of a typical factory town, including the numerous cottages of the twine and net makers, the Georgian townhouses of the merchants in the town centre and the larger detached houses of the most successful merchants and factory owners in the surrounding countryside. Several of the merchants' houses were attached to walks or workshops, and external taking-in doors indicate that warehousing was located close to the living area (Fig 5.39). The most grandiose of the 18th- and 19th-century houses, sited in their own grounds around the town, are of equivalent scale and architectural treatment to those found near the large industrial conurbations, a clear indication of the unusual wealth generated by Bridport's staple industry in the 19th century. Far more numerous are the small cottages, workshops and walks of the twine spinners that front the main streets, many of which still retain the long, narrow yards and gardens that were formerly used as walks (Fig 5.40). The varied materials and detailing of their 18th- and 19th-century elevations indicate that the cottages remained in separate ownership in the period when more uniform types of factory housing were appearing in other areas. A result of the unusual history of the flax and hemp industry in Bridport was that the industrial community did not quickly adopt the regimented way of life that was a feature of the 19th-century factory system.

The small size of many of the twine and net businesses in the 19th century also led to the construction of a variety of workshops and warehouses. Warehouses were the first buildings erected at the early factory sites, and several of the factory owners later used larger warehouses in the town or at the harbour (Figs 5.41 and 5.42). The continued use of the open walks meant that workshop extensions were added to many of the artisans' cottages, while

Fig 5.39
The main streets in the centre of Bridport contain a variety of merchants' town houses and offices associated with the flax and hemp trade, some combining domestic and industrial features, such as this example on Downe's Street. [AA045006]

Fig 5.40
Former walks and workshops are better preserved outside the town centre, such as these behind East Street, along with their adjoining artisans' houses. [DP001483]

Fig 5.41
The warehouse of the merchant and manufacturer Stephen Whetham, close to the centre of Bridport, was built as the backdrop to the gardens of his early 19th-century town house on South Street.
[DP000782]

small independent workshops were built close to the newly laid-out walks. These were typically of three storeys and three bays with central taking-in doors, of similar size to contemporary weavers' cottages in other areas (Fig 5.43).

The most conspicuous buildings dating from the expansion of the industry from the late 18th century are the mills and warehouses which still dominate parts of the town. The expansion of the factories and the open walks throughout the 19th and early 20th centuries, particularly those on the west side of the town, represented a significant extension of the built area of Bridport beyond its traditional boundaries. The more progressive flax and hemp merchants in Bridport had started to expand their businesses by constructing warehouses and workshops from around the middle of the 18th century. Successful family firms such as Gundrys, the Hounsells and Whethams all started as merchants and manufacturers, contracting out most of their production to the spinners and net makers in the town.[43] The result was that the factories encouraged the continuation of the traditional industry based in walks and workshops. Bridport manufacturers used the factory sites for warehousing, preparation and finishing processes, but continued to put out the spinning of rope and twine to the privately owned walks. The use of outworkers enabled the large firms to quickly supply a wider range of specialised products, which may have suited the demand from the ship building and fishing industries. Later in the 19th century, steam-powered machinery for net making, power-loom weaving and other processes was installed at the factories, and several firms built their own rope and twine walks at the factory

Fig 5.42
This early 19th-century warehouse on St Michael's Lane, probably converted from a pair of cottages, stands at the head of a series of open and covered walks dating from the expansion of the industry into new suburbs around the town centre.
[AA049072]

a

b

Fig 5.43a and b
A variety of workshops combined with loading doors for warehousing indicate the continued importance of the smaller twine and netting businesses in Bridport in the early 19th century, such as these examples on (a) St Michael's Lane and (b) Folly Mill Lane.
[AA045004, DP139283]

sites, but the use of outworkers for specialised types of netting and twine continued, ensuring the preservation of buildings from all stages in the development of the industry.

Court Mills, Bridport

The earliest factory building in Bridport is the front block of Court Mills, which later expanded into the largest textile mill complex in Dorset (Fig 5.44). The site is historically associated with the firm of Bridport-Gundry, a late 20th-century amalgamation of the town's main surviving textile manufacturers. The firm originated in the mid-17th century and occupied Court Mills under Joseph Gundry by the 1760s. The early building, by the site entrance, was probably built as a warehouse or workshop in the mid-18th century but is now used as offices. Several extensions were added later, two of which are dated 1838 and 1844. It was not water- or steam-powered, indicating that when it was built the firm relied on hand-powered processes and operated as a putting-out business, outsourcing much of the work. From the mid-19th century Court Mills was greatly enlarged in several more phases of building over a large area to the north. Unusually, by the end of the century the complex did not include any of the multi-storeyed mills that typified other textile-producing areas. The extensive one- and two-storeyed sheds were built for flax and hemp preparation, spinning, new types of netting machinery, for the finishing of nets and twine and for making-up drift and trawl nets (Fig 5.45). By the late 19th century the buildings were powered from a central engine and boiler house with an attached two-storeyed engineering workshop, which is now Bridport's only example of cast-iron framed fireproof construction.

Gundry's took over other firms during the 20th century, notably Bridport Industries based in the St Michael's Lane area, after which it traded as Bridport-Gundry from the 1960s. More recent changes have seen the site managed as part of a global business by Bridport Aviation in the 1990s and by AmSafe Bridport, the current occupiers, from 2002. Court Mills is still used for the manufacture of specialised aircraft cargo and military netting products today, representing an exceptionally long period of continuous manufacturing for an English textile mill.

Fig 5.44
The oldest factory site in Bridport is probably Court Mills, established by Joseph Gundry in the late 17th century. The main building at the site entrance, currently offices, was built as a late 18th- to early 19th-century warehouse, dating from the period when most of the firm's production was outsourced. [AA031007]

Fig 5.45
The rear part of Court Mills was an extensive late 19th- to early 20th-century steam-powered factory, primarily developed for machine-net making. The largest 19th-century industrial site in Dorset, it remains in production for specialist types of cargo-restraint and camouflage netting. [AP26487/012]

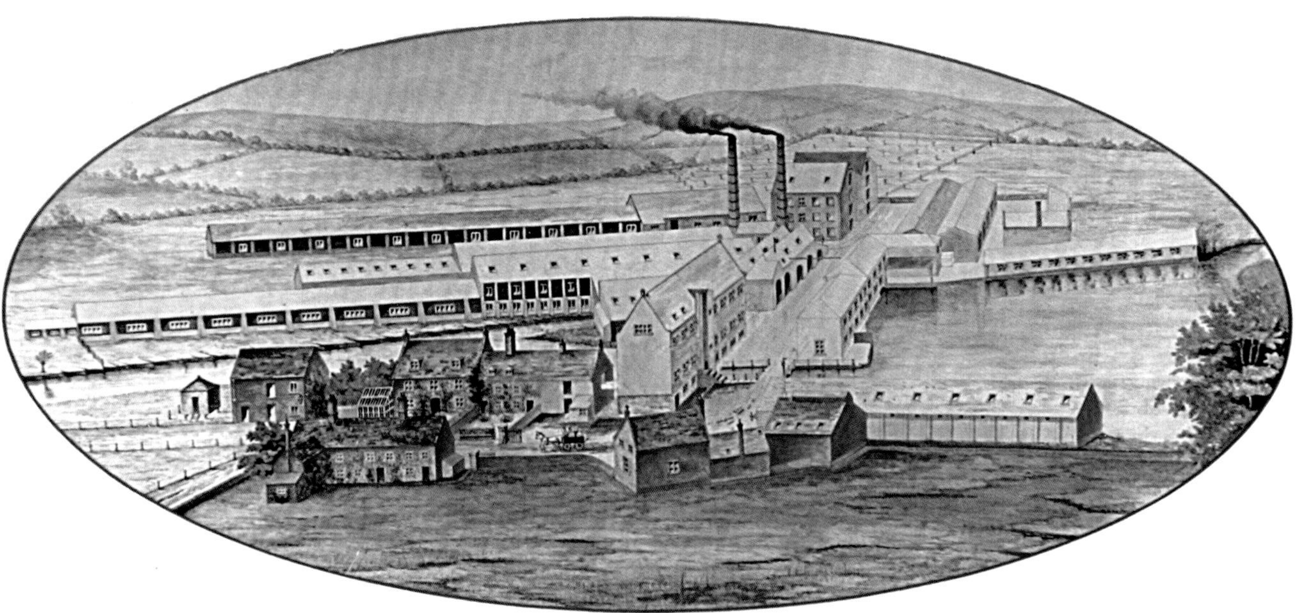

Fig. 5.46
North Mills, Bridport, originated in the early 19th century as the factory of the netting, twine and sailcloth manufacturer William Hounsell. By the early 20th century, it included a wider range of building types than Court Mills, reflecting its wide variety of products and use of both water and steam power.
[Reproduced courtesy of the Museum of Net Manufacture, Uploders. DP004871]

North Mills, Bridport

To the north of Court Mills, North Mills was established in the 1820s as a large water- and steam-powered complex, just beyond the northern edge of the town (Fig 5.46). It was used for the manufacture of twine, netting and sailcloth by William Hounsell and Company, another well-known Bridport firm which was founded in the 17th century. In the mid- to late 19th century Hounsell's developed an extensive international trade in cordage and netting products. By that time North Mills had developed into a substantial site, including several powered mills, flax warehouses, north-light sheds and covered walks. In the mid-20th century the site was absorbed into the residential suburbs of Bridport and many of its earliest buildings were demolished, including the original water-powered mill with its adjoining pond. The largest extant building is a large, well-preserved three-storeyed warehouse, built in two phases during the mid-19th century (Fig 5.47). To the north of this, the complex comprises a series of late 19th- and 20th-century sheds with an attached engine house. The surviving part of the covered walks at North Mills now forms the largest walk building in Bridport.

Fig 5.47
Imported hemp being loaded into the North Mills warehouse, c 1945.
[Reproduced courtesy of the Museum of Net Manufacture, Uploders. DP000579]

Priory Mill, Bridport

Priory Mill, marking the southern end of Bridport's western industrial suburbs, is a well-preserved integrated steam-powered factory, built in 1838, which by 1840 was the first site in the town to use power looms (Fig 5.48). In comparison with the other local factories, its architecture, power system and internal construction are all more similar to the textile mills

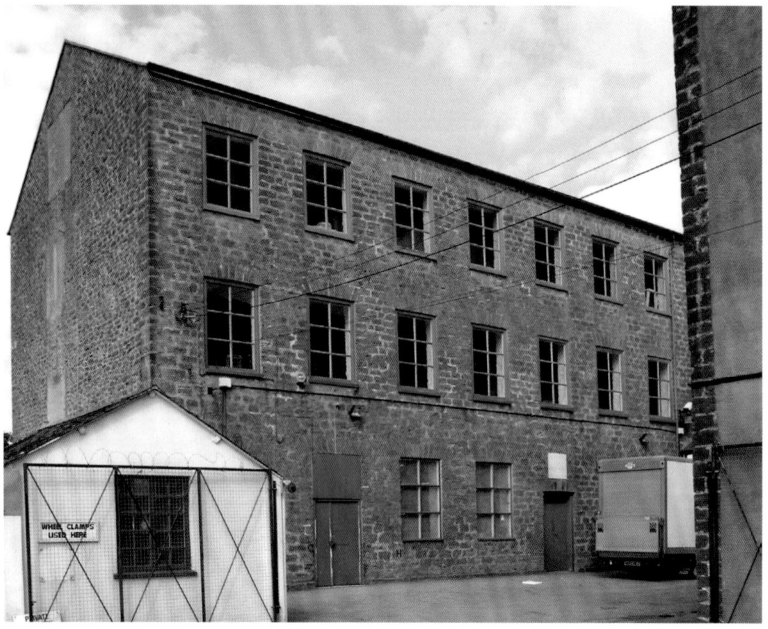

Fig 5.48
Priory Mill on St Michael's Lane was built by Stephen Whetham in the 1830s as a steam-powered factory for making sailcloth on power looms. It was the first power-loom factory in the area, its steam-power system and architecture being perhaps more typical of the towns in other regions. [DP000773]

of other regions, suggesting that the use of power looms enabled a more conventional factory design than was possible in sites built for net and twine making. It was built by Stephen Whetham and Sons, one of the most prominent 19th-century firms in Bridport. As an integrated factory, Priory Mill carried out all stages in the manufacture of twine, netting and sailcloth from raw flax and hemp.

The stone-built principal buildings comprise a three-storeyed mill of eight bays and a parallel three-storeyed ancillary building of seven bays (Fig 5.49). The mill was powered from an internal beam-engine house in the north-end bay, with steam supplied by an attached external boiler house. The floors are of heavy-timbered construction, with thick planks mounted directly on the beams, without using joists, which was intended to improve their strength and fire resistance. The ancillary building may have originally been a workshop or warehouse, but steam-powered shafting was inserted later into its ground floor. The two buildings are linked at the north end by a later north-light shed of three bays. A mid-19th-century house stands by the north boundary of the site, its position suggesting it was built to accommodate a site manager.

West Bay, Bridport's harbour

One of the main factors in the long-term success of the industry in Bridport was the development of Bridport Harbour. This was greatly improved and extended in the late 18th and early 19th centuries, including new quays, warehouses, a ship-building yard and workers' housing, and benefited from its location which allowed it to serve a large part of the flax and hemp area (Fig 5.50). The harbour gave Bridport's manufacturers a competitive advantage in the period when factory-based industries were expanding in other regions. Local firms could export directly to the North American market, and had ready access to imported hemp, flax, seed and other raw materials. The value of the harbour to the local industry declined from 1857, when the Great Western Railway was extended to Bridport. A local branch line leading directly to

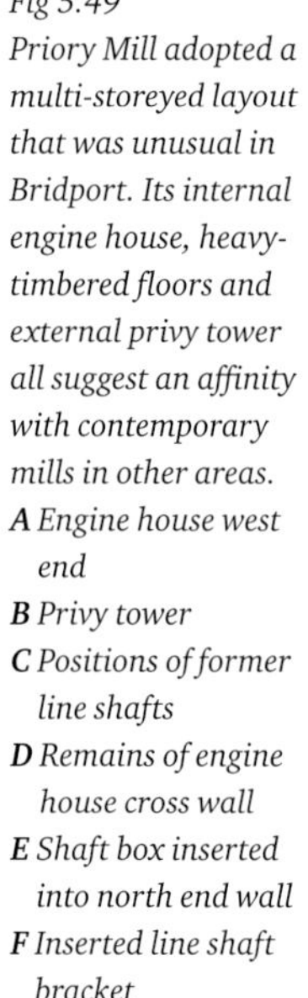

Fig 5.49
Priory Mill adopted a multi-storeyed layout that was unusual in Bridport. Its internal engine house, heavy-timbered floors and external privy tower all suggest an affinity with contemporary mills in other areas.
A *Engine house west end*
B *Privy tower*
C *Positions of former line shafts*
D *Remains of engine house cross wall*
E *Shaft box inserted into north end wall*
F *Inserted line shaft bracket*

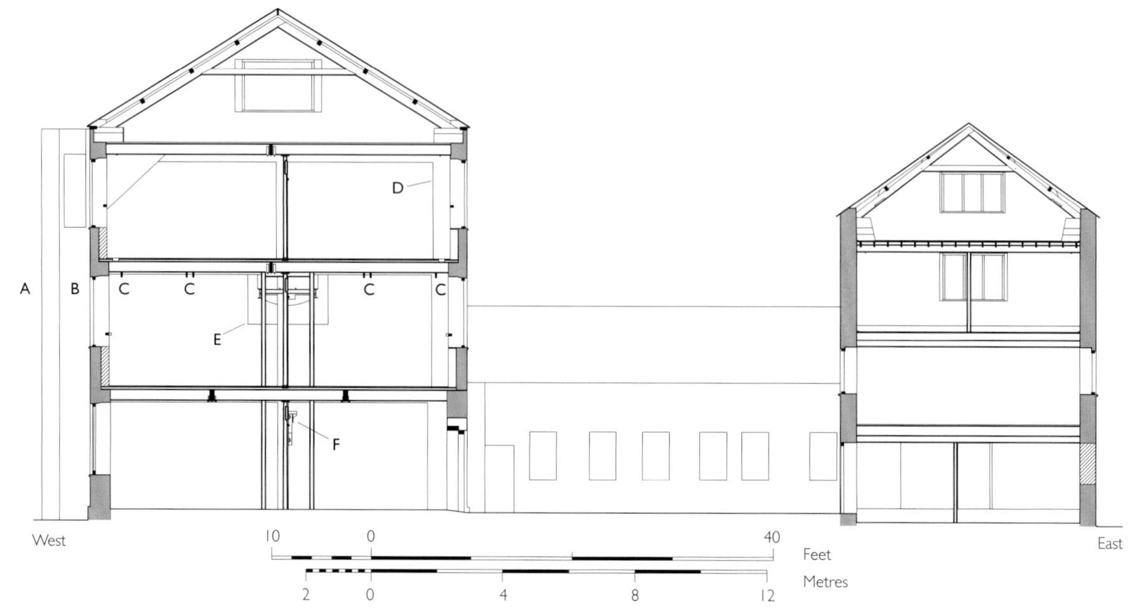

Fig 5.50
Improvements to Bridport Harbour from the late 18th century were central to the great success of the town's flax and hemp industry in the 19th century. Its relevance to the industry declined after the Great Western Railway was extended to Bridport, and in the 1880s was renamed West Bay. Late 19th-century photograph.
[Reproduced courtesy of Bridport Museum W32.]

the harbour was added in 1884, when the settlement was renamed West Bay to encourage tourism.

Conclusion: The context and significance of the flax and hemp industry

The traditions of the flax and hemp industry have been rooted in the countryside and towns of Somerset and west Dorset for an exceptionally long period, and it can be argued that this is the earliest South West textile industry to remain in its original location. Its buildings have developed to combine the area's vernacular materials and features with a different set of functional requirements to those of the region's other textile industries. The mills, warehouses and housing of the 19th century are found alongside the farm buildings, artisans' cottages, walks and workshops of a much older industry which, by the late 18th century, was too efficient to be quickly replaced by the factory system. The transition to factory working was also distinctive in comparison with other industries. The standard concept of the factory system sweeping away earlier forms of industry does not fit well into the history of this area, where the particular requirements of the specialist trades led to a different course of development.

By the 18th century, the pre-factory industry had a fully developed system of outworking, including the cultivation and preparation of flax and hemp by tenant growers, twine and rope spinning in the open walks, the extensive handloom weaving of sailcloth and the braiding of a wide range of nets in the cottages of towns and villages. The seasonal nature of flax and hemp farming, together with fluctuations in the demand for the industry's products, meant that these trades were frequently conducted on a part-time basis, often combined with other types of work by members of the same household. The varied nature of employment in the industry, contrasting strongly with the way of life in a typical factory town, was the main factor influencing the diversity of its buildings.

The history of international trade was of great importance to the prolonged success of the industry, and can be seen to have directly influenced the development of its historic buildings and landscapes. The varied use of locally grown and imported raw materials was one of the main factors in the long-term development of the industry. Favourable local conditions for growing flax and hemp, together with the proximity of the area to the coast, helped establish the early industry, but the later expansion into factory working was much more dependent on the use of imported raw materials. Local flax and hemp remained an important supplement to imports, especially when international trade was interrupted by wars, but local supplies alone could not provide the quantities of raw materials needed by the 19th-century factories. The industry's access to harbour facilities, including those at Bridport, was one of the main reasons for its later success, both by ensuring a steady supply of raw materials (including the seed used by the local growers), and by connecting manufacturers with expanding overseas markets.

6

The silk industry

Silk was a relatively late addition to the textile industries of the South West but occupied a wide geographical area, including parts of Gloucestershire, Dorset, Somerset and Wiltshire. The pioneering silk firms introduced some of the earliest examples of mechanisation to the region, the few surviving early buildings including good examples of the adaptation of traditional vernacular styles for new types of workshops and factories. As the industry spread around the region, however, most of the silk firms adapted existing buildings instead of constructing completely new sites. These included disused woollen or grist mills which were made available by the changes taking place in other industries. By re-using empty mills and employing redundant textile workers the industry became an important part of the economies of both towns and rural areas, and helped preserve industrial buildings which would otherwise have disappeared. The industry was established in some areas in the 17th century, and was widely scattered around the South West by the late 18th century, but it was strongly influenced, and to some extent controlled, by the silk trade in the major centres of London and Coventry (Fig 6.1).

Raw silk could not be produced in commercial quantities in the English climate, and

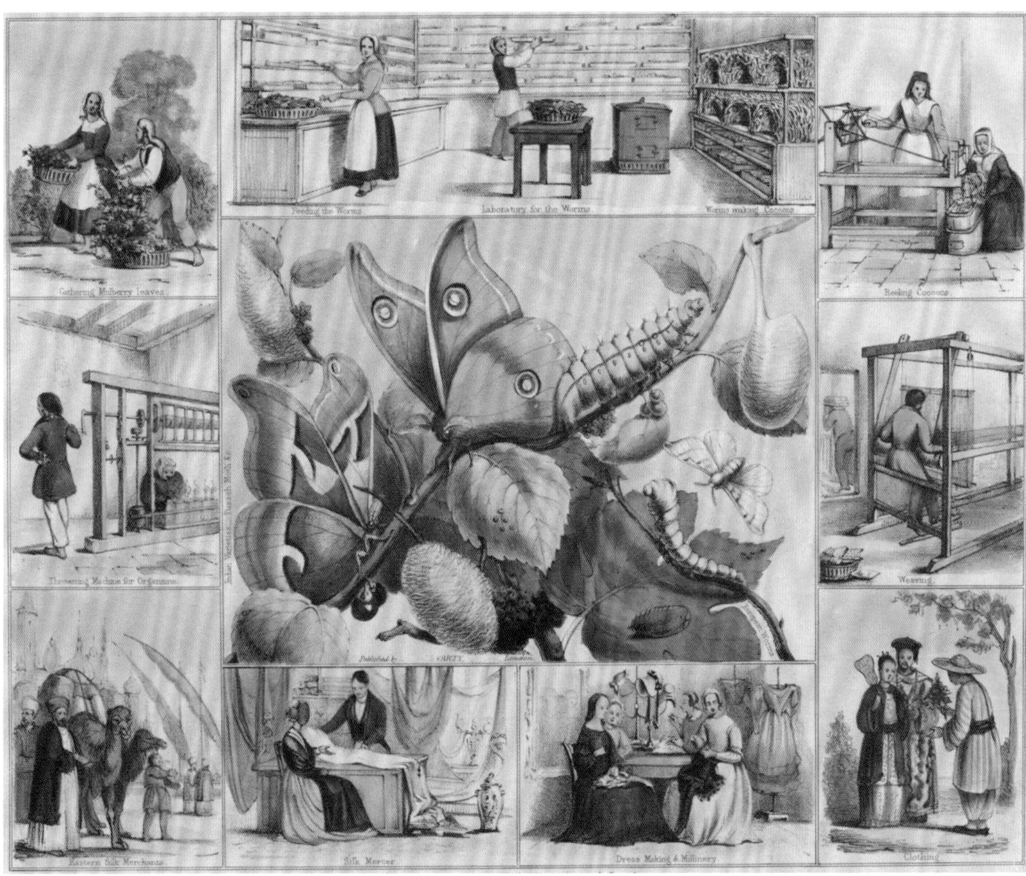

Fig 6.1
The Silk Worm, *published by Thomas Varty, drawn by W Hawkins, mid-19th century. Silk was obtained from the warmer climates of central and southern Europe, and the use of imported fibre for weaving in England did not begin until the 15th century. This lithograph illustrates the cultivation and processing of silk fibre, still an object of curiosity to the Victorian public.*
[© Victoria and Albert Museum, London]

in the medieval period most silk cloths were imported. The English silk-weaving industry, using imported fibre, originated in the 15th century but was not significant until the 17th century, when the migration of large numbers of skilled French weavers established silk weaving in London and the South East. The main centres of the industry in the 17th century were Spitalfields in London, Coventry and Norwich, each of which developed communities of specialised silk weavers. In the early to mid-18th century the successful use of Piedmontese silk-throwing machines in Derbyshire was an important step in the expansion of the industry into the regions, although silk production on a smaller scale was already established by then in parts of the South West. The further development of silk spinning, throwing and weaving was favoured by import duties and influenced by legislation between the late 18th and the early 19th centuries, which encouraged merchants and manufacturers in London to expand into other areas. In the South West, merchants established silk factories and workshops in

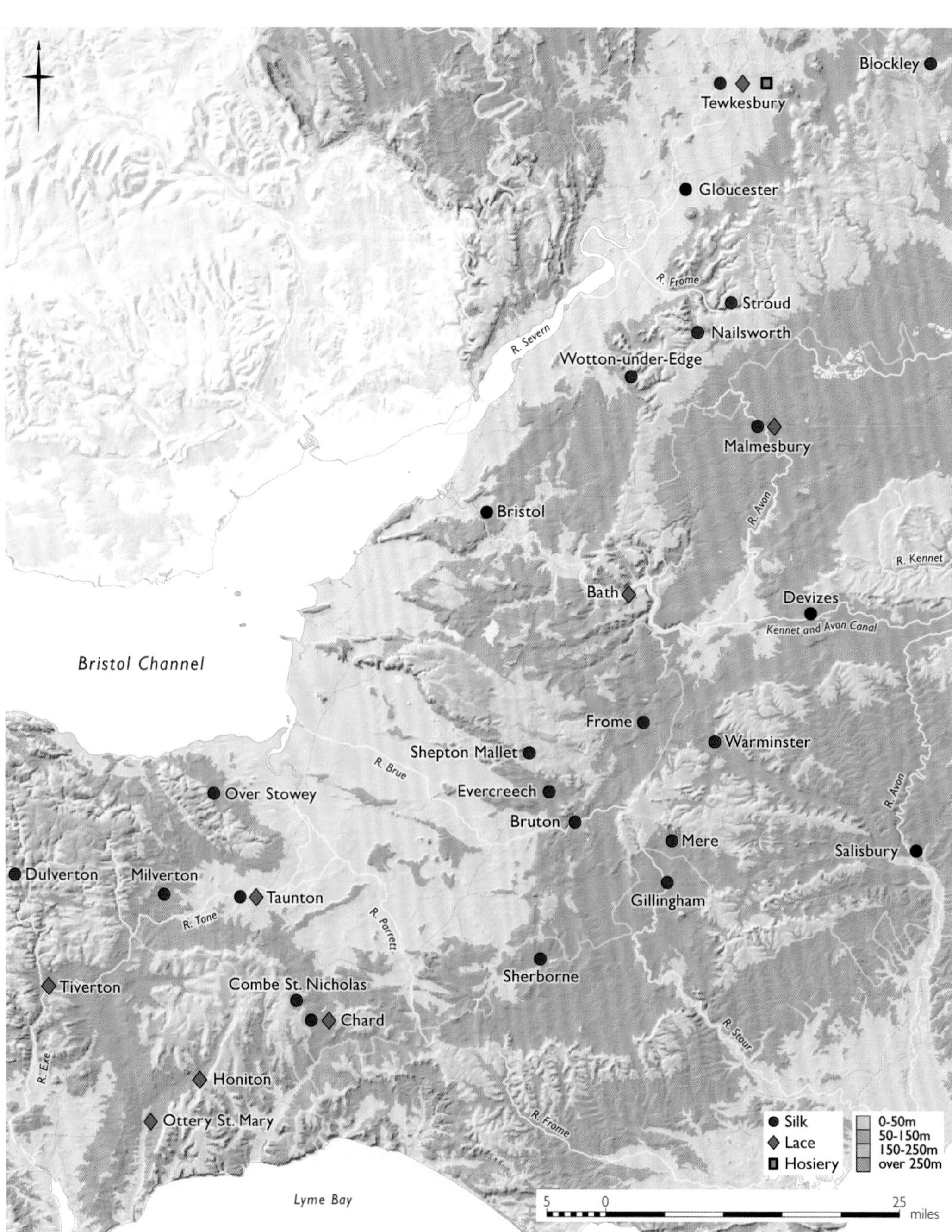

Fig 6.2
The silk, lace and hosiery industries were widely distributed across the region, often in areas where the earlier textile industries were in decline (see Chapter 7).
[90m SRTM Topography data courtesy of the CGIAR, http://srtm.csi.cgiar.org]

districts which had suffered from the decline of the traditional woollen and worsted industries. Later in the 19th century, further changes in legislation made the English silk industry far less competitive, however, after which silk production in the region saw a similar contraction to the other textile industries. Many of the mills which had been adapted for silk were then converted again for other uses.

The silk industry expanded in a period when increasing numbers of South West textile mills were empty, and mill workers and outworkers were available for re-employment. Silk production was not restricted by the same topographical factors that had influenced the location of the woollen, hemp and flax industries, and the use of redundant mills meant that silk firms could be set up in most of the earlier textile areas (Fig 6.2). Documentary evidence points to a silk industry in the Blockley area of Gloucestershire by the end of the 17th century, but the main period of expansion in the rest of the region was from the mid-18th to the early 19th century. Early silk factories were established around Sherborne, west Dorset, in the mid-18th century, expanding into adjoining rural parts of Somerset and later into the towns of Taunton, Bruton, Shepton Mallet and Frome. In the late 18th and the 19th century the industry was more widely seen in Gloucestershire, including some purpose-built mills and converted woollen mills in the Stroud Valleys,[1] and other converted silk factories in market towns such as Tewkesbury. The early to mid-19th century saw similar expansion in Wiltshire, using both converted and new buildings, for example at Malmesbury, Mere and Warminster.

Former textile mills could be readily adapted for all but the most specialised of silk processes, but a wide range of other building types were also converted for the industry, including grist mills, houses, warehouses, and in one case even a theatre.[2] The amount of conversion work needed ranged from minor alterations to provide workshop space, such as the provision of loading doors, to the addition of a power system or the complete rebuilding of a traditional grist mill.[3] Many silk processes remained hand powered until well into the 19th century, and could be located in a variety of suitable buildings, but throwing and spinning were usually located in mill buildings with an available water-power system. In most of the South West, the emphasis on the re-use of existing sites and on manual work in workshops or cottages meant that the silk industry did not significantly alter the existing landscape in the early 19th century. The small scale of the industry, and its continued use of traditional buildings, contrasted with the construction of new types of large factories by other textile industries in the same period.

Silk mills provided employment for large numbers of women and children in the 19th century, and the industry has often acquired an important place in local community history (Fig 6.3). In many cases, however, the industry employed a displaced workforce for lower wages than were common in the other textile industries. The low cost of labour, and

Fig 6.3
Silk outworkers at Darshill, near Shepton Mallett, c 1910. By the 19th century the silk industry was a significant employer in towns and villages, particularly of women and children in areas where other textile industries were in decline.
[Reproduced courtesy of Christine Marshman. DP148231]

the absence of local restrictions on the industry, were frequently cited as the main reasons for the expansion of silk throwing and weaving in the South West.[4] In the 18th century some silk firms recruited the inmates of local workhouses, while others transported children from workhouses in London to work in the South West.[5]

The silk industry was significantly influenced by events outside the region. The new types of machinery used in the factories were developed in other areas, and derived from machines used in other countries. The silk trade was also greatly affected by international politics and economics, such as the need to locate new sources of raw silk in the 18th century as a result of the wars in Europe. In 1773, legal restrictions were introduced to protect the long-established silk industry in London, but these Spitalfields Acts had the effect of encouraging the London merchants to develop their businesses at new sites in the regions, including the South West. Between 1776 and 1825 the industry was also favoured by high duties on imported silk goods, but not on raw silk. All these changes encouraged the development of a new, factory-based silk industry outside London from the mid-18th century.

Products and processes

The English silk industry was dependent on imports of raw silk – various attempts were made to cultivate silkworms from the 17th century but met with little commercial success.[6] The sources of raw silk varied, and it was imported in different periods from China, India, Italy and France. The initial processes took place at a 'filature' in the country of origin, a building where the cocoon made by the silkworm was soaked in warm water and the filament carefully reeled off to form a bundle or 'skein', which was the raw material used at a silk mill (Fig 6.4). In addition to raw silk, an important branch of the industry concerned the processing of waste silk, which was equivalent to almost 50 per cent of raw silk production in the mid-18th century. Waste silk was a valuable commodity in itself. It was obtained both from the silk farms and during the spinning of raw silk, and was delivered to the mills in the form of compressed bales. By the 19th century mills specialised in either raw or waste silk, since they required a different sequence of processes and were used for different types of cloth.

The production of thread from raw silk was a specialised form of spinning, and involved a different sequence of processes for threads that were to be used for warp or for weft. Silk spinning was complicated by the delicate nature of the filaments and required higher amounts of twist than other fibres. Until the early 18th century, the stronger warp thread, known as organzine, had to be imported, and this greatly inhibited the development of the silk industry in England. A key event in the development

Fig 6.4
Silk filament was obtained in a filature, often attached to a silk farm, by soaking and unravelling the cocoons made by the silkworms. Individual filaments could be up to 900m long. From A Diderot 1751–2 Pictorial Encyclopedia of Trade and Industry, reprinted 1959, Dover Publications, Plate 315.
[DP139051]

of the English industry was the obtaining of detailed information on the machinery used in Piedmontese throwing mills, arguably by less than fair means, by Thomas Lombe in 1717.[7] Throwing was the final stage in the spinning of organzine, in which doubled threads were twisted together to form a stronger thread that was suitable for a warp. The early water- or animal-powered throwing machines were highly distinctive, and probably not directly related to the later spinning machinery developed in other textile industries. They occupied two floors of a mill, comprising a pair of concentric cylindrical frames, typically measuring 19ft (5.9m) high and 12ft (3.66m) in diameter, with the outer cylinder fixed to the floor and the inner cylinder revolving on a vertical shaft (Fig 6.5). The wooden mechanism was arranged to produce the high rate of twist required by the delicate silk fibres. Lombe obtained English patents for the machines and installed them in a successful water-powered factory in Derby in 1721, probably the first purpose-built textile factory in England. Restrictions on the use of the machines by other firms were removed in 1732, after which water-powered throwing mills were built in other parts of the midlands, the north-west and, from the 1750s, the South West. The weaker silk thread that was used for weft, sometimes referred to as tram, was produced at an intermediate stage, before throwing, by doubling two or more threads of twisted filament.

Silk mills carried out a complex sequence of processes before the actual throwing. The skeins of raw silk were washed and dried and then taken to the winding rooms, often located in the upper floors of the mill or in separate buildings. Different types of winding frames were used to remove the knots from the silk, known as cleaning, and to wind it onto swifts, a type of collapsible wooden reel which enabled the silk to be transferred to other machines (Fig 6.6). The production of thrown silk was divided into three stages using separate groups of machines. Spinning involved twisting the raw silk at up to 80 turns per inch to produce 'singles', using spinning frames that were similar to those used in the cotton industry. The next stage was doubling, or combining two or more singles into a thread; this was the tram that could be used for weft. In the final stage, two or more tram threads were combined in the opposite direction in the throwing machines to form the stronger organzine. In waste silk

Fig 6.5
Piedmontese silk-throwing machines were used by the 15th century to spin a consistent quality of silk filament and doubled organzine thread, which required very high rates of twist in comparison with other textiles. They were arguably the first stage in the development of mechanised spinning in powered factories, but were not used in England until the early 18th century. From A Diderot 1751–2 Pictorial Encyclopedia of Trade and Industry, reprinted 1959, Dover Publications, Plate 316.
[DP139050]

Fig 6.6
A variety of winding frames were used in silk mills or workshops to unravel the skeins of raw silk, clean it and prepare it for use on spinning or throwing machines. From Rees's Manufacturing Industry, *1819–20, reprinted 1972, vol 4, 475.*
[DP139053]

spinning, sometimes referred to as spun silk, the bales of compressed silk were broken open, prepared and chopped to form a fibre with a consistent staple. This was then carded, formed into slivers and spun using spinning frames.

In the 19th century improvements to the full range of silk-processing machinery paralleled those in the other textile industries. The Piedmontese-type throwing machines were obsolete by the early 19th century and were superseded by more compact throwing frames (Fig 6.7). New machinery was of particular benefit to waste silk production, which was the dominant branch of the silk industry by the mid-19th century.[8] The complexity of the industry, and its continuing links with the London silk merchants, is illustrated by the production of Marabout silk, which was used for crepe weaving, at Milverton, Somerset, in the 1820s. The raw silk was prepared and doubled at the mill, then taken to London for dyeing, before being returned to the mill for throwing.[9]

Fig 6.7
By the 19th century new types of spinning frames had replaced the Piedmontese machines, for both raw and waste silk spinning. From Rees's Manufacturing Industry, *1819–20, reprinted 1972, vol 4, 475.*
[DP139053]

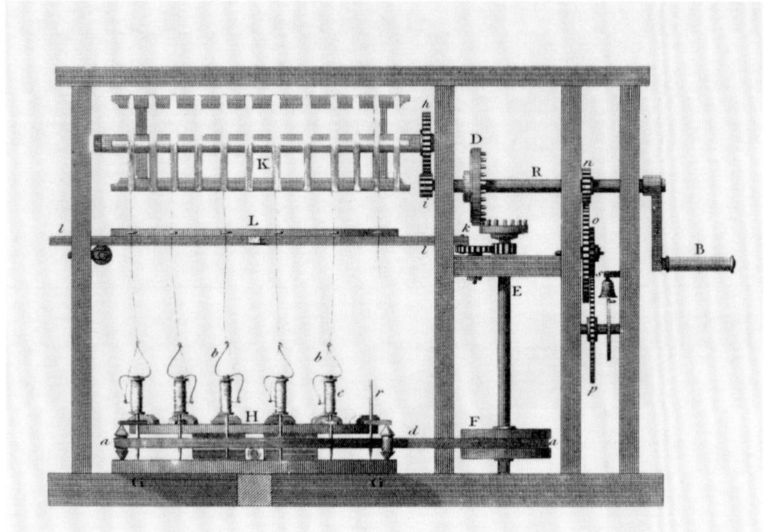

The weaving of silk ribbons and tapes using distinctive types of narrow looms in workshops was a significant branch of the English industry from the 17th century (Fig 6.8). A notable ribbon-weaving industry had developed in Coventry by the early 18th century, and probably influenced the further development of the silk industry in the Blockley area of Gloucestershire (*see* p 159). Other parts of the South West seem to have concentrated on silk throwing, to supply thread to the London weavers. Silks were prestigious, high-value fabrics woven by a specialist class of skilled handloom weavers. From the 17th century the use of the drawloom, in which groups of warp threads could be raised or lowered in a predetermined sequence, enabled the weaving of patterned or 'fancy' silks, and these continued to be produced on handlooms into the late 19th century.[10] From the early 19th century, patterned weaving was facilitated by the addition of the treadle-operated Jacquard machine, in which the sequence of raising the warp threads was controlled by a belt of pegged boards passing through a mechanism mounted on top of the loom. Power-loom weaving of silk was introduced from the 1830s, but was mainly used for plain cloths. In the mid-19th century, the weaving of crepe, normally on power looms, was a significant part of the output of several South West silk mills.

In some areas, notably Taunton, silk weaving was extensive in the late 18th century but was scarce by the 1820s. Its decline was related to the repeal of the Spitalfields Acts in 1824, which had protected the wages of the London weavers and encouraged silk merchants to employ handloom weavers in the region, where wage costs were lower. From the 1820s, however, the Spitalfields weavers were paid the same low wages as those elsewhere, removing the competitive advantage of the South West industry. Another significant factor in the early decline of silk weaving in the region was the introduction of power-loom weaving in other industries by the late 1820s. This meant that towns which were converting to power looms had many redundant handloom weavers who could be employed by the silk industry, further undercutting the silk weavers in the South West.[11]

The origins of the silk industry in the South West

The early history of the industry was strongly influenced by London-based merchants who imported the raw silk, with the manufacturing processes controlled by master throwers or weavers. The commerce of the merchants financed the industry, but the merchants themselves had little direct contact with silk manufacturing. It was the master throwers and weavers who established the industry in the South West, often in partnership with either a London merchant or one of their agents. The other early centre of the industry to influence the South West was Coventry, where the silk industry was established by the late 17th century.[12] Coventry was an important centre for silk ribbon weaving from the mid-18th to the late 19th century, providing a demand for thrown and spun silk produced in Gloucestershire and the Cotswolds. Throughout the South West, the masters set up production in locations with available buildings, a suitable workforce and good road communications with London or Coventry. The origins of the local silk industries can often be traced back to individuals who had direct connections with silk merchants based outside the region. In several cases the masters of the local silk mills, or their relatives, initially migrated from the London silk-weaving district centred on Spitalfields, and remained dependent on contract work for the London merchants thereafter. These external influences were reflected in both the histories of individual firms and in the development of some building features that had more in common with other areas than with the local vernacular.

Fig 6.8
Handloom silk weaving was a skilled and relatively prosperous industry in some areas by the 18th century, notably at Spitalfields in London and Coventry. The production of silk thread in South West mills was often connected with the merchants who financed these industries, but silk weaving in the region did not reach the scale of that in the main centres. From F. Warner, 1921, Silk Industry in the United Kingdom, *Plate XV. [DP137649]*

The silk industry in Blockley, and adjoining parts of Gloucestershire

Villages in different parts of the South West provide contrasting examples of the influence of the silk industry on the local economy and on local buildings. The earliest known example of the silk industry associated with a mill was in the Cotswold village of Blockley in the late 17th century. Together with the surrounding villages and the nearby market town of Chipping Campden, the industry in this area remained a significant employer until the mid-19th century. The 1851 census for Blockley indicates that 405 people were still employed in the industry, mostly as factory operatives, of which 84 per cent were female and 41 per cent were children under the age of 16.[13] In the 19th century, silk factories were also set up in converted woollen mills in other parts of Gloucestershire, but those in Blockley are more representative of the small scale of buildings that were associated with the silk trade in rural areas.

Situated in the valley of Blockley Brook, a tributary of the River Stour, Blockley seems to have been a preferred location for water-powered grist and fulling mills from an early date, with 12 mills listed in the area in the Domesday survey.[14] The village developed in a roughly linear pattern on the higher ground to one side of the valley, with a parallel line of mills along the stream. Its association with the

Fig 6.9
The silk industry in Blockley, Gloucestershire, originated before the introduction of Piedmontese-type machines to England in 1717. The traditional buildings of the village include several late 18th- to late 19th-century silk throwing mills. [DP137107]

Fig 6.10
Snugborough Mill, still located close to a former mill pond, illustrates the extent to which Blockley silk mills were disguised by their conversion to domestic use. [DP137198]

silk industry started in *c* 1680, possibly when the merchant and diplomat Sir James Rushout moved to the nearby Northwick Park house and estate. Rushout was descended from immigrants thought to have had connections with the London silk trade.[15] Documentary evidence suggests that the silk industry in Blockley originated shortly after Rushout moved to the area. In 1688 a former grist mill in the village, which was described as a 'spinning mill' in contemporary deeds, was leased to an Edward Whatcott, whose family were referred to as silk throwsters by 1712.[16] These are the earliest known references to a powered spinning mill of any kind in the South West, but its exact location in Blockley is not known. Other small mills in and around the village were converted to silk throwing and spinning in the 18th century, with eight separate factories in use by the early 19th century. Only one was associated with weaving, suggesting that the Blockley mills were supplying silk thread to weavers elsewhere; the Coventry silk ribbon industry had expanded enormously by the early 19th century, with a claimed 13,000 looms in use, and is likely to have been an important source of demand for the Blockley throwers.[17] The local mills declined, along with much of the South West silk industry, following the removal of duties on silk imports in the 1820s, although the largest site remained in use until the 1890s.

Most of Blockley's silk mills have been converted to residential and other uses, disguising their industrial origins but retaining many of the architectural details associated with smaller industrial buildings in the Gloucestershire Cotswolds (Figs 6.9 and 6.10). They mostly date from the mid-18th to the early 19th centuries and are attached to houses, in layouts typical of smaller grist or fulling mills. The mills themselves are smaller than contemporary woollen mills, and of similar scale and locally sourced stone to the other village buildings nearby, but are distinguished by their use of similar proportions and architectural features to the early factories. These include the regular fenestration of small flat- or segmental-headed windows, plain-gabled roofs and taking-in doors. Other physical clues to their non-domestic origins include the absence of internal walls and original chimneys, and their position adjoining a stream or culvert. Steam power does not appear to have been used in the local silk industry, although one mill was used as an early electricity generating station after it closed as a silk mill.[18] Waterwheels were external, breast or under-shot and supplied by small ponds. In some cases wheel pits appear to have been enclosed beneath later extensions of the mill. Blockley did not develop the elevated leats or other large-scale earthworks associated with water power in other parts of Gloucestershire.

Blockley Court (Westmacott's Mill)

The largest silk mill in Blockley, and the only one that is of comparable scale to other Gloucestershire textile factories, is Blockley Court, also known as Westmacott's Mill (Fig 6.11). It has been suggested that this may have been the site of the watermill of Edward Whatcott, used for spinning in the late 17th century, but the extant

Fig 6.11
Westmacott's Mill, built in the early 19th century, was the largest of the Blockley silk mills, employing 120 operatives in 1849. It remained in use as late as the 1890s.
[DP137157]

buildings mostly date from the early 19th century and later. Recent research suggests that the nearby Malvern Mill, now a house, could in fact have been the site of the 17th-century mill.[19] By the early 19th century Blockley Court was run by Martin Westmacott, and continued to be used for silk throwing throughout most of the 19th century. It comprises two parallel ranges of three- and four-storeyed factory buildings built across the stream. Both have segmental-headed windows that are wider and shallower than those seen in other early 19th-century textile factories in Gloucestershire, suggesting that the site was built to contain a high proportion of workshop space. The three-storeyed upstream range was built in two phases and appears to be of slightly earlier date; in 1990 it contained two internal waterwheel pits, one of which may have been retained from an earlier mill.[20] A three-storeyed early 19th-century house for the owner or manager is attached to the west end, an unusual arrangement by that date which may reflect the position of an earlier mill house. This was the last silk mill to remain in work in Blockley. In the 1890s it was converted for processing ramie fibre, which was grown locally.

Chipping Campden Silk Mill

Chipping Campden, three miles north of Blockley, had a smaller silk trade in the 18th century, but retains one of the best-preserved early silk industry buildings in the region.[21] Chipping Campden Silk Mill is built across the River Cam, close to the town centre, and comprises two ranges of workshops added in a complex sequence of development around parts of an earlier watermill (Fig 6.12). The workshops were probably built between the mid-18th and the early 19th centuries. The surviving parts of the earlier mill include the wheel position and one side of the wheel chamber, now used as a through passage, indicating that the silk-mill conversion was intended to contain both powered and unpowered processes. The earlier mill was initially raised to its present height of three storeys and a workshop extension added to the north, followed by a longer south extension. Most of the earlier mill was removed when the extensions were added, leaving just two bays of its east side (Fig 6.13). The most distinctive feature of the building is its well-preserved workshop windows, employing 18th-century

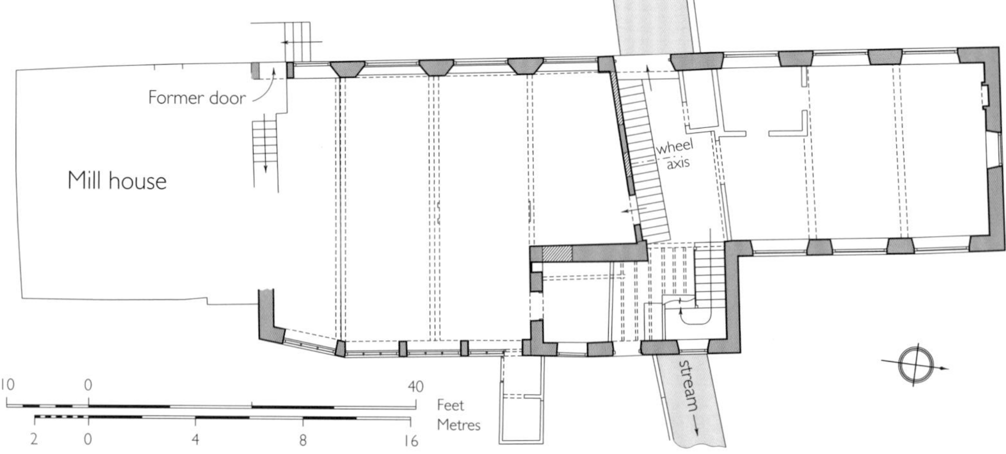

Fig 6.12
Chipping Campden Silk Mill comprises two ranges of late 18th- to early 19th-century workshops added to either side of the waterwheel chamber of an earlier mill.

Fig 6.13
The wide workshop windows of Chipping Campden Silk Mill are built in traditional materials and are clearly distinguished from those of contemporary woollen factories, suggesting more emphasis on hand-powered processes.
[DP025458]

Cotswold vernacular in a style that clearly predates the fenestration of the early factories. The wide, flat-headed form of the windows, with wooden casements, seems to be more influenced by 18th-century workshops in the north and the midlands than the woollen mills of Gloucestershire. The complicated development, with many small additions, reflects the scale of the local silk industry in the 18th century, with small businesses that did not require the construction of a large powered factory. In the 1780s the mill was used by the thrower John Franklin, who also occupied Snugborough and Conygre Mills in Blockley.[22] It was used for throwing until the mid-19th century and retained its close association with the silk industry in Blockley. In the 1850s it was owned by Lucy Russell, the widow of a silk thrower who also owned Malvern Mill in Blockley, and was occupied by another thrower from Blockley, John Long.[23]

The silk industry in Sherborne, Dorset

Sherborne was perhaps the most important of the early centres of the silk industry in the South West, pre-dating the expansion of weaving around Taunton with the construction of throwing factories that were on a larger scale than those being built in Gloucestershire and the Cotswolds. The first Sherborne site was established by a Spitalfields silk thrower in 1755 and had developed into one of the largest silk factories in the region by the 1840s. Three other local watermills had been converted for silk by the early 19th century, and even the refectory building of Sherborne Abbey was extended into a silk factory. The firms established here in the mid-18th century formed the centre of a business network which extended over a large area, constructing new factories and converting existing buildings in Dorset, Somerset and adjoining parts of Wiltshire. The connections with the London silk merchants, and the dependence on the international silk trade, were maintained up to the collapse of the industry in the late 19th century; as in other parts of the South West, the local industry declined following the repeal of the Spitalfields Acts in the 1820s and the later removal of duties on imported silk goods.

Westbury Silk Factory

The first Sherborne silk factory started in *c* 1755, when the London thrower John Sharrer acquired the leasehold of a grist mill and house at Westbury, just outside the town, from Lord William Digby.[24] The lease included an agreement to rebuild the old watermill for silk throwing, Sharrer investing £2,500 in new buildings and machinery.[25] From the early 1760s the factory was being managed by his nephews, George Ward and William Willmott, and it was they who expanded the business throughout the surrounding area in the late 18th century. In 1769 the firm split, after which William Willmott and his descendants ran the Westbury Factory along with other mills and workshops at Sherborne, Cerne Abbas and Stalbridge.[26] Willmott also took over the early Taunton silk factory of Vansommer and Paul in 1783 (*see* p 169). In the same period, George Ward established another successful silk business with several factories in the Bruton and Evercreech area, 12 miles north of Sherborne.

No completely intact buildings survive from Sharrer's original factory, but the early development of the site is illustrated by estate maps of the 18th and early 19th century.[27] The earlier grist mill was a long, narrow building straddling a leat, but by the early 19th century this had been replaced by a wider mill in the same position, and the leat and tailrace rebuilt to supply a wheel house attached to its north end. The water-supply system was probably altered in 1778, when William Willmott purchased a new, larger waterwheel. Smaller factory buildings were added upstream and downstream of the main mill, and the waterwheel was supplemented by a horse wheel from 1781.[28] In the 1770s the factory was already throwing a range of silks on commission for two London firms, using 'Italian' throwing machines.[29] An inventory of 1787 listed 14 throwing machines with winding engines and 43 'tram wheels', which were presumably a machine used for doubling singles into tram.[30]

Three bays of the early 19th-century factory survive, but had to be substantially repaired in the 1980s, including the rebuilding of the roof, after a fire which destroyed the rest of the building (Fig 6.14). The surviving section includes distinctive wide windows, with segmental heads and cast-iron glazing bars, which suggest that this part of the building may have been used as a workshop for hand-powered

Fig 6.14
The two-storeyed part of the Westbury Factory, Sherborne, which was destroyed by fire in 1981, was built across a watercourse and probably contained powered machinery. 'Italian' throwing machines were used at this site by the 1770s. The adjoining three-storeyed building, which survives, contained workshops.
[BB65/01956]

Fig 6.15
This early 19th century steam-powered addition to the Westbury Factory was one of the few purpose-built silk factories in the South West. [DP025834]

processes. The roof was rebuilt in its former appearance, comprising a series of transverse hipped ridges instead of the plain gabled roofs that are commonly found on mill buildings. The largest extant part of the site is a major extension that was added across the road to the north of the original mill in the mid-19th century, and separately named the Westbury Silk Throwing Factory. This comprises a long two-storeyed range with a similar transverse-ridged roof to the earlier mill, and was built for steam power with an engine house at its south end (Fig 6.15).

Silk works at Sherborne Abbey

The main local rival to Willmott's factory was an unusual silk works set up in the buildings of Sherborne Abbey. Parts of the cloister and refectory ranges and the Abbey House were in use as a silk factory from the 1770s, initially occupied by the firm of Cruttwell and Stidson.[31] The nearby abbey grist mill was added to the works in the early 19th century. As was usual in the silk-throwing industry, the factory mainly employed women and children; many workers left Willmott's factory to work at the abbey site, which apparently also employed children from workhouses in London.[32] The business was in difficulties by the 1790s, but the works was sold to more successful firms and continued to be used for silk throwing until the 1870s. In the early 19th century the thrower John Gouger occupied the Abbey House and used the former refectory as a 'silk house' (probably a workshop), adding the Abbey Mill to the factory by the 1830s. New workshops were added, which

Fig 6.16 (below left)
The development of the silk industry in Sherborne included adapting parts of the abbey and its nearby mill into another silk factory. The industrial buildings were later altered or demolished in the conversion of the site into Sherborne School. [DP137205]

Fig 6.17 (below right)
Some industrial buildings were retained when the former Abbey buildings were taken over by Sherborne School in 1851. [DP137203]

must have given the site an odd mix of medieval and early industrial architecture. From the 1840s to the 1870s the site was occupied by the silk throwers Rawlings and Robinson, whose additions included a new two-storeyed factory, an engine house, washing house and drying house.[33] From 1851 the refectory and adjoining abbey buildings reverted from their industrial use to become parts of the newly founded Sherborne School, which developed alongside the continued operation of the silk factory. The remaining silk industry buildings were added to the school in 1872, and some were subsequently demolished.[34]

Sketches of 1850 show some of the refectory building shortly before it was acquired for use by the school.[35] An upper floor had been inserted into the building, but was later removed during its conversion into the school library. Parts of several early to mid-19th-century silk factory buildings remain intact at the Abbey Mills part of the school, all built in local stone with similar details to the other silk industry sites in Sherborne. These include a two-storeyed factory building added by Rawlings in 1854 in compensation for the loss of the refectory; its roof comprises multiple transverse hipped ridges, notably similar to the roofs at the Westbury factory site (Figs 6.16 and 6.17).

The silk industry in Gillingham and Mere, Wiltshire

Another early silk industry which had connections with Sherborne and the London trade developed in the Gillingham and Mere area of south Wiltshire. The Gillingham Silk Company was founded by Stephen Hannam when he took over and extended the town corn mill in 1769. The mill was extended into an L-plan, giving a factory layout but with vernacular construction; the attractive building remained in use until 1895, and was demolished in the 1980s (Fig 6.18). In the village of Mere, silk was an important local employer in the early and mid-19th century, with several mills and other buildings converted for a business started by Isaiah Maggs and subsequently run by his relatives Charles and Henry Jupe.[36] These included a large workshop on Water Street, known as

Fig 6.18
The Gillingham Silk Company occupied the town mill from the mid-18th to the late 19th century. [AA48/09639]

the Silk House, which was established by the Willmotts of Sherborne in 1814 before being acquired by Maggs in *c* 1830; the building was damaged by fire in the 1850s and later converted into a house, but its industrial origins are still discernable. The nearby Lordsmeade Mill was initially a flax mill but used by the Jupe family for the manufacture of silk bobbins in the mid-19th century.[37]

The silk industry in the Bruton area, Somerset

The division of John Sharrer's Sherborne silk business between his nephews George Ward and William Willmott led to the dispersal of the silk industry across a large area of Dorset and Somerset. George Ward started silk throwing at Bruton in 1769, initially in a factory that was already owned by John Sharrer. Bruton had been an early centre of the woollen industry, with clothiers running fulling mills from the 14th century and woollen goods exported via Bristol, but by the 18th century the production of woollen and mixed cloths was in decline.[38] By the late 18th century, John Sharrer Ward (George's son) occupied two factories in the town and had been joined by at least three other silk manufacturers as Bruton developed into the centre of a network of small factories and workshops located in many of the surrounding villages. Most of the relatively small silk industry buildings in the Bruton area have been demolished, but Evercreech retained one of the last silk loomshops to remain in use, and Gant's Mill in the adjoining parish of Pitcombe survives as one of the best-preserved silk factories in the region. The silk factories themselves were usually set up in existing water-powered mills, although extensions were often added for silk machinery and one of the factories leased by J S Ward was described as newly built in 1792. Water power was used to drive the silk-throwing machines, Ward's factories containing 15,700 spindles in 1821, with most of the preparatory winding processes carried out by children in off-site workshops, or silk houses. In the early 19th century Ward's business employed about 1,000 people in the area, one-third under 18.

Gant's Mill, Pitcombe

Gant's Mill to the south of Bruton is an exceptionally well-preserved industrial site with very early origins (Fig 6.19). It may be the site of the 13th-century fulling mill of John le Gaunt, and was used as a grist and fulling mill up to the 1730s. Various clothiers leased the mill, notably William Yerdbury of Trowbridge in the early 17th century. It was rebuilt as a woollen factory in 1740, under the ownership of William, Lord Berkeley, and in 1812 was sold to a French immigrant, Theophilus Percival, a Parisian silk thrower. The extant buildings mostly date from the late 18th to early 19th centuries, when the woollen mill

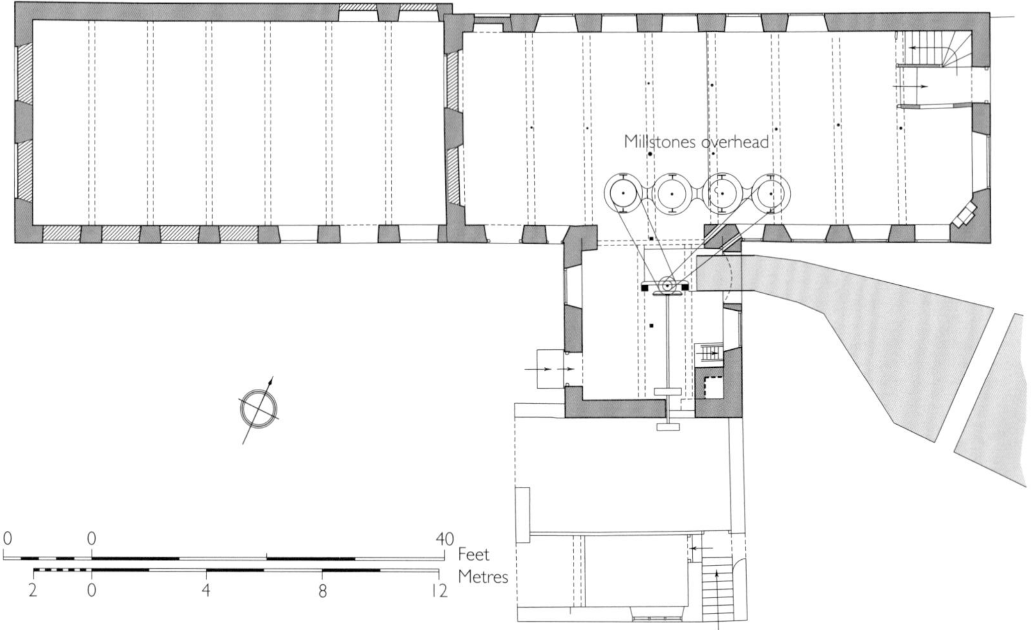

Fig 6.19 (left)
The site of an ancient fulling mill, Gant's Mill, near Bruton, retains several phases of 18th- and 19th-century buildings reflecting its use for different industries.

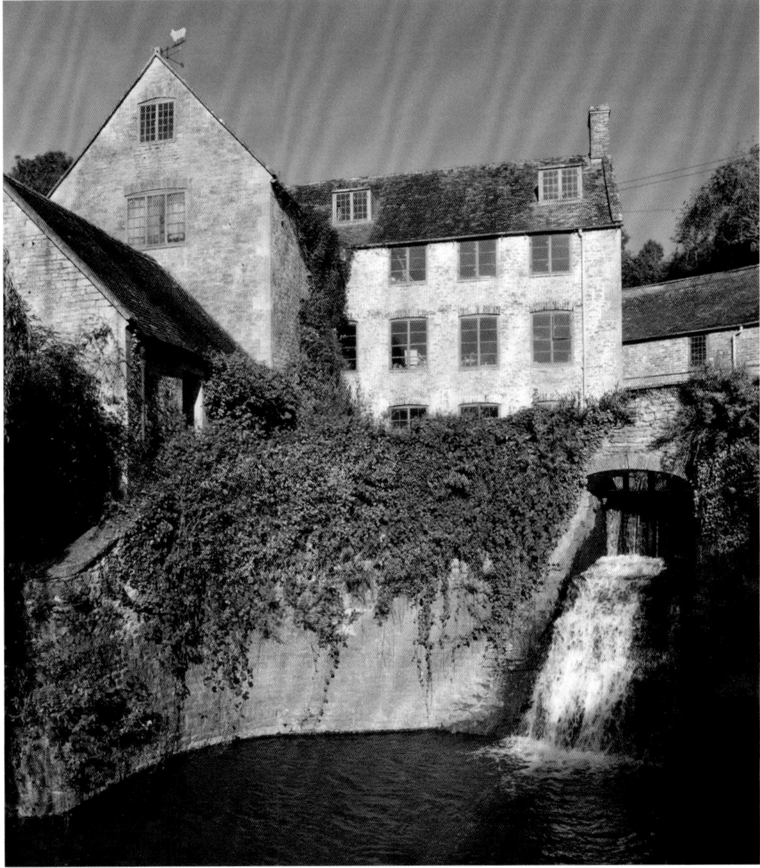

was substantially rebuilt as a water-powered throwing factory employing up to 200 workers. It prospered in the favourable trading conditions of the early 19th century, when Percival also occupied a silk mill in nearby Bruton, but was converted again for corn milling in *c* 1840 (Figs 6.20 and 6.21).[39]

The silk industry in Evercreech, Shepton Mallet and Frome

Two silk factories were started in Evercreech in the late 18th to early 19th centuries, and another added in the late 19th century. Albion Mill was formerly located on the River Milton to the south of the village. It was a four-storeyed water-powered factory in use for silk production by 1788, which was leased to the London throwster James Hoddinott in 1799. Early 19th-century improvements included a six-horse-power Boulton and Watt engine and an accommodation block, known as The Crescent, for up to 150 workers.[40] Closer to the edge of the village, J S Ward extended his Bruton business with the construction of a two-storeyed workshop, known as Ward's Silk Factory, which remained in the silk industry until the mid-19th century, employing 80 girls in 1851.[41] The building survives as an unpowered silk-winding workshop, probably dating from the early 19th century (Fig 6.22). It combines vernacular materials and construction, similar to those used in contemporary agricultural buildings, with the regular fenestration of small windows associated with the early factories. Facing it across the street is a very late example of a silk-weaving loomshop, the two sites now forming a rare group of surviving silk workshops (Fig 6.23). This was built by William Kemp in *c* 1860, a member of a prominent family of Spitalfields silk manufacturers.[42] Kemp's factory has the distinction of being one of the last sites to remain in use in the South West, being used for the weaving of high-quality silk fabrics until 1919.[43]

The Evercreech factories were also connected with the silk industry in Shepton Mallet and Frome, where the re-use of former woollen mills for silk throwing and weaving was widespread from the early 19th century. Both towns had important woollen industries in the early 18th century which had since declined, partly because of competition from the industry in the Trowbridge and Bradford-on-Avon area. In the hamlets of Darshill and Bowlish, to the west of Shepton Mallet, at least six small woollen mills sited along the valley of the River Sheppey were converted to silk by the firm of Nalder and Hardisty in the 1820s and 1830s. To the east, a larger woollen site known as Jardine's Factory was sold to a silk manufacturer in 1826.[44] Silk weaving in particular remained an important local employer in the late 19th century, when most of the town's mills were acquired by the firm of Thomas Kemp and Sons, who also operated the loomshops in Evercreech. In Frome, the decline of the woollen industry was offset by the construction

Fig 6.20 (above left)
The well-preserved interior of Gant's Mill, with floor beams supported by early cruciform-section cast-iron columns.
[DP085827]

Fig 6.21 (above)
Gant's Mill was rebuilt as a woollen mill in the mid-18th century, and extended for silk throwing in the early 19th century. The enlarged building was driven from an external waterwheel chamber supplied by a long, elevated leat.
[DP085804]

Fig 6.22
The silk industry was a significant employer, mainly of women and children, in Somerset villages in the 19th century. Ward's Factory in Evercreech was a workshop built for silk winding by the thrower J S Ward of Bruton. [DP139934]

Fig 6.23
Located opposite Ward's Factory in Evercreech, Kemp's Factory was a late 19th-century loomshop built by a London firm which also occupied silk mills in Shepton Mallet. [DP139932]

of one of the few purpose-built silk mills in the region, at Merchant's Barton. The earliest building at this large, town-centre site is a four-storeyed, steam-powered mill built in 1823 by the silk throwsters Lawrence and John Hagley, which is now one of the best-preserved early steam-powered mills in the area (Fig 6.24). Two long three-storeyed extensions were added in the late 19th century, when the site was run as a silk and crepe factory by William Thompson, originally from Spitalfields, London, in a firm known as Thompson and Le Gros.[45]

The silk industry in the Taunton area, Somerset

The Taunton silk industry was established between the late 18th and the early 19th centuries by merchants and manufacturers who were directly connected with the silk trade in London and Sherborne. As stated earlier, the high labour costs associated with the Spitalfields silk weavers in this period encouraged London firms to relocate to areas with plentiful cheap labour and suitable buildings. In Taunton this initially led to the conversion of a wide variety of buildings for winding, throwing and handloom weaving, including houses and several water-powered mills. Taunton developed into the main hub of the industry in the area, with at least 8 factories employing 500 people in throwing and around 800 handlooms in the early 19th century.[46] From the 1820s, however, the advantage of low wage costs for weavers was removed, and weaving in Taunton declined as the local firms concentrated more on the production of silk thread. As a major local industry, the silk factories influenced the development of the town and also the re-use of

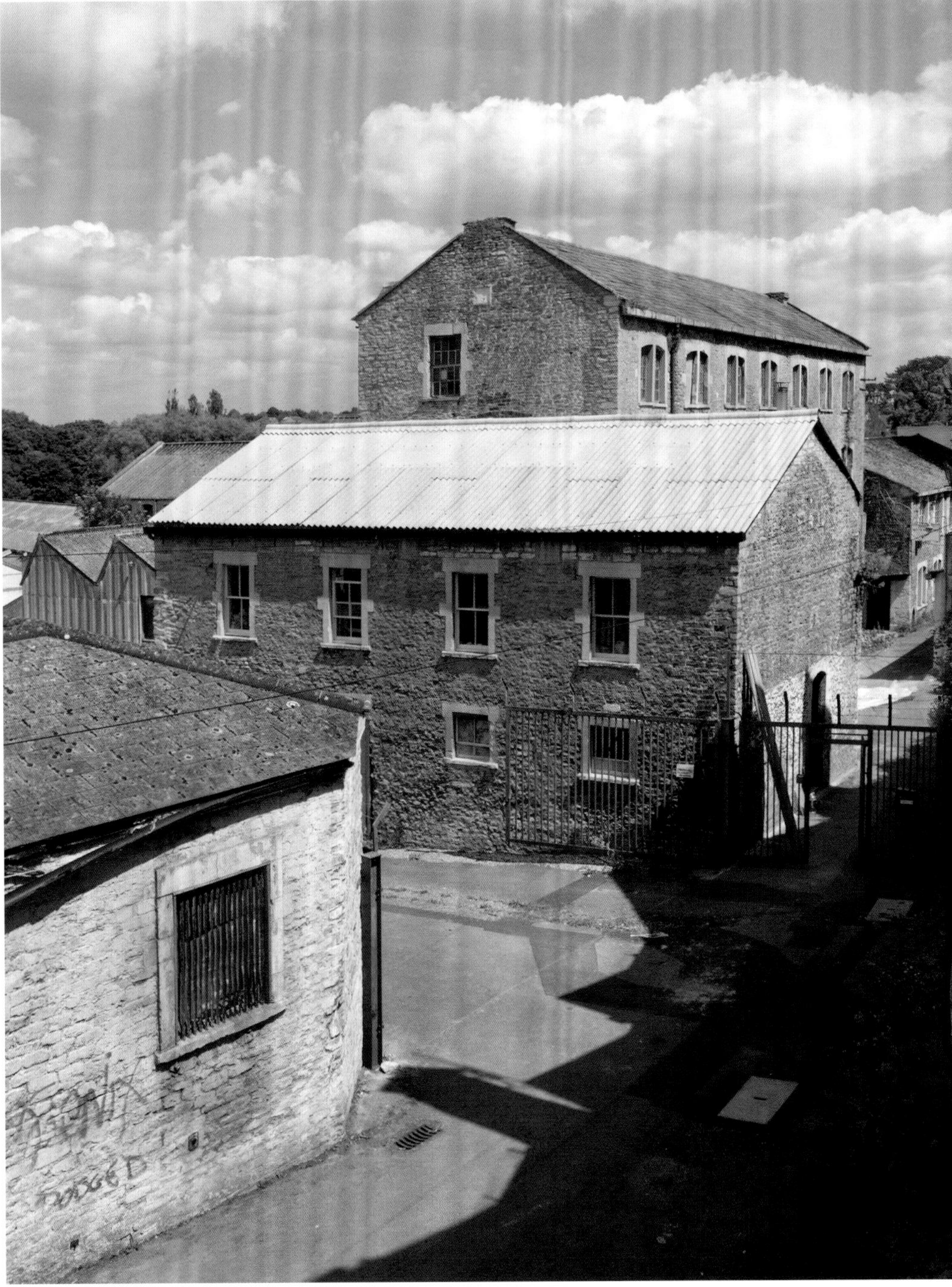

Fig 6.24
The decline of the woollen industry in Frome also provided opportunities for enterprising silk firms in the early 19th century. Merchant's Barton mill is architecturally similar to the town's woollen mills, but was built for silk throwing by John and Lawrence Hagley in 1823.
[DP139938]

buildings in the surrounding countryside. With the decline of the trade in the regions in the mid-19th century, however, the Taunton factories were extensively converted or demolished, and today only one silk mill building is known to survive in the town centre (Fig 6.25).

The first silk business in Taunton was a weaving firm established by Messrs Forbes and Wasdale in 1778, probably on the site of an early 19th-century factory on East Street.[47] In the 1830s this was the factory of the throwster John Jones, who claimed that the falling price of labour in London had undermined the silk-weaving industry in Taunton, forcing his business to concentrate on throwing. His factory had previously been used mainly for weaving, with additional weaving put out to home workers.[48] Another early silk factory was that of the London merchants Vansommer and Paul, who converted a former brewhouse

Fig 6.25
The former silk thread factory on Tancred Street is the last mill building associated with Taunton's extensive silk industry, which included several London-based firms from the late 18th century.
[DP139957]

Fig 6.26
The South Street Mill, Taunton, demolished in the late 1990s, was established by a Spitalfields silk weaver in the late 18th century, but like most of the Taunton firms it concentrated on throwing by the 1830s.
[BB98/11741]

for silk production in 1781. Their factory was not initially successful, and was taken over by the Sherborne silk thrower William Willmott and his Taunton partner John Norman in 1783. Willmott's correspondence with London silk suppliers describes how he improved the throwing machines, probably of the Piedmontese type, to be used for the production of tram using a variety of different types of silk.[49] The business also set up workshops for silk winding, referred to as 'winding houses', at Chard and Combe St Nicholas. The early Taunton factories made extensive use of hand-powered machinery, often in workshops located away from the factory site, but most also used power on a small scale for throwing. One site in the 1780s was powered by a treadwheel.[50] Several were using small steam engines from the early 19th century.

South Street Mill

One of the last surviving silk factories in Taunton was South Street Mill, run by the firm of John Balance and John Heudebourck from *c* 1813, and demolished in the late 1990s (Fig 6.26).[51] The business had been established by William Heudebourck, a Spitalfields silk weaver, in the mid-1790s. By the mid-1830s it comprised a silk-throwing factory powered by a six-horse-power engine and with a workforce of 80, three-quarters of whom were female and only 12 adults. In the 1990s the site retained early and late 19th-century wings and a rebuilt mid-19th-century engine house, but had been extensively altered during its later use as a shirt factory.

Marsh Mills, Over Stowey

Several of the London-based firms who established silk factories in the main towns of the South West soon expanded further with workshops or mills in the parishes surrounding Taunton. These included the early 19th-century extension of Marsh Mills, the site of a 17th-century fulling mill, into a water-powered silk factory by Thomas Ward and Tom Poole in 1812. The silk factory was of three storeys, comprising two wings in an L-shaped plan with an internal wheel chamber fed from a long pond via a stone-built launder. By the 1850s it had been converted again into a corn mill, and is now a house of two storeys.[52]

Dulverton Mill

The firm of Henry Smith, son of the London silk manufacturer Leny Smith, expanded the family business from Hackney to Taunton in 1795.[53] This was claimed to be one of the largest silk manufacturers in the country around the turn of the 19th century, employing 600 to 700 weavers in Taunton and a similar number at a throwing factory in Hackney.[54] Henry Smith later started a crepe factory at Dulverton, 20 miles west of Taunton, in the 1820s (Fig 6.27). Crepe was a fashionable black cloth which was made by applying a gum to the silk during the dyeing process, after weaving, causing the thread to unwind and give the cloth a distinctive crinkled texture.[55] The Dulverton factory is of only three storeys and five bays but appears to have been purpose-built for crepe production. It reflected some of the latest principles of factory design of the 1820s, combining local stone with walls of distinctive

Fig 6.27
Dulverton Mill was built by the London silk manufacturer Henry Smith to produce the fashionable crepe fabrics, probably in the late 1820s. Continuing the tradition of large workshop windows in a water-powered silk mill, it is distinguished by its use of pier-and-panel wall construction.
[DP139294]

pier-and-panel construction. The building was clearly intended to provide the maximum level of natural lighting. The narrow stone piers supporting the floor beams enabled the use of wide casement windows in the intervening wooden panels. This gave an unusually high proportion of glazing in the side elevations. The ground floor of the building was water powered from a breast-shot wheel in an external wheel house, allowing more efficient layout of machinery than in the earlier mills with internal wheels. An inventory of 1859 indicates that the ground floor contained 11 power looms, with the other crepe processes in the upper floors. The mill employed up to 70 workers, mainly women and girls, but the silk industry had left Dulverton by the 1870s.[56] By the 1890s the building was converted to its present use as a laundry.

Conclusion: The pioneering role of the silk industry in the transition to the factory system

The silk industry colonised extensive areas of the South West in the 18th and 19th centuries, providing low-paid work for communities where the traditional textile industries and other forms of rural employment were in decline. The early silk firms expanded from centres such as Sherborne, Taunton and Blockley, and were contemporary with the expansion of the industry in other regions, typically using similar machinery to that introduced by Lombe at Derby. From the mid-18th century the silk industry can be seen to have adopted the approach to organising production that was shortly to be used by the other textile industries, with powered processes in factories accompanied by the extensive use of manual processes, either in parts of the factory or in detached or domestic workshops. Most of the silk factories were set up at existing mills, although these were frequently extended or rebuilt to accommodate the new processes. The early factories and workshops introduced some functional details that were new to the architectural vocabulary of the South West, such as particular types of workshop windows and factory roofs, but by the early 19th century the emphasis was firmly on the re-use and conversion of a wide variety of existing buildings.

Throughout its history, the industry was financed from outside the region, principally by silk merchants and manufacturers in London, and was strongly influenced by developments in national politics and international trade. The external control of the industry was another prelude to the changes affecting other textile industries in the 19th century. The masters of the new factories frequently relocated to the South West, but most continued to do contract work for London firms. The local workforce was mainly female, with a large proportion of children; the employment of children in the silk industry continued after it was legally restricted in the other textile industries in the 1830s. The low cost of labour ensured that the silk trade maintained the involvement of rural communities with textiles long after other industries had disappeared, and thus enabled the survival of smaller types of industrial buildings that had been made redundant by the transition to factory working in the other textile industries.

7

The lace, hosiery and cotton industries

Some of the largest and most advanced 19th-century textile mills in the South West were built for the manufacture of lace and cotton, although the industries were much less widespread than in the midlands and the north. Lace, hosiery and cotton were historically connected, since lace and hosiery used cotton thread (in addition to other fibres), and the machinery in the lace factories developed from the framework-knitting machines used in the cottage workshops of the hosiery industry.[1] All three industries were widely distributed across the region, with little evidence of the dependence on local topography that had influenced the woollen and serge industries (*see* Fig 6.2). They saw a similar emphasis on investment from outside the region to that which had influenced the growth of the silk industry from the early 18th century. In comparison with the earlier silk mills, however, the lace and cotton factories represented a new generation of industrial architecture, and were directly comparable to the latest types of construction, power systems and machinery being introduced in other areas. They were mostly built by manufacturers who were already established elsewhere, and were either attempting to regenerate industry in the South West, in partnership with local investors, or avoiding the excessive competition and workers' unrest that was afflicting the factory system elsewhere. Throughout the 19th century, most of the lace and cotton firms in the South West maintained strong connections with the main centres of their industries in other regions. The hosiery-knitting industry was similarly connected with the extensive hosiery trade of the East Midlands, which was the national centre of the industry. It operated on a smaller scale in the South West, being locally important but without much large-scale investment in factories. It remained dependent on hand-powered framework-knitting machinery in workshops and cottages until the 1820s, as was the case in other areas.

Factory-made lace in particular made a dramatic impact on Devon and Somerset in the early 19th century, where the buildings of the industry still dominate parts of Tiverton, Chard and Barnstaple (Fig 7.1). Their construction caused the decline of a long-established hand-made lace industry and its replacement with a new style of business using the latest types of machinery and mill buildings. They were built by pioneer industrialists who migrated to the region from the East Midlands. Their factories were built in urban settings and were associated with the creation of new industrial suburbs, characterised by a regular street pattern with housing and related buildings which contrasted markedly with the older market town buildings nearby. The earliest sites were re-used woollen mills, the availability of redundant buildings and unemployed workers being an important factor in the relocation of the industry to the region.

Fig 7.1
Old Town Mill, Chard, Somerset, built 1825. Lace and cotton factories were a new style of mill building in the South West, more typical of the textile industries in other regions, and incorporated some of the latest developments in construction and machinery.
[AP26127/015]

The origins of the lace industry

Before the introduction of the factory system, a successful handmade lace industry had become established over a long period in several parts of the South West. The production of handmade lace was a specialised and skilled cottage industry, often employing women and children, with a developed system of outworking. It was usually located in areas that were also associated with other textile industries. Notable cottage industries developed in Malmesbury in north Wiltshire,[2] in Bath, and in Yeovil and Taunton in Somerset,[3] but by the 17th century the best-known area for the production of hand lace was centred on Honiton in east Devon. By 1698 over 4,600 lacemakers were located in villages across east Devon, including over 1,300 in Honiton, 800 in Ottery St Mary and 350 in Colyton.[4] Honiton lace was a valuable product that continued to be an important source of employment during the decline of the woollen and serge industries in the second half of the 18th century (Fig 7.2). In contrast to other South West textile industries, however, there was no gradual transformation from traditional hand processes to the later factory system. High-quality, handmade lace was not suited to conversion into factory working and did not result in the construction of distinctive types of buildings, thereby complementing other aspects of the rural economy rather than dominating it. The machine-made lace of the factories was initially limited to plain netting, and was aimed at a different market, but the vastly increased output of the factories was to

Fig 7.2
The production of ornate handmade lace was a well-established industry in some areas by the 18th century. Although the cottage workers made a completely different product to the factories, the cheaper machine-made lace eventually caused the downfall of this highly skilled traditional industry. Engraving dated 1804.
[© Bodleian Library. John Johnson collection.]

Fig 7.3
Traditional Honiton lace in a christening robe of c 1870, part of the collection of the Allhallows Museum, Honiton.
[DP139924]

have a dramatic impact on the traditional production of handmade lace.

The traditional industry seems to have been organised along comparable lines to the woollen industry, with so-called 'manufacturers' having a similar role to the clothiers, putting out the various stages of production to specialist cottage workers. Handmade lace was known as pillow lace, bone lace or bobbin lace, referring to the technique of winding the thread onto slender bobbins, often made of bone, and of working it around pins on a lacemaker's pillow to construct the desired pattern. Lace thread was spun using a range of fibres, including silk, wool and cotton. The lacemakers used it to make a wide variety of ornamental motifs, which were then stitched together to form the finished articles (Fig 7.3). The manufacturers sold the finished goods to dealers, who were known as lace men in east Devon.[5] This system of outworking, in which specialist trades were independent of each other but entirely controlled by the manufacturers, was well developed by the end of the 18th century, but few if any of the traditional firms were directly involved with the transition to factory working. The value of handmade lace fell dramatically in the early 19th century, and the traditional industry experienced a slow decline while nearby factories produced the new types of lace in vast quantities.

The manufacture of machine-made lace in factories effectively began in the South West in 1816, with the transfer of the lace business of John Heathcoat from Loughborough in the East Midlands to Tiverton. As mentioned, the factories did not produce the same type of highly decorated lace as the cottage industry, but their vast output and low prices changed the demand for the whole range of lace products, and the traditional industry declined thereafter (Fig 7.4). Heathcoat's firm initially occupied a disused textile mill on the outskirts of Tiverton and created an extensive settlement of industrial housing. Similar lace factories were established by other East Midlands manufacturers in Barnstaple and Chard, some by associates of John Heathcoat, creating a type of planned industrial townscape that was unusual in the South West.

John Heathcoat is widely recognised as one of the great innovators of the factory system during the classic period of the Industrial Revolution, patenting a series of complex and very effective types of lace machinery, but he was also significant for his adoption of a paternalistic concern for the good management of his workforce (Fig 7.5). Many accounts have been published of the relocation of Heathcoat's business from Loughborough to Tiverton in 1816, including the 200-mile journey on foot of about 40 of the most loyal factory workers. Several of Heathcoat's partners and associates also relocated to the South West, including around 10 other lace manufacturers, so the region's machine-lace industry originated with the migration of an entire community of pioneering industrialists, led by Heathcoat, rather than by an individual firm.[6]

The ownership and management of the new factories reflected a complex network of business relationships, with most of the key

Fig 7.4
Machine-made sheet net is still produced at Perry Street Works in Somerset using machinery based on the main principles of John Heathcoat's early 19th-century patents. These machines were made in the East Midlands, and date from the early 20th century. [Reproduced courtesy of Swisstulle UK Ltd. DP101383]

Fig 7.5
Copy of portrait of John Heathcoat by William Beetham, English School. [© National Trust Images/ John Hammond. 69958]

figures having started in the East Midlands lace industry. The various businesses were probably connected by their use of Heathcoat's patented machinery. Heathcoat's main partner, John Boden, moved into another disused woollen mill at Barnstaple in 1822 and built a second nearby lace factory in 1825 (Fig 7.6, *see* p 183). Other firms from the East Midlands were connected to factories at Chard in this period. John Boden moved back to a lace factory in Derbyshire in 1831, after which the Barnstaple site was run successfully by John Miller, another East Midlands lacemaker who had previously been a partner in one of the new factories at Chard. The personal and business connections between the two regions were maintained thereafter. In the late 19th century several South West mills transported their lace goods to be sold at Nottingham warehouses, although John Heathcoat appears to have sold most of his goods via London.[7]

The ready availability of redundant industrial buildings and a suitable workforce clearly influenced the relocation of John Heathcoat's business to the South West, but this was not the only factor. The move was also prompted by issues relating to the highly competitive nature of the lace industry in the East Midlands, where the lace and hosiery-knitting trades had been established for centuries. One reason may have been the desire to obtain the decorative motives produced by the Honiton lacemakers for stitching onto the plain machine-made net.[8] Heathcoat's machinery was complex and innovative, but in addition to his own innovations it also utilised numerous ideas from previous machines, particularly those developed for hosiery knitting. This led to ongoing legal proceedings relating to the licensing of his machinery, including dealing with over

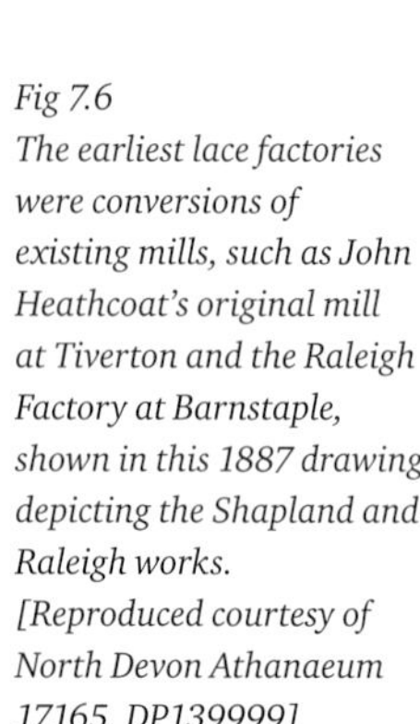

Fig 7.6
The earliest lace factories were conversions of existing mills, such as John Heathcoat's original mill at Tiverton and the Raleigh Factory at Barnstaple, shown in this 1887 drawing depicting the Shapland and Raleigh works. [Reproduced courtesy of North Devon Athanaeum 17165. DP139999]

200 patent infringements by 1819.[9] By moving to the South West, an area which had not seen the development of new types of lace machinery, Heathcoat was avoiding the difficulties encountered by the early factory system in the East Midlands lace industry.[10] His business in Loughborough was also affected by serious unrest amongst the hosiery and lace workers. The most dramatic event prior to the move was the violent destruction by Luddites of much of the firm's machinery in a Loughborough mill in 1816.[11] Heathcoat's acquisition of a recently disused woollen mill and housing at Tiverton was already underway by that time, suggesting that the well-reported machine-breaking incident was not the only reason for relocating the business, but industrial unrest in the East Midlands seems to have been an important factor in establishing the most progressive sector of the early 19th-century lace industry in the South West.

The origins of the Tewkesbury hosiery industry

Hosiery knitting was a local cottage industry in market towns across the South West by the early 18th century. In Gloucestershire, the industry became established in the Vale of Evesham and was a significant employer at Tewkesbury in particular, where it was founded by the 1640s and saw gradual expansion throughout the 18th century.[12] The Tewkesbury industry probably originated independently to that in the East Midlands,[13] but with an emphasis on hand-knitted and woven hosiery.[14] From the early 18th century, however, it was organised along similar lines with similar types of framework-knitting machinery. The local hosiery industry was noted for its extensive use of cotton and worsted, in addition to the fine wools that were used in other parts of Gloucestershire.[15] In 1779 it was stated that 650 stocking frames were in use in the town, employing 700 to 800 knitters and controlled by 15 to 20 hosiers.[16] In the early 19th century hosiery was the main local industry, with 800 frames in use by 1810 employing about a quarter of the population.[17] Framework knitting was a domestic industry organised by hosiers in a system of outworking that differed from other South West textile industries but was comparable to that used in the East Midlands. The hosiers rented the stocking frames to the knitters, sold them the raw materials and then bought back the finished goods at the current market price. Frame rents were a significant source of additional income for the hosiers, and the knitters retained a degree of independence, both of which were a disincentive to convert to factory working.[18] The Tewkesbury industry was much smaller than that of the East Midlands, but was perceived to be a significant source of competition; in the 1760s the Nottingham framework knitters petitioned Parliament because their trade was being undermined by the Tewkesbury hosiers.[19] Framework knitting expanded gradually in the first half of the 19th century, with about 930 frames and 12 hosiers in the town by 1842,[20] but declined thereafter until the trade finally ended in the first decade of the 20th century.

The connection with the main centre of the hosiery and lace trade in the East Midlands had a stronger influence on the Tewkesbury industry in the 19th century. By the middle of the century framework knitters were migrating north from Tewkesbury, but several manufacturers also moved into the town, helping to both sustain and diversify the hosiery industry. New products included net lace, thrown silk and clothing. The most notable was George Freeman of Radford, Nottinghamshire, who in partnership with his neighbour John Brown had developed the traverse-warp bobbinet machine in 1810–11.[21] The new machine was intended to circumvent the patent restrictions protecting John Heathcoat's lace-net machinery. It was patented by John Brown in 1811, but because of litigation the patent was not validated until 1816. Following Brown's death in *c* 1819, Freeman moved to Tewkesbury and built the East Street Lace Factory in 1825 to contain 37 of the machines (*see* p 196).

The cotton industry in the South West

Perhaps the most conspicuous feature of the cotton industry in the South West was its rarity. Only four purpose-built factories have been identified, contrasting with the thousands that were built in the North West and the midlands from the late 18th to the early 20th century. Bristol was the main regional centre, containing four cotton factories by *c* 1800, three of which were re-used mills.[22] The reasons for this strong regional bias are complex, but include the dominance of the established woollen and serge manufacturers in the South West, the greater use of cotton in the pre-factory fustian industries of other regions, the development of importing facilities in the ports of Liverpool and London, and possibly the more humid climate and soft water in other areas, which were beneficial to cotton spinning and finishing. The most notable site in the South West was the Great Western Cotton Factory in Bristol, a state-of-the-art integrated factory that was built in the 1830s as part of an attempt to regenerate the port of Bristol and its related industries (*see* p 198). Other examples included an early cotton factory built to use Arkwright's machines near Exeter (Fig 7.7), while in Gloucestershire the production of cotton thread by cottage workers is said to have helped establish the Tewkesbury hosiery-knitting industry. The Tiverton mill bought by John Heathcoat was also built as a cotton mill in the 1790s, but had been converted into a woollen or serge factory before it was again converted by Heathcoat into a lace factory in *c* 1817.[23]

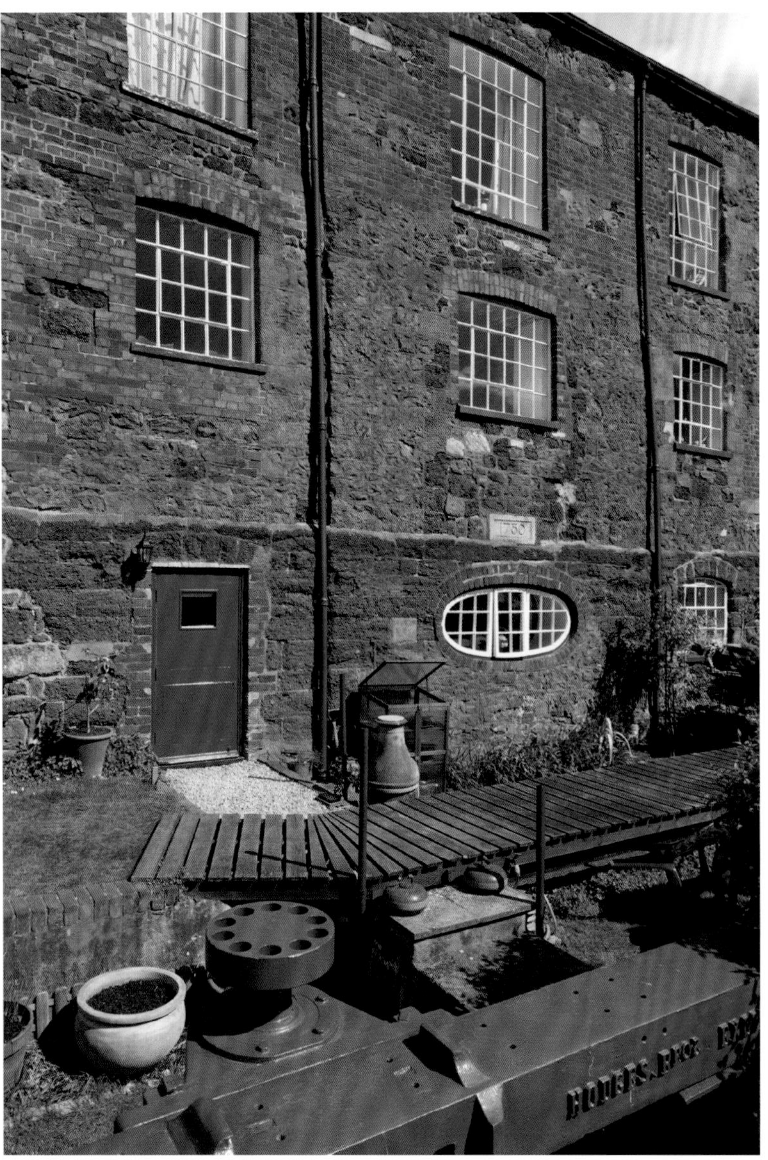

Fig 7.7
Trew's Weir Mill, near Exeter, was adapted for cotton spinning and weaving in 1793 but had closed by 1812. In contrast to the great success of the industry in the north, very few cotton mills were built in the South West.
[DP139556]

The introduction of new technology

In Devon and Somerset, handmade lace was an intricate and expensive product made from flax, silk, wool or cotton and used mainly for clothing and household goods. The demand for lace was subject to changes in fashion, but the trade had generally remained buoyant during the 17th and 18th centuries. The early inventions by John Heathcoat, notably the bobbinet machine patented in 1809, were intended to mimic handmade plain lace, known as tulle, but at much lower prices. Initially, decorative features still had to be added by hand, but the use of machinery effectively transformed the market for the whole range of lace products. Later improvements, including many by Heathcoat, enabled machines to be powered by water or steam, increased the width of the lace, enabled the machine production of patterned lace and improved the methods of preparing thread for use on lace machines. One of the main changes in the early 19th century was the increased use of cotton thread for machine lace, much of which was obtained from the cotton industry in the north. Silk and other fibres also continued to be important, however, and the new lace factories were equipped with multiple preparation departments to enable thread made from different fibres to be used on the same type of lace machines. John Heathcoat's firm eventually set up a silk factory in France and a 'filature' in Sicily, together with a cotton mill in Lancashire, to achieve better control of the production of lace thread.[24]

The invention of the bobbinet machine represented a significant step forward in the development of textile machinery, involving a much more complex sequence of operation than the spinning machines of the 18th century and receiving admiring comments from 19th-century observers (Fig 7.8). Heathcoat's improvements required a high standard of engineering and precise metal working in the manufacture of the machines. Skilled engineers had a significant competitive advantage in the early lace industry, and most of the lace factories included in-house facilities for the fabrication or maintenance of machinery. The patents of 1808 and 1809 reflected Heathcoat's earlier experience of working with framework knitting machines, which had originated in the 16th century and were being widely developed by mechanics in the East Midlands during the late 18th century. Heathcoat acknowledged that his bobbinet machine combined earlier improvements with his own new ideas.[25] The machine combined the use of vertical warp threads, wound onto revolving upper and lower beams similar to a conventional loom, with a large number of weft threads manipulated by a complex mechanism. The weft threads, of which there might be several hundred on each machine, were wound onto lightweight flat bobbins, made of brass, that were each mounted in moveable steel frames, known as carriages (Fig 7.9). Heathcoat's machine used two tiers of carriages, the lace being formed by the overlapping movements of the bobbins with the warp threads. This was not the first attempt to use multiple bobbins on net-lace machines, but Heathcoat greatly refined their design, and similar bobbins remain in use. The original bobbinet machines were said to involve 24 distinct motions to complete one mesh, but later improvements simplified their operation.[26]

The use of water and steam power enabled the South West lace factories to operate on a large scale and undoubtedly gave the industry a major competitive advantage. Heathcoat was apparently using water power from around 1816, for example, which pre-dated the widespread adoption of the power loom in the cotton industry by about 13 years.[27] The development of machinery also continued in the East Midlands, however, where around 60 lace machinery patents were in force by the 1830s.[28] Amongst the most significant were those invented in 1814 by John Leavers of Nottingham, which could be adapted to make patterned lace using a Jacquard system, and several developments of Heathcoat's machines which were later also used in the South West; these included the traverse warp machine used at Tewkesbury from the 1820s, and the roller-locker machines used at the Derby Lace Factory in Barnstaple from the 1870s. The East Midlands contained more lace manufacturers than the South West in the early 19th century, but most were smaller businesses, still based in workshops and using hand-powered machines that were not as competitive as those of John Heathcoat and his associates. From 1816 to around 1850, the South West machine-lace industry was arguably the most technically progressive in the country, although it was less extensive than the industry in the East Midlands.[29] In the second half of the century, however, the East Midlands industry also adopted new types of machinery in powered factories, and regained its former position at the forefront of developments in the lace industry. By the end of the century the South West lace manufacturers were transporting their products back to the East Midlands for sale in the Nottingham lace market.

Fig 7.8
A 19th-century bobbinet machine formerly used in John Heathcoat's Tiverton factory. Nineteenth-century observers admired the complexity of Heathcoat's patented machines, while their commercial success was envied by other manufacturers.
[Reproduced courtesy of the Trustees of the Tiverton and Mid Devon Museum. DP148469]

Fig 7.9
Heathcoat's patents greatly improved the use of light metal 'bobbins', mounted in mobile carriages, to interlace the hundreds of weft threads to the vertical warp. Similar brass bobbins are still used in the traditional net machinery at Perry Street Works.
[Reproduced courtesy of Swisstulle UK Ltd. DP101342]

Tewkesbury hosiery was mostly made from cotton, contrasting with the fine-woollen industry in other parts of Gloucestershire, although cotton was also widely used for hosiery in the East Midlands. In the 17th and 18th centuries the cotton thread was obtained locally, and it was claimed that the hosiers benefited from the Gloucestershire tradition of spinning short-staple wool, since the spinners could readily adapt to using cotton.[30] The hand- and foot-operated framework-stocking machine had been used for hosiery knitting from the late 16th century (Fig 7.10), and was probably the most sophisticated textile machine of the pre-factory era. It was first invented by William Lee in 1589, and was improved by a variety of mechanics in the 17th and 18th centuries.[31] The specialised nature of the machines may have contributed to the continued independence of the framework knitters and to the system of outworking and frame-rents that was retained by the hosiers, both of which were factors in the relatively slow adoption of factory methods. Tewkesbury knitting frames may not have included some of the later technical improvements used in other areas, but the industry nevertheless continued to employ around a quarter of the local population until the second half of the 19th century. In the 1860s competition from the expanding hosiery trade in the East Midlands, where the factory system was now being adopted on a larger scale, led to attempts to diversify the Tewkesbury industry, and to the conversion of some sites for new uses. The East Street Lace Factory (*see* p 196) was re-opened for the production of hosiery and shirts in 1860, but was only partially successful until its closure in 1870. In this period it operated as part of an outworking system with the framework knitters still based in the town.[32] The building was later used for silk throwing.[33]

Fig 7.10
The framework knitting machine originated in the 16th century and was greatly improved in the East Midlands, where it was widely used in the workshop-based hosiery trade. Manufacturers from that region established a similar industry in Tewkesbury, Gloucestershire. Early 19th-century engraving. [© Bodleian Library. John Johnson collection.]

In the cotton industry, the overall range of processes was broadly similar to that used for fine woollens, but the many technical differences at each stage of production meant that cotton developed into a largely specialised industry. Detailed accounts of the historical development of cotton processes have been published elsewhere.[34] The main differences were in the preparation and finishing stages, which excluded the scouring, drying and fulling processes of the woollen industry but involved additional processes such as the 'conditioning' of the raw fibre in damp cellars prior to spinning and various developments in cloth printing. In general, cotton was used to manufacture light mass-market cloths, often for export, with cotton mill design showing a strong emphasis on maximising output by enabling the most efficient layout of machinery. As an imported raw material, which prior to the 1860s was chiefly obtained from the slave plantations of the southern United States, cotton was subject to fluctuations in international trade, and cotton-manufacturing areas needed to have good access to the major ports. The South West was hindered in this respect; the Great Western Cotton Factory, for example, was intended to use cotton imported via the recently improved port of Bristol, but the proprietors soon found it was cheaper to use cotton brought overland from the more extensive port facilities at Liverpool. Like wool, raw cotton was grown in many varieties that were often blended and used to manufacture a vast range of textiles. In this case, however, the long-staple varieties were used for fine yarns and muslins, while shorter-staple cotton was used for a wider range of mass-market goods.

Buildings associated with the machine-lace industry

The first lace factories in the South West were conversions of existing mills built for the local textile industries, but within a decade the lace manufacturers were constructing new types of mills that were clearly influenced from outside the region. The existing sites were chosen for their suitability to be adapted for the use of powered lace machinery on a large scale, and for their proximity to an available workforce for both factory work and outworking (Fig 7.11). They were recently built water- or steam-powered mills, mostly sited close to an urban population, that were available because of the decline of the woollen and serge industries.

From the mid-1820s, the purpose-built lace factories and their associated workers' housing had a considerable impact on local townscapes, representing the introduction of mill-town architecture to Devon and Somerset. The mills of the mid-1820s embodied many of the latest aspects of factory design, reflecting the progressive approach of their owners and the new types of machinery they were built to contain. They were notably similar to the architecture, functional design and internal organisation of contemporary textile mills being built in other regions, such as cotton spinning mills. They were of fireproof construction, with cast-iron internal frames and roofs, and were designed to be fully powered using internally housed beam engines.[35] Exterior details, including the use of brick as the main building material and the design of windows and doors, were also more similar to cotton mills in other regions.

The South West lace factories initially concentrated on the production of plain net in large quantities, and fully adopted the principles of the factory system. They contained carefully arranged groups of machinery and processes to achieve an efficient flow of materials in a period when the other South West textile mills were still dependent on handlooms located off the factory site. The lace factories brought in thread from other mills, which was then prepared to give the consistent standards of weight and quality that were needed for lace manufacture; the factories carried out a similar range of processes to a late 19th-century power-loom weaving mill. One exception to the extensive use of machinery in factories, however, was the continued importance of outworking for most of the 19th century, mostly for mending defects in lace net, with some of the lace factories employing more outworkers than factory workers.

The townscapes created alongside the lace factories were a distinct form of planned urban development that differed from the more gradual development of townscapes associated with the other South West textile

Fig 7.11
John Heathcoat's Tiverton Factory was a converted serge mill, which was itself a conversion of a cotton mill. The existing factory housing formed the basis of the worker's community that Heathcoat developed close to the site. Engraving, c 1820, R Marlan & Co. [Reproduced courtesy of the Trustees of the Tiverton and Mid Devon Museum. DP148461]

industries. In Tiverton and Barnstaple, streets and housing were laid out around the town on greenfield sites that were purchased with the intention of establishing an industrial community; in Chard, development took place on sites closer to the centre of the town. The small terraced cottages in these communities were built for industrial workers who were employed away from the home, although some of the early housing bought with the existing mills may have included domestic workshop space.[36] The surviving housing mostly dates from the mid- and late 19th century and shows a clear architectural development revealing the employer's concern for the welfare of the workforce. At Tiverton, the layout of Heathcoat's housing from the mid-19th century also showed an awareness of effective urban design, including the use of a variety of open spaces to provide allotments and public gardens.

John Heathcoat's Tiverton lace factory

The mill purchased by Heathcoat had been built in 1791 as a cotton mill, probably water powered, by the wealthy Tiverton merchants Thomas Heathfield and Nicholas Dennys.[37] Cotton production was unusual in the South West and the mill was soon transferred to new owners and converted for wool or serge; it had probably been built as a cotton mill in response to the decline of the traditional serge industry in Tiverton. The building was destroyed by fire in 1936, but the early site is illustrated in a contemporary painting (Fig 7.12). It was built in an area with a long history of water-powered mill building, with several fulling mills located along this stretch of the Exe valley. Water was supplied to the site by a leat running from a weir on the River Exe to the north of the town. The mill was of five storeys, built to a long,

Fig 7.12 (right)
This c 1790 view of the mill before it was purchased and extended by Heathcoat shows a typical large serge factory. The louvred top storey of the ancillary building suggests it may have included combing shops.
[Reproduced courtesy of the Trustees of the Tiverton and Mid Devon Museum. DP148464]

Fig 7.13 (below)
The extension of the mill into a lace factory, and the installation of powered machinery, required the addition of an efficient suspension wheel in 1824, shown here before it was dismantled in 1897.
[Reproduced courtesy of the Trustees of the Tiverton and Mid Devon Museum. DP148462]

narrow plan that was typical of the period. An earlier four-storeyed building, possibly a workshop or fulling mill, stood close to its east end. This building included a tall louvred dry loft, suggesting that it may have been associated with worsted combing for the local serge industry.

Heathcoat took over the mill in 1815 and soon began to expand the site. A full-height wing was added to the east end and in 1824 a large suspension wheel purchased from the well-known firm of Hewes and Wren in Manchester (Fig 7.13), both clear indications that the site was to be developed for powered processes on a large scale. Engineering facilities were also added from an early date. By the

Fig 7.14
The original Heathcoat factory, shown in Figure 7.11, was destroyed by fire in 1936, but both the site and the name survived as the firm developed into one of the region's major manufacturers of textile products.
[DP139749]

1830s a detached foundry, a gas works and an engineering department had been built to the north of the mill, the gasworks supplying both the factory and parts of the town. Other additions included the Heathcoat School of 1843, a pair of gatehouses flanking the site entrance and Exeleigh House, a residential villa built for John Heathcoat in *c* 1820, which was later absorbed by the expansion of the site (*see* p 191). The site remains in use for the production of a range of modern textiles, some related to the later developments of the lace industry, but few of the early industrial buildings survive. The main mill and wing were replaced by the extant concrete-framed buildings after the 1936 fire, although the site retains buildings dating from the expansion of the factory to the north of the original mill in the late 19th century (Fig 7.14).

The Barnstaple lace factories

Raleigh Mill and the Derby Lace Factory

The lace industry expanded to the north Devon coast in 1822 when John Boden, a partner of John Heathcoat, converted a woollen mill at Pilton on the northern outskirts of Barnstaple. Boden had been the manager of Heathcoat's London warehouse; his partner at Barnstaple was Thomas Heathcoat, John's brother. Raleigh Mill (also known as Rawleigh) was a substantial five-storeyed building, powered by two waterwheels, but is no longer extant (*see* Fig 7.6). John Boden left the partnership by 1825 when he built the nearby Derby Lace Factory, which survives largely intact. Housing and new streets were constructed at the same time, partly by Boden and partly by speculative developers, but was later thought to be inadequate and was replaced by the mid-20th century.[38] In 1828 Boden sold the new site to John Miller, another East Midlands manufacturer, after which it was run as a successful lace factory by the Miller family until the early 1920s. It was later acquired by Small and Tidmas, another firm with factories in the East Midlands.

The Derby Lace Factory is built to a U-shaped plan with a four-storeyed main block flanked by two-storeyed wings (Fig 7.15). The main block is of fireproof construction, with cast-iron beams, columns and roof trusses that are remarkably similar to the contemporary lace factories in Chard (*see* Figs 7.17 and 7.18). Fireproof mills of the 1820s often exhibit local variations in the design of the cast-iron components, and the presence of near-identical features in the South

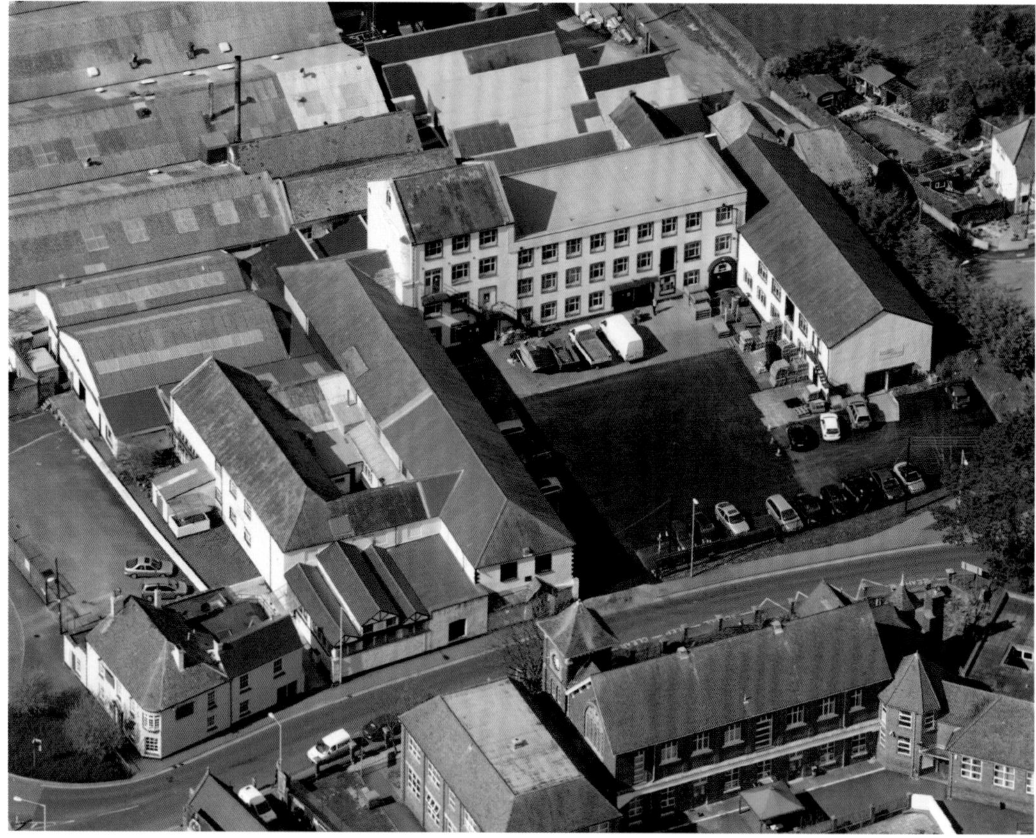

Fig 7.15
Derby Lace Factory, Barnstaple, Devon, was built in c 1825 by John Boden, one of Heathcoat's associates, after establishing his business a few years earlier at the nearby Raleigh Factory.
[AP26642/006]

West lace factories suggests that they probably obtained their ironwork from the same source, and that the factories were designed to perform similar functions. Other notable similarities include the complete reliance on steam power, the need for engineering departments in ancillary buildings and the proportions of the main production areas, which were generally nine bays long.

A detailed description of the operation of the Derby Lace Factory was made in 1889, which states that the functions of the main buildings had not significantly altered since the 1820s.[39] The mill was producing large quantities of plain lace net which was transported by rail for sale at the Nottingham lace market. Cotton thread and silk were brought to the site and prepared separately for use on the lace machines. The north wing of the mill was added in the late 19th century, and the original 16-horse-power engine replaced by one of 60 horse power, to accommodate roller-locker machines, one of the many later developments of Heathcoat's original bobbinet machines. Defects in the finished net were still repaired by hand, either in the mill's mending department or by outworkers in the cottages close to the site.

The Chard lace factories

The machine-lace industry was started in Chard by East Midlands manufacturers at about the same time as it was being established in Barnstaple. Three mills were built or rebuilt in the town in the 1820s and several others in the surrounding villages, sometimes in partnership with local property owners. The Chard firms concentrated on the production of plain lace net using powered bobbinet machines. Lace factories soon dominated the older town centre, and although the local firms did not operate on the same scale as Heathcoat at Tiverton, Chard acquired more lace factories than any other town in the South West. Forty-nine lace machines were said to be in use in Chard in 1826, increasing to 360 machines in 1862.[40] In the 1830s lace factories were the main local employers, with 'about seven' firms in the area employing 1,500 workers,[41] but by the 1870s Chard itself contained only two factories.[42] The Chard industry acquired a far less favourable reputation for the welfare of its workers than the Heathcoat factory in Tiverton. A parliamentary survey of working conditions in the 1830s made scathing remarks about some of the factories, and although a few examples of workers' housing were built, the early local manufacturers did not appear to share Heathcoat's enlightened approach to housing the workforce.[43] Some improved factory housing appeared in the 1890s, however, when the Derby-based firm of Boden and Co took over one of the mills (*see* below). Most of the Chard factories retained commercial links with the East Midlands and were also connected with other lace manufacturers in the South West, either through business partnerships or by their use of similar machinery.

Old Town Mill (later Boden's Mill)

The five-storeyed mill on the north side of Mill Street was built in *c* 1825 by the firm of Wheatley and Co, one of the most prominent lace manufacturers in Chard in the 19th century (Fig 7.16). It was built on the site of an earlier textile mill, which had been converted by Wheatley and Co *c* 1822, but was destroyed by fire in 1825. The rebuilt mill was of similar proportions, with fireproof construction and a steam-power system, to the Derby Lace Factory at Barnstaple, and comparable to the latest developments in textile mill design in other regions. The installation of machinery was supervised by John Riste, a partner in the firm with mechanical expertise in lace machinery. The mill was equipped with 72 lace machines, and by 1833 employed 500 workers and a further 200 outworkers.[44] A gasworks was added to the mill in 1837, which supplied both the factory and parts of the town.[45] Wheatley's remained at the site until the late 19th century, becoming the longest surviving lace manufacturer in Chard, and also operated premises in Nottingham.

The main block is partly built on a stone plinth which may survive from the earlier mill at the site.[46] Straight joints indicate the positions of cross-walls that segregated the internal engine house at the west end and a four-bay extension at the east end. Parts of the original boiler house remain attached to the west end, next to the engine house, along with the full-height plinth of an attached chimney. All four storeys and the attic retain evidence that they were originally powered from the engine house. Internally, the cast-iron columns, floor beams and roof trusses (Figs 7.17 and 7.18)

Fig 7.16
Old Town Mill, Chard, reflected some of the latest thinking in factory design in the mid-1820s, with a fireproof structure, internal steam-power system and external proportions that were notably similar to contemporary cotton mills. [DP148460]

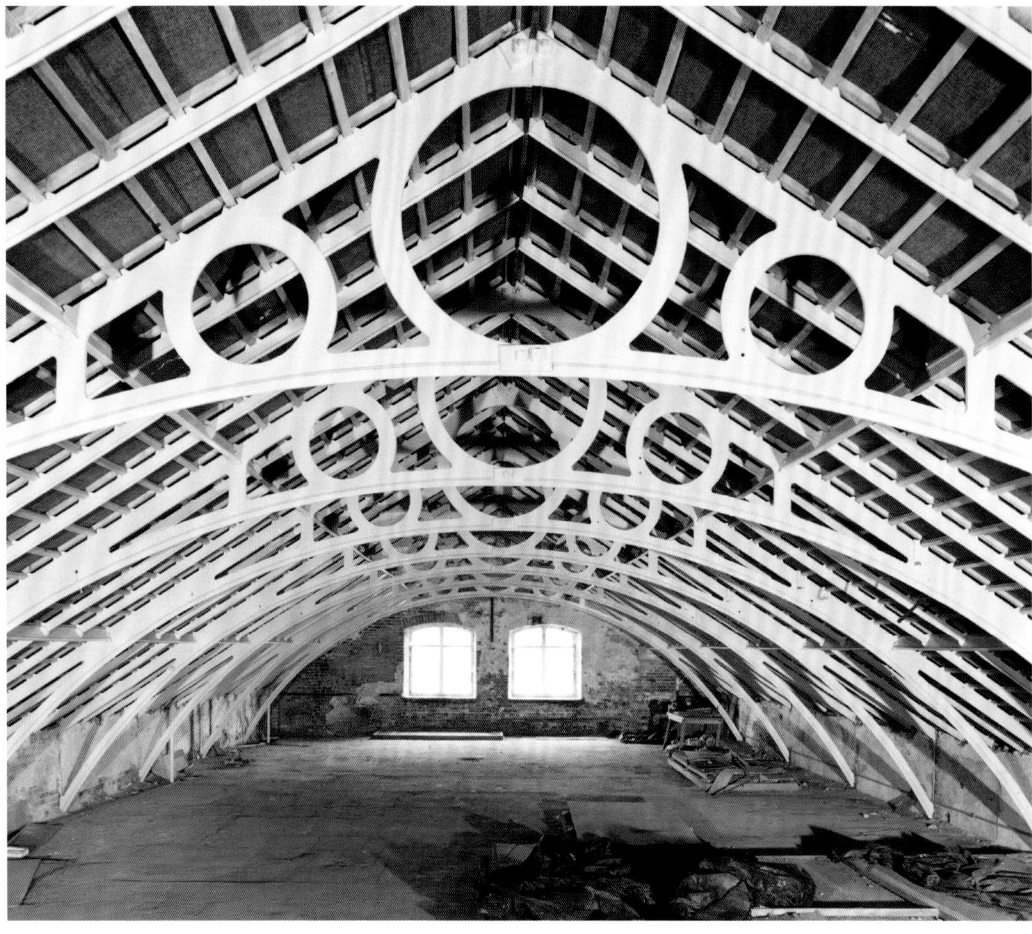

Fig 7.17
The cast-iron roof trusses of Old Town Mill, Chard, are almost identical to those at the nearby Holyrood Lace Factory and the Derby Factory in Barnstaple.
[DP100705]

Fig 7.18
The cast-iron columns and floor beams of Old Town Mill are also very similar to the other lace factories, reflecting the early connections between the three firms.
[DP100706]

are all of very similar design to the contemporary Barnstaple mill and the nearby Holyrood Mill, suggesting that all three sites may have obtained their ironwork from the same foundry. The four-bay extension was of conventional non-fireproof construction, however, with timber floors and roof trusses. The original entrance was a rusticated arched door in the north elevation, adjoining the cross-wall, which gave access to the fireproof main staircase.

Boden and Co, the firm that had earlier established the lace industry in Barnstaple under John Boden, acquired the site in 1891, and built new housing and a workers' institute, dated 1892, on nearby Boden Street. Alterations to the mill itself included an extension to the north end of the engine house, presumably to accommodate a larger engine, and the addition of a gatehouse with rusticated archways, dated 1901, to the west end of the yard (Fig 7.19).

Holyrood Mill (later the Gifford-Fox Lace Factory)

The former lace factory currently used as Chard Library and the offices of South Somerset District Council was built in *c* 1827, possibly on the site of an earlier mill, for the firm of Sparks and Company, and remained a lace factory until the 1960s.[47] By 1833 it was owned by the Holyrood Mill Company, employing about a 160 workers on site and another 300 outworkers.[48] It was partly empty in the 1840s, when the fourth

Fig 7.19
Towards the end of the 19th century the Old Town Mill, Chard, was developed further under the ownership of Boden and Co, including a grand new site entrance and an extended engine house. The firm also built a nearby institute and housing. [DP148457]

storey was the location for the first powered flight by John Stringfellow, a lace machinery maker.[49] In *c* 1854 it was bought by the lace manufacturer James Gifford, previously of Blacklands Mill outside Chard, who employed about 300 workers. Account records from the 1850s indicate that powered lace machinery was located in the lower three floors, with bobbin winding, engineering and storage in the upper floors.[50] From 1857 Gifford was in partnership with M Fox, a relative of Fox Brothers of Tonedale Mills near Wellington.

This mill is of five storeys but is otherwise of very similar functional design to the Old Town and Barnstaple lace factories, with similar cast-iron floor and roof structures and a similar steam-power system separated by a cross-wall near the north end (Fig 7.20). In this case the chimney plinth is attached to the east side and retains its cornice and the moulded base of the circular stack. Marks on the outside wall indicate the former position of the gabled external boiler house, near the base of the chimney. The site of the internal engine house, in the

Fig 7.20
The Holyrood Mill was the largest working lace factory in the Chard area until the 1960s, and still dominates the town centre. Its fireproof structure has been well preserved in a recent conversion to a library and offices by South Somerset District Council.
[DP139889]

north end bay, is indicated by blocked openings in the end wall. Unusually, the original beam engine was saved in the 1950s and exported to the United States for display in a museum.[51] The building has some architectural contrasts with the other lace factories, notably the larger, flat-headed windows and prominent finials to the gable coping. Later alterations included the addition of an external stair tower, a six-bay extension to the south end and a group of detached two-storeyed ancillary buildings to the west, some recently converted into housing.

Perry Street Works

Perry Street Works is an example of the early lace factories that were established in the countryside around Chard, and is now distinguished as one of the few sites in the English lace industry still using machinery which evolved from that invented by Heathcoat. The mill was probably built in the mid-1820s for the firm of G W Cuff, lace manufacturers. It has remained in use for lace production with a succession of owners. It was bought by J B Payne by the 1850s, who had connections with the South West flax industry,[52] and Small and Tidmas in the late 19th century, the latter with connections in the East Midlands lace industry. In 1983 the firm was taken over by the forerunners of its present owners, Swisstulle UK Limited of Nottingham.

The factory originally comprised a complex of water-powered buildings, supplied from a large reservoir adjoining the north end of the site, including a three-storeyed main block with attached offices, several ranges of single-storeyed sheds, a detached warehouse and houses for workers and the site manager (Fig 7.21). Most of the main building and sheds were demolished in *c* 1954 and replaced by new sheds which now contain the historic machinery. In comparison with the other Chard lace factories it was architecturally distinctive, being built to a long, narrow plan of 19 bays with unusual Dutch gables and wide lunette windows to the end walls. The water power was estimated at just 25 horse power in the 1840s, steam power not being added until the late 19th century. The unusual plan shape, and the relatively small size of the power system, suggests that the mill was not built with the emphasis on powered machinery seen at the other South West lace factories, and may have been only

Fig 7.21
The partly rebuilt exterior of the Perry Street Works, which contrasted with the Chard lace factories in its plan form, architecture and its relatively small water-power system. Steam power was added later. [DP101392]

Fig 7.22
At Perry Street Works specialised types of sheet lace are still made using machinery and processes which have changed little since the late 19th century. One of the key features of bobbinet lace machines is the delicate bobbins, made of thin brass and steel, which hold the weft threads. Several hundred bobbins are mounted on each machine. Specialised machinery is used to load and prepare the bobbins. The initial processes involve loading the bobbins with a precise amount of weft yarn, which is bought from external suppliers. The warp is prepared in a similar way to power looms, with the spools of yarn mounted on a creel from which they are wound onto the beams which are mounted on the bobbinet machines. [Reproduced courtesy of Swisstulle UK Ltd. DP101336]

partly powered. Another distinctive building is a two-storeyed fireproof warehouse added in the mid-19th century, of Classical proportions and details, including offices decorated with original ornate plasterwork.

The range of processes and machinery at Perry Street Works is similar to that carried out at other South West lace factories in the 19th century (Figs 7.22–7.26). It involves all the stages in the production of a range of tulle nets from natural and man-made fibre. The lace net machines are probably of early 20th-century date and of the rolling-locker type, manufactured by Newton and Pycroft of Nottingham, although some were obtained from other sites.[53] They utilise the basic principles of Heathcoat's early 19th-century machines, including the use of flat bobbins mounted in carriages and a rotating warp beam, along with numerous developments that were introduced later in the 19th century. They are electrically powered and produce lace in widths of up to 17m; spare parts are no longer manufactured, so the firm has been forced to obtain disused machines from Europe and North America. Thread is brought in from other mills and prepared by winding onto the warp beams and bobbins, involving similar processes to those described in the late 19th century.[54] Repairing imperfections in the net is a manual process, little changed since the 19th century, and carried out either in the mill's mending department or sent to homeworkers.

Fig 7.23 (right)
Trays of carriages containing several thousand brass bobbins, awaiting installation on bobbinet machines.
[Reproduced courtesy of Swisstulle UK Ltd. DP101367]

Fig 7.24 (far right)
Carriages with bobbins containing the weft yarn, installed on a bobbinet machine.
[Reproduced courtesy of Swisstulle UK Ltd. DP101376]

Fig 7.25 a (right) and b (opposite page)
Two views of the roller locker machines, a later development of the Heathcoat bobbinet machines.
[Reproduced courtesy of Swisstulle UK Ltd. DP101372, DP101369]

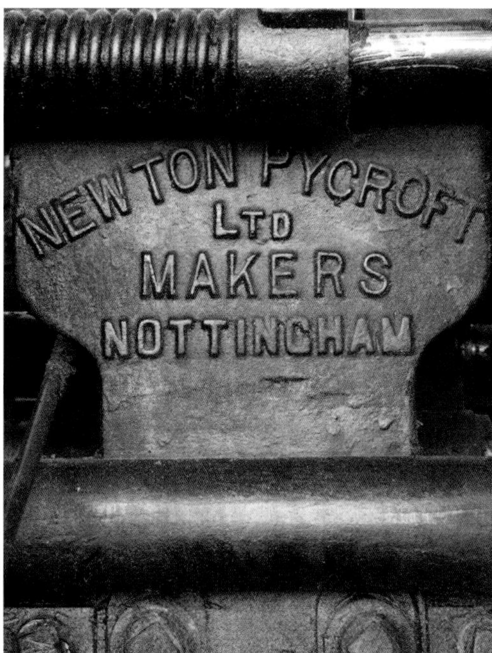

Fig 7.26
Newton and Pycroft manufactured lace and plain net machines in Nottingham from 1888 until 1973. Spare parts now have to be sourced from second-hand machines obtained from factories around the world.
[Reproduced courtesy of Swisstulle UK Ltd. DP101377]

The townscapes of the South West lace factories

The three main lace factory towns in the region all saw significant expansion as a direct result of the new industry. The lace factories were associated with rows of new housing and other community buildings, some of which formed industrial suburbs with newly laid-out streets. The housing was sometimes built by the factory owners, and in other cases by speculative developers responding to the demand from an expanding workforce. Significantly, these were not colonies of workers' housing, restricted to employees of the mill, as are often associated with 18th-century factory building elsewhere. The housing was occupied by people involved in a wide range of trades, in addition to lace factory workers, and John Heathcoat clearly stated that he wanted to encourage the development of a mixed community in his housing at Tiverton.[55] Some of the earliest houses were soon recognised to be inadequate, and from the 1830s the expansion of the Tiverton factory was matched by the provision of improved housing along with schools, an institute, chapels and parks, most of which were paid for by the factory owners or their associates. The other pioneers of the machine-lace industry in the South West adopted a somewhat less benevolent approach to their workers, however, with conditions of employment and standards of housing that were no better than those noted in other regions in the first half of the 19th century.

The lace factories at Barnstaple and Chard were associated with the construction of rows of small terraced workers' cottages. At Barnstaple, the suburb of Derby developed close to the factory from the 1820s, comprising seven streets of housing by the 1840s and acquiring a dense urban character by the late 19th century. Most were built by speculators to meet the increased demand for industrial workers' housing. Only one street, Boden's Row, was built by the mill company, and actually contained some of the smallest and most inadequate houses, with no water supply.[56] All of this first generation of industrial housing has been demolished, much of it replaced by later road building, although some terraces that were extant by the 1840s survive in nearby streets. In Chard, similar small early 19th-century cottages associated with the lace factories formerly stood on Mill Street.[57] In both towns, later improved terraced housing was built in street patterns influenced by the layout of the earlier housing, maintaining the mix of factories and residential buildings that characterised the industrial suburbs.

The housing provided for the employees of John Heathcoat in the Tiverton suburb of West Exe was much more extensive, and together with the growth of the factory it represented

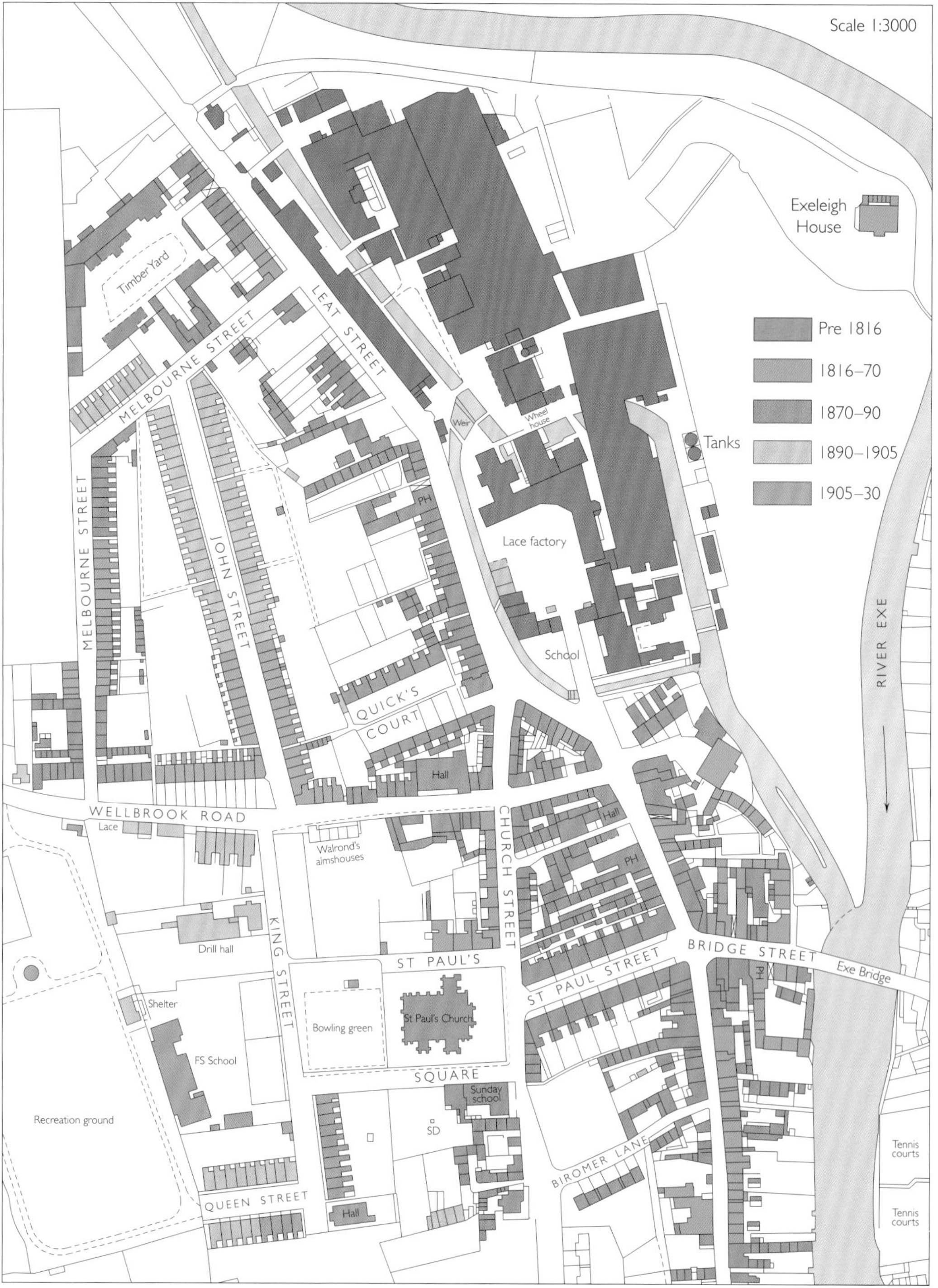

Fig 7.27
Heathcoat factory housing, Tiverton. The architecturally distinguished suburb of West Exe was created by John Heathcoat and his descendants to provide a high standard of housing for both the factory workforce and for other residents who were not employees. Heathcoat's concern for public welfare is reflected in the high quality of architectural details, the provision of a range of community buildings and the relatively spacious street layout.

a significant expansion of the town (Fig 7.27). Heathcoat can be compared with other well-known enlightened factory owners of the 19th century who adopted a paternalistic concern for the welfare of the working classes. As an employer, and later as a Member of Parliament, he repeatedly stated the benefits of encouraging the good health and general wellbeing of the workforce, including the provision of dignified housing and education.[58] The purchase of the woollen mill in 1816 had included up to 75 existing cottages, but during the following decades large plots of land were purchased to the west of the mill to increase the housing provision. By the 1840s, 1,218 workers were employed in the factory, plus hundreds of outworkers, and Heathcoat started an ongoing campaign of housing development which was continued by the firm into the 20th century. Heathcoat also bought or built several houses for his own or his family's use, notably 48–50 St Peter Street (Fig 7.28) and Exeleigh House close to the factory. In 1869 his grandson Sir John Heathcoat-Amory, of apparently grander means and ambitions, built Knightshayes Court to the north of Tiverton, a spectacular High Victorian Gothic Revival country house by the architect William Burges (Fig 7.29).

A substantial group of the houses purchased by Heathcoat in 1815 survives as Heathcoat Square, to the west of Leat Street (Fig 7.30; formerly Quick's Court). This comprises two parallel terraces of three-storeyed cottages, separated by gardens or allotments, which illustrate something of the character of industrial housing in Tiverton before the Heathcoat era. They have no architectural embellishment but may have included top-floor workshops,[59] and are notably larger than the early factory housing in Barnstaple or Chard. They were later improved with rear extensions, and were retained when most of the other early industrial

Fig 7.28
This Georgian town house on St Peter Street was one of several houses occupied by John Heathcoat in the Tiverton area, including Exeleigh House, which has now been absorbed within the factory site.
[DP139742]

Fig 7.29
Knightshayes Court was built in 1869–74 by John Heathcoat's grandson, Sir John Heathcoat-Amory, on a terrace with a vista towards the Tiverton lace factory. An exercise in High Victorian Gothic by the noted architect William Burges, the house and gardens have been managed by the National Trust since 1973.
[DP139712]

Fig 7.30
Heathcoat Square contains some of the earliest factory housing in Tiverton, which was contemporary with the worsted mill purchased by Heathcoat in 1817. The relatively large size of the houses suggests they may have originally included domestic workshops. [DP139723]

housing was demolished. In the 1840s, plans were made for the expansion of housing on the adjacent farmland, adapting existing houses where possible but adding new streets which were aligned with the old field boundaries (*see* Fig 7.27). Housing was built along these streets in phases, starting with those close to Heathcoat Square, with a succession of materials and architectural details. The whole development maintained an open character that contrasted with the generally congested nature of industrial housing of the period, including large spaces for allotments behind most of the main streets.

In addition to housing, John Heathcoat and his successors provided a range of institutional and religious buildings. The local architect G A Boyce was commissioned to design the Heathcoat School, built next to the factory

Fig 7.31
John Heathcoat's concerns for the welfare and education of his workforce came to fruition with the opening of the Heathcoat School next to the factory, designed by the local architect G A Boyce, in 1843. [DP139744]

and opened at a ceremony in 1843 (Fig 7.31).[60] Heathcoat Hall was built as a working men's institute in 1876. A workmen's hall designed by John Hayward was opened in 1877. In a related development, St Paul's Church and its associated middle-class town houses on St Paul Street (none of which were occupied by factory workers), were built by Heathcoat's daughter and son-in-law on a site to the south of the industrial housing in 1854–6 (Figs 7.32 and 7.33);

Fig 7.32
In the late 19th century John Heathcoat's descendents added new streets of middle-class housing in the area around St Paul's Church, developing the architectural style of the workers' housing closer to the factory. [DP139736]

Fig 7.33
Heathcoat's concern for public welfare was reflected in the architectural detailing used in the earlier factory housing, and this continued in the spacious layout of the later extensions to the residential area. Rounded corners and small front gardens are used to enhance the relatively open design (for the 19th century) of the later streets. [DP139719]

G A Boyce was the supervising architect.[61] These houses show a more prominent use of similar detailing and materials to the nearby factory housing, with which they were clearly intended to form a visual group.

The hosiery and lace industry in Tewkesbury

Tewkesbury is widely recognised for the fine quality of its traditional market-town architecture, but the narrow alleys between the brick and timber-framed townhouses also contain a wide variety of industrial workshops. In spite of the widespread demolition of smaller houses and industrial buildings, many of the surviving workshops date from the period when hosiery was the town's main industry, and are likely to have been used by some of its 1,500 or so workers. The scale of the framework-knitting businesses, and the continued use of domestic workshops, did not result in extensive rebuilding. In many cases, the smaller industrial buildings of the town have details suggesting a stronger connection with the industrial vernacular of the East Midlands than with other parts of the South West. The most distinctive domestic workshops are in a block of three late 18th- or early 19th-century cottages on St Mary's Lane, known locally as framework-knitters' cottages (Fig 7.34). These may have been the cottages sold by the hosier Thomas Bayless, who went bankrupt in *c* 1812.[62] The cottages appear to have been originally one room deep, later enlarged with rear extensions, but their most distinctive feature is the six-light workshop windows to the middle storeys. The wide, segmental-headed form of these windows, and the location of the workshops in the middle storeys, are both unusual in the textile workshops of Gloucestershire.

The East Street Lace Factory, built for George Freeman in 1825, is also dissimilar to other contemporary factories in the area in its functional design and architectural details (Fig 7.35). It was built as a large unpowered workshop, with an attached manager's house or offices, to contain the traverse-warp lace machines patented by Freeman's partner, John Brown. The main building is a long, narrow two-storeyed range overlooking an enclosed yard, with the arched main gate through the offices at the front end of the site (Fig 7.36). It was comparable with lace and hosiery buildings in the East

Fig 7.34
The distinctive cottages in St Mary's Lane are the best preserved hosiery-knitters' workshops in Tewkesbury. The wide workshop windows are of a form more common in the East Midlands hosiery industry than the Gloucestershire woollen industry.
[DP137245]

Fig 7.35
The East Street Factory was built as a large workshop to contain an improved type of hand-powered lace machine, as illustrated in 1860, although steam power was added later. Engraving of the Patent Renewable Stocking Factory, Tewkesbury, Illustrated Times, *24 November 1860. [© The British Library Board]*

Fig 7.36
The workshop range of the East Street Factory was later converted into a row of houses, inserting party walls and chimneys but retaining the original fenestration. [DP137247]

Midlands, where much of the lace and hosiery industry remained located in workshops until the middle of the 19th century.[63] The lace factory operated successfully from 1825 to 1853, employing about 150 workers to manufacture a range of plain and patterned net lace. Steam power had been added by the 1860s, when the site was extended and converted into a hosiery and shirt factory. Its most distinctive architectural feature is the use of wide, closely spaced windows to each storey, indicating that it was designed for good internal lighting and was unlikely to have originally contained heavy-powered machinery and shafting.

Cotton industry buildings in the South West

Cotton was imported via Bristol throughout the 18th century, albeit in much smaller quantities than the other major ports, and various attempts were made to establish a cotton industry in the area from the 1690s.[64] One of the four sites manufacturing cotton in Bristol by *c* 1800 employed about 250 people, but the local industry suffered from the high costs of using the harbour and from competition from other ports, notably Liverpool. From the late 1820s, the cotton industry was promoted as of great potential benefit to Bristol, leading to the construction of the Great Western Cotton Factory a decade later. The large scale of investment in the factory was part of a coordinated effort to revive the trade and industry of Bristol, which included the construction of the Great Western Railway and the Great Western Steamship Company, and by making good use of the port facilities which had been improved in 1809.[65]

The Great Western Cotton Factory, built at Barton Hill in the suburbs of Bristol, was one of the most significant mid-19th-century textile mills in the region.[66] The spectacular site, now mostly demolished, was built in 1837–8 by a partnership involving a Manchester cotton manufacturer, J B Clarke, with 10 Bristol investors, to form the business of Clarke, Acramans, Maze and Company (Fig 7.37). The local partners included wealthy entrepreneurs who were also connected with the Great Western Railway, the port of Bristol, and the Great Western Steamship Company. In a dramatic contrast to the small scale of the rest of the cotton industry in the South West, this was a state-of-the-art factory that was comparable

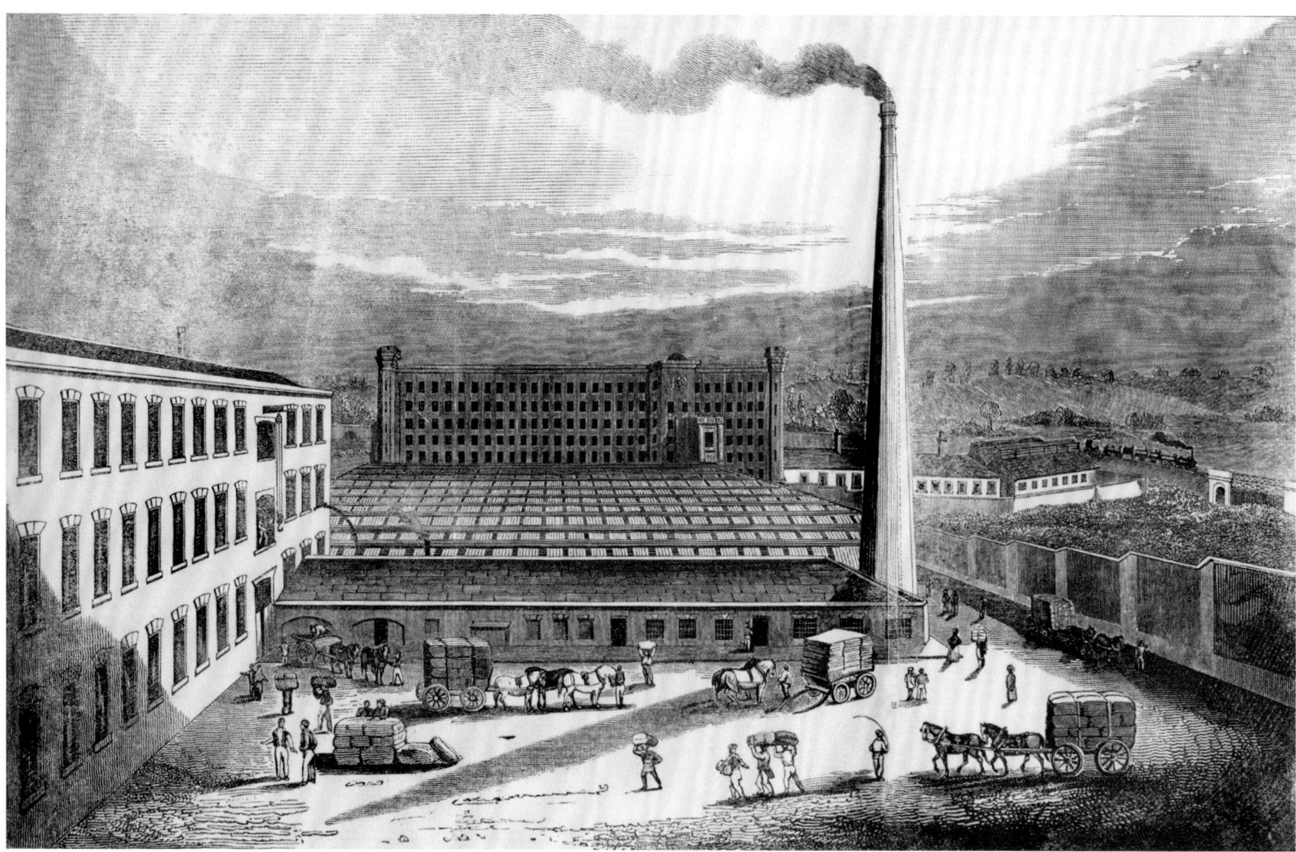

Fig 7.37
The extensive Great Western Cotton Factory was a collaboration between a group of wealthy Bristol merchants and an ambitious Manchester cotton manufacturer. An attempt to revive Bristol's industries and commerce in the 1830s, it was associated with other initiatives including the Great Western Steamship Company and the nearby Great Western Railway. From Chilcott's Descriptive History of Bristol *or* A Guide to Bristol, Clifton and the Hotwells. *5th edn, improved, opposite p 86. [Reproduced courtesy of Mike Bone. DP139049]*

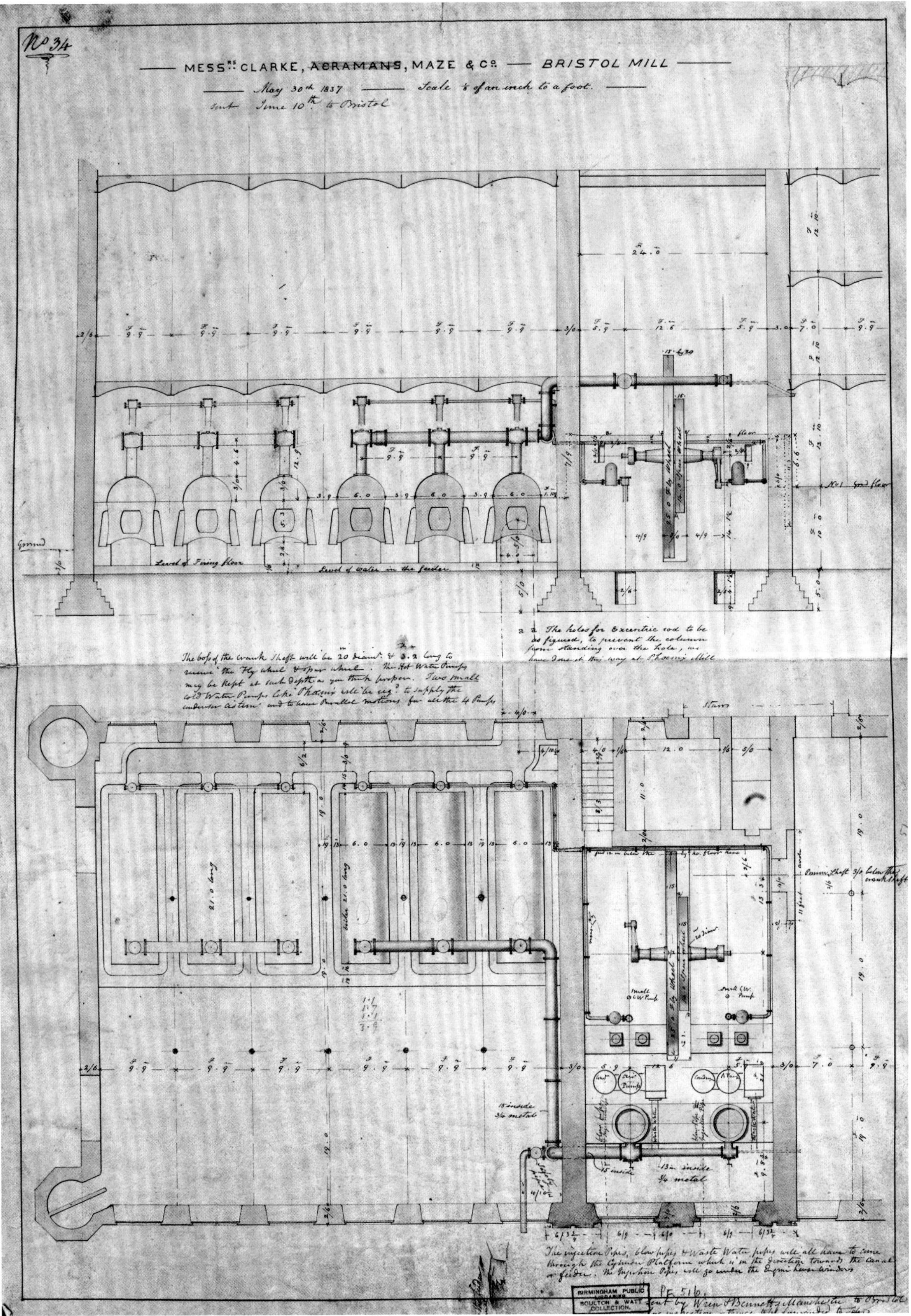

Fig 7.38
The Great Western Cotton Factory was designed as a state-of-the-art integrated factory, comparable in size to the largest mills in the Lancashire cotton industry. The Boulton and Watt double-beam engine, with adjacent internal boiler house, was one of the largest steam-power systems installed at a cotton mill in the 1830s. [Reproduced with the permission of Birmingham Archives & Libraries, Boulton and Watt Archive, Portfolio 516_c. DP137103]

to the latest types of cotton mills being built in the north, and was much larger than Clarke's Manchester mill.[67] It was a fully integrated complex, with a five-storeyed fireproof spinning mill, an attached power-loom weaving shed containing 1,000 looms (one of the largest in England in the 1830s), a bleach works, foundry, engineering works and a community of workers' housing. The steam-power system comprised three Boulton and Watt engines and seven boilers (Fig 7.38). The mill was located alongside the Feeder Canal, built in 1804–9 as part of the improvements to Bristol harbour, which served as the water supply for steam plant and processes, and for the transport of coal, cotton and finished goods. The first bales of cotton used at the site were said to have been imported in the maiden voyage of the SS *Great Western*.[68] However, it proved cheaper to transport cotton overland from Liverpool, and other technical issues hindered the business, including the hardness of the local water. Although it was one of the largest and most advanced textile mills in the region, the factory did not lead to an expansion of the cotton industry, similar to that in the north, and no other large cotton mills were built in the South West. It was converted to artificial silk production in the 1920s, and the spinning mill and weaving sheds were not demolished until the late 1960s.

Conclusion: The significance of the South West lace factories, hosiery workshops and cotton industry

The lace, hosiery and cotton industries together accounted for a much smaller number of sites than the older woollen industries, but their buildings have nevertheless made an important contribution to the industrial heritage of the South West. The development of the three industries reflected a broader redistribution of manufacturing that was one of the defining features of the Industrial Revolution in England. From the mid-18th century, migrations of both factory builders and industrial workers were widespread, often from rural areas to the expanding industrial towns, as new factory-based industries prospered and traditional industries declined. Of particular significance to the South West textile industries was the mobility of the relatively new class of wealthy industrialists, who actively sought the most favourable areas to develop their businesses. In many cases, the migrations of factory builders were directly related to the spread of innovation and the transfer of new technologies around the country. The early 19th-century developments in lace, hosiery and cotton manufacturing, while the traditional industries were in decline, were all connected to the enterprise, innovation and mobility of these pioneers of the factory system.

Although the three industries were related, they resulted in a notably diverse range of building types. The hosiery trade of Tewkesbury represented an unusual continuation of domestic industry well into the mid-19th century, and a relatively late transition into a form of factory working that was more typical of the East Midlands than other parts of the South West. In contrast, the huge lace and cotton factories were not the result of the long development of a local industry, but included some of the most progressive types of early 19th-century factory building in the region, dating from a period when the construction of new mills in the traditional industries was in decline. The transfer of John Heathcoat's business to Tiverton was a dramatic example of the redistribution of industry in the early 19th century, and for a few decades the new type of lace factory he pioneered contained some of the most complex machinery in any of the textile industries. In Bristol, the Great Western Cotton Factory was a massive investment in the latest types of buildings and machinery which, in combination with parallel investments in railways and shipping, reflected the city's confidence in its unique position as the historic centre of the region's industry and trade.

Of great interest is the influence of these industries on local townscapes, in particular the housing built by John Heathcoat and his descendants for their Tiverton workforce. As a reflection of Heathcoat's paternalistic and, by the standards of the early 19th century, progressive concern for his employees, the factory housing at Tiverton is of comparable significance to better known examples in other areas, including Saltaire in West Yorkshire, Houldsworth's Mills in Greater Manchester, and New Lanark in Scotland. In the South West, Heathcoat's planned residential suburb represents one of the most distinctive townscapes of the textile industries, contrasting with the piecemeal development of workshops in Trowbridge and the preservation of ancient rope and twine walks in Bridport.

8

The legacy of the South West textile industry

Textile industries persisted throughout the South West for eight centuries by adapting their buildings, techniques and methods of business to suit the evolving markets for textile goods. Evidence of this development is readily seen in the diverse range of textile buildings and landscapes which have become key features of the region's heritage. The contribution of the textile industries to the history of the South West has therefore been profound. They employed men, women and children in mills, cottages, workshops, walks, factories, farms and warehouses, with hundreds of businesses located in market towns, countryside, cities and ports. The vast range of goods they produced, many of which were exported, provided a nationally important source of revenue from the 14th to the 20th century, and their enterprising clothiers, merchants and manufacturers played a prominent role in shaping the history and identity of the region. Employment in the textile industries was often part-time and sometimes seasonal, so textiles have long been vital to the mixed economies of the countryside and its market towns. The long-term adaptability of the textile industries is strongly reflected in their historic buildings, but will also continue to be important in the survival of their rich legacy for future generations.

Textile mills are the most conspicuous buildings of the industry, particularly the factories of the 18th and 19th centuries, but they were historically associated with a much larger number of earlier vernacular buildings (Fig 8.1).

Fig 8.1
Damsel's Mill, Painswick, Gloucestershire, has been converted into a house, but still illustrates the size and vernacular details of Gloucestershire's 17th-century fulling mills. The great variety of vernacular industrial buildings dating from before the factory system are an intrinsic part of the historic landscapes of the South West.
[DP025346]

Manufacturing industry was in decline nationally throughout the second half of the 20th century, resulting in the loss of much of the nation's industrial heritage. The South West textile industries have been relatively fortunate, however, as the tradition of adapting sites for new uses has resulted in the survival of an unusually wide variety of historic buildings, landscapes and townscapes.

The historical significance of the textile industries in the South West

The textile industry in the South West, in comparison with other regions, appears to have been remarkably widespread, diverse and long lived. Those industries which were original to the South West, such as wool, flax and hemp, began to develop local specialisation from an early date, but the production of textiles in general was not constrained to particular parts of the region, limited to certain periods of its history, or dominated by industries using a particular raw material. The diversity of the South West industries is illustrated in their widely varied origins, and their inherent connections to the region's landscapes and townscapes.

The west of England woollen industry, for example, saw an early emphasis on different products in the contrasting landscapes of Gloucestershire, Wiltshire and Somerset, probably by the 16th century. The Gloucestershire valleys are closely associated with the distinctive vernacular architecture from that period, centred on the rural water-powered fulling sites, to which were added the workshops of the early factory system, followed by larger water- and steam-powered factories, and later the full range of building types in the large integrated complexes. In Wiltshire and Somerset the early industry developed a wider variety of woollen cloths, with less emphasis on prolonged fulling, and its clothiers were traditionally based in the historic wool towns. By the 19th century their factories were architecturally and functionally distinguished from those in Gloucestershire, resulting from a gradual development of workshop buildings that culminated in closely packed groups of steam-powered mills in mainly urban settings (Fig 8.2). The construction of entirely steam-powered mills in Wiltshire and Somerset also led to the continued use of domestic workshops in both towns and villages until well into the 19th century.

The rural textile industry of Devon and Somerset originally produced similar woollens

Fig 8.2
By the late 19th century, urban steam-powered mills, such as Abbey Mill, Bradford-on-Avon, used similar technology to those in other regions, but their internal organisation often reflected the histories of the local industries. [AP26219/005]

to other regions, but from the late 16th century it gave more emphasis to the weaving of serge cloths using a combination of long and short wool. By the 18th century serge production in the area had developed into one of the largest cottage industries in the country. It later experienced a dramatic transition to the factory system, as the extensive outworking industry declined and consolidated into a much smaller number of integrated factory firms, notably those in the wool towns of south Devon and the exceptionally large complexes of Fox Brothers at Wellington. The ancient hemp and flax industry seems to have been based in Somerset and Dorset from as early as the 13th century. It remained closely linked to the local countryside, even after imported raw materials exceeded the use of locally grown crops. Its distinctive mill complexes and twine walks were built with vernacular materials to house processes that were completely different to those of the woollen industries.

The new textile industries which appeared in the South West in the 18th and 19th centuries reflected a national redistribution of manufacturing associated with the growth of the factory system, but by adapting old mills they often colonised the same areas used by the earlier industries. The silk and machine-lace factories brought new machinery and processes, along with different approaches to industrial organisation and building types that were clearly influenced from outside the region. Lace factories represented the last stage in the protracted development of an industry that had started over a century earlier in the East Midlands. The silk industry was established by firms based in London, its early buildings pioneering the nascent factory system and introducing new architectural details. In the 19th century it continued to provide employment for women and children in many rural communities after most of the traditional textile industries had disappeared.

Historic landscapes and townscapes of the textile industries

The influence of the textile industries on the historic buildings of the South West goes far beyond the easily recognisable architecture of the factories. The traditional vernacular architecture in many parts of the region is closely related to textile history, either because the buildings were built to accommodate textile workers, clothiers or merchants or (in fewer cases) because they were actually used for industrial processes. Evidence of the former industrial uses of vernacular buildings can be disguised by their later conversion for purely domestic use. Documentary research has demonstrated that the houses of artisans, clothiers and merchants often included rooms used for industrial processes or storage that later served a domestic function; the provision of utility space that could be readily adaptable for multiple uses was a common requirement of traditional house builders. The long development of the early factory system resulted in a wide range of proto-industrial workshops and loomshops, and created a greater mix of early industrial architecture than that seen in those regions where the factory system had a more immediate impact. Factories in the South West often represented the latest of many phases of development at a mill site, their size and location being influenced by existing buildings and landscape features. They adopted similar design principles and technologies to the early factories in other regions, but with a strong emphasis on the continued use of vernacular materials and features. The later generations of factories, such as those built for the lace and cotton industries, contrasted markedly with the conservative architecture of the older industries by importing the latest forms of fireproof construction, steam-power systems and machinery layouts from other areas.

The landscapes and geography of the South West offered clear advantages to the early textile industries, but some industries remained in the same area after the original factors of location were no longer an advantage. The flax and hemp industry remained in its original location for an exceptionally long period, even after its factories were more dependent on imported raw materials and produced large quantities of goods for export. The favourable local growing conditions remained an advantage in periods when imports of raw materials were restricted. In the Gloucestershire woollen industry, the large numbers of water-power sites in the western Cotswolds offered suitable locations for fulling mills from the 16th century, and the availability of water for both power and processes remained the main factor of location for the following two centuries (Fig 8.3). In the 19th century, however, when steam became the

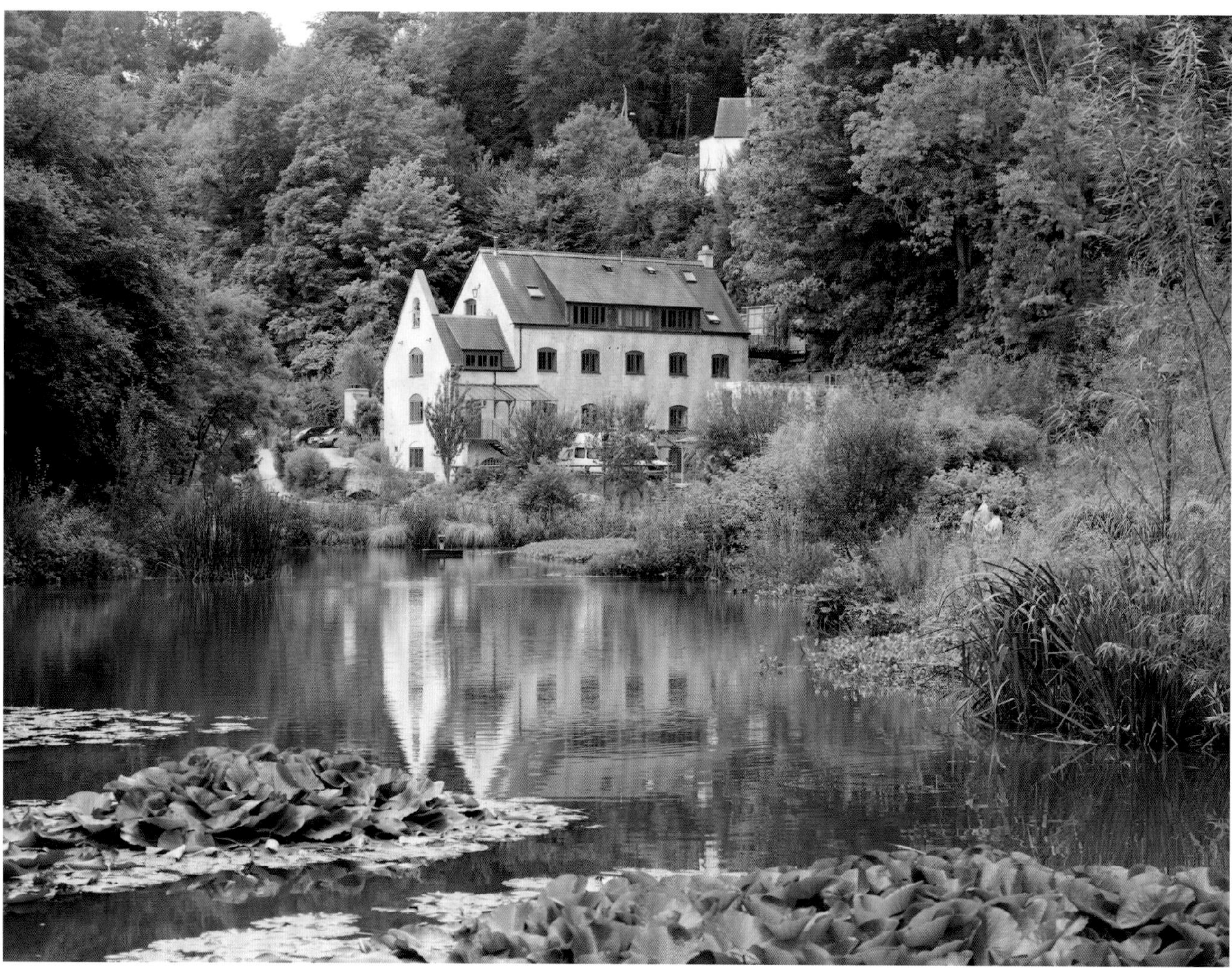

Fig 8.3
The extensively restored Horsley Lower Mill was one of the many woollen mills sited along the valleys converging on Nailsworth. Gloucestershire's landscape was clearly suited to the construction of large numbers of water-powered mills, but was no longer an advantage when steam power became more important in the 19th century.
[DP025278]

preferred power source for textile factories, the industry remained in the valleys, and saw far less new mill building than the towns of Wiltshire. The new types of factories no longer required water-power sites, and those built in the larger towns benefited from the availability of better infrastructure and commercial facilities. As the importance of steam power increased, along with the size of the new factories, the restricted valley floors of the early water-power sites eventually became a disadvantage. Other geographical factors had more influence on the locations of the later textile industries. The serge trade in Devon and Somerset benefited from its isolation from London, which enabled the development of Exeter into a major regional port and the commercial hub of the industry. The silk and machine-lace industries both relocated to the region to avoid machine breakers, competitors, legal restrictions or high wages in other areas. These industries emphasised the re-use of existing mills, however, so while they offered new employment to local communities they did not result in the expansion of textiles into new areas.

The landscape features of water-power systems are not the main focus of this book, but are perhaps the earliest and the most extensive physical evidence of the region's industrial history. The prolonged importance of water power, which greatly exceeded the duration of the factory system, and the continual occupation of water-power sites in areas such as Gloucestershire, has often resulted in a complex development of leats, ponds, races and bypass channels. Water power was also closely related to the history of farming, settlement and infrastructure. The archaeological potential of water power in the region is considerable but has not yet been fully assessed. The subject could add significantly to the understanding of the importance of industry in the history of land use.

The textile industries have also been a major influence on the historic townscapes of the

South West. In many parts of the region, textile trades complemented the other traditional industries in market towns, but in the areas occupied by the main industries the buildings of textile workers and clothiers became dominant features of the townscape. Two contrasting examples show the varied influence of the textile industries on the market towns in the South West. In Bridport, the unique processes of twine, rope and net making, in particular the use of spinning walks by small businesses, led to the retention of property boundaries and the old patterns of land use after the introduction of factories, which were mostly built on the edges of the town. In Trowbridge, the gradual adoption of machinery in the woollen industry saw the incremental addition of workshops to clothiers' houses, culminating in the construction of large factories on the adjoining plots. This piecemeal development from workshops to factories has also been recognised as a characteristic feature of industrial townscapes in other regions. Complementing these alterations to existing townscapes was the construction of factories and related buildings in new industrial suburbs around several towns from the late 18th century. Industrial suburbs were another characteristic feature of the spread of the factory system, particularly its use of steam power, with similar developments appearing in the other regions. They were differentiated, however, by building types that were suited to the local industries. A completely different type of development took place at Tiverton. John Heathcoat's paternalistic concern for his workers saw the extension of the housing acquired with his first factory into a formally laid out residential area, in which the domestic architecture reflected the organised social structure of the factory.

The historic significance of international trade

One of the main conclusions to be drawn from the economic history of the South West textile industries is their strong connection with international trade. The origins of several of the main industries were related to the availability of export markets and imported raw materials, and fluctuations in trade have also indirectly influenced the development of mill sites. The overseas demand for wool, and the commercial success of English merchants, was central to the establishment of the medieval woollen industry. The post-medieval expansion of the industry around the region was linked to changes in the statutory controls of imports, exports and taxation, and clothiers concentrated on products that were specifically aimed at exports, such as undyed cloths sold for finishing in Europe. Other statutory controls ensured that the quality of their goods suited the export markets. By the 17th century, the greater use of imported wools had influenced the transition to the production of new types of lighter cloths, which resulted in a complete reorganisation of the late medieval industry and created a distribution of mill sites that remained largely unaltered in some areas during the factory-building period.

From the 18th century, the growth of factory working in the regional textile industries was also closely related to international trade. Imports of hemp and flax were central to the development of that industry, providing the quantities and qualities of raw material that were needed by the factory system. Local growing remained important in parts of the South West, particularly when imports were restricted, but was dependent on the use of imported seed and could not match the huge quantities and low cost of imports. Much of the output of the factory-based twine and netting industry was exported via Bridport Harbour, and other regional ports. Wool imports were vital to the branches of the fine-woollen industry from the 17th century, and imports of longer-staple wools became increasingly important in the worsted and serge industries. British and Irish wool production continued, however, and significantly influenced the development of local industries, notably the South West serge industry; the blending of wools from different sources to achieve particular characteristics was an important preparation process in the factories.

The general growth of international commerce in the 18th century enabled the expansion of textile industries that were totally dependent on imported raw materials, notably silk and cotton. The factory-based English silk industry originated in the 1720s to circumvent the high costs of imported Italian organzine, its expansion into regions such as the South West being supported by favourable duties on imports and exports. In most of the textile industries, the output from the 18th- and 19th-century factories was largely aimed at export markets, often in Europe or further destinations connected with the colonies. The South West serge industry, for example, was largely dependent on the East India Company by the late 18th century, which used the relatively cheap cloth finished at Exeter to support its lucrative export trade with the Far East. The only large cotton mill in the region, the Great Western Cotton Factory in Bristol, was built at huge expense specifically to utilise cotton imported at the nearby harbour and to manufacture large quantities of calico for export.

The character of textile industry buildings

The buildings of the early factory system

The transition to the factory system was arguably one of the most important episodes in industrial history, but a consequence of the later redevelopment of many industrial areas is that intact examples of early factory buildings are rare and therefore of great interest. In comparison with other regions, the South West retains unusually good evidence of how the textile industries converted to factory working. Each of the region's industries adapted differently to the use of new machinery and methods of organisation, with some processes located in factories by the late 18th century while others continued to be outsourced to domestic workers for much longer, in some cases up to the late 20th century. The transition was characterised by a gradual introduction of new buildings and functional features in many successive stages, often spanning a period of more than a century.

In Gloucestershire, the factory system was introduced gradually by clothiers improving the processes that were used in the superfine woollen trade. In a prelude to the later development of the fully integrated textile mill, processes such as raising, shearing, dyeing, spinning and weaving were being concentrated close to the clothier's house or fulling mill well before the construction of the first factories. In contrast, the early 19th-century introduction of steam-powered factories to Trowbridge and other parts of Wiltshire and Somerset had a more sudden impact on local townscapes, and was more comparable to the changes taking place in the northern mill towns. In the silk industry, the extensive use of manual processes meant that the early factories did not need to be fully powered, with the result that the industry colonised redundant small mills as it expanded across the region. Perhaps the most dramatic transition to the factory system was in the machine-lace industry. Most of the development of lace machinery had taken place in the East Midlands, where workshop-based industry

Fig 8.4
Textile workshops and loomshops provided an open, well-lit interior and are readily adaptable to new uses, as seen here at Frogmarsh Mill, Gloucestershire. [DP025953]

continued on a large scale even after the patented machines were installed in factories in the South West.

The most common transitional-period buildings were the wide variety of workshops that were built in vernacular style to contain warehousing and hand-powered processes (Fig 8.4). By combining traditional building methods with features aimed at improving the efficiency of production, workshops show the progress of the early factory system in each of the industries. In the woollen industry the workshops (or unpowered rooms in the early factories) were used for spinning on jennies and handloom weaving from the mid-18th century, with water power used mainly for fulling and teazle-raising gigs. In the hemp and flax industry the preparation of the fibre took place on farmland, with processes such as breaking and scutching in nearby cottage workshops or small mills. The early silk mills only used power for throwing, the last stage in the production of silk thread. A wide range of small buildings were converted into workshops for the preceding winding processes, as well as the handloom weaving of silk cloths.

Evidence of functional development in textile mill buildings

The architecture of textile mills was largely determined by the relationship between external form and internal function. Contemporary architectural fashions usually influenced the external and internal embellishment, but the building's main purpose was to enable the efficient layout of machinery and processes that would ensure a profit for the business. The external features of a mill therefore often provide direct evidence of its original intended use. The ongoing alterations to machinery and power systems that were essential to remain competitive were also reflected in the adaptations to the building. Evidence of functional alterations is therefore widespread in historic textile mills, and it is unusual to find buildings which only reflect a single period in the development of an industry.

The complete rebuilding of a textile mill was not uncommon, and could be prompted either by the need to increase production, by the conversion of a mill for use in another textile industry or damage by fire. The rebuilding of vernacular mills was particularly widespread during the spread of the factory system around the region in the late 18th and early 19th centuries. The new factory buildings were a radically different form of architecture, but were often influenced by the locations of the smaller traditional mills they replaced. In rare cases, the old mill remained attached to the factory, or was incorporated within it.

In the 19th century, the larger factories were more compatible with improvements to textile machinery, and extensions became more common than wholesale rebuilding. In thriving textile industries, wings or extra storeys were frequently added to mills in periods of high demand. The fenestration and floor construction of the extensions usually reflected the ongoing development of industrial building techniques. In general, the internal width of mills increased to contain ever-larger machinery, and was accompanied by increasing ceiling heights, larger windows and stronger floor construction. Joisted timber floors remained the most common type in the South West, and were improved from the mid-19th century by the use of cast-iron columns, heavier or paired beams and deeper joists. Brick-vaulted fireproof construction was used at some larger modified or rebuilt woollen mills in the early 19th century, including Stanley Mill and Tonedale Mills, and also for the new lace factories, but remained far less common than in other regions. Examples of the improved types of fireproof construction that were developed in the late 19th century are rare in the South West.

Functional features were added or modified throughout the working life of a mill. Taking-in doors with external hoists were often included in mills, warehouses and workshops, and were formed later by enlarging windows. Floor traps were used for the internal movement of goods, and could be re-sited following the installation of new machinery. Doors and windows were also subject to alteration. Factories and large workshops were usually built with external stair towers, and the internal straight stairs of smaller buildings were often removed to provide more floor space. From the early 19th century factories were commonly equipped with attached privy towers and had internal goods lifts driven from the line shafting; such features illustrate the ongoing development of factory design, but were often replaced later. Other early alterations included the installation of gas lighting at larger sites, which would require the addition of a retort house and gas holder, and the insertion of piped steam heating to the main floors and the tentering rooms.

Fig 8.5
The development of window types over four centuries illustrates the exceptional range of architectural detail in textile industry buildings. Dates are approximate.

A *Harnham Mill, Salisbury, early 16th century [DP025781]*
B *Longfords Mills, Nailsworth, mid-18th and early 19th century [DP155151]*
C *Royal Wilton Carpet Factory, Wilton,* c *1800 [DP025883]*
D *Avon Mills, Malmesbury,* c *1791, windows replaced [DP137176]*
E *Hosiery knitters' cottages, Tewkesbury, early 19th century [DP155152]*
F *Old Mill, Tonedale, Wellington,* c *1800, window converted to loading door [DP139884]*
G *Castle Mill, Trowbridge, 1820s [DP137732]*
H *Ebley Mill, Stroud* c *1818 [DP137228]*
I *Dulverton Mill, 1820s [DP139295]*
J *Former Silk Works, Sherborne School* c *1854 [DP137204]*
K *Chipping Campden Silk Mill, late 18th century [DP137148]*
L *Lodgemore Mills, Stroud,* c *1872 [DP137238]*

A

B

C

D

E

F

G

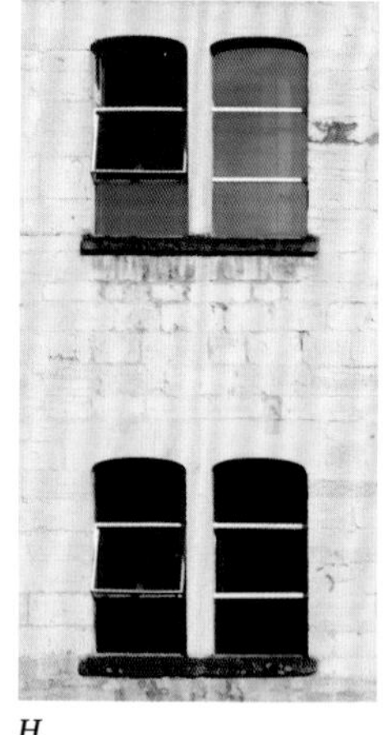
H

I

J

K

L

The development of mill sites also involved the addition of more specialised building types. The form and external features of such buildings are a good indication of the wide range of functions at an integrated textile mill. As discussed in chapter 2, the addition of new buildings to fulling mills generally predated the construction of the first factories, and continued with the further development of integration. Perhaps the most functionally distinctive new building type in the 19th century was the north-light shed, usually built for power-loom weaving or cloth finishing. North-light sheds represented a fresh and highly efficient approach to industrial design, and were arguably the forerunners of the single-storeyed factories of the 20th century. In the hemp and flax industry, the traditional open twine and rope walks were also improved in the 19th century. Open walks were increasingly protected with long-gabled roofs, similar roofs being original features of the new walks. Two-storeyed walks were added in some areas to enable the 'wet' sizing processes to be separated from the production of twine or rope. Many smaller specialised buildings were added in the same period, including bucking houses (for bleaching), turn houses, warehousing and net-making workshops.

Changes to power systems were among the most common developments at textile mills. These involved alterations to the prime mover, usually a waterwheel or steam engine, and also to the shafting used to transmit power around the mill, or to groups of buildings at a large complex. Improvements to the power system usually accompanied building extensions or the installation of larger or additional machinery.

Water was the most important source of power in the South West textile industries, and alterations to water-power systems at some sites could span a date range of several centuries. Repairs to watercourses, wheels, gearing and shafting were needed regularly, but an increase in power normally entailed raising the head of water or installing an improved type of waterwheel. The rebuilding or extension of a mill might require the construction of a larger pond and bypass channel, and probably a raised leat extending a considerable distance upstream of the mill. In some cases a larger wheel was installed by deepening the wheel pit and extending the tailrace. The landscape features of water-power systems are probably the most extensive physical evidence of the textile industry in the South West countryside. Another frequent cause of rebuilding or modification to a water-powered mill was flood damage, which could be an almost annual occurrence at some sites. Flood-prevention measures could significantly influence the location of a mill.

Waterwheels rarely survive *in situ*, but wheel pits usually contain physical evidence of the alterations to the wheel. Many improvements were made to waterwheels in the 19th century, but the most significant for textile factories was probably the introduction of the suspension wheel. These were larger than earlier types and were usually installed in external wheel houses. They were accompanied by carefully built wheel pits with close-fitting ashlar breastwork and improved types of mechanical penstocks to enable precise control of the flow of water into the wheel. The technology of the suspension wheel represented a significant improvement in water-power systems, and at sites with a good water supply it was a viable alternative to a small steam engine. At some textile mills the use of water power was extended into the late 19th century by the replacement of the waterwheel with a turbine, which required other modifications such as water-feed pipes. Turbines were not commonly used to drive textile machinery directly, however, but were an efficient means of driving DC generators for electric lighting.

Steam power was used to supplement water power by the turn of the 19th century, and has left its own distinctive features and building types. The early beam engines were often smaller than those used in other regions and of the free-standing or 'independent' type, requiring a less substantial engine house. Engine houses added to water-powered mills were usually external and sited to facilitate the connection of steam power to the earlier water-powered shafting. The early engines would need upgrading after a few decades of use, and were often compounded by adding a second high-pressure cylinder. Factories built specifically for steam power, such as the Trowbridge woollen mills and the purpose-built lace factories, had larger engines and a similar layout of boilers and chimney to the early steam mills in other regions; this was in part because the early engines were often from the same maker, typically Boulton and Watt of Birmingham. Mid-19th- to early 20th-century mills were equipped with improved types of engine, including double-beam engines and horizontal-tandem and cross-compound engines. These specialised types of textile mill engines

Fig 8.6
The external form and architectural details of textile mill buildings strongly reflect the processes and machinery they were built to contain.

A Attic used for sorting raw wool, Tonedale Mills, Wellington, late 19th century [AA96/3931]
B Stair tower with sprinkler tank, Tonedale Mills, 1873 [BB96/8578]
C Fireproof staircase, Tonedale Mills, c 1820 [BB96/8561]
D Power-loom weaving shed, John Boyd's Factory, Castle Cary, c 1871 [BB01/5829]
E Detail of iron footbridge, Longfords Mills, Nailsworth [DP137170]
F Twine walks and warehouse, Bridport, late 19th to mid-20th century [DP001484]
G External beam-engine house, Tonedale Mills, mid-19th century [AA96/03930]
H External compound engine house, Lodgemore Mills, Stroud, c 1872 [DP137422]
I Boiler and economiser house, Coldharbour Mill, Uffculme, late 19th to early 20th century [AA024543]
J Cottage wool-combing lofts, Buckfastleigh, early 19th century [DP140073]

A

B

C

D

E

F

G

H

I

J

Fig 8.7
Mechanical features in situ *are now extremely rare, but they are relatively well preserved in some South West textile mills.*

A Waterwheel and ring gear, St Mary's Mill, Minchinhampton, early to late 19th century [DP025136]
B Dismantled suspension wheel and penstock, Tone Works, early 19th century [AA96/00684]
C Blocked engine-house windows, Tonedale Mills, 1873 [AA96/03825]
D Horizontal compound steam engine, 1904, St Mary's Mill [DP025118]
E Intact line shafting system, Tone Works, c 1894 [DP043907]
F Waterwheel governor, Dunkirk Mill, Nailsworth, late 19th century [DP085692]
G Construction detail, Tonedale Mills, 1873 [AA96/03835]
H Interior of a milling machine, Tone Works, mid-20th century [DP043832]
I Warehouse wall crane, Goods Yard, West Bay, early 19th century [AA049599]

A

B

C

D

E

F

G

H

I

were associated with much larger boiler houses, usually for double-flue Lancashire boilers, with economisers and taller free-standing chimneys.

Powered mills of all types required a power-transmission system, comprising horizontal and vertical shafting attached to ceilings, walls, floors and columns, which drove the machinery throughout the mill. Shafting systems were a form of complex, heavy engineering that was prone to vibration and needed to be accurately set up; they were a major influence on the design and construction of mill buildings. The power-transmission system would be altered to suit changes in the machinery layout and extended to power new buildings. In almost all cases the line shafts, gears and pulleys were completely removed when the mill was converted to electric drive or non-textile uses, but features such as bearing boxes and bolting faces on columns enable the former layout of shafting to be reconstructed. Exceptionally well-preserved power systems survive at Tone Works, Wellington, and Coldharbour Mill, Uffculme.

The conversion of mills to non-textile uses

In addition to the adaptation of mills by some of the textile industries, notably silk, the conversion of mills for completely new uses was common in some parts of the South West by the early 19th century, when the practice was less common in other regions. It has continued to the present day. Early examples of the use of mills by other industries included the manufacture of walking sticks and furniture in several of the Stroud Valleys mills (Fig 8.8), and the conversion of mills for machine makers and brush-making in Somerset. The conversion of mills for housing also started relatively early in the South West. When applied to smaller vernacular mills, such as the Blockley silk mills, domestic conversion can retain much of the original character and layout of the building. The conversion of the larger factory mills or warehouses into domestic accommodation started in the South West and other regions in the early 19th century. This often involved more subdivision and internal alteration, and sometimes the removal of smaller ancillary buildings, which can be more detrimental to the historic character of a textile mill. The early conversion of the region's textile mills was probably a reflection of the traditional combination of textiles with other trades or with farming. Dual economies developed in several areas, in which households would be engaged in both farm work and employment in a textile

Fig 8.8
South West textile mills began to be converted for completely new uses in the 19th century, helping to preserve the buildings. St Mary's Mill, Minchinhampton, was one of many Gloucestershire sites adapted for the manufacture of walking sticks, shown here, or furniture.
[Reproduced courtesy of Audrey Penrose. DP025128]

Fig 8.9
Chipping Campden Silk Mill was a notable example of the deliberate conservation and conversion of a textile mill. In 1902 the buildings were bought by C R Ashbee, a notable proponent of the Arts and Crafts movement, and carefully adapted for use by members of the Guild of Handicraft. Their descendents, Hart Silversmiths, still occupy the former silk workshops. [DP025476]

trade, and continued well into the 19th centuries in industries such as silk and flax. In the late 19th century only the largest mills in the most suitable locations were likely to be competitive with firms in other regions, although some of the smaller mills remained in use for the more specialised textile industries. As the number of firms in the main industries declined, the conversion of mill buildings increased (Fig 8.9). The demand for adaptable industrial buildings was higher in areas with a wide variety of rural trades, such as in the industrialised countryside in parts of Gloucestershire and in the larger market towns.

In the late 20th century the refurbishment and conversion of historic mill buildings became widespread in the South West, with architects and developers combining traditional industrial architecture with modern structures to enable a much wider range of new uses. Conversions range from small fulling mills that have been adapted for use as housing or commercial premises, to some of the largest 19th-century mills that have seen new life as apartments or local authority offices. Creative new uses have been found for most of the building types associated with the industry (Fig 8.10). Mills have been converted into libraries

Fig 8.10a
New Mills, Kingswood, is an outstanding example of the creative re-use of a wide variety of textile mill buildings by Renishaw plc, manufacturers of high-quality metrology systems. The late 19th-century weaving sheds and ancillary buildings have provided space for a canteen and gymnasium. [DP025237]

Fig 8.10b
Modern dining facilities in a converted north-light shed.
[DP025233]

Fig 8.10c
The first floor was partly removed to create a spacious, well-lit entrance foyer with a mezzanine gallery.
[DP025252]

Fig 8.11
Ruskin Mill, Nailsworth, formerly named Millbottom Mill, was more extensively altered in a recent conversion into an educational trust, one of the great variety of new uses that have been found for South West mills. Most of the changes still reflect the architectural character of a Gloucestershire woollen mill; the angled pediment is a recent addition.
[DP025281]

and art galleries, north-light sheds used for housing, canteens and fitness centres, and wool-drying stoves reborn as tourist information centres. Throughout the region, historic textile mill complexes have become frequently visited destinations, some as museums but far more as efficient space for small businesses or retail units (Fig 8.11).

Conserving the heritage of textile industry

The wealth of textile mill buildings surviving across the South West is a testament to the durability of their construction and adaptability to new uses. Their historical significance is widely recognised, and it is now generally accepted that good examples are worthy of preservation, but the re-use of historic mills has involved a range of different approaches to their conservation. In some cases mills are retained in more or less their original condition, with few alterations needed to adapt them to a new use, but others have seen more extensive removal of industrial or architectural details. This can result in the loss of the most important historic features of textile-industry buildings.

Textile mills are essentially functional buildings, and appreciating their heritage value requires an understanding of how their architecture and design relates to their former use. The architecture of textile mills is largely defined by their functional features, and the development of these features effectively documents the history of the industries. Various approaches to architectural embellishment were used in textile factories, ranging from the Palladian influences of the late 18th century to the flamboyant use of polychromatic brickwork in the late 19th century, but to the mill builders the ornamentation was of secondary importance to achieving an efficient functional design. Earlier mills and workshops, which combined industrial features with vernacular materials and techniques, may show a less clear relationship between form and function, but are of great historic interest because they reveal the first evidence of the transition to the factory system.

Although a wide range of textile industry buildings have been protected and conserved, there are still some historically important building types that have seen less effective conservation. These include transitional-period workshops and other industrial extensions to clothiers' houses, both of which were of great importance in the early development of the factory system, and textile industry buildings in town centres, where land use has changed considerably since the decline of the textile industry. The smaller, specialist ancillary buildings at the integrated complexes are also more vulnerable to loss, but are essential in understanding the adjoining larger buildings.

Conversely, larger mills and factories have proven to be more adaptable. The simple, robust construction of the larger mill buildings, and their well-lit, open-plan interiors, means that these structures are generally regarded as the most versatile for alternative uses and have a better rate of survival. The rarest historic features, and some of the most significant, are the machines themselves. The rate of survival of specialist machinery and fittings is considerably lower than that of mill buildings, and where they remain *in situ* such features are generally seen as an impediment to practical re-use. Intact buildings that still contain the original types of machinery are the rarest type of historic textile mill.

Unsurprisingly, sites that have remained in continuous industrial use, even where the nature of that industry has altered, have tended to better preserve the functional elements and their overall character even though the buildings may not be as highly maintained as those that have been converted to other uses. Once mill sites fall into disuse their buildings can quickly deteriorate, and the amount of investment needed for repairs means that conversion to higher value uses becomes almost inevitable unless substantial grant aid is available. Another legacy of long-standing industrial use can be a significant further constraint on the reuse of such sites, as the almost unavoidable need for decontamination and flood prevention works escalates the cost of conversion. As a result, some of the most impressive and well-preserved textile mill complexes can be subject to overly intensive or destructive conversion schemes, or left empty and neglected.

Fig 8.12
The recently refurbished exterior of Chipping Campden Silk Mill, with conserved loading doors and leaded workshop windows.
[DP025466]

Conversion of textile mills to commercial uses, such as storage, offices, shops or galleries, is more likely to preserve the internal as well as external characteristics of the buildings, since there is less pressure to subdivide the large open spaces (Figs 8.12–8.15). Such schemes do not always generate sufficient revenue to pay for the major repair and infrastructure costs required to rescue a site from a condition of extreme dilapidation. In these cases, more radical solutions are difficult to avoid, such as those involving elements of demolition or conversion to residential use, or even both, except in the rare instances where significant grant aid can be obtained. Where a major conversion scheme is being contemplated, restoration efforts often become too focused on the buildings that are either most architecturally impressive or easily convertible, and structures that are of a more modest or less easily adaptable form are regarded as dispensable. In this way the historic character of the large integrated sites can be eroded as elements that are critical to an understanding of their function are lost or altered beyond recognition. In a large redevelopment scheme it is important to obtain a thorough and authoritative understanding of the function and significance of both the overall site and its individual components at an early stage.

Fortunately, the South West has several examples of large textile sites that have been the subject of exemplary restoration schemes by enlightened owners with the assistance of grant aid, which also provide public access. These include Coldharbour Mill at Uffculme, Devon; Gants Mill at Bruton, Somerset; and Higher Flax Mill in Castle Cary, Somerset, one of the few sites which still functions as a textile manufactory. Other successful examples include the pioneering conversion of Ebley Mills, Stroud, Gloucestershire, into local authority offices; the conversion of the Gifford-

Fig 8.13
The more radical conservation of Horsley Lower Mill included a new gable wall (with bell). The building originally extended to the left of this wall, although it had been reduced to its present length before the refurbishment. Well-designed new features convey the intention to creatively re-use the building, while respecting its industrial character. [DP025271]

Fox Lace factory in Chard, Somerset, into local authority offices and a public library; and the re-use of New Mills near Wotton-under-Edge, Gloucestershire, including the creative adaptation of most of the ancillary buildings, as the international headquarters of a manufacturer of analytical equipment. In difficult economic times grant aid for the conservation of large industrial buildings is increasingly hard to obtain, and the pressures to find commercially viable developments will become more acute. It will be increasingly important to understand the historical characteristics of textile mills, to recognise their significant features and prioritise the remaining sites. As successful conservation schemes have already demonstrated, inventive solutions are needed to avoid further losses of important historic mill sites, potentially involving the use of enabling developments to secure the funding for building conservation.

For several decades the conservation of this industrial heritage has been underpinned by new fieldwork and research, which has greatly enhanced our understanding of one of the most complex periods in our history. The early factories were radically different, and are now widely recognised as of great historic interest, but they only tell one part of the story. The character and distribution of factory buildings was influenced by many factors, including the early development of processes, the history of international trade, the varied methods of clothiers, merchants and industrialists, and by

Fig 8.14
The late 19th-century attic of Frogmarsh Mill, Gloucestershire. Many mills can provide well-lit, spacious interiors without significant alteration to their historic features.
[DP025948]

the migrations of factory workers. The nature and progress of the Industrial Revolution thus varied significantly across the South West, and the heritage of the region's textile industries cannot be explained solely as a conversion to factory methods at the end of the 18th century. It is often assumed that the factories represented a more uniform type of architecture, but these studies have shown that the diversity of the early factory system was far greater than that of the vernacular industry that preceded it.

Textile mills are a fundamental part of the historic character of the region, connecting its different landscapes with a common heritage that crosses boundaries and geographical divisions. Their historical development was more prolonged and more diverse than that of the textile industries in other regions. The longevity of these industries has shaped the character of buildings, landscapes, villages and towns, their surviving sites giving us a rare insight into the emergence of a manufacturing society from the ancient traditions of craft industry.

Fig 8.15
The effective conversion of mill floor space to accommodate modern information technology or media businesses is increasingly common, as seen at St Mary's Mill, Gloucestershire.
[DP025173]

A SELECTION OF HISTORIC TEXTILE INDUSTRY SITES

The following sites comprise a small sample of the wide variety of surviving historic buildings related to the South West textile industry. Some of these sites are either fully open to the public, with visitor facilities, or are accessible by the public because of their function (eg retailing). Others can be well viewed from nearby streets or footpaths but cannot be accessed by the public. Inclusion in this book does not indicate public access is possible.

Devon

Coldharbour Mill, Uffculme (ST 061 121). Very well-preserved working woollen mill, built by Thomas Fox, now an outstanding working museum. Includes *in situ* water- and steam-power systems, combing and spinning machinery, gift shop and café.

Allhallows Museum, Honiton (ST 163 007). Not a textile mill, but the museum includes a superb collection of handmade Honiton lace.

Tuckers Hall, Fore Street, Exeter (SX 917 923). The 15th-century meeting hall of the Company of Weavers, Tuckers and Shearmen, restored in the 19th century and still in use.

Tiverton Museum, Beck's Square, Tiverton (SS 954 123). Not a textile mill, but includes displays on John Heathcoat and machinery from the Tiverton lace factory.

Heathcoat factory housing, West Exe, Tiverton (SS 950 126). The distinctive and very well-preserved housing built by John Heathcoat of the nearby lace factory (no public access). The residential and industrial suburb of West Exe paralleled the development of the mill, and is perhaps the best example of a factory settlement in the South West.

Dorset

Mangerton Mill, Mangerton (SY 490 957). Well-preserved combined corn and flax mill, with museum display.

Poole History Centre and Archives, attached to Poole Museum (SZ 008 903). Part of a 15th-century wool warehouse, with 19th-century alterations.

Folly Mill Lane–Riverside path, Bridport (SY 469 927). This route from South Street to East Street gives good views of the best-preserved group of open and covered walks in Bridport, most of which probably originated as burgage plots. It includes workshops and other small industrial buildings associated with the walks. Many are now private gardens. No public access.

Gloucestershire

Bourne Mill, off the A419 in the Stroud Valley (SO 872 021). Early to mid-19th-century woollen mill complex, recently restored, in use for retailing and workshops.

Chipping Campden Silk Mill, Sheep Street (SP 149 389). Late 18th- to early 19th-century workshops, conserved and in use as café, gallery and offices. Includes the historic workshops of Harts Silversmiths.

Day's Mill, Old Market, Nailsworth (ST 850 996). Early to late 19th-century woollen mill complex in a town-centre location, partly converted for retailing.

Dunkirk Mill, off A46 in the Nailsworth Valley (SO 844 005). Imposing multi-phase woollen factory, late 18th to early 20th century, externally well preserved in a 1990s conversion to apartments. Includes the visitor centre of the Stroudwater Textile Trust, with three preserved waterwheels. Access by appointment.

Ebley Mill, off Westward Road, Stroud (SO 829 045). Early to late 19th-century woollen mill complex, exceptionally well preserved in the early 1990s when it was converted into the offices of Stroud District Council.

Egypt Mill, Station Road, Nailsworth (ST 849 998). Late 18th- to early 19th-century fulling and grist mill, with adjoining 17th-century clothier's house. Converted into restaurant, pub, B&B and conferencing facilities.

St Mary's Mill, Minchinhampton, off A419, Stroud Valley (SO 885 021). Privately owned site which is not accessible to the public, but can occasionally be visited on Heritage Open Days. An exceptionally well-preserved early 19th-century woollen mill, including an internal waterwheel and a compound steam engine.

Longfords Mills, off B4014, Nailsworth (ST 866 992). Largest woollen mill complex in Gloucestershire, mid-18th to late 19th century, extensively converted into housing. Privately owned, but the earliest buildings retain their industrial character and can be viewed from the public road which passes through the site.

Ruskin Mill and Horsley Lower Mill, Horsley Road, Nailsworth (ST 846 990 and ST 844 986). Two recently preserved but extensively altered woollen mills set within the conserved landscape of the Horsley Valley. The whole area was converted by the Ruskin Mill Educational Trust. Ruskin Mill includes a gallery and café.

Tetbury Market House, Church Street, Tetbury (ST 890 931). One of the largest and best preserved of the Cotswold market halls formerly used by the woollen industry.

St Mary's Lane and East Street, Tewkesbury (SO 890 325 and SO 895 328). Well-preserved hosiery-knitters workshops and the unusual East Street factory, both suggesting architectural influence from the East Midlands lace industry. No public access.

Hampshire

Southampton Maritime Museum, The Wool House, Town Quay Road, Southampton (SU 418 110). The museum is located in an early 15th-century wool warehouse, associated with the export trade in raw wool.

Whitchurch Silk Mill, Winchester Street, Whitchurch (SU 462 479). A working silk mill museum. The exceptionally well-preserved building was built as a fulling mill and converted to silk in the early 19th century. Includes displays of silk weaving; also an attached water-powered corn mill.

Somerset

Holyrood Lace Mill/Gifford Fox Factory, Holyrood Street, Chard (ST 322 084). Chard's last working lace factory, now converted into Chard Library and offices for the district and county councils.

Gant's Mill and Garden, Gant's Mill Lane, Bruton (ST 674 342). Well-preserved woollen mill, silk mill and corn mill, with working leat and turbine, on the site of an ancient fulling mill. Open for day visits, functions and B&B.

Old Town Mill/Boden's Mill, Chard (ST 323 084). Probably the best preserved of the early 19th-century lace factories in Chard, retaining most of the architectural features of its steam-power system and fireproof construction. No public access, but visible from adjoining roads.

Tourist Information Centre, Justice Lane, Frome (ST 777 482). This has been adapted from a circular drying stove.

Wiltshire

Harnham Mill, Town Path, Salisbury (SU 135 294). Iconic 15th-century watermill which has been used for paper, corn and fulling. Currently a pub, restaurant and hotel.

Royal Wilton Carpet Factory, Wilton (SU 099 314). Substantial parts of the historic factory survive, including early 19th-century workshops. Carpet production continues in a nearby modern factory, the older buildings having been converted into the Wilton Shopping Village and a small museum.

Former Drying Stove, Church Street, Melksham (ST 903 637). This has been converted for commercial use.

Trowbridge Museum, The Shires Shopping Centre, Court Street (ST 855 579). The museum is located in the middle floors of the main building of Home Mills, which forms the central feature of the shopping mall. Highly informative displays on the local woollen industry and early textile machinery, including a handloom and a spinning jenny.

Court Street area, Trowbridge (ST 855 578). An impressive group of early 19th-century steam-powered textile mills and related buildings, mostly well preserved, representing the addition of a new industrial suburb to the earlier workshops and housing of the town centre. No public access to mill sites.

Avon Mills, Malmesbury (ST 935 868). Very impressive and externally well-preserved early woollen factories, later converted for silk. Visible from the road but no public access.

LOCATIONS OF SITES MENTIONED IN THE TEXT

MILL SITE	GRID REFERENCE
Abbey Mill, Bradford-on-Avon, Wiltshire	ST 8250 6094
Albion Mill (site of), Evercreech, Somerset	ST 6597 3773
Angel Mill, Westbury, Wiltshire	ST 8732 5125
Ansford Factory, Castle Cary, Somerset	ST 6433 3250
Anstie's Factory, Devizes, Wiltshire	SU 0043 6164
Ashton Mill, Trowbridge, Wiltshire	ST 8607 5771
Avon Mills, Malmesbury, Wiltshire	ST 9358 8688
Belford Mill, Ashburton, Devon	SX 7535 7153
Bitham Mill, Westbury, Wiltshire	ST 8754 5134
Blockley Court, Blockley, Gloucestershire	SP 1665 3500
Bourne Mill, Brimscombe and Thrupp, Gloucestershire	SO 8722 0214
Bowbridge Dye Works, Stroud, Gloucestershire	SO 8576 0425
Brick Mill, Trowbridge, Wiltshire	ST 8552 5784
Bridge Mills (site of), Trowbridge, Wiltshire	ST 8541 5795
Brimscombe Upper Mill, Brimscombe and Thrupp, Gloucestershire	SO 8662 0242
Buckfast Higher Mill, Buckfastleigh, Devon	SX 7391 6736
Buckfast Lower Mill, Buckfastleigh, Devon	SX 7412 6724
Cam Mills, Cam, Gloucestershire	SO 7524 0006
Castle Mill, Trowbridge, Wiltshire	ST 8555 5778
Charfield Mills, Charfield, Gloucestershire	ST 7222 9299
Chestnut Hill, Nailsworth, Gloucestershire	ST 8481 9951
Chipping Campden Silk Mill, Gloucestershire	SP 1495 3897
Clothier's house, British Row, Trowbridge, Wiltshire	ST 8541 5826
Clothier's house, Fore Street, Trowbridge, Wiltshire	ST 8554 5807
Coker Sail Cloth Works, Crewkerne, Somerset	ST 4399 1016
Coldharbour Mill, Uffculme, Devon	ST 0619 1219
Coppice Hill workshop, Bradford-on-Avon, Wiltshire	ST 8272 6109
Court Mills, Bridport, Dorset	SY 4641 9300
Cricklepit Mill, Exeter, Devon	SX 9184 9218
Damsel's Mill, Painswick, Gloucestershire	SO 8772 1103
Dawe's Twine Walk, West Coker, Somerset	ST 5121 1369
Day's Mill, Nailsworth, Gloucestershire	ST 8500 9965
Derby Lace Factory, Barnstaple, Devon	SS 5618 3365
Domestic workshops, Newtown, Trowbridge, Wiltshire	ST 8521 5755
Domestic workshops, St Mary's Lane, Tewkesbury, Gloucestershire	SO 8905 3257
Domestic workshops, Yerbury Street, Trowbridge, Wiltshire	ST 8598 5803
Downes Street, Bridport, Dorset	SY 4664 9298
Dry loft, Chapel Street, Buckfastleigh	SX 7380 6612
Dry loft, Kingsbridge Lane, Ashburton, Devon	SX 7550 6989
Drying stove, Bradford-on-Avon, Wiltshire	ST 8239 6150
Drying stove, Frome, Somerset	ST 7773 4820
Drying stove, Melksham, Wiltshire	ST 9038 6375
Dudbridge Dye Works, Dudbridge, Gloucestershire	SO 8359 0452
Dulverton Mill, Dulverton, Somerset	SS 9128 2776

MILL SITE	GRID REFERENCE
Dunkirk Mill, Nailsworth, Gloucestershire	SO 8447 0052
East Street Factory, Tewkesbury, Gloucestershire	SO 8955 3279
East Street Walks, Bridport, Dorset	SY 4696 9280
Ebley Mill, Cainscross, Gloucestershire	SO 8296 0457
Egypt Mill, Nailsworth, Gloucestershire	ST 8495 9987
Frogmarsh Mill, Woodchester, Gloucestershire	SO 8407 0179
Gant's Mill, Pitcombe, Somerset	ST 6744 3427
Gillingham Town Mill (site of), Gillingham, Dorset	ST 8079 2659
Gould's Twine Walk, West Coker, Somerset	ST 5204 1333
Great House, Tiverton, Devon	SS 9539 1257
Great Western Cotton Factory, Bristol	ST 6105 7272
Greenland Upper Mill (site of), Bradford-on-Avon, Wiltshire	ST 8310 6060
Grove Mill, Burton Bradstock, Dorset	SY 4906 8971
Ham Mill, Brimscombe and Thrupp, Gloucestershire	SO 8606 0319
Handle House, Trowbridge, Wiltshire	ST 8538 5793
Harbertonford Mill, Harberton, Devon	SX 7823 5621
Harnham Mill, Salisbury, Wiltshire	SU 1353 2940
Heathcoat Square, Tiverton, Devon	SS 9509 1267
Heathcoat's Factory, Tiverton, Devon	SS 9515 1276
Higher Flax Mills, Castle Cary, Somerset	ST 6351 3235
Holyrood Mill, Chard, Somerset	ST 3223 0844
Horsley Lower Mill, Horsley, Gloucestershire	ST 8442 9867
Iford Mill, Hinton Charterhouse, Bath and North East Somerset	ST 7994 5885
Inchbrook Mill, Minchinhampton, Gloucestershire	SO 8434 0092
Jardine's Factory, Shepton Mallet, Somerset	ST 6264 4359
Kemp's Silk Factory, Evercreech, Somerset	ST 6482 3897
Kingston Mill (site of), Bradford-on-Avon, Wiltshire	ST 8279 6084
Lodgemore Mills, early buildings, Stroud, Gloucestershire	SO 8435 0498
Lodgemore Mills, late 19th-century mill, Stroud, Gloucestershire	SO 8446 0498
Longfords Mills, Minchinhampton, Gloucestershire	ST 8669 9920
Loomshop, Woodchester, Gloucestershire	SO 8408 0282
Lordsmeade Mill, Mere, Wiltshire	ST 8158 3189
Malmesbury Abbey House, Malmesbury, Wiltshire	ST 9334 8738
Malvern Mill, Blockley, Gloucestershire	SP 1622 3458
Mangerton Mill, Netherbury, Dorset	SY 4901 9572
Market Hall, Tetbury, Gloucestershire	ST 8906 9312
Marsh Mills, Over Stowey, Somerset	ST 1905 3836
Merchant's Barton Mill, Frome, Somerset	ST 7781 4790
Naish's Street, Frome, Somerset	ST 7717 4819
New Mills, Kingswood, Gloucestershire	ST 7375 9296
New Mills, Stroud, Gloucestershire	SO 8598 0565
North Mills, Bridport, Dorset	SY 4657 9356
North Tawton Mill, North Tawton, Devon	SS 6573 0158
Old Mill, Longfords Mills, Minchinhampton, Gloucestershire	ST 8666 9920
Old Mill, Tonedale Mills, Wellington, Somerset	ST 1287 2135
Old Town Mill, Chard, Somerset	ST 3239 0845
Parrett Works, Martock, Somerset	ST 4463 1866
Perry Street Works, Tatworth and Forton, Somerset	ST 3355 0492
Pitchcombe Upper Mill, Pitchcombe, Gloucestershire	SO 8483 0792
Priory Mill, Bridport, Dorset	SY 4639 9270
Pymore Mills, Bradpole, Dorset	SY 4707 9462
Raleigh Mill (site of), Barnstaple, Devon	SS 5638 3415
Royal Wilton Carpet Factory, Wilton, Wiltshire	SU 0096 3147
Ruskin Mill, Nailsworth, Gloucestershire	ST 8468 9902

MILL SITE	GRID REFERENCE
St Mary's Lane workshops, Tewkesbury, Gloucestershire	SO 8904 3257
St Mary's Mill, Minchinhampton, Gloucestershire	SO 8857 0215
Silk House, Mere, Wiltshire	ST 8154 3231
Silk Thread Factory, Taunton, Somerset	ST 2321 2463
Silk Works, Sherborne Abbey, Dorset	ST 6368 1654
Snugborough Mill, Blockley, Gloucestershire	SP 1677 3514
South Street Mill (site of), Taunton, Somerset	ST 2337 2450
Stanley Mill, King's Stanley, Gloucestershire	SO 8119 0425
Staverton Factory, Staverton, Wiltshire	ST 8563 6099
Stone Mill, Trowbridge, Wiltshire	ST 8547 5787
Studely Mill, Trowbridge, Wiltshire	ST 8536 5792
Tail Mill, Merriott, Somerset	ST 4493 1235
Tone Works, Wellington, Somerset	ST 1259 2185
Tonedale Mills (centre of site), Wellington, Somerset	ST 1280 2131
Town Mill, Buckfastleigh, Devon	SX 7385 6623
Town Mill, Ottery St Mary, Devon	SY 0947 9532
Trew's Weir Mill, Exeter, Devon	SX 9252 9162
Twerton Lower Mills (site of), Bath, Bath and North East Somerset	ST 7239 6486
Twerton Upper Mill (site of), Bath, Bath and North East Somerset	ST 7270 6476
Upper Steanbridge Mill, Painswick, Gloucestershire	SO 8788 0787
Viney Bridge Mills, Crewkerne, Somerset	ST 4487 0914
Ward's Silk Factory, Evercreech, Somerset	ST 6483 3895
Warehouse, St Michael's Lane, Bridport, Dorset	SY 4635 9286
West Lavington Mill, West Lavington, Wiltshire	SU 0081 5358
Westbury Factory, Sherborne, Dorset	ST 6356 1592
Westford Mills (site of), Wellington, Somerset	ST 1201 2032
Weston Lower Mills (site of), Bath, Bath and North East Somerset	ST 7247 6489
Weston Mills (site of), Bath, Bath and North East Somerset	ST 7279 6481
Whetham's Warehouse, Bridport, Dorset	SY 4648 9280
Whitchurch Silk Mill, Whitchurch, Hampshire	SU 4625 4790
Woodchester Mill, Woodchester, Gloucestershire	SO 8429 0287
Wool House (Maritime museum), Southampton	SU 4186 1106
Wool House (Poole History Centre), Poole	SZ 0085 9031
Workshop, Folly Mill Lane, Bridport, Dorset	SY 4669 9276
Workshop, St Michael's Lane, Bridport, Dorset	SY 4635 9297
Workshops, Fore Street, Trowbridge, Wiltshire	ST 8546 5801
Worsted Factory, Ottery St Mary, Devon	SY 0944 9529
Yarn Market, Dunster, Somerset	SS 9915 4381

GLOSSARY

Throughout the glossary words in *italics* denote terms which can be cross-referenced. Words in **bold** have been used to highlight additional terms defined within a single entry. The glossary is derived from sources in the bibliography and is included to provide basic definitions and background information for technical terms used in the text. The definitions have been selected as the most appropriate for this book; the terminology of the textile industries was extensive, and in many cases terms varied both regionally and chronologically.

Axminster carpet *See* carpet

bleaching; including bucking and lye The cleaning and removing of colour from raw fibres, yarn or fabric through washing and the application of natural or artificial chemical agents. In the woollen industry bleaching was undertaken as part of the *scouring* of the wool fibres or the finished cloth. The term bleaching therefore is more typical of the cotton and flax industries, and was usually part of the finishing process, although yarn could also be bleached. In both industries the stages of the process were similar, involving **bucking** (or bowking – that is, boiling) the material in a **lye** (or lay – an alkaline solution, often made using wood ash), and grassing or crofting the material by laying it out in fields to allow the sun and dew to help the process. These two stages could be repeated as necessary to produce the desired colour. The final stage was souring which entailed soaking the cloth in a weak acid solution – sometimes buttermilk or sour milk. Cloth or yarn was then washed to remove the traces of the bleaching agents. This process could take months, and innovations in the 18th century included the use of new solutions, such as sulphuric acid, which considerably shortened the bleaching time.

bobbin net; including plain net A machine-made version of plain lace net. The bobbinet machine was patented in 1809 by John Heathcoat of Loughborough. It was significant as the first mechanisation of the lacemaking process, although only capable of the plainest version of the handmade system (hence its alternative name of **plain net**). The machine operated on the principal of a stationary *warp* thread running up from a beam, with two sets of *weft* threads descending diagonally from both sides. The weft threads were mounted on narrow brass bobbins which twisted around each warp thread in turn, by means of shifting the bobbins in carriages across and along the base of the machine. The plain net produced could then have more elaborate motifs attached to create a product similar to handmade decorative lace, or could be used in its plain form for products such as net curtains.

braiding The process of producing net from flax or hemp yarn. The process of braiding was largely undertaken by hand, and some types of net are still hand produced despite the invention of net-making machinery in the mid-19th century. Braiding is similar to knitting, with the yarn threaded onto a timber needle and the mesh created by a series of loops which are knotted together.

breaking (flax and hemp) Also known as bolling, this was the first stage of flax dressing, which normally followed the *retting* of the cut crops. The hard stem of the plant was broken and loosened ready for removal from the useful fibres by *scutching*. Originally this was done by hand, beating the flax stems against a solid base with a rounded mallet known as a flax breaker. The process was mechanised from the early 18th century with the invention of the 'bolling mill' where metal stamps were lifted by the action of the waterwheel to beat the stems. In the 19th century the stamps were replaced with rollers to undertake the same process.

broadcloth The term originally applied to cloths made on a *broadloom* but later simply referred to a type of fine cloth. A noted product of the west of England trade from the late medieval period, broadcloths were usually *fine woollens* the size of which was regulated by statute. The statute size varied, but was typically from 26–28yds (23.17–26.6m) long and 45in (1.14m) wide.

broadloom *See* handloom

Brussels carpet *See* carpet

bucking *See* bleaching

burling In the woollen and worsted industries burling was the inspection of cloth and the removal of knots or small items of vegetable matter, during the *dressing* or finishing of the cloth. It was usually an occupation for women and was done with tweezers of varying fineness, known as burling irons.

carding (wool and cotton) The process of opening and straightening raw wool or cotton fibres to prepare them for *spinning*. By the 13th century this was done by hand cards – wooden boards with iron teeth which were worked in pairs by hand. The growth of the cotton industry in the 18th century led to the invention of a hand-powered carding machine in which the fibre was drawn over a large cylinder with wire teeth. This was quickly improved upon by Richard Arkwright in the late 18th century who patented a water-powered carding engine in which the cotton fibre was passed into and over the cylinder continuously and out via a secondary cylinder which formed a continuous line of untwisted fibre. The fibre was then ready for *slubbing*. The fine woollen industry adopted similar machinery.

carpet; including Brussels carpets, Wilton carpets and Axminster carpets The production of carpets in western Europe was well established by the 18th century with the production of oriental style carpets on horizontal looms. These were referred to as Savonnarie or **Brussels carpets**, produced using a linen *warp* and coloured, looped worsted for the pile. It is possible that some Brussels carpets were being produced in the South West in the early 18th century, but the industry was given impetus when the Duke of Pembroke opened a carpet factory at Wilton. **Wilton carpets** were similar to the earlier Brussels type but with a deeper pile and cut to produce a velvet finish. In contrast **Axminster carpets** were created using a system which followed the Turkish tradition, where individual woollen tufts were hand knotted.

cassimere; including kerseymere A fine-woollen cloth made using a twill weave. Cassimere was patented by Francis Yerbury of Trowbridge in 1766 and became a specialism of the Wiltshire trade. The name is sometimes corrupted as **kerseymere**, due to an erroneous association with the cloth type *kersey*; however, kerseys were a coarse cloth and very different from the fine cassimere cloth.

clothier An entrepreneur engaged in the production of cloth, usually woollens, often combining the roles of manufacturer and merchant. The term was often applied to those who dealt with the buying of raw materials, organised the various stages of outworking required to produce wool cloth and arranged the sale of the finished goods. Clothiers could be quite modest in scale and wealth employing a few people and perhaps undertaking some work themselves, but the term has become more commonly associated with the affluent clothiers of the 16th to 18th centuries, who invested their wealth in houses, estates and charitable endowments.

combing The process of straightening *worsted* fibres, similar to the carding process used for short wool. Combing was designed to remove the short fibres (or noils) from the longer fibres (known as top) as well as straightening them. Originally this was done by hand using a pair of heavy metal combs which were heated on a stove. One comb was fixed to a wall or post to hold the wool, while the second was used to carefully separate the fibre. Combing was one of the last processes to be mechanised. The inventor of the *power loom*, Edward Cartwright, patented a combing machine in the 1790s which aimed to copy hand combing but this was never particularly efficient. The process was finally mechanised from the 1840s, with James Noble creating the most successful version in 1853.

conditioning (cotton) A process intended to improve the handling of raw cotton or cotton yarn by storing in a controlled humid environment, often a damp room or cellar.

creel A wooden or metal framework onto which spun yarn is mounted, for feeding onto carriages, bobbins or warp beams ready for weaving.

crepe Typically a black silk fabric with a gauze-like appearance, woven using highly twisted thread, often *marabout*. It often had a crisp or crinkled finish that was created by treating the fabric after it was woven. It was popular as a fabric for mourning dress in the late 19th century. In the 18th century the term was used for a fine worsted fabric often used in clerical dress.

doubling (silk, cotton, wool, flax and hemp) The process of twisting together two or more slivers of prepared fibre or spun yarn. The slivers were combined in this way to even out irregularities in the fibre, which might then be drawn and doubled again. Yarns were combined to former stronger thread. In silk, doubled thread was suitable for weft but not strong enough for warp (*see* organzine). Until the 18th century doubling was done on a hand-operated doubling wheel, but from the 1770s mechanised versions were used, although in many places the early stages of thread production appear to have remained hand powered into the 19th century.

drawloom A development of the handloom, in use by the 17th century, in which multiple heads were used to raise and lower the *warp* threads in sequence, enabling the weaving of patterned cloths. The *Jacquard loom* was a later development of this type.

dressing (flax and hemp) A general term for the processes used to remove the straw (or stem) of flax or hemp from the useful fibres and prepare the fibres for spinning. It usually incorporated the processes of *breaking*, *scutching* and *heckling*.

dressing (wool) A collective term for the *raising* and *shearing* processes which produced the fine finish of woollen cloth.

drying Various processes for producing fibre, yarn and cloth involved wetting or dampening the material, necessitating drying. Drying of raw wool fibre after scouring or dyeing could take place in the open air but from the 17th century wool *drying stoves* were developed, in which heat was used to speed up the process. Cloth drying required more space so was typically done outside. In some mills ventilated drying rooms were provided to allow for this as part of the finishing process. After the introduction of steam power in the 19th century, the areas associated with *boiler houses* were often used for drying cloth. *Tentering* was a distinct drying process.

dry house A specialised building used for the controlled drying of woven or finished cloth pieces. Usually of one or two storeys and a long, narrow plan, dry houses were used from the early 19th century, before the introduction of *tentering* machinery. They often combined warm-air heating with natural ventilation using opening louvres, the cloth being attached to internal racking with tenter hooks.

drying stove; including wool stoves Typically a small circular or hexagonal detached building with a conical roof. Drying stoves (also called **wool stoves**) were designed to allow the heating, and therefore rapid drying, of scoured wool. Internally they had slatted floors, often arranged into two or three storeys each up to 8ft (2.44m) in height, with a central iron stove. Drying stoves appear to have developed in the west of England industry in the 17th century, with surviving examples typically of 18th century date. In some cases their use extended into the 19th century. Early examples could be associated with clothiers' houses or fulling mills and later some were incorporated into mill complexes and specialist dye works.

dyeing Dyeing could be undertaken at two different points in the cloth-making process. The most common practice was to dye the cloth after it was woven (also known as piece dyeing) which produced a more even finish. This could take place some distance from the earlier processes. The early cloth industry in the west for example, tended to produce 'white' cloth which was then dyed in London or even exported for finishing abroad. In the 18th century Stroud became famous for its scarlet-dyed woollen cloth, which was considered superior due to the qualities of the river water. The dyeing of wool fibre (also known as dyeing 'in the wool') was required when patterned cloth was to be produced, or for the medley type cloths of the *New Draperies* in which different coloured wools were blended before they were spun. For both types of dyeing the process was essentially the same. Specialist dye houses were typically used, with the cloth and dyestuffs placed in heated coppers and the cloth subsequently stood in wooden vats of water to help fix the dye. Colouring was achieved using natural dyes. Artificial dyes were introduced in the 19th century.

engine house; including engine types The building or room designed to contain a steam engine in a mill complex. Early steam-powered mills had internal engine houses, but external engine houses were common for the later, larger engines. Engine houses could be placed either at one end or sometimes centrally to the building. Early engine houses were characterised by a tall, narrow space, which allowed for the upright, single main cylinder. The earliest **engine types** in use in the South West were the rotative beam engines pioneered by Boulton and Watt, who supplied a number of engines to South West mills from the 1790s. More efficient compound engines were introduced from the mid-19th century and from the 1860s engines with horizontal cylinders began to be used prompting the provision of broader and longer engine houses. Although the size of the later engines varied they were typically larger necessitating the enlarging of older engine houses or the addition of a new one. The investment and importance of the engine to the mill complex meant that engine houses could be architecturally quite ornate spaces.

fine woollen *See* woollen

filature (silk) The factory or building where silk was wound from cocoons, almost always located in the country where the silk was produced. Silkworms were raised on mulberry bushes, which were never successfully cultivated in England on a commercial scale, and thus the filatures which supplied the British silk industry were in mainland Europe, particularly in Italy, or Asia.

finishing A general term for the series of processes carried out on cloth or other fabrics after weaving. For woollen cloth this could include *fulling*, *raising* and *shearing* to improve the weight, texture and feel of the cloth. Finishing could also include *bleaching* or *dyeing*.

flannel A woollen or worsted cloth produced with a particular emphasis on *milling* (or *fulling*) to produce a soft finish. Typically grey in colour. In the South West it became one of the specialist products of the industry in Devon and parts of Somerset, produced by large-scale 19th-century firms such as Fox Brothers.

flax Crop widely cultivated for its seed (linseed) but also for its fibres which were broken down and used to produce yarn. Cultivated and processed for cloth in the South Somerset area since at least the medieval period. By the 18th century large amounts of flax were imported into the area to supply the industry.

flock (wool) Chopped or short woollen fibre obtained as a waste by-product from factories. In the 19th century Gloucestershire developed a niche market in flock production, using it in wallpaper or as stuffing for furniture.

fulling; including milling and rotary fulling An important stage in the finishing of *fine woollens*, fulling was the process of shrinking and thickening cloth by beating and washing. Fulling was the first woollen process to be mechanised with water-powered mills on record from the 12th century. The process, as it developed in the medieval period, involved the use of large timber hammers or stocks which were raised and dropped with the action of the wheel and pounded the cloth which sat in the water-filled 'box' at the base of the stocks. By the 17th century fulling stocks were also used for the *scouring* process, which immediately preceded fulling. After fulling the cloth would be dried, usually by *tentering*. The early origins of the technology meant that a variety of regional names are applied to the process including 'tucking' in some western areas. The basic principle of the fulling stock continued in use until the 20th century, although in most places it was replaced by **rotary fulling** after the invention of the rotary fulling machine by John Dyer of Trowbridge in 1833. In rotary fulling the cloth was stitched into a continuous loop which passed between heavy rollers to create friction and therefore heat, which caused it to thicken and shrink. This was also known as the rotary milling machine and the term **milling** became an alternative term for fulling in the 19th century.

framework knitting; including the stocking frame The term for knitting carried out on a **stocking frame**, invented by the Reverend William Lee in 1589. The frame copied the techniques of hand knitting, which it slowly superseded, using foot treadles to operate a system where the knitting was suspended and worked by a series of hooked needles. Lee's machine was initially only capable of knitting coarse wool, but he later refined the design to enable it to knit silk and, later still, it was improved again to allow it to work cotton. Stocking frames were not powered until the 1840s, and despite improvements the basic principles still remained those of Lee's original machine.

handle house A building used for the drying and storing of the teazle handles which were used in the *raising* process. The buildings are characterised by the generous provision of ventilation, often through walls formed of slatted wood, or brick laid in an open pattern. Early handle houses could be associated with clothiers' houses or workshops, but they were also built as part of factory complexes in the early 19th century.

handloom; including broadloom, narrow loom The horizontal wooden-framed handloom was used in England from the 13th century, employing a system whereby alternate *warp* threads were lifted using foot-operated treadles and the *weft* thread was thrown between the warp by hand in a shuttle. From the later medieval period the **broadloom** was used, which was simply a wider version of the horizontal loom, and usually required two operatives to pass the shuttle. The **narrow loom**, worked by a single operative, remained in use for some specialist cloth types and was better suited to the loomshops that became common from the later 18th century. The productivity of the handloom was greatly enhanced by the invention of the flying shuttle by John Kay in the 1730s. This mechanised the movement of the shuttle and allowed even broadlooms to be operated by a single person. From the early 19th century handlooms were increasingly replaced by *power looms* although they remained in use for some specialist branches of weaving until the early 20th century.

headrace *See* leat

heckling (flax and hemp) The final stage of *dressing* flax or hemp, heckling (or hackling) was comparable to *combing* or *carding* in the woollen and worsted industries. It sorted the fibres and laid them parallel, ready for *spinning*. The scutched fibres were aligned by drawing them through sets of hackles or pins fixed to a bench. This also separated the shorter fibres (*tow*) from the longer fibres (known as line). The hackles could be graded from coarse to fine, to allow for the production of different grades of fibre.

Heckling was not mechanised until the mid-19th century, and hand heckling continued in some areas well into the 20th century.

hemp A tall woody plant cultivated for its fibre, used to produce a strong yarn. Hemp fibre was typically used for cord and rope, and some coarse fabrics, and was cultivated and processed in the south Somerset and west Dorset area from at least the medieval period.

hosiery Originally a collective term for hose, the leggings commonly worn in England up to the early 19th century, the term also encompasses other items created using the same knitting techniques, such as stockings. From the late 16th century the hosiery industry mainly emerged in the East Midlands area, around Nottingham and Loughborough, but notable examples were also found in areas of the South West.

integration The bringing together of processes that were previously carried out at separate sites, and sometimes in different areas. The integration of spinning with weaving is associated with the 19th-century development of powered factories, but the combining of other processes was also a feature of the pre-factory industries.

Jacquard loom The Jacquard loom was patented by Joseph Marie Jacquard in Lyon in 1801 and was a type of *handloom*, rapidly replacing the earlier *drawloom* as a more efficient means of producing complex woven designs. It was introduced to England in 1820, gaining popularity with an improved version patented by Stephen Wilson of Spitalfields. The main feature of the machine was a mechanism mounted above the loom which used a belt of pegged boards or punched cards to activate the raising and lowering of the *warp* thread. The loom was quickly adopted in England, and from the mid-19th century powered versions were produced resulting in complex weaving becoming *factory* based.

jute A fibre harvested from the bark of a plant in the *Corchorus* genus. The fibre was grown mostly in India, and though not widely adopted in the South West, it was used for some specialised cloth types. It was used in the late 19th century for some specialist cloth types in south Somerset and west Dorset as part of the diversification of the flax and hemp industries.

kerseymere *See* cassimere

kerseys A coarse wool cloth traditionally produced in East Anglia and which developed into a standard product of the Yorkshire woollen industry. In the South West it was one of a diverse range of fabrics produced in Devon in the late medieval period, before the emergence of the serge industry.

knapping machine *See* raising

lace; including bobbin lace, pillow lace and bone lace An open-work fabric in flax (linen), cotton or silk originally created by hand by operatives, typically women. In the South West the hand-lace industry was focused around Honiton in Devon, with Honiton lace becoming a nationally renowned product. The Honiton work was typically **pillow lace** (also referred to as **bobbin lace**, or **bone lace**), that is, lace created on a pillow using wooden or bone bobbins. It was usually made using linen thread. The product was often highly ornate incorporating intricate naturalistic designs.

launder A trough carrying a *headrace* to the wheel, typically at high level to feed a breast-shot or over-shot wheel.

leat; also headrace and tailrace A watercourse used to direct water from a river or stream into the mill pond or directly to the wheel. The term **headrace** was often used for the watercourse above (or before) the wheel. The **tailrace** was below the wheel as water issued back into the stream or river. Leat systems were the most common way to feed a water-powered mill as they allowed control of the water supply, often through allowing water storage in the mill pond or reservoir. Depending on the topography of the site and the power required, leat systems and the associated water storage areas could involve substantial earthworks and infrastructure, representing a significant investment for the mill owner.

light serge *See* serge

line The longer fibres of flax separated from the shorter fibres (tow) during the *scutching* process.

line shafting; including power transmission The means of **power transmission** around a mill complex by a series of horizontal shafts running through the building. Line shafting was sometimes powered from a main upright shaft or by ropes or belts, to transmit power up through a multi-storey mill and along the various levels. Shafting could be powered by the waterwheel, the steam engine and, from the early 20th century, electric motors, all of which provided the rotation required to turn the main shaft. Machinery was then powered from the line shafts by belts and pulleys.

long-staple wool *See* staple (wool)

loomshop A building in which handlooms were organised prior to the development of power-loom weaving. Loomshops could belong to the pre-factory era, but due to the continuation of *handloom* weaving after the mechanisation of other processes they also featured in factory complexes. In size, a loomshop could range from a small extension of a weaver's or clothier's house to a much larger detached building, sometimes within a factory complex. As with *workshops*, loomshops typically had generous light provision to assist the weavers.

lye *See* bleaching

marabout A specialist type of silk thread typically used in the production of *crepe* or gauze ribbon. Marabout was produced from a specific type of high-quality Italian white raw silk, and was a type of *tram* created using three threads.

medleys Types of cloth produced in Wiltshire and north Somerset from the late 16th century onwards, particularly popular in the 17th century. The product was a *fine woollen* created using fibres which were dyed in the wool and then mixed in different proportions prior to spinning, creating a wide variety of colours in the finished cloth.

milling *See* fulling

mixed cloth Cloth produced using two different types of fibre. In the South West, for example, *serge* was woven from a long-fibre warp of worsted and a short-fibre weft of fine wool.

mule *See* spinning

muslin A lightweight cotton fabric with a plain weave.

napping *See* shearing

narrow cloth Widths of cloth, variously classified as under 52in (1.32m) or under 44in (1.12m). The term is sometimes used to refer to woollens that were narrower than the traditional broadcloths, such as those produced in loomshops, or to more specialised products that were made to specific weight and width, such as sailcloth.

narrow loom *See* handloom

net braiding *See* braiding

New Draperies A wide variety of mostly woollen and worsted cloths introduced throughout England from the late 16th century, which differed in their light weight, colour and finish to the traditional heavily fulled woollens.

north-light shed A single-storeyed factory building, often used for power-loom weaving. The north-light shed was distinguished by its characteristic saw-tooth roof profile. This was created by parallel ranges of pitched roofs comprising longer south-facing pitches and glazed shorter, steeper north-facing slopes. This was intended to provide an even light for the weaving undertaken inside. Typically north-light sheds would be attached to a multi-storey spinning mill, the later mechanisation of the weaving process meaning that the mill would often pre-date the sheds.

organzine Silk thread made of *singles* or *tram*, twisted in the opposite direction to the twist of the fibres in the singles. This stronger thread was often used as the *warp* thread in silk weaving. The specialist process required to make organzine was a secret of the Italian silk trade until the early 18th century, forcing English producers to import all their organzine. In 1717 Sir Thomas Lombe controversially managed to obtain knowledge of the method, and brought the water-powered 'Piedmontese' machine, which produced organzine, to England where he set up a mill in Derby. From the 1730s the technology was employed more widely in England allowing a significant growth in the domestic production of silk thread.

piece A standard length of cloth or other type of woven fabric. The standardised length varied depending on the product.

plain net *See* bobbin net

power loom A loom which used a source of motive power, typically either water or steam power. The concept of a powered loom was pioneered by Edward Cartwright, who patented his first machine in 1785. This was followed by a series of improved versions which had limited success and his steam-powered mill ultimately failed despite his innovative attempts. The principles of his second patented design, however, were employed in other designs in the early 19th century. In 1822 Richard Roberts patented a metal-framed loom, which allowed for mass production and was widely adopted in the cotton and worsted industries. Other branches of the textile trade were slower to adopt the ideas, particularly those which used more fragile thread types, such as wool, or more complex designs, typical in the silk industry.

power transmission *See* line shafting

puttee A piece of cloth (or leather) wound around the lower leg to provide protection and support. In the late 19th and early 20th century puttees formed part of military field uniform and were worn by sportsmen and others who spent long periods in rough terrain. Fox Brothers of Somerset became important producers of puttees during the First World War.

raising; including the teasel gig and the knapping machine The vigorous brushing of woollen cloths to extend the surface fibres which could then be carefully removed by *shearing* to create a smooth finish in which the *warp* and *weft* were not visible. The early technique for raising involved the cloth being rested over a bar (or perch) and the nap raised with teazles affixed to a wooden handle. The cloth could be wet or dry for the process, producing different finishes. The teazles used were an imported variety known as Fullers' teazles, which had a hooked barb. A **teazle gig**, or gigmill, was in use by the late medieval period, in which the teazles were placed on a rotating drum that was turned against the cloth. This was banned by statute in the 16th century in order to preserve the work of the raisers, but probably continued in use in some areas, notably Gloucestershire. Their increased use in the late 18th century led to significant unrest. Gigs were improved in the early 19th century, and for some cloth types the teazles were replaced with wire hooks, but for others natural teazles were still used in the 20th century. The **knapping machine** or knapping engine (not to be confused with the later 19th-century machine of the same name, which was used for shearing) was invented in 1743 by the Gloucestershire clothier Onesipherous Paul, and provided a mechanised means of raising the nap in parallel bands which produced a specific ridged finish used for certain types of woollen cloth.

ramie A plant of the nettle family with a fibrous bark. Ramie has been associated with textile production for an exceptionally long period, but was not widely used in the British textile industries.

retting (flax and hemp) The process of softening the cut flax or hemp after harvesting, usually done either by spreading out the fibres in the fields (dew retting) or by soaking the fibres in water pits or tanks (water retting).

ring frame *See* spinning

rope walk *See* walk

rotary cutting machine *See* shearing

rotary fulling machine *See* fulling

roving *See* slubbing

scouring The process of washing or cleaning in the preparation of wool (or worsted) cloth. The term was used to describe both washing raw wool and washing finished cloth *pieces*. The scouring of raw wool removed impurities and also the natural oil (lanolin) from the wool. The scouring process was originally undertaken by applying an alkaline substance (or lye) to the wool, typically stale urine. The wool was then rinsed to remove the lye and the impurities. By the 19th century the original alkaline substances were replaced with artificial detergents and rinsing was undertaken in bowls. After scouring raw wool would go for *scribbling* and/or *carding*, while worsted would go for *combing*. Scouring of cloth pieces was intended to remove the oils and other substances added during the spinning and weaving of the fibre. The scouring of cloth pieces typically took place in the fulling mill immediately prior to *fulling*, again by applying the lye and then rinsing in water. Rinsing cloth pieces was done either with a gentle action by the fulling stock, or from a separate set of driving stocks intended for the purpose. From the late 19th century cloth scouring was undertaken on scouring machines, in which the cloth was passed through a vat of heated liquor and squeezed between heavy wooden rollers.

scribbling The opening and oiling of scoured wool before *carding*. This was originally achieved by adding butter to the wool by hand, but by the late 18th century types of olive oil were used when the process was carried out in a scribbling machine. From the late 17th century the process was aided by a scribbling horse, a frame with a leather covering set with iron teeth, through which the wool could be drawn with a hand card. In the late 18th century this system was again superseded by a scribbling machine, but from the early 19th century scribblers were generally attached to carding engines.

scutching (flax and hemp); including swingling The second part of the flax *dressing* process, scutching removed the broken stem sections from the useful fibres. The hand technique was to place the broken fibres against a wooden board and to beat them with a bat or flail sometimes referred to as a swingler. Scutching was mechanised in the South West in 1803 by Richard Roberts of Burton Bradstock, west Dorset, although it had been mechanised by 1740 in Ireland. Irish scutching machines involved the use of water power to turn a shaft on which timber blades turned within a box. The flax was pushed into the box and beaten until the stems and woody parts had been separated. It is likely that the early South West machinery was similar in principle.

serge; including light serge The most successful product of the Devon cloth trade, serge was originally produced with a *worsted warp* and a woollen *weft*. From the early 19th century the serge industry developed forms of **light serge** by varying the preparation and finishing processes to produce cloths which were of lighter weight with a soft finish.

shearing; including napping and the rotary cutting machine Shearing (sometimes referred to as **napping**) removed the nap of the woollen cloth after *raising*. This achieved a finer finish to the cloth and for some cloth types the process of raising and shearing would be repeated several times. The original hand-shearing process involved resting the raised cloth on a padded table and passing large iron shears over the top of the cloth. One blade was fixed and the second was moved against it to remove the nap. The shearing process was mechanised in 1815 with the invention by John Lewis of Brimscombe, Gloucestershire, of the **Rotary Cutting Machine** (sometimes referred to as the Lewis Cloth Cutting Machine), based on an earlier machine invented by an American, Samuel Dore, in 1794.

short-staple wool *See* staple (wool)

single (silk) A single thread of raw silk, twisted to increase its strength and give it a better texture. Singles could be used as a form of thread, but were also spun or thrown to form other types of silk threads such as *tram* and *organzine*.

sizing The application of a protective coat of a starch-based mixture or glue, known as size, to yarn, twine or cloth in order to strengthen it. Size was often applied to *warp* threads in order to prevent breakages during weaving. Sizing could also help prolong the working life of fabric by making it more resistant to water and abrasion.

skein (silk) A bundle of raw silk prepared at the *filature* for delivery to the factory in packs known as books or bales.

skirders A horizontal bracket placed on a post used to support the lengths of twine or rope along a *walk*.

slubbing (wool, cotton); including roving The initial stage of preparing carded fibre for spinning, in which it was formed into a sliver and lengthened by drawing. It was followed by later stages of *drawing* and *doubling* on successive machines, after which the sliver was twisted to produce a **roving**. This was wound onto bobbins which were transferred to the spinning machines which produced the yarn.

Spanish cloth A type of *medley* cloth produced in north Somerset in the 16th century. In the 17th century it was produced throughout Wiltshire and Gloucestershire and replaced much of the earlier broadcloth trade. The name apparently derives from the use of imported fine wool, largely from Spain.

Spanish wool Very fine wool imported from Spain from the mid-16th century onwards, usually associated with Merino sheep. The value placed on this wool type led many English producers to try to copy its qualities, including the importing and cross-breeding of Merino sheep.

spinning; including the spinning jenny, water frame, mule, throstle and ring frame The drawing and twisting of prepared raw fibre to produce a yarn. Spinning was originally carried out by hand on a drop spindle, where the thread was twisted by hand action, with a weight drawing the yarn downwards. This was replaced, in the 14th century, by the spinning wheel where the hand-turned wheel spun the spindle, and the fibre was drawn on at an angle to create the twist. The spinning wheel was gradually developed over a long period, including a number of significant improvements before the introduction of spinning machines. Spinning was one of the first textile processes to be mechanised with the invention of the **spinning jenny** by James Hargreaves in 1764. Although this, and subsequent inventions, were largely associated with the cotton industry they were quickly adapted for use with wool and some other fibres. Mechanised processes for longer fibres, such as flax took longer to develop, although by the late 18th century mechanisation had started. The spinning jenny used the same principal as the spinning wheel, but with multiple spindles to significantly increase the amount of yarn produced. The success, and limitations, of the jenny led to a number of innovations in the late 18th century. Richard Arkwright's **water frame** allowed for the continual drafting and twisting of the fibre and enabled water-power to be applied to the system. The most successful machine was the **mule,** a hybrid of the jenny and the water frame invented by Samuel Crompton in 1779. Alternative machines were largely improvements on Arkwright's water frame, the most successful being the **throstle** and, from the late 19th century, the **ring frame**.

spinning jenny *See* spinning

spinning (twine and rope) The traditional process of spinning flax and hemp to create twine and lay a rope was different than that for yarn spinning and involved the use of a *walk*. A bundle of prepared fibre was manually twisted to form a yarn that was suspended on brackets along the full length of the walk. Twist was applied using a hand-cranked machine called a jack at the end of the walk. Multiple yarns were combined using the same technique to form a twine; twines were combined to form a rope.

staple (wool, also cotton, silk); including long-staple, short-staple A classification of the average length of individual fibres in the raw material. In the wool trade, for example, the main distinction was between the shorter, finer wool varieties and the longer, coarser types. Short staple (fine) wool was most valued in the late medieval period and 16th century for the production of *fine woollens*. However, from the 17th century England specialised in the longer, coarser wool staples which were required for use in the *serge* industry (particularly in Devon) and in the *New Draperies* pioneered in Wiltshire and Somerset. The raw fibre of cotton and silk was also sometimes classified according to its staple, although the classification systems were completely different from those for wool.

stocking frame *See* framework knitting

superfine woollen *See* woollen

swingling *See* scutching (flax and hemp)

tailrace *See* leat

tarring In the hemp and flax industry, rope or twine could be coated with tar in order to prolong its working life, particularly for the lines and rigging of ships.

tentering The drying of woollen or worsted cloth after fulling by stretching the fabric between tenterhooks mounted on wooden racks. The hooks were intended to control the amount the cloth shrank as it dried, in order to meet standardised proportions. As this was typically done outside, tenter fields were a common feature of the landscape around fulling mills. From the early 19th century tentering was increasingly carried out in the more controlled conditions of *dry houses*.

teazle gig *See* raising

throstle *See* spinning

throwing (silk) A general term for the spinning of silk including twisting into *singles*, the various means of *doubling* and, if required, the additional twisting required to create the stronger *organzine* or *warp* thread. The term was also used to refer to the use of tram threads to create organzine.

throwster (silk) A person who throws raw silk to produce silk thread. As with the term *throwing*, there was a dual meaning. Throwsters (or sometimes throwers) were the individuals responsible for the manual processes of producing silk thread, but the term was also used by the owner of a firm. In this case, throwster referred to a business that concentrated on the production of silk thread, and was distinguished from a silk manufacturer, who also produced the fabric. The two types of silk business appear to have remained separate in many cases.

tow (flax and hemp) Short fibres of flax and hemp which were separated out from the long fibres during the *heckling* process. Tow was used for different products that required a softer yarn.

tram (silk) Two or more *singles* twisted together through the *doubling* process. Tram was typically used as the *weft* for silk weaving, with the stronger *organzine* thread as the *warp*.

twill weave A type of weave where the *weft* is passed under more than one *warp* thread in order to create a diagonal pattern of parallel ribs on the surface of the cloth.

walk (rope and twine) A long and narrow yard or building used for the traditional method of spinning twine or laying rope from flax or hemp. Walks could be up to 100yds (91.44m) long. Open walks could be features of towns or rural areas, usually defined by boundary walls, and were often accompanied by small ancillary buildings at each end. Some were later covered by awnings or roofed over. Purpose-built covered walks were usually one- or two-storey buildings, the largest of which were fireproof structures built in the late 18th century.

warp The thread running along the length of the cloth.

waste Discarded raw material or partly processed fibre collected for use in by-products such as lower-grade yarns or cloth. Specialised industries could emerge around the processing of waste material, for example, in the processing of waste wool to produce *flock*.

water frame *See* spinning

waterwheel; including suspension wheels The waterwheel provided the rotary motion to turn shafting and machinery. Wheel types varied depending on the power required, and the topography and the design of the associated watercourse. Basic waterwheel types include undershot (turned by water flowing underneath the wheel), breast-shot (turned by water feeding in on the side of the wheel) or over-shot (turned by water feeding in at the top of the wheel). From the late 18th century waterwheels powered the first factories, and on some sites they continued as a power source into the 20th century, as where there was a regular water supply the power derived from the system was comparable to that of steam power. The 18th and 19th centuries saw considerable improvements to the basic technology including the use of iron rather than wood for various parts of the structure and the development of the **suspension wheel**, where the wheel turned the main shaft through gearing on the rim (or shroud) of the wheel (*see* Fig 2.54). Along with the use of wrought-iron rods in place of the arms, this allowed suspension wheels to be considerably lighter in construction and therefore larger, both in diameter and in width, considerably increasing the power that could be derived from the system.

weaving The forming of cloth or other fabric by interlacing the *warp* and the *weft* threads, typically on a loom. The development of weaving techniques was a major influence on the history of the textile industry. For detail on the evolution of the loom see handloom and powerloom.

webbing (flax, hemp and cotton) A variety of fibres spun into hard-wearing or decorative yarns were used for a wide variety of webbing, either woven by hand or with specialist *narrow looms*. Webbing made from flax, hemp or cotton was used for a variety of purposes including upholstery and industrial products as well as forming part of military uniforms and other clothing.

weft The thread running across the cloth, typically carried in a shuttle on a *handloom* or *power loom*.

weir A bank or dam constructed in a stream or river, raising the level of the water and diverting it to feed the leat or headrace of a mill water system.

winding house (silk) A building in which raw silk skeins were wound onto swifts or bobbins. In the silk industry this process was hand powered for longer than other stages of the throwing process, and as such often appears to have been conducted in buildings separate from the main mill complexes, even in different towns or villages. *See* workshop.

woollen or woollen cloth; including fine woollen and superfine woollen The term woollen covers a wide range of different cloths produced from short-staple wool, typically fulled after weaving to produce a denser surface in which the weave was not visible. **Fine-woollen** cloth was the traditional product of the Gloucestershire, Wiltshire and northern Somerset industries, although different areas specialised in different types and finishes. **Superfine woollens** became the speciality of Gloucestershire's clothiers and their early woollen mills and were produced using the highest grades of imported wool.

wool stove *See* drying stove

workshop A room, or building, without a power system in which mechanical processes and workpeople could be efficiently organised. Workshops could be converted from other building types or purpose built. In industrial history the term is most commonly applied to buildings in the period before the development of factory buildings, when processes were still largely hand powered. In this phase workshops were often associated with clothiers' houses, built in attached or detached blocks to the rear of the main domestic accommodation. Such workshops can be distinguished by the provision of ample lighting through large windows, large open internal spaces without domestic features and in some cases the presence of external loading doors for bringing in goods. After the development of the early factories, workshops often continued to be built and used where specific parts of the process were not yet mechanised, for example in the provision of *loomshops* or *winding houses*.

worsted Yarn or cloth produced using long-staple wool. Worsted was used in the early Devon and Somerset *serge* industries, but was more widely used from the 17th century in the lighter fabric types which became popular. Worsted production required a different preparation process to short-staple wool, most notably in the need for *combing* to straighten the fibres and in specialised *spinning* machinery designed to give worsted a different twist and draw.

NOTES

Chapter 1

1 Palmer and Neaverson 2003, 155.

Chapter 2

1 Tann 1967 identified 256 sites in the Gloucestershire woollen industry; a study by RCHME in 1999 (Williams and Stoyel 1999) identified 220 textile industry sites, 150 of which were extant.
2 Pioneering works on the Gloucestershire woollen industry included Tann 1967; Mann 1971; and Ponting 1971. Appraisals of mill buildings include Mills and Reimer 1989, and Falconer 1993. The extensive and ongoing local research includes the valuable publications of the Gloucestershire Society for Industrial Archaeology and the Stroudwater Textiles Trust. A revision of Tann's 1967 work was published as this book was going to press. Tann, J 2012 *Wool & Water: The Gloucestershire woollen industry and its mills*. Stroud: The History Press.
3 Tann 1965, 58.
4 Tann 1967, 83–138, identified 91 woollen industry sites in this area, including workshops.
5 Mann 1971, xvi–xviii.
6 Ibid 13.
7 Tann 1967, 17.
8 Ponting 1971, 30; Mann 1971, 25.
9 For a more detailed account of processes in the west of England *see* Mann 1971, chapter 10; for a summary in a national context *see* Ponting 1971, 36–8.
10 Tann 1967, 17.
11 Mann 1971, 14.
12 Haine 1981, 30–1; Wilson 1989, 32–5; Falconer 1993, 64–7.
13 One example was Jeremiah Cother of Pitchcombe; Gloucester Archives D1815, Box 18, Bankruptcy, Bargain and Sale..., 10 May 1806.
14 Walrond 1964, 9–11. On the importance of fulling to the South West *see* Palmer and Neaverson 2005, chapter 2.
15 Tann 1967, 23.
16 Ibid 33; Rogers 1976, 17.
17 The knapping machine was said to have been introduced to Gloucestershire by Sir Onesiphorus Paul, clothier, of Southfield Mills, Woodchester, in 1743; Randall 2008; Moir 1957a.
18 Patent No. 1737; Ponting 1971, 70.
19 Mann 1971, xv.
20 18th-century ledgers for Brimscombe Dye Works, Gloucester Archives D1241 Box 79 Bundle 2; early 19th-century stock books for Dudbridge Dye Works, Gloucester Archives D1181/3/3.
21 Tann 1967, 29.
22 Tucker, Josiah (Dean of Gloucester), 1757, *Instructions to Travellers*, 37, quoted in Moir 1957b, 226.
23 Macintosh 1985, 29–30.
24 Tann 1965, 60.
25 On the influence of the clothiers *see* Moir 1957b.
26 On clothiers' houses *see* Palmer and Neaverson 2005, 51–67.
27 Kingsley 1992, 10–11.
28 Ibid 294; Fisher 1871, 216–17.
29 Hopf 2006, 164–5.
30 Tann 1967, Fig 2, 47.
31 Ibid 226.
32 Patterson and Mills 1997.
33 Tann 1967, 229.
34 Ibid 231; English Heritage Archives file, Egypt Mill, BF033611.
35 Tann 1967, 177–82.
36 *See* note 12.
37 *VCH Gloucestershire*, 11, 1976.
38 Gloucester Archives TS 267/2, Plan of Land & Premises at Dudbridge in the County of Gloucester, T. Croome, 1825; Boulton and Watt Archive, Birmingham Central Library, Portfolio 1330.
39 Falconer 1993, 67–71.
40 English Heritage Archive file, Longfords Mills, BF083415.
41 Gloucester Archives D1815, Box 18, Mortgage and Assignment of fire assurance, 5 Jul 1792, Jeremiah Cother and Wife to Stephen Woodifield.
42 Gloucester Archives D1815, Box 18, Lease dated 14 Nov 1789, Joseph Cooper to George Connibeere.
43 *Gloucester Journal*, 18 Jul and 15 Aug 1814; referenced by Haine 1984, 29.
44 Gloucester Archives D1815, Box 18, Bankruptcy, Bargain and Sale issued against Jeremiah Cother, 10 May 1806.
45 Haine 1984, 29.
46 The Bisley and Stroud Tithe Map of 1842 shows the building divided into domestic and industrial uses, Gloucester Archives P47 SD 2/3/2.
47 Existing waterwheels often remained in use in the late 19th and early 20th century, usually supplemented by steam power, and at some sites were replaced by turbines. No completely new water-power installations are known which date from after the early 19th century.
48 Contemporary publications on the late 19th century development of textile mill architecture include Nasmith and Nasmith 1909 and Fairbairn 1865.
49 Portfolio 1061, Boulton and Watt Archive, Birmingham Central Library.
50 Tann 1967, 232.
51 Falconer 1993, 71–4; further information courtesy of the Stroudwater Textile Trust, which runs a museum at Dunkirk Mill.
52 Investigation of water-power features by Alan Stoyel, May 2009.
53 Falconer 1993, 75, referring to answers given to the Factory Commission in 1834; kerseymeres, or cassimeres, were patented by Francis Yerbury of Bradford-on-Avon in 1766; Mann 1971, 50–1.
54 The most detailed report to date is by Stratton and Trinder 1988.
55 For comparison, the largest steam engine in use in a Manchester textile mill in 1813 was 100 horse power, at Chorlton New Mill; English Heritage Archive NBR 53338.
56 Tann 1967, 184.
57 Ibid 170–2; report and research on Ham Mill, September 1997, Ian Mackintosh, Stroudwater Textile Trust.
58 Tann 1967, 66.
59 On Lancashire mill architects, for example, *see* Holden 1998, 46–7.

Chapter 3

1 Of particular importance are the many publications of K H Rogers (1976, 2005, 2006, 2008), which have pioneered the study of the area's woollen industry and remain the standard source of historical research.
2 Defoe 1724–6, 260.
3 Rogers 1976, 56.
4 There was no firm division between areas

producing either dyed or undyed cloths; most parts of the west of England industry produced a variety of cloths, but local emphasis had developed in particular products by the 18th century.

5 Mann 1971, xvii.
6 Palmer and Neaverson 2003, 128–9.
7 Mann 1971, 50–1. Cassimeres were also known as kerseymeres, and were widely produced in Yorkshire as well as the South West.
8 Rogers 1976, 52–3.
9 Ibid 17.
10 Palmer and Neaverson 2003, 155.
11 One of the earliest examples of power looms in the area was at the Staverton Factory in 1839; Rogers 1976, 99.
12 Rogers 2008, 39–41.
13 The principal French weaver was Anthony Dufosee; Britton 1801, 137–9; Rousell 2006, 21.
14 Patent No. 578, granted to Ignatius Couran, merchant of London, John Barford, upholder of Wilton, and William Moody, clothier of Wilton, for making 'French carpeting or Moccadoes', *VCH Wiltshire* 4 1959, 148–82.
15 *VCH Wiltshire* 4 1959, 148–82.
16 Ponting 1971, 16–17.
17 Hurst 2005, 97.
18 Ibid 126.
19 An Act towching the making of woollen clothes, AD 1557–8 4 & 5 Phil. & Mar.c.5, *Statutes of the Realm*, Volume 4, 1547–1624, 323–6.
20 Ponting 1971, 15–16.
21 Ibid 18.
22 Rogers 1976, 50.
23 Defoe 1724–6, 260. Daniel Defoe's descriptions of the woollen trade were not complete or technically informed, but give a perceptive overview of the character of the industry just prior to the introduction of factory methods.
24 Defoe 1724–6, 261.
25 Ibid 262–3.
26 Defoe 1761 (6th edn), 38.
27 The use of rooms at the inn for storing cloth to be sold at the fair was described in legal proceedings of 1585, quoted in Brett 2002.
28 Palmer and Neaverson 2005, 105–6.
29 Defoe 1724–6, 261.
30 Leech 1981, 9; also population survey of 1785, *A Particular Account of the number of Families & Inhabitants within the Town and Parish of Frome Selwood…*, Longleat MS, WMR Box 29.
31 Leech 1981, 9.
32 For lists of textile machinery used in Wiltshire workshops *see* Rogers 1976, 29.
33 Weaving in domestic workshops probably also exceeded that in loomshops in the early 19th century; Palmer and Neaverson 2003, 145.
34 For an 1823 description of wool-drying stoves *see* Partridge 1823, 34–6.
35 Rogers 2005, site 14.
36 Ibid.
37 Haycock 1991, 14; Rogers 1976, 105.
38 *Wiltshire Notes & Queries*, Vol VIII, 347, quoting *The Gentleman's Magazine*, Vol XXXIX, 1769.
39 *VCH Wiltshire* 4 1959, 148–82.
40 Rogers 1976, 71–4.
41 The site was investigated by RCHME before conversion to flats in 1983. English Heritage Archive file BF008213.
42 Rogers 1976, 96–104.
43 Ibid 152–3.
44 English Heritage Archive NBR file 90891.
45 Rogers 1986, 168–72.
46 Teazles were attached to rectangular boards known as handles; Rogers 1976, 63.
47 Rogers 1986, 82.
48 Rogers 1976, 224–5.
49 Portfolio 462, Boulton and Watt Archive, Birmingham Central Library.
50 NBR file 90934; Rogers 1976, 158–61.
51 Rogers 1976, 49.
52 Ibid 113–48.
53 Ibid 49 and 124–6.
54 MS 3147 / 5 / 996, Boulton and Watt Collection, Birmingham Central Library.
55 Extensive groups of commercial warehouses were built in the late 19th century to service some of the other regional textile industries, such as in Bradford and Manchester.
56 Palmer and Neaverson 2003, 149.
57 Rogers 1976, 43.

Chapter 4

1 Lysons and Lysons 1822, 298-306, quoting from Thomas Westcote 1630, *A View of Devonshire in MDCXXX.*
2 Celia Fiennes description of 1698: Morris 1947, 246–7.
3 Specialist combing and top-making firms were a feature of the Yorkshire worsted industry in the late 19th century; Giles and Goodall 1992, 111.
4 The first combing machine was patented by Edmund Cartwright in 1790 but was not a success; a series of improvements were made in the early 19th century, including Platt and Collier's machine patented in 1827. Combing machines patented from the 1840s more efficiently separated the long- and short-staple fibres and were more widely used, notably the Heilmann comb of 1846, Listers's of 1851 and the Noble comb of 1853. Lemon 1972, 95–100.
5 Youings 1968, 2. The cloth was named after Kersey in Suffolk, where it originated. The length, width and weight of kerseys were determined by statute from the mid-16th century; *VCH Somerset* 2 1911, 415.
6 Lysons and Lysons 1822, 298–306, refers to trade problems due to the quality of the cloth.
7 Warren 1993, 9.
8 Hoskins 1935, 30.
9 Ibid 36–7.
10 Mann 1971, 26.
11 Described by Celia Fiennes in 1698: Morris 1947, 246.
12 Lysons and Lysons 1822, 298–306.
13 Hoskins 1929, 42.
14 Westcote, 1630, *A View of Devonshire in MDCXXX*, 61.
15 The organisational differences between the established fine woollen industry and the emerging serge industry are summarised in Hoskins 1935, 12–13, quoting a comparison of the South West with the Yorkshire woollen industry by Mantoux 1928, 66–7.
16 Fox 1958, 109–10.
17 Hoskins 1935, 68.
18 Lysons and Lysons 1822, 298–306.
19 Hoskins 1935, 52.
20 Hoskins 1935, 83.
21 Described by Celia Fiennes in 1698: Morris 1947, 245–6.
22 Pye *et al* 1995, 7–15.
23 Pye *et al* 1995, 17; Parker 1996, 16–22.
24 Youings 1968.
25 Jenkins 1806, 489.
26 Hoskins 1935, 47–9.
27 Amery 1876, 329; Hoskins 1929, 5; Westcote's description of 1630 was probably of the industry in this area.
28 Amery 1876, 334.
29 Ashburton Tithe Map, 1839, Devon Record Office; Phoenix Fire Assurance Register, policies 740248, 1837, and 905077, 1845, Devon Record Office, 924B/B9/1.
30 Buckfastleigh Tithe Map, 1839, Devon Record Office; Phoenix Fire Assurance Register, policy 740397, 1837, Devon Record Office, 924B/B9/1.
31 Chimmo – Hamlyn, Deeds and schedule, 1848, Devon Record Office, 924B/L7/3.
32 Phoenix Fire Assurance Register, policy 740399, Devon Record Office, 924B/B9/1.
33 Harris 1992, 122–3.
34 Ibid 121–2.
35 Amery 1876, 335.
36 Gosling and Harris 2004, 70.
37 Hoskins 1935, 46; Gray 1998, 88–9.
38 Ibid; quoting Rev John Swete, who stated in 1794 that the factory had cost £36,000 to build and was sold for £11,000.
39 Hoskins 1935, 29: map showing local specialisation in the serge industry.
40 Auction catalogue, late the property of Sir George Yonge, 1794; Somerset History Centre, DD\MY/35.

41 Fox 2009, 110–12.
42 Lease, 1815, John Lavers, serge maker, to Thomas Windeatt, serge maker; Devon Record Office, 924B/L45.
43 Ottery St Mary Tithe Apportionment 1843; William White's 1850 *Directory* (1968 reprint), 350; *Kelly's Directory of Devonshire* 1883, 312; Auction catalogue 1882, 62/9/2 Box 6/44; Devon Record Office.
44 Hoskins 1929, 59.
45 Lease and schedule 1815; 924B/L45, Devon Record Office.
46 RCHME Historic Buildings Report, 'North Tawton Mill', English Heritage Archive NBR 88996.
47 Murless 2003; site survey by Exeter Archaeology, 2007.
48 Fox 1958, 15, 70.
49 Ibid 109–10.
50 Ibid 69. Serge was woven for the East India Company in pieces 25yds long, known as Long Ells.
51 Fox 1958, 100.
52 Anon 1912, 13–18.
53 Fox nd, 44.
54 Jessop and Williams 2007, 6.
55 Information from *Valuation of Machinery*..., June 1916, Fox Brothers and Company Archives.
56 Jessop and Williams 2007.

Chapter 5

1 Over 1988, 26; Pahl 1960, 144. The early trade in Bridport is summarised in detail in Sims 2009, 19–22.
2 Nathan 1957, 133 and 401.
3 Crick 1908, 347; Pahl 1960, 144–6.
4 The importance of international trade and the demand from the navy is summarised in Buchanan 2008, 8–9.
5 Coad 1989, 197–201.
6 Nathan 1957, 404, 423.
7 Ibid 404–5. For a list of the flax bounties in Dorset parishes *see* Trenchard 2000.
8 Crick 1908, 348; Pahl 1960, 150; Perry 1964.
9 Nathan 1957, 401, 404–5 and 423; large quantities of Coker sailcloth were supplied to the naval dockyards in 1809.
10 Trenchard 2000, 2.
11 Way 1812, 404.
12 Some flax manufacturers also invested in other textile industries in the region. Sparks (of Sparks and Gidley, Crewkerne), for example, was connected with one of the earliest lace factories in Chard in the 1820s, and the Jupe family, flax manufacturers of Mere in Wiltshire, moved into the silk industry in the mid-19th century. *See* chapters 6 and 7.
13 Rimmer 1960, 239.
14 Ibid 74–5.
15 Ibid 242–3; Billingsley 1798, 213.
16 Way 1812, 404.
17 Rimmer 1960, 242.
18 Warden 1867, 32 on the rotation of flax; Way 1812, 404 on the rotation of hemp.
19 Warden 1867, 30–1.
20 Roberts 1980, 11.
21 Bone 1985, 24.
22 Powered flax-spinning machinery was in use in Burton Bradstock and Bridport by the first decade of the 19th century. Roberts 1980, 11–12; Sims 2009, 25.
23 Open walks were formerly common features of industrial areas and could be set up informally on any available ground, including temporary walks in fields, alleys and along pavements.
24 Flax-spinning machines were first patented by Kendrew and Porthouse of Darlington in 1787, and improved and patented by Mathew Murray of Leeds in 1793; Rimmer 1960, 31. Murray's machines were used in the Leeds mills of John Marshall in 1793, and in Ditherington Mill, Shrewsbury, from *c* 1797.
25 Buchanan 2008, 16–17; bleaching was important in the South West but did not result in the development of specialised bleach works, such as those built in the Irish linen industry, possibly because of the declining emphasis on cloth production in the early 19th century. *See* McCutcheon 1980, 283–325.
26 Posts for yarn drying in fields were still present in the Crewkerne area in the 1940s. Hurlbutt Albino 1948–50, 77.
27 Bone 1985, 25.
28 Hurlbutt Albino 1948–50, 77.
29 For an indication of the extent of the industry in west Dorset in the late 18th century *see* Dewar 1969, 216; for the Coker area of Somerset in the 17th and 18th century *see* Nathan 1957, 401–5.
30 Roberts 1980, 11.
31 Ibid 12–13.
32 Balling mill sites are identified in Bone 1985, 24–31.
33 English Heritage Historic Buildings Report, 'Tail Mill, Merriott', English Heritage Archive NBR 98658; Buchanan 2008, 21–30.
34 English Heritage Historic Buildings Report, 'Tail Mill, Merriott', English Heritage Archive NBR 98658.
35 Buchanan 2008, 23.
36 Collier 1998, 34; Buchanan 2008, 21.
37 English Heritage Historic Buildings Report, 'Higher Flax Mills, Castle Cary', English Heritage Archive NBR 105517.
38 Buchanan 2008, 34–8.
39 Nathan 1957, 404 and 422.
40 English Heritage Historic Buildings Report, 'Ansford Factory, Castle Cary', English Heritage Archive NBR 106473.
41 Buchanan 2008, 26.
42 For an overview of Bridport's flax and hemp industry buildings *see* Williams 2006.
43 Detailed accounts of individual Bridport firms in Sims 2009.

Chapter 6

1 In the upper part of the Stroud Valley, for example, at least 13 former woollen mills were used for silk in the mid-19th century; Conway-Jones 1980.
2 Adcock 1973, 30.
3 Whitchurch Silk Mill in Hampshire is a well-preserved example of the conversion of a large fulling mill to silk weaving, and later to grist milling. *See* chapter 3.
4 One example was evidence given by John Jones of Taunton; First Royal Commission on the Conditions of Children's Employment 1833 (450) B.1. 72.
5 Weinstock 1953, 94–5, quoting Willmott's correspondence on the use of children in Sherborne silk mills; Stephen Hannam of Gillingham Mill employed children from the London Borough of Lambeth in the late 18th century, Tighe 1997, 40.
6 For useful background on types of silk and the development of processes in the silk industry *see* Lardner 1831; Schober 1930; and Gaddum 1948.
7 Calladine 1993, 82–7.
8 Warner 1921, 403–16.
9 *VCH Somerset* 2 1911, 423.
10 Warner 1921, 466–7.
11 Ibid 151.
12 *VCH Warwickshire* 2 1965, 257–8.
13 Information from 1851 census; the silk industry was the largest employer after farming, with 405 people in the trade compared to roughly 449 labourers and farmers.
14 For more background on Blockley and its mills *see* Icely 1974 and Marshall 1988.
15 RCHME Historic Buildings Report, 'Blockley Court', English Heritage Archive BF081995.
16 Leases of land tenanted by Edward Whatcott, 1688, Northwick Papers, 705:66 BA228 XLVII/1.4 and XLVII/1.5, Worcestershire Records Office; MS3197/ ACC 1919-025/280751, Birmingham City Archives.
17 *VCH Warwickshire* 2 1965, 157–63.
18 Marshall 1988, 30.
19 Research based on late 18th- to mid-19th-century deeds to properties in Blockley; Gloucester Archives, D1395/II/T/5.
20 RCHME Historic Buildings Report, 'Blockley Court', English Heritage Archive BF081995.
21 The 1851 census indicates the mill was occupied by the throwster John Long.

22 Historical research kindly provided by Stephen Nixon (Nixon 2008).
23 Kelly's 1851 *Directory of Gloucester*, 262; the 1851 census identifies Long at the site, and 62 employees, 59 of whom were women.
24 Symonds 1916, 67.
25 Ibid 71.
26 Agreement of 1769; D/WIL/A1/2, Dorset History Centre.
27 1733 estate map SHR/B53 and 1834 map with the Sherborne Terrier SHR/B56, Sherborne Castle Archive.
28 Symonds 1916, 76.
29 Weinstock 1953, 85.
30 Symonds 1916, 81; Spinning wheels used for silk doubling are illustrated in Doble *et al* 2001, 60.
31 Symonds 1916, 74.
32 Weinstock 1953, 94–5, quoting Willmott's correspondence.
33 1856 Agreement between J B Rawlings and the Executors of Earl Digby; Sherborne Castle Archive, SHR/C/P167.
34 Surveyor's report to the Charity Commissioners describing the silk factory site in 1872; Dorset History Centre, S235 D2/2/1(78).
35 Gourlay 1971, opp. 265.
36 Tighe 1997, 40–1.
37 Ibid 43.
38 *VCH Somerset* 7 1999, 18–42.
39 Historical research and leaflets on Gant's Mill, courtesy the owner, Brian Shingler.
40 Doble *et al* 2001, 11.
41 Ibid 31.
42 Ibid 37.
43 Ibid 40.
44 Bodman 2009, 2–15; Rogers 1976, 178.
45 National Archives PRO HO107/1654/18.
46 Savage 1822, 382.
47 Ibid.
48 First Royal Commission on the Conditions of Children's Employment 1833 (450) B.1. 72.
49 Dorset Records Office, Letter Willmott to Tatlock 19 Jul 1784 in D/WIL/A5/28.
50 Savage 1822, 381.
51 RCHME building report, 'South Street Mill, Taunton', English Heritage Archive NBR 96942.
52 Riley 2006, 145–6.
53 Savage 1822, 382.
54 *VCH Middlesex* 10 1995, 92–101.
55 Porter 1831, 297.
56 Toulson 1995, 136.

Chapter 7

1 Mason 1994, 2.
2 Blanchard 1990.
3 *VCH Somerset* 2 1911, 426–7.
4 Yallop 1992, Appendix 1, 245.
5 Ibid 135–6.
6 Mason 1994, 85.
7 Felkin 1867, 333.
8 Palmer and Neaverson 2005, 27.
9 Mason 1994, 23.
10 Varley 1968, 17.
11 Felkin 1867, 237.
12 *VCH Gloucestershire* 8 1968, 144; Rath 1976.
13 The earliest known hosiers in Tewkesbury originated in London; Adcock 1973, 5.
14 Rath 1976, 141.
15 Ibid 142.
16 Adcock 1973, 8, quoting the House of Commons Journal, 1779, Vol 37, 370.
17 *VCH Gloucestershire* 8 1968, 145.
18 Adcock 1973, 19.
19 Ibid 6.
20 Ibid 22.
21 Felkin 1867, 215.
22 Jones 1947, 65–7.
23 Keene 2004, 43.
24 Felkin 1867, 256.
25 Heathcoat's description, quoted in Felkin 1867, 193.
26 Varley 1968, 13; Mason 1994, 24.
27 Mason 1994, 24.
28 Ibid.
29 Ibid 84–5.
30 Adcock 1973, 6, quoting Henson 1831, 360. Any advantage accruing from the skills of the local spinners would be reduced following the development of cotton spinning machinery in other areas in the late 18th century.
31 Lewis 1986, 129.
32 Adcock 1973, 33.
33 Ibid 45.
34 General sources include Mann 1958 and Catling 1970.
35 John Heathcoat was interested in factory design and may have influenced the use of fireproof construction in the South West lace factories; one of his innovative factory designs was patented in 1824; Mason 1994, 115.
36 Brayshay 1991, 85.
37 Keene 2004, 43.
38 Christie and Gahan 1997, 66.
39 Strong 1889, 28.
40 Felkin 1867, 333, 397.
41 First Royal Commission on the Employment of Children in Factories 1833 (450) B.1. 70; Pigot's Directory 1830, 702.
42 Kelly's *Directory of Somerset* 1875, 355.
43 First Royal Commission on the Employment of Children in Factories 1833 (450) B.1. 70.
44 First Royal Commission on the Employment of Children in Factories 1833 (450) B.1. 84.
45 Anon 1998.
46 RCHME Historic Buildings Report, 'Boden's Mill, Chard', English Heritage Archive BF060156.
47 Nance 2006.
48 First Royal Commission on the Employment of Children in Factories 1833 (450) B.1. 83.
49 For more information on Stringfellow *see* Penrose 1988.
50 Somerset History Centre A\ACL/2 1843–1865.
51 Nance 2006.
52 John Bellamy Payne ran a sacking and twine works at Knapp Mill in Perry Street (Somerset History Centre DD\PTR/8; Buchanan 2008, 66). He was also an engineer, and worked with Gundrys in Bridport to develop new netting machinery (Sims 2009, 85). He patented machinery associated with hemp breaking, apparently based on traditional fulling stocks (Denis Chapman, quoted in Buchanan 2008, 66).
53 Factory manager, pers comm.
54 For example in Strong 1889.
55 Brayshay 1991, 96.
56 Christie and Gahan 1997, 64.
57 Chard History Society 1973, 36.
58 Felkin 1867, 261; Brayshay 1991, 88.
59 Brayshay 1991, 85.
60 Ibid 88.
61 Cherry and Pevsner 1989, 811.
62 Adcock 1973, 16.
63 Mason 1994, 85.
64 Jones 1947, 62.
65 Ibid 73.
66 Buchanan and Watkins 2001; Jones 1947, 73–8.
67 J B Clarke's Manchester business was based at Hope Mill, Pollard Street, which survives as a well-preserved fireproof mill of the late 1820s. English Heritage Archive NBR file B/047/2002.
68 Jones 1947, 72–3.

BIBLIOGRAPHY

A wide range of published work has been indispensible to this study of textile industry buildings, of which the following is a necessarily brief selection. The aesthetic qualities of the industrial heritage of the South West have long been appreciated by locals and visitors, and some of the pioneering work on industrial history and industrial archaeology was carried out in the region. Amongst the contemporary publications were those written by well-known travellers, which can shed light on early perceptions of the textile industries, notably the accounts of Fiennes of the 1690s (Morris 1947) and Defoe (1724–6). Other early sources convey a fresh perspective on the expanding industries and some technical details which have since been lost. These include 18th-century descriptions of agricultural practices, such as those of Billingsley (1798) and Way (1812), and the early industrial encyclopaedias of Diderot (1751–2) and Rees (1819–20).

From the late 19th to the mid-20th century, highly detailed studies established the importance of the economic and social histories of the national textile industries, at a time when the buildings themselves were not widely threatened with demolition. These included the major volumes by Felkin (1867) on the factory-lace industry and Warner (1921) on the silk industry. More specific early studies included those on the cotton industry in Bristol by Jones (1947), and the role of the 'gentlemen clothiers' of Gloucestershire by Moir (1957b).

Other research has increasingly concentrated on the histories of the separate industries within the region. Of particular note is the very early work of Hoskins (1929 and 1935) on the Devon serge industry. From the 1960s a series of seminal publications revealed the nuances of the early history of the west of England fine-woollen industry, collating extensive research into individual mill sites which remain the main sources of historical information today. These publications helped establish what was the relatively new subject of industrial archaeology. They included the publications by Tann (1965, 1967) on the Gloucestershire mills, by Rogers (1986) on the Wiltshire and Somerset mills, and the regional studies by Ponting (1971) and Mann (1971). Additional pioneering work furthered the study of machinery and power systems, such as the records of hundreds of mill engines in the George Watkins Collection, held at the English Heritage Archive. Recent local publications have provided more detail on the local development of particular industries, including the studies of Sims (2009) in Bridport and Buchanan (2008) on the flax industry in Somerset.

From the 1980s more publications have specifically focused on mills as historical monuments, combining documentary research with the analysis of physical evidence obtained in fieldwork. In the northern textile industries, this work was pioneered by articles by Fitzgerald (1987–8) and the publication of RCHME textile mill surveys by Giles and Goodall (1992) in Yorkshire, Williams and Farnie (1992) in Greater Manchester and Calladine and Fricker (1993) in East Cheshire. In the South West, an appraisal of RCHME's work on the Stroud Valleys textile mills, highlighting their national importance, was published by Falconer (1993), together with a study of Gloucestershire mills of all types by Mills and Riemer (1999). An assessment of the surviving textile mills across the whole region was compiled for English Heritage by Williams and Stoyel (1999). More recent work by Palmer and Neaverson (2003, 2005) has provided a more detailed analysis of the social archaeology of the textile industries, focusing on the influence of processes and adding to the history of the region's industrial communities.

One of the most significant developments in recent years has been the wealth of local publications (including websites) that provide an increasingly valuable source of historical information throughout the region. Of particular note are the publications by museum trusts, such as the Stroudwater Textiles Trust in Gloucestershire and Coldharbour Mill Museum in Devon, the many articles published by the industrial archaeology societies of Gloucestershire, Somerset and Bristol, and those of the vernacular buildings research groups, for example in Wiltshire and Somerset.

Adcock, J A 1973 'The Tewkesbury Hosiery Industry 1760–1900'. Unpublished report in the archives of the Western Archaeological Trust, Gloucestershire Archives, D4784/5

Amery, P F S 1876 *Sketch of Ashburton and the Woollen Trade*. Report of the Devonshire Association Vol III, 323–37

Anon 1912 'The Manufacture of Woollen Goods: Messrs Fox Brothers and Company Limited'. *The Gentleman's Journal,* 24 Feb 1912, 13–18

Anon 1998 'The Chard Gas Industry'. *Somerset Industrial Archaeology Bulletin* 48 (August 1988), 7

Billingsley, J 1798 *General View of the Agriculture of the County of Somerset with Observations on the Means of its Improvement. Drawn up in the Year 1795*, 2 edn. Bath: R. Cruttwell

Blanchard, J 1990 *Malmesbury Lace.* London: Batsford

Bodman, M 2009 'Mills on the Sheppey – Part Two. Shepton Mallet, Darshill to Draycott'. *Somerset Industrial Archaeology Society Bulletin* 110, April 2009, 2–15

Bone, M 1985 'The Bridport flax and hemp industry'. *Bristol Industrial Archaeology Society Journal* 18, 19–31

Brayshay, M 1991 'Heathcoat's Industrial Housing in Tiverton, Devon'. *Southern History* 13, 82–104

Brett, C J 2002 'The Fairs and Markets of Norton St Philip'. *Somerset Archaeological and Natural History Society Proceedings* 144

Britton, J 1801 *The Beauties of Wiltshire, Vol.1.* London: Vernon and Hood

Buchanan, A and Watkins, G 2001 'The Great Western Cotton Factory'. *Bristol Industrial Archaeology Society Journal* 34, 3–10

Buchanan, C A 2008 *From Field to Factory, Flax and Hemp in Somerset's History after 1750*. SIAS Survey no 18

Bush, S 1987 *The Silk Industry*. Princes Risborough: Shire (Shire Album 194)

Calladine, A 1993 'Lombe's Mill: An Exercise in Reconstruction'. *Industrial Archaeology Review* XVI, Autumn 1993, 82–99

Calladine, A and Fricker, J 1993 *East Cheshire Textile Mills*. London: RCHME

Catling, H 1970 *The Spinning Mule*. Newton Abbot: David and Charles

Chard History Society 1973 *A History of Chard.* Chard History Group Publication series, no 4

Cherry, B and Pevsner, N 1989 *The Buildings of England, Devon.* London: Penguin

Christie, P and Gahan, D 1997 *Barnstaple's Vanished Lace Industry*. Bideford: Edward Gaskell Publishers

Coad, J G 1989 *The Royal Dockyards 1690–1850: Architecture and Engineering Works of the Sailing Navy, Studies in Naval History 1.* Aldershot: Scholar Press

Collier, W 1998 *Classic Sails*. Cowes: Ratsey and Lapthorne Limited

Conway-Jones, H 1980 'The Silk Industry in the Chalford Valley'. *Gloucestershire Historical Studies* XI, 44–9

Crick, M M 1908 'The Hemp Industry'. *The Victoria County History of the County of Dorset Vol 2*, 344–53. London: Constable

Defoe, D 1724–6 *A Tour through the Islands of Great Britain…* , Rogers, P. (ed) 1971. London: Penguin

Defoe, D 1761 *A Tour through the Islands of Great Britain …*, vol II, 6 edn

Dewar, H S L 1969 'Flax, Hemp and Their Growers in West Dorset'. *Proceedings of the Dorset Natural History and Archaeological Society* 91, 216–19

Diderot, D 1751–2 *A Diderot Pictorial Encyclopedia of Trades and Industry.* Reprinted 1959. Gillespie, C C (ed)

Doble, J, Hodgson, B, Lindsay, G, Shingler, B, Snelgrove, L, and Stokes, P 2001 *The Silk Industry in Evercreech* (Evercreech & District Local History Society). Wells: St Andrews Press

Fairbairn, W 1865 *Treatise on Mills and Millwork.* London: Longman

Falconer, K 1993 'Mills of the Stroud Valley'. *Industrial Archaeology Review* XVI (Autumn 1993), 62–81

Felkin, W 1867 *A History of the Machine-Wrought Hosiery and Lace Industries*. London: Longman, Green and Co; reprinted 1967 Centenary edition with introduction by S D Chapman. Newton Abbot: David and Charles

Feltwell, J 1990 *The Story of Silk.* Stroud: Alan Sutton

Fisher, P H 1871 *Notes and Recollections of Stroud, Gloucestershire,* reprinted 1986. Stroud: Alan Sutton

Fitzgerald, R S 1987–8 'The Development of the Cast-iron Frame in Textile Mills to 1850'. *Industrial Archaeology Review* 10, 127–45

Fox, C 2009 *The Arts of Industry in the Age of Enlightenment.* New Haven: Yale University Press.

Fox, F H nd *Fox Brothers and Co. Ltd.: Fifty Years' History*. Undated typescript, courtesy Fox Brothers

Fox, H 1958 *Quaker Homespun: The Life of Thomas Fox of Wellington, Serge Maker and Banker, 1747–1821.* London: Allen and Unwin

Gaddum, H T 1948 *Silk How and Where it is Produced.* Macclesfield: H.T. Gaddum and Company Limited

Giles, C and Goodall, I H 1992 *Yorkshire Textile Mills, 1770–1930*. London: HMSO

Goodall, R 2009 *The Industries of Frome.* Frome Society for Local Study

Gosling, G and Harris, P 2004 *The Book of Ottery St Mary with West Hill and Escot: the birthplace of Samuel Tayler Coleridge.* Tiverton: Halsgrove

Gourlay, A B 1971 *A History of Sherborne School.* Dorset: Sawtells

Gray, T (ed) 1998 *Travels in Georgian Devon: The Illustrated Journals of the Rev. John Swete (1789–1808) Volume II.* Exeter: Devon Books

Haine, C 1981 'Wool Drying Stoves along the Painswick Stream'. *Gloucestershire Society for Industrial Archaeology Annual Journal 1981,* 30–1

Haine, C 1984 'The Cloth Trade along the Painswick Stream Part IV'. *Gloucestershire Society for Industrial Archaeology Annual Journal 1984,* 19–36, 52

Harris, H 1992 *The Industrial Archaeology of Dartmoor*, 4 edn Newton Abbot: Peninsula Press

Haycock, L 1991 *John Anstie of Devizes 1743–1830, an Eighteenth-Century Wiltshire Clothier*. Stroud: Alan Sutton

Henson, G 1831 *A Political and Mechanical History of the Frame Work Knitters*, reprinted 1970. Nottingham: David and Charles Reprints

Holden, R 1998 *Stott and Sons, Architects of the Lancashire Cotton Mill.* Lancaster: Carnegie Publishing

Hopf, P M 2006 *The Turbulent History of a Cotswold Valley. The Upper Slad Valley and The Scrubs.* Stroud: Nonsuch

Hoskins, W G 1929 *The Rise and Decline of the Serge Industry in the South-West of England, with Special Reference to the Eighteenth Century*. University of London MSc thesis

Hoskins, W G 1935 *Industry, Trade and People in Exeter, 1688–1800, with Special Reference to the Serge Industry*. University College of the South-West of England, History of Exeter Research Group, monograph no. 6

Hurlbutt Albino, H 1948–50 'Sailcloth Weaving, A Somerset Industry'. *The Somerset Countryman* XVI, 75–8

Hurst, D 2005 *Sheep in the Cotswolds; the Medieval Wool Trade*. Stroud: Tempus

Icely, H E M 1974 *Blockley Through Twelve Centuries.* Kineton: Roundwood Press

Jenkins, A 1806 *Civil and Ecclesiastical History of the City of Exeter and its Environs: from the Time of the Romans to the Year 1806,* 3 edn. Exeter: W Norton

Jenkins, D T and Ponting, K G 1987 *The British Wool Textile Industry 1770–1914.* Aldershot: Scolar Press

Jessop, L and Williams, M 2007 *Tone Works, Wellington, Somerset. Survey and analysis of buildings, power systems and machinery*. Research Department Report, ser no. 72/2007, English Heritage

Jones, S J 1947 'The Cotton Industry in Bristol'. *Transactions and Papers (Institute of British Geographers)* 13, 61–79

Keene, B 2004 *The Watermills of Tiverton*. Leat Press: Tiverton

Kerridge, E 1972 'Wool growing and wool textiles in medieval and early modern times' in Geraint Jenkins, J (ed) *The Wool Textile History in Great Britain.* London: Routledge & Kegan Paul

Kingsley, N 1992 *The Country Houses of Gloucestershire, Volume II.* Chichester: Phillimore

Lardner, Revd D 1831 *A Treatise on the Origin, Progressive Improvement, and Present State of the Silk Manufacture.* London: Longman, Rees, Orme, Brown and Green

Leech, R 1981 *Early Industrial Housing: The Trinity Area of Frome*. Supplementary ser 3, RCHME. London: HMSO

Lemon, H 1972 'The Evolution of Combing' in Geraint Jenkins, J (ed) *The Wool Textile Industry in Great Britain.* London: Routledge and Keegan Paul

Lewis, P 1986 'William Lee's Stocking Frame'. *Textile History* 17(2), 129–48

Lysons, D 1811 *Supplement to the First Edition of the Historical Account of the Environs of London*. London: T Cadell and W Davies

Lysons, D and Lysons, S 1822 'Manufactures'. *Magna Britannia: Being a Concise Topographical Account of the Several Counties of Great Britain Volume the Sixth containing Devonshire*, 298–306. London: Thomas Cadell

Mackintosh, I 1985 'Laying the foundation, Stroud in the 16th century'. *Gloucestershire Society for Industrial Archaeology Annual Journal 1985*, 29–37

Mann, J, De L 1958 'The Textile Industry. Machinery for Cotton, Flax, Wool, 1760–1850', in C Singer *et al* (eds) *A History of Technology, Volume IV, The Industrial Revolution, c 1950 to c 1850*, 277–307. Oxford: Clarendon Press

Mann, J De L 1971 *The Cloth Industry in The West of England from 1640 to 1880* (1987 edn). Gloucester: Alan Sutton

Mantoux, P 1928 *The Industrial Revolution in the Eighteenth Century*. London: Jonathan Cape

Marshall, N 1988 *Blockley and the Silk Trade*, 3 edn. Stratford-upon-Avon: Bloomfield and Son

Mason, S A 1994 *Nottingham Lace 1760s–1950s: The Machine-made Lace Industry in Nottinghamshire, Derbyshire and Leicestershire*. Stroud: Alan Sutton

McCutcheon, W A 1980 *The Industrial Archaeology of Northern Ireland*. Belfast: HMSO

Mills, S and Riemer, P 1989 *The Mills of Gloucestershire*. Buckingham: Barracuda Books

Moir, E L 1957a 'Sir George Onesiphorus Paul', in Finberg H P R (ed) *Gloucestershire Studies*, 195–224. Leicester: Leicester University Press

Moir, E L 1957b 'The Gentlemen Clothiers, a Study in the Organisation of the Gloucestershire Cloth Industry, 1750–1835' in Finberg H P R (ed) *Gloucestershire Studies*, 225–66. Leicester: Leicester University Press

Morris, C (ed) 1947 *The Journeys of Celia Fiennes*. London: Cresset Press

Murless, B J 2003 *Westford Mills, Wellington, an introduction*. Report by SIAS for Taunton Deane Borough Council

Nance, D 2006 'A Chard beam engine in America'. *Somerset Industrial Archaeological Bulletin* 101 (April 2006), 5–9

Nasmith, J and Nasmith, F 1909 *Recent Cotton Mill Construction and Engineering*, 3 edn. Manchester

Nixon, S 2008 *Interim Report on the History of the Old Silk Mill, Chipping Campden*. CADHAS, May 2008

Nathan, Sir M 1957 *The Annals of West Coker*. Cambridge: Cambridge University Press

Over, L 1988 *Bridport: The Evolution of a Town*. Publication no. 1. Bridport: Bridport Museum

Pahl, J 1960 'The Rope and Net Industry of Bridport: some aspects of its history and geography'. *Proceedings of the Dorset Natural History and Archaeological Society* 82, 143–54

Palmer, M and Neaverson, P 2003 'Handloom weaving in Wiltshire and Gloucestershire in the 19th century: the building evidence'. *Post-Medieval Archaeology* 37(1), 126–58

Palmer, M and Neaverson, P 2005 *The Textile Industry of South-West England, A Social Archaeology*. Stroud: Tempus Publishing

Parker, R 1996 *Archaeological Survey of Cricklepit Mill, Exeter, Part 2: The buildings*. Exeter Archaeology, Report no. 96.37

Partridge, W 1823 *A Practical Treatise on Dying of Wool, Cotton and Skein Silk with the Manufacture of Broadcloth and Cassimere*, reprinted 1973. Edington: Pasold Research Fund

Patterson, N and Mills, S 1997 'Cloth Pins and Leather – An examination of Frogmarsh Mill, Woodchester'. *Gloucester Society for Industrial Archaeology Journal 1997*, 3–13

Penrose, H 1988 *Ancient Air: A biography of John Stringfellow of Chard, a Victorian Aeronautical Pioneer*. Shrewsbury: Airlife Publishing

Perry, P J 1964 'Bridport Harbour and the Hemp and Flax Trade, 1815–1914'. *Proceedings of the Dorset Natural History and Archaeological Society* 86, 231–34

Ponting, K G 1971 *The Woollen Industry of South-West England*. Bath: Adams and Dart

Porter, G R 1831 *A Treatise on the Origin, Progressive Improvement, and Present State of the Silk Manufacture*. London: Longman, Rees, Orme, Brown and Green

Pye, A R, Collings, A G and Harper, S 1995 *Cricklepit Mill, Exeter, Documentary Sources and History, 1220–1989*, Exeter Archaeology, Report No. 95.60

Randall, A 2008 'Paul, Sir Onesiphorus, first baronet (*bap.* 1706, *d.* 1774)'. *Oxford Dictionary of National Biography*, Oxford University Press

Rath, T 1976 'The Tewkesbury Hosiery Industry'. *Textile History* 7, 140–53

Rees, A 1819–20 *Rees's Manufacturing Industry*, 5 Vols, reprinted 1972. Newton Abbot: David and Charles Reprints

Riley, H 2006 *The Historic Landscape of the Quantock Hills*. Swindon: English Heritage

Rimmer, W G 1960 *Marshalls of Leeds, Flax Spinners*. Cambridge: Cambridge University Press

Roberts, P P 1980 'Richard Roberts, Flax Spinner'. *Dorset Natural History and Archaeological Society Proceedings for 1977* 99, 11–28

Rogers, K H 1976 *Wiltshire and Somerset Woollen Mills*. Edington: Pasold Research Fund

Rogers, K H 1986 *Warp and Weft, the Story of the Somerset and Wilts Woollen Industry*. Buckingham: Barracuda Books Limited

Rogers, K H 2005 *Clothier's Workshops in Trowbridge*. Trowbridge: The Friends of Trowbridge Museum

Rogers, K H 2006 *Woollen Industry Processes: I The Domestic Industry*. Trowbridge: The Friends of Trowbridge Museum

Rogers, K H 2008 *Woollen Industry Processes: II The Factory Industry*. Trowbridge: The Friends of Trowbridge Museum

Rousell, C 2006 *The Book of Wilton*. Tiverton: Halsgrove

Ryder, M L 1972 'The Wools of Britain' in Geraint Jenkins, J (ed) *The Wool Textile Industry in Great Britain*. London: Routledge and Keegan Paul

Sampson, M 1995 *A Dictionary of Wool*. Tiverton: The Wool Exhibition Group

Savage, J 1822 *The History of Taunton in the County of Somerset, Originally Written by the Late Joshua Toulmin. A New Edition Greatly Enlarged and Brought Down to the Present Time*. Taunton: John Poole

Schober, J 1930 *Silk and the Silk Industry*. London: Constable & Co Ltd.

Sims, R 2009 *Rope, Net & Twine, the Bridport Textile Industry*. Wimborne Minster: The Dovecote Press

Singer, C *et al* (eds) 1958 *A History of Technology, Volume IV, The Industrial Revolution,* c *1750 to* c *1850*. Oxford: Clarendon Press

Stratton, M and Trinder, B 1988 'Stanley Mill, Gloucestershire'. *Post-Medieval Archaeology* 22, 143–80

Strong, H W 1889 *Industries of North Devon*, reprint of 1971, with introduction by B D Hughes. Newton Abbot: David and Charles

Symonds, H 1916 'The Silk Industry in Wessex'. *Dorset Natural History and Archaeology Field Club* 37, 66–93

Tann, J 1965 'Some problems of water power – a study of mill siting in Gloucestershire'. *Transactions of the Bristol and Gloucestershire Archaeological Society 196,* 53–77

Tann, J 1967 *Gloucestershire Woollen Mills*. Newton Abbot: David and Charles

Tann, J 2012 *Wool & Water: The Gloucestershire woollen industry and its mills.* Stroud: The History Press

Tighe, M F 1997 *Silver Threads, a Study of the Textile Industries of Mere*. Mere Papers 3. Mere: Friends of the Church of St Michael the Archangel.

Toulson, S 1995 *Somerset with Bath and Bristol*. London: Pimlico County History Guides

Trenchard, D 2000 *Dorset People Involved in the Growing of Flax and Hemp, 1782–1793*. Bridport: The Somerset and Dorset Family History Society

Varley, D E 1968 *John Heathcoat 1783–1861. Founder of the Machine-made Lace Industry.* Newton Abbot: David and Charles

VCH Gloucestershire 8 1968 *The Victoria County History of the County of Gloucestershire, Vol 8.* Oxford: Oxford University Press

VCH Gloucestershire 11 1976 *The Victoria County History of the County of Gloucestershire, Vol 11*. Oxford: Oxford University Press

VCH Middlesex 10 1995 *A History of the County of Middlesex, Vol 10.* Oxford: Oxford University Press

VCH Somerset 2 1911 *The Victoria County History of the County of Somerset, Vol 2.* London: Constable

VCH Somerset 7 1999 *The Victoria County History of the County of Somerset, Vol 7.* Oxford: Oxford University Press

VCH Warwickshire 2 1965 *The Victoria County History of the County of Warwickshire, Vol 2.* Oxford: Oxford University Press

VCH Wiltshire 4 1959 *The Victoria County History of the County of Wiltshire, Vol 4.* Oxford: Oxford University Press

Walrond, L F J 1964 'Early Fulling Stocks in Gloucestershire'. *The Journal of Industrial Archaeology* 1/1 (May 1964), 9–16

Ward, J T 1970 *The Factory System Vol 1 Birth and Growth.* Newton Abbot, David and Charles

Warden, A 1867 *The Linen Trade Ancient and Modern,* 2 edn. London: Longman, Green, Longman, Roberts and Green

Warner, F 1921 *The Silk Industry of the United Kingdom, Its Origin and Development* (facsim edn published on request by Kirtasbooks 2010)

Warren, D 1993 'The Woollen Trade Around Exmoor'. *Somerset Industrial Archaeological Society Bulletin* 63 (August 1993), 9–15

Watkins, G 2003 *Stationary Steam Engines of Great Britain Vol 7 The South & South West.* Ashbourne: Landmark Publishing

Way, H B 1812 'Account of the Culture and Preparation of Hemp, in Dorsetshire; by H.B. Way, Esq., of Bridport Harbour'. *Belfast Monthly Magazine,* Vol 9, 403–6

Weinstock, M 1953 'Portrait of an Eighteenth Century Sherborne Silk Mill Owner'. *Studies of Dorset History*, Chapter 7. London: Longmans

Wells, F A 1935 *The British Hosiery and Knitwear Industry: Its History and Organisation.* Newton Abbot: David and Charles

Williams, M and Farnie, D A 1992 *Cotton Mills in Greater Manchester.* Preston: Carnegie

Williams, M 2006 *Bridport and West Bay, The Buildings of the Flax and Hemp Industry*. Swindon: English Heritage

Williams, M and Stoyel, A 1999 *The South-West Textile Mill Survey, A Project by RCHME for English Heritage*. Swindon: NMR

Wilson, R 1989 'Circular wood drying towers'. *Gloucestershire Society for Industrial Archaeology Journal* 1989, 32–5

Yallop, H J 1992 *The History of the Honiton Lace Industry*. Exeter: University of Exeter Press

Youings, J 1968 *Tuckers Hall Exeter*. Exeter: University of Exeter and the Incorporation of Weavers, Fullers and Shearmen

INDEX

Page numbers in **bold** refer to illustrations and their captions. Where figures are scattered throughout the text this is indicated by (*illus*). The letter n following a page number denotes that the reference will be found in a note.

A

B

C

Y